WORKING with VIOLENT FAMILIES

a guide for clinical and legal practitioners

Frank G. Bolton and Susan R. Bolton

SAGE PUBLICATIONS
The Publishers of Professional Social Science
Newbury Park   London   New Delhi

To the memory of Emily and Stanley,
our loyal friends

For information address:

SAGE Publications, Inc.
2111 West Hillcrest Drive
Newbury Park, California 91320

SAGE Publications Ltd.
28 Banner Street
London EC1Y 8QE
England

SAGE Publications India Pvt. Ltd.
M-32 Market
Greater Kailash I
New Delhi 110 048 India

Printed in the United States of America

Library of Congress Cataloging-in-Publication Data

Bolton, Frank G.
    Working with the violent family.

    1. Family violence—United States. 2. Family
violence—Law and legislation—United States.
3. Problem families—Counseling of—United States.
I. Bolton, Susan R. II. Title.
HQ809.3.U5B65   1986   362.8′2   86-13510
ISBN 0-8039-2586-7
ISBN 0-8039-2587-5 (pbk.)

THIRD PRINTING 1990

Contents

Part VI: Capturing the Family Violence Practitioners' Environment (III): Special Issues in Working with the Violent Family—Attorney and Clinician

Preface:
The Practitioner's Use of This Book

This book is directed at two groups of practitioners: attorneys and clinicians. It was also written for academic researchers and students in both areas and is designed to inform both the expert and the novice. For the novice it is intended to describe what has preceded entry into professional practice with violent families. For the expert it will prove a ready reference. Although ideally the book should be read from cover to cover, it is doubtful that busy practitioners, researchers, or students will have the time. Therefore we offer the following general guide.

For the practitioner new to family violence or the experienced individual struggling to find a point of entry to a specific family, the first part of the book ("The Violent Family: An Introduction") will prove vital. The purpose of the early chapters is to provide a framework through which the practitioner may organize his or her thinking about a family exhibiting violent behavior.

The second part ("Capturing the Critical Environments") should be useful to all practitioners. The chapters in this section review current knowledge of the social and psychological environments of the violent family. Critical to this section is a view of the lore of family violence—axiomatic beliefs that may no longer be considered scientifically valid. These points should prove especially helpful to the attorney seeking to assess the quality of an expert's current knowledge of the area or one seeking to build a cross-examination strategy.

Part III ("Violent Family Personalities and Processes") examines the individuals in violent families and the processes that define their dysfunctional behavior. An unusual feature of this section is a perspective on "special" victims and perpetrators (e.g., the male sexual abuse victim). These individuals present continuing dilemmas for the practitioner. Extant information about these special persons can be found here.

The fourth part ("Capturing the Family Violence Practitioner's Environment (I): Legal Work and the Violent Family") is intended to serve both attorney and clinician in their understanding of violent families. Recent research on legal practice reforms and logistical changes in courtroom procedure are reviewed. A rationale for specific approaches to the issues confronting the attorney is also presented. For the clinician, this section is informative in increasing understanding of attorneys' choice of a given stance or practice in working with a violent family.

Part V ("Capturing the Family Violence Practitioner's Environment (II): Clinical Work and the Violent Family") is the "how-to" portion of the book. Professionals in all relevant fields will gain by the research indicating just how well or how poorly legal and/or clinical practitioners are doing with violent families. This section was written specifically to enable the legal practitioner to understand the clinician's view of the problem as well as the interventions most commonly (sometimes erroneously) applied. This section should be reviewed by anyone who is preparing to work with the violent family.

The sixth and final part of the book ("Capturing the Family Violence Practitioner's Environment (III): Special Issues in Working with the Violent Family, Attorney and Clinician") describes the problems common to both attorneys and clinicians in their work with violent families. Included in this section are practical suggestions for interviewing children, working with hostile and aggressive individuals, predicting violence and dangerousness, the special case of the low-income or minority family, approaching the personality disordered or affectively disordered family member, and the joint responsibility of clinician and attorney in the development of effective expert witnessing strategy. Following these sections are appendices intended to aid the researcher in locating the references most appropriate for discussion of individual issues presented throughout the book.

It was our hope, in writing this book, to provide practitioners, students, and researchers from both the legal and clinical perspectives with a substantial body of knowledge from which to conduct professional activities with violent families. This work represents the thinking, research, and practice of literally thousands of legal, clinical, and academic professionals. Obviously, it is not possible to include in this relatively limited space every deserving work; providing a reference text through language that is understandable across disciplines demands a sharp editorial knife. What has been included here are the works that we have found most useful in our own day-to-day interactions with violent families. Our only hope is that others will find this information useful as well.

Phoenix, Arizona—
F.G.B.
S.R.B.

Acknowledgments

There were many people who helped form the thoughts that appear in this book—some directly, some indirectly. For many of the readers of this book, the names of the authors of the studies it references are just that, names in a book. We have been fortunate enough to know many of these "names" as people and the times and thoughts we have shared together really contributed more to this book than they might think. For those readers who only know these people as names, understanding some of the "human" aspects of their lives might help to make their "academic" thoughts less imposing and more real.

Consider the fact that Richard Gelles is the world's most fanatic baseball fan, that Eli Newberger plays in one of the most popular jazz bands around, that Robert Burgess loves Penn State football as much as any Nittany Lion fan around, that Michael Wald is more than an avid ornithologist, that Jon Conte is an Oreo cookie fanatic, that Roland Summit collects carousel horses, that David Finkelhor folk dances and Murray Straus sails, that Jay Belsky has a twin brother who's the only person in the world who talks faster than Jay, that James Garbarino spends his summers on a secluded island, that Donald Bross and John Johnson were both Naval officers, that Michael Lamb is the Utah Jazz's biggest fan, that Harold Martin smokes little black cigars like a well-known cowboy, that Ken Robson is a trout fisherman, and that Brandt Steele was the first psychiatrist on Normandy beach. Most of all, think how lucky we've been to know and learn from each of these people. Their thoughts are in this book. We thank them.

Part I

The Violent Family:
An Introduction

1

Unkept Promises of Family Violence Research and Practice

Family members can harm each other in many ways. We are now in our third decade of attempting to discover why they do. Research has sought to approach this seemingly illogical problem from a logical perspective. Clinicians have tried to provide external reasons when families have been unable to find internal reasons. *Neither attempt is working very well, and we are running out of time.*

Law professor Michael Wald (1985) suggests that the public is becoming impatient and he sees a "groundswell of pressure" seeking to alter the therapeutic orientation that has guided practice in the family violence area. In its place will be a more punitive prosecutorial and criminal justice response. Psychiatrist Roland Summit (1985) echoes Wald's warning of an impatient public in stating, "We have not matured to the point that we meet standards for conventional expertise—we are so 'young' in what we know." Researchers too have joined in this warning. Cohn, for example evaluated multiple intervention strategies in child maltreatment and concluded that these programs are "not as successful as society has been led to expect" (1979, p. 516). Similar statements of concern will be found in the literature on child sexual abuse (Lanyon, 1985), conjugal violence (Fleming, 1979), and elder mistreatment (Kosberg, 1983a). It is clear that neither research nor clinical practice has provided us with one answer.

Public impatience should be no surprise. Neither is it surprising that a greater emphasis upon prosecution would be seen as an immediate form of relief. The court provides a concluding statement; the court provides a decision about these cases and in short, something is done about "those people." But, according to pediatrician Eli Newberger (1985b), the attraction of prosecution extends even beyond decision making. He suggests eight roles for prosecution that the public finds attractive:

(1) It punishes offenders, which allows the public to vent rage and sadness.
(2) It provides public entertainment for those fascinated by such things.
(3) It provides aspiring prosecutors political opportunity by allowing them to be on the "right" side of an "apple pie" issue.
(4) It provides in general, more work for attorneys.
(5) It allows us to abandon the expensive social welfare approaches that focus on poor "people" who are too expensive anyway.
(6) It fosters our image of good prevailing over bad and that the courts will punish those who are wrong allowing the rest of us to feel righteous about how we treat our children.
(7) It allows us to punish the social workers who cannot seem to fix the problem.
(8) And, finally, it allows us to view the strange things that occur in a violent home.

Some of these elements clearly victimize the family involved, but that seems to be a price the public is willing to have them pay.

Clinicians and researchers unfortunately are not moving quickly enough toward an alternative that is acceptable to the public. Why have two decades of practice and study with violent families not led to an answer? Perhaps the problem may have been that too many promises were made that were not kept.

The Unkept Promises of Two Decades

The legacy of family violence over the past two decades may be described as a collection of partially met promises. Some of these promises, perhaps unrealistic from the outset, will be reviewed in this chapter.

Promise 1: Research will answer the difficult questions and lead to the development of efficient and effective treatments.

In reviewing family violence research, Hornung and colleagues (Hornung, McCollough, & Sugimoto, 1981) have concluded only that we are becoming more knowledgeable about less. In reviewing child maltreatment, Garbarino (1984b) provides a similar perspective, contrasting the large number of clinical/empirical studies with the relatively small number of facts produced. For some, the problem is methodological inadequacy (Cicchetti & Rizley, 1934 p. 192). Gelles (1982) suggests a difficulty in translating research findings into clinical practice. All describe problems.

It would be difficult to describe the child maltreatment literature as "knowledge" in the strict scientific sense, in as much as it has not met traditional standards for scientific inquiry (Bolton, Laner, Gai, & Kane, 1981). More than ten years ago, Gelles (1973) described this literature as repetitious and trapped in a circular examination of itself. At the same time, Polansky and colleagues described the child neglect research as "rudimentary" (Polansky, Hally, & Polansky, 1975). A 1980 review (Gerbner, Ross, & Zigler, 1980, p. vii) agreed that the work was "rudimentary" and "isolated from the mainstream of scholarship." These views only hint at the methodological shortcomings.

Across the whole study of family violence, research has suffered from methodological and design flaws (Hornung et al., 1981). Various reviews have found problems in sample size and selection, comparison and control group absences, single-case insights, imprecise definitions, over-reliance upon official records, and bias toward lower socio-economic status subjects. These are problems found in the work on child maltreatment (Garbarino, 1984b; Gelles & Pedrick-Cornell, 1985; Newberger, Newberger, & Hampton, 1983) sexual abuse (Chandler, 1982; Finkelhor, 1984), conjugal violence (Ulbrich & Huber, 1981), and elder mistreatment (Douglas, 1983; Pedrick-Cornell & Gelles, 1982). There are accompanying problems in application.

In his experience as a clinician, following a research career, Gelles discovered fundamental incompatibilities between research and practice in family violence cases. First, research is nomothetic (broad); practice is idiographic (individualized). Second, research categories and typologies are too general to help in understanding specific situations. Third, the researcher seeks closure (i.e., the answer), while the clinician remains open to new information (Gelles, 1982, p. 14). As confirmation, Schumm and colleagues (Schumm, Martin, Bollman, & Jurich, 1982) have found the broad social indicators used in research to have little predictive value in distinguishing violent from non-violent families. Much of what we *know* of violent families may have an *association* with the problem, but not be causally related to the actions of a specific family (Burgess & Youngblade, 1985). And when the possibility of being misled by the research is added to our inability to define adequately the problems in violent families, the dangers are multiplied.

Promise 2: The types of family violence can be delineated through specific and comprehensive definitions.

Family violence is at the same time a criminal, social, behavioral, and medical problem (Conte, 1981). In addition, the public holds a generalized belief that violence in families is uniformly systematic and intentional, which gives the topic a stronger criminal justice flavor than might be deserved (Newberger, 1985b). Quite simply, too many systems and persons have the opportunity to generate or influence definitions, and these are systems and individuals that vary enormously in their perspective (Wolfe, Fairbank, Kelly, & Bradlyn, 1981, p. 11). The result is a lack of consensus (Faller, 1981, p. 2), definitions that are more abstract than operational (Burgess & Garbarino, 1983, p. 88), and clinical and statutory definitions that conflict (Bourne & Newberger, 1979, p. 6). Despite the need for uniform definitions in the building of a service delivery system, this uniformity has proven elusive within the study of family violence.

Specificity in definitions in family violence also proves itself a problem (Faller, 1981, p. 7). A lack of precision in definitions is seen by some as an open invitation to intrusion into individual and family rights (Bourne & Newberger, 1979a; Wald, 1976). Clinicians, on the other hand, view more open definitions as helpful in reaching a greater number of families at risk at an earlier stage in the violence (Jason, 1981, p. 281). This is a clinical versus legal conflict that is also found in issues of "parental intent," the definition of "overt signs" and the boundaries of "parental responsibility" (Bourne & Newberger, 1979, p. 5). The definition of child maltreatment today is so much broader than the original concern over physically battered children that there is virtually no hope that child welfare agencies will ever serve the full range of mandated child problems. As Newberger (1985a, p. 5) notes, it is a "paradoxical and troubling issue" that definitions for child maltreatment are expanding so broadly (for example, inclusion of the Baby Doe case and out-of-home assault) at a time that resources to deal with the problem are increasingly in short supply. The definitional problems in other areas of family violence provide no fewer dilemmas.

Clinicians working in sexual abuse seek flexible definitions due to the variety of perpetrator roles (for example, father versus stranger) and severity of outcomes that they see (Kempe & Kempe, 1984, p. 10). Beyond that general point of agreement, however, lies chaos. Disagreement is particularly evident between the two groups most responsible for the recognition of child sexual abuse: the child maltreatment specialists ("child protectors") and the women's movement ("feminists"); (Finkelhor, 1984, p. 3).

The child protector's view of sexual abuse is that it is a family problem akin to other forms of child maltreatment; a problem grounded in family-system pathology. The feminist view finds greater commonality with rape; an act of aggression originating in a patriarchical society and male socialization (Finkelhor, 1984, p. 4). These are difficult differences to capture within a single statute.

Feminist theorists (Russell, 1984, pp. 187–188) would extend definitions of sexual abuse beyond their current focus on specific sexual acts and include less overtly sexual behavior. Clinically, Brandt and Tisza (1977; Schultz, 1980) have described the polarities as *sexual abuse*, a genuinely sexual act that results in perpetrator satisfaction, and *sexual misuse*, a quasi-sexual act that may or may not involve sexual contact and/or satisfaction. The official response to this broadening of definitions is that the system would be overwhelmed if all such cases were included. This is a political battle also being waged within the study of conjugal violence.

The feminist view of conjugal violence is that it is a problem of a societal nature in which male dominance has given license to violence toward women (Walker, 1979). Clinical perspectives define conjugal violence in terms of conflict, psychopathology, and anger/impulse control (Deschner, 1984). The court's definitional structure, having been limited by criminal statutes and minimal victim protection, has been less than acceptable to both feminist and clinical groups.

Current efforts to establish a meaningful definition for elder mistreatment have been even less successful. Here, even the drawing of battlelines is not yet possible. Pedrick-Cornell and Gelles (1982, p. 3) have reviewed the research on elder mistreatment. They found the definitions used in the studies to be so varied that comparison was impossible. It is not clear, for example, that institutional and noninstitutional mistreatment are qualitatively different. It is uncertain whether abuse or neglect is the pivotal problem. Beyond traditional types of maltreatment, abuse of material possessions remains a problem; what type of problem is as yet unclear. Finally, the separate roles of victim and perpetrator in elder mistreatment are muddled (Block & Sinnott, 1979; Lau & Kosberg, 1979; Rathbone-McCuan, 1980). Perhaps this is an issue of too recent discovery to expect adequate definition. On the other hand, it may be that violence in the family is so much a part of family operations that the expectation of a definition apart from normal family functioning may be too much to ask.

Promise 3: Family violence problems will be found to be so different from each other that new theories, techniques, systems, and experts will be required to deal with each (i.e., child maltreatment, sexual abuse, conjugal violence, and elder mistreatment).

We are only now beginning to take a broad look at family violence. Prior to this time, we have been busy building experts, treatments, and service delivery systems that focus upon single issues. Curiously, persons who study one area of family violence tend not to communicate with those who study other areas. Even those in what appears to be a single area do not communicate well, for example, incest versus child molestation (Conte, 1984). Across practitioner types, in the management of a single case, "turf" battles are a recurrent barrier to success. The result is a set of experts who know a great deal about a small area and little of the wider social world that the violent family inhabits. These clusters of experts produce research, theory, and practice guidelines that answer some phase of the family violence question, but separately, they have yet to provide *the* answer.

Promise 4: Violent families will be found to be so different from other families that new and exclusive systems and treatments will be required.

Finkelhor (1979), Summit (1985), and Wald (1985) have all commented on the need within people to view violent families as different than their own and others they know. This is a belief that persists despite the awareness of the universal nature of intra-familial violence in our society. That violent families are different enough to require totally new forms of intervention, and that violent families that manifest violence of a given type (i.e., child maltreatment) are different from those manifesting another type (i.e., conjugal violence), are both open questions.

Family violence research and clinical work were initiated through an "illness" model. The illness model is useful for it distances the problem from those who are not seemingly afflicted with the contagion (Summit, 1985). And there is always hope that a new technology will find a way to cure it (Summit, 1985; Wald, 1985). But, as regards violence in the family, the technology for cure has not come about as yet.

It could be that violent families are not as unlike nonviolent families as once thought. It could be that those manifesting one form of violence are not as different from those manifesting other forms of violence. In either case, the problem has outstripped our technological ability to find a new treatment that will eliminate the problem. Perhaps, the problem is that the cooperative set of laws we were promised, laws that would allow us to get these special families to our new treatments and to protect the victims within them, have never arrived.

Promise 5: New laws will be written, and legal strategies designed, which will offer protection and treatment to families involved in violence of all types.

All fifty states have mandatory child maltreatment reporting. Some communities now allow law enforcement officers to press charges in conjugal violence situations. Unprotective mothers, as well as perpetrating fathers, are being prosecuted in sexual abuse situations. The number of mandatory reporting statutes related to elder mistreatment is increasing. This seems to be progress; unfortunately, these evidences of progress are, at least partially, empty promises.

The growth in the legalization of family violence is what Newberger and Daniel (1979, p. 19) call "humane rhetoric" because what lies beyond this reporting system is a service delivery system that is overwhelmed. Solnit (1980, p. 135) straightforwardly defines the problem as "too much reporting: too little service." The public may believe that services automatically follow reporting; those who work in the area know better.

It is not wrong to develop mandatory reporting, but it is wrong to promise a treatment where there is none. There is a treatment system, but the identification of increasing numbers of cases in every form of family violence occurred so quickly that it was impossible to keep pace. The result is a system often unable to protect the victim (Bourne & Newberger, 1979). We simply did not anticipate the need and build a system that could handle such a large proportion of our families (Kahn & Kammerman, 1980). Today, our broad statutory mandates to respond and the increased reporting of cases are threatening to bankrupt the system entirely. The only solution seems to be to do a better job in gaining the cooperation between the legal and treatment system that was promised at the outset.

Promise 6: Legal and treatment professionals will work together to bring the efforts of both areas to bear upon the protection of family members.

In the past, the framework used to conceptualize family violence (i.e., the medical/treatment model) directed the response away from "coercive" treatment involving legal sanctions or cooperation. In some areas there has been an almost antilegal mind set. In fact, the two most common features of the response to discovery of violence in a family were often described as if they were antagonists (e.g., criminal versus social interventions) rather than partners (Bailey & Bailey, 1983). These approaches can be antagonists no more.

Public opinion seems to be moving away from social/treatment intervention and toward criminal/legal intervention in family violence. Similarly, professionals who recognize the difficulty in gaining cooperation from violent families are finding increasing logic in the cooperative inclusion of the legal system in planning and treatment for violent families (Rosenfeld & Newberger, 1979, pp. 144–145). It is only through such cooperation that some balance between the unmet therapeutic promises of yesterday and the coercive approaches of tomorrow will be reached.

As Bourne (an attorney) and Newberger (a physician) write, "In all cases, there is a need for a balance and coordination of compassion and control" (1979, p. 85). Although Bourne and Newberger were writing of child maltreatment, this is a requirement that can be extended to all forms of family violence. What is to be gained in this partnership is a reasonable assessment as to the prognosis for therapeutic intervention, an assessment as to the most appropriate form of legal leverage for gaining cooperation and monitoring attendance in treatment, an assessment of the ability of the family to protect the victim, and information for the various therapeutic and legal interventions that will occur during the process of family rebuilding or dissolution. To date, this is a partnership not well formed, but it is one that must exist in the future.

Promise 7: Violence in the family is outside the realm of normal family functioning and, consequently, its etiology will be easy to explain.

There is a dangerous reluctance to accept the potential for violence in families. That it exists is known to almost everyone. Yet there remains a denial that such families can be found in the neighborhoods, friends, or professional acquaintances that are most familiar to us. When family violence occurs with sufficient approval and prevalence to be described as a "normal" (i.e., naturally occurring) part of our world (Gelles & Straus, 1978, p. 549) such distancing is inappropriate.

Behavior standards seem to be differentially applied in the family. There is a recognition that, outside the family, aggression and violence is a shared potential across individuals. Outside the family there is an expectation that individuals will seek to meet their own needs before attending to those of others. Yet inside the family these expectations are softened and made more positive. Inside the family, the individual is expected to suppress his or her own needs for the greater good of family survival. This is not always a realistic view. Added to this sometimes unrealistic view of families is the overabundance of theories available to explain the general phenomenon of violence in families. This not only sustains a sense that these families are unique, it clouds our ability to make fundamental discriminations between those who might become violent and those who seem to be insulated.

The violent family is easy to describe, but difficult to explain. There is scarcely any discipline not able to descriptively explain violence in families through the application of the theories of their discipline. A variety of answers have been offered by medicine (Kempe & Helfer, 1972), sociology (Gelles & Straus, 1978, 1980), psychology (Feshback, 1980), social work (Gil, 1970), and the law (Besharov, 1985). There is no problem in arriving at a theoretical basis for family violence. The problem is in selecting from the myriad theories the one that applies to the family sitting in the office at that moment. Explaining family violence is not difficult. Discovering a starting point for work with the family sitting across the room sometimes seems impossible.

Today, practitioners must juggle competitive and unsupported theory, inadequate research, and a confusing legal system in their attempts to benefit violent families. There does not seem to be a juncture at which all these areas have successfully met. Fortunately, there are some commonalities and parallels within these families that may, at least, bring the practitioner closer to understanding a given family. But first there must be an "un-learning" of an over-expectation of a protectiveness in the family.

Promise 8: There will be a normal family structure that can be identified that will promise continuous protection against internal violence.

The family is a social organization. This organization was designed to maximize the potential for the survival, survival of the individuals within it. Finding violence in a family should not lead to a mourning over lost "familiness." This family has not lost some mystical psychological adhesive. This family may simply be demonstrating a poor fit. It is demonstrating a structural incompatibility between its members, between itself and its environment, or both.

If the individuals in a family are to survive, each must balance the achievement of their own needs against the cost to the family unit. This requires an altruistic ability to sacrifice, to enter reciprocal relationships with other family members, and an ability to invest in the family's overall progress. Our social-biological mix has provided the greatest possible probability that these skills will be available. But, in some individuals, they are not. In most cases, it is the most powerful member of the family whose needs are met first. This is even more clear in the violent family. Practitioners must understand this competitiveness and temper their view of the family as a consistently safe place to be for all concerned.

All families have inherent stress points. These common features are the foundation upon which life-threatening actions are built. Straus (1979), for example, has noted that the intensity of involvement between family members is unparalleled in any other relationship. These individuals spend a great deal of time together engaged in an enormous range of activities. Each of these activities is subject to the judgments and criticisms that are learned as the right of family membership. Bourne (1979, p. 7) simply suggests that we are taught to be ourselves in our families. This gives license to both positive and negative interaction, both thought to be safe. In some families this is a dangerously inaccurate assumption.

Straus (1979) cites the involuntary nature of family membership as a stressor. The family member is an individual trapped in a long-term commitment to a group he or she did not seek to join (Gelles, 1974,

p. 27). But even involuntary membership provides extraordinary knowledge of other family members. Gelles (1979, p. 14) describes the "social biographies" of family members as being too familiar to other family members. With this information comes the knowledge of individual vulnerabilities. This is knowledge that can be used against others during times of anger and competitiveness.

Garbarino (1977, p. 569) completes the litany of probable points of family conflict with a description of the psychological costs of family membership. In his view, there is no privacy in the family. In the family each member's time and/or resources are assumed to belong to all members; activities are scrutinized and commented upon, and obligations are manipulated continuously.

Through these views the family can be seen as a group of individuals who have an exaggerated level of personal/emotional involvement, potentially destructive information about others' strengths and weaknesses, permission to act as they please, and involuntary membership. If that mixture is not explosive enough, additional strain can be found in the age differences, sex differences, role conflicts, and lack of privacy that are also predictable features of family life (Gelles, 1974, p. 27; Straus, 1979).

It is clear that costs are extracted by membership in a family. Yet the family members who isolate themselves from these burdens also isolate themselves from the most predictable (in most cases) sources of warmth and security (Garbarino, 1977b). The dilemma for family members, and the practitioners working in their behalf, is that of determining at what point the costs of participation exceed the benefits.

A Summary View

In looking at the problems in the family violence research and practice, it may be asked, "is it too soon for a clinical/legal issues review such as this book represents?" In looking at the intractability of the legal system and poor definitions that exist within it, it may be asked, "is it too late for a clinical/legal issues review such as this?" Both answers are *no* because, despite some of the unkept promises, many violent families have been helped. Those experienced in working with violent families know that they have helped, at least in some cases.

The difficulty rests with the fact that many practitioners have found that it has been instinctive responses, also known as "common sense," that have helped the most. Thus, many of the most successful interactions with violent families (clinical or legal) have gone unreported, as common-sense responses are thought to be "recalcitrant to analysis" (Fletcher, 1984, p. 212). Therefore, it is the intent of this work to report (not support or condemn) the clinical and legal research of the past two decades and juxtapose some of the practitioner's common sense and lore upon that reporting.

The research in family violence has not proven to be all that had been promised or hoped. That does not mean that learning has not taken place. The difficulty for practitioners, as Gelles (1982) has pointed out, has been in selecting and synthesizing those elements of the research that apply to their task. Once discovered, this synthesis must be displayed in some framework that is not only familiar, but easily used by the practitioner. That is what has been attempted in this work both for clinician and attorney.

Finally, if the legal or clinical practitioner does confront a violent family, three questions must be answered relative to their fundamental operations:

(1) What is the potential for dysfunction in this family compared to other families?
(2) How closely do the characteristics of this family approximate those of other families engaging in violence?
(3) What are the unique features of this family that allow its members to be dangerous to one another?

The suggestion from child maltreatment research is that each family's "ecology" (comprehensive internal and external world) must be examined in total to answer these questions (Garbarino & Gilliam, 1980). That comprehensive view is the goal of the practitioner's assessment.

A good initial assessment is nothing more than an examination of the critical environments within which the family must operate. A comprehensive view of these critical environments of risk (i.e., social, psychological, and family operations) will enable the practitioner to become familiar with critical variables in the family. Once isolated and prioritized, these family environment variables become the basis for cooperative legal and clinical resolution of family problems. A discussion of these critical environments of risk will be provided through the chapters that follow.

2

Getting to Know You: Fundamentals about the Family

The first meeting with a family suspected of being violent is an imposing task. The practitioner will often have a sense of being overwhelmed by the information-gathering task. These families tend to occur at the extremes of the information continuum; they are either silent and difficult or hyper-verbal. Most practitioners find some data-gathering model to be a useful addition to their armament in these cases. This chapter will offer a model that seems to hold some functional promise.

The basic question the practitioner must answer about a given family is whether it is able to prevent ordinary life events from escalating into violence, whether the traditional protective mechanisms within families are being impeded by the individual or environmental characteristics (i.e., "marker" variables that correlate with increased risk) that describe the family suspected of being violent. There are some specific marker variables that aid the practitioner in reaching this decision. However, since the information is likely to be either hard to acquire or hard to keep up with, a framework for collection will be helpful.

Assessing the Diathesis-Stress Continuum

Some practitioners prefer to place the information they acquire in an initial interview in a somewhat static perspective—taking a "snapshot" of the family. Cicchetti and Rizley (1984) have a useful model for this data harvesting. These child maltreatment researchers view the family in terms of "challenges" (problem areas) and "buffers" (compensating mechanisms). They further divide these areas into short-term and long-term problems. Such a four-square design allows the practitioner to see just how much weight the family is carrying and the resources they have to deal with the problems. Other practitioners prefer a somewhat more dynamic model of the family. The "diathesis-stress" continuum seems to offer such a perspective.

"Diathesis" in this model refers to an increased likelihood of being afflicted with a problem or engaging in a problematic behavior. It is often interpreted as a "propensity for." "Stress," as used here, describes individual, environmental, or relationship pressures that may overwhelm the individual's or family's ability to respond to events in a balanced manner. In this model, if an individual has a high propensity for a problem (i.e., diathesis) and is also highly stressed, he or she is at risk. Conversely, if the individual has a high propensity and very little stress, the problem may never surface. In some situations, extraordinary stress is sufficient to bring the problem about even in the absence of a pre-existing propensity. However, this model does help the practitioner begin to measure anticipated risk levels.

What remains necessary in the application of either model is gaining sufficient information to enable the practitioner to determine whether the individual/family is responding to an internalized propensity (e.g., psychopathology) or to situational stress (e.g., unemployment). It is this discrimination that dictates the degree of compassion (e.g., reducing situational stress) or control (e.g., restricting the opportunity for this propensity to manifest itself) to be applied in the practitioner's planning for the individual/family (Newberger & Bourne, 1979). Fortunately, key questions do exist that help to encourage the reluctant family reporter or control the over-enthusiastic talker.

Critical Questions at First Meeting:
Sample Guidelines

The initial meeting with the violent family is often conducted in the midst of a crisis due to the recent and sudden disclosure of the problem. The ability to conduct a structured assessment often becomes lost in the pace, emotionality, and volume of the initial interview. The practitioner must have some quick mechanism for organizing facts, observations, and social histories that arrive from multiple family members in a rush. Consider Table 2.1 as a general guide to some of the more important issues to be captured at the outset. These practitioner keys represent nothing more than the requirements of a functional family restated in question form. There is no claim to statistical reliability or validity in their organization. The maximum utility of these keys is in their ability to aid the practitioner in the identification of issues in families; families whose problems have exceeded the bounds of their ability to help themselves.

The ideal among families being initially assessed in this way is one in which the psychological attachment between its members is sufficiently strong to afford a balanced competitiveness. The individual members of this family will not jeopardize others in order to meet their needs. There is an ability to nurture when the need for nurturance is communicated. The parents in this family respond to the children both spontaneously and upon reasonable demand from the child. The family's members both enjoy and make sacrifices for each other. No single member has a disproportionate share of the power in the family, nor is there a single member who is either idolized or denigrated. The environment of the family is capable of supporting its needs, and the family is capable of using the environment to acquire necessary goods and services. Most importantly, the practitioner is not left with a lingering doubt that there is a problem in the family that eluded detection in this initial interview. For the most part, in professional work with violent families, few of these positive signals will be found. A similar set of keys may be used to evaluate the family's environment in an effort to determine the stress component of the diathesis-stress continuum.

This second set of keys, like the first, is no more than a collection of issues critical to violent families representing the probable stress points in the family's environment. To the extent that poverty provides a fertile field for crisis, isolation prevents adequate help from reaching the family, and intellectual or educational problems prevent the learning of adequate responses to crisis, these issues predict trouble. The parent attempting to do the work of two is chronically stressed. So, too, is the adolescent parent who has entered that role too soon. If the two are combined in one family, managing

TABLE 2.1
Practitioner Keys to Propensities (Diathesis) in
Family Functioning

(1) Has this family demonstrated a past willingness/capacity to nurture and protect *all* its members? Have their been any *major* failures in nurturance or protection in the past?

(2) Do the members of the family seem to be able to make their needs known to the other family members?

(3) Do the adult members of the family that have any *obvious* mental illnesses/ delays/incapacities that might inhibit their ability to understand a family member's needs or respond to them?

(4) Do the children in the family seem to be able to elicit caregiving from either or both parents? By report? By observation?

(5) Do family members seem to engage in altruistic exchanges or is there the constant presence of competition or expectation of repayment or reward?

(6) Are the relationships in the family reciprocal?

(7) Do family members seem to be able to find positive elements in other members and positive aspects of their interactions?

(8) Are the family members given permission to operate as individuals or do they seem to be fused into a single undifferentiated pattern of thought and behavior?

(9) Does it seem that one family member is continuously asked to sacrifice for the others or delay gratification of their own needs until others are satisfied?

(10) Is there a single family member who seems be the recipient of all positive or negative exchanges and attention?

(11) Does the competition within the family seem manageable? for physical resources? space? emotional support?

(12) Is the physical environment in which the family lives capable of supporting this family given its relative strengths and weaknesses?

(13) Is there a completely dominant family member? adult male? adult female? child?

(14) Did you (the practitioner) have a nagging sense that something was wrong with family interaction after completing the interview?

TABLE 2.2
Practitioner Keys to Critical Environmental Issues
in the Violent Family

(1) Does their environment repeatedly expose family members to crisis situations of all types?

(2) Would this environment be considered poverty-ridden by most persons?

(3) Is the family physically isolated from formal and informal sources of support?

(4) Is the family emotionally isolated from formal and informal sources of support? Are personal and kinship support systems weak?

(5) Are both the personal and official support systems that are available appropriately used in times of need?

(6) Can nuclear family members count on each other in times of crisis? Is there evidence of past problem-solving capacity?

(7) Is this family chronologically out-of-step with other families (e.g., early childbirth, early marriage, too many children too quickly)?

(8) Did the adults in this family terminate their education prematurely?

(9) Is there evidence of relationship disruption among adult family members (e.g., dissolution, marital disruption or separation, prior removal of children from parental care by family or official agency)?

(10) Are there problematic employment patterns in adult members?

(11) Does there seem to be a reasonable understanding of child care, child development, parenthood skills, and discipline on the part of the parents?

(12) Is there an over-reliance upon physical punishment? Or a belief that increasing the severity of corporal punishment increases the effectiveness of learning?

(13) Are any of the children in the family described as different, hard to handle, or troublesome?

(14) Is misbehavior on the part of the child ever described as being intentional or purposeful?

(15) Is there a belief system (in adult members) that seems rigid, inflexible, and drawn along absolute polarities (i.e., black-and-white thinking)?

(16) Is there a sense of deprivation or violence in the childhood or background of adults in the family? If so, how does this influence their knowledge or acceptance of violence?

(17) Are the extended family members or other non-kin adults in the home who are not part of the nuclear family?

the environment may be an impossibility. Finally, the frustration of employment difficulty may be expressed in the family through an aggressive act directed at any member. These are the elements of stress in the family that tend to breed violence. A family may contain both normal and abnormal stress.

Stress in the Family Environment

Most families survive normal stresses with a minimum of difficulty (Garbarino, 1977b, p. 572). It is when such stresses come upon the family too rapidly (Justice & Justice, 1976), too chronically (Steele & ·Pollack, 1972, p. 8), or from too many sources at once (Pagelow, 1984, p. 125) that it becomes "abnormal" and unmanageable without outside assistance (Garbarino, 1977a, p. 727).

The failure to manage stress and crisis successfully is a recurrent element of violent families (Bourne & Newberger, 1979, p. 10; Garbarino, 1977a, p. 727; Howze & Kotch, 1984, p. 401). Violent families seem to be those families least able to prevent stress from escalating into crisis. This crisis overwhelms an already fragile family balance (Burgess & Garbarino, 1983; Conger, Burgess, & Barrett, 1979).

The violent family becomes imbalanced and internally competitive in the face of stress. This rapid decay in stability grows out of a lack of fundamental social skills (Wolfe, Kaufman, Aragona, & Sandler, 1981, p. 17), isolation from support (Howze & Kotch, 1984, p. 1), and an inability or unwillingness to seek outside help (Garbarino, 1977b, p. 572). Two features of this decay in stability will be noted by the practitioner. First, this family will move quickly from *the perception of stress* to *the experience of crisis* and will demonstrate inertia or panic unnecessarily. Second, this family, even in the midst of crisis, will isolate itself from sources of aid and support that might help to reduce the stressful conditions. It is critical to separate the genuinely isolated family from that family that *chooses* to isolate itself (Garbarino, 1977a, p. 727). The family that isolates itself is demonstrating a pattern of *over-reaction* and *under-response* that must be broken if problem-solving skills are ever to be introduced in this family. The next section will reveal just how common the over-stressed position of the violent family is across all forms of family violence.

Differential Stress Patterns
by Type of Family Violence

The reporting of stress and crisis is one of the more repetitive elements of the *child maltreatment* literature (Garbarino, 1977a; Steele & Pollack, 1972; Wolfe, Kaufman et al., 1981). The personal stability of the parent in this family is questioned as the day-to-day stresses of family management overwhelm the adult who feels worthless and incapable (Alexander, 1972, p. 26; Steele & Pollack, 1972, p. 8). The poor quality of the social networks and supports available to the maltreating family are seen as contributing to a prolongation of this crisis (Garbarino & Gilliam, 1980) and there is a generalized social incompetence both within and outside the family (Wolfe et al., 1981) which results in accumulated pressures that eventually overwhelm the parent's protective mechanisms (Bolton, 1983; Steele, 1982). This pattern of overwhelming stress takes its toll in other types of violent families as well.

Conjugal violence has been described by Ganley and Harris (1978) as *direct* evidence of stress in the perpetrator's extra-familial environment. Neidig, Friedman, and Collins (1984, p. 8) find such violence to be the result of intra-familial stress due to poor marital adjustment. Whether internally or externally generated, most experts find stress-management skills a pivotal feature of any conjugal violence treatment program.

The stresses of caring for an older person are a recurrent theme in the work on *elder mistreatment*. The family may be stretched to, and beyond, the breaking point by this demand (Douglas, 1983, p. 183). This is not only physical stress, but constant social/emotional depletion that leaves the caretaker unable to cope (Steinmetz, 1983, p. 138). And while alternative care is available (Cazenave & Woodburn, 1981), the financial and psychological costs of such care frequently restrict its use.

Steinmetz (1983, p. 138) has called the caretakers in this stressful situation *Generationally Inversed* for the child now becomes a parent to their parent. Giordano and Giordano (1984b) describe five patterns of stress that may accompany such an inversion. First, the internal family dynamics may have been dysfunctional for some time. The stress, in this case, is a continuation. Second, the increasing dependency of the older person may increase risk. Third, individual pathologies may surface in this new relationship. Fourth, economic drain or the need to leave a career to become a caretaker creates stress. Finally, external stress such as substance abuse, unemployment, or medical problems may push this struggling family past its ability to cope.

Some families respond to the stress of an older person in their home with overcommitment and burn-out. Others may provide only minimal care and unintentional neglect. Still others reject the caregiver role, strike out against it, and bring overt violence into the family (Douglas & Hickey, 1983, p. 175). In any case, stress is introduced by inescapable circumstance and violence may be the result.

A Summary View

Stress does play a role in the violent family. *The assessment of past and present stress, as well as the family's demonstrated capacity and techniques for coping with it, are vital factors of the practitioner's initial knowledge of the violent family.* However, while stress remains a necessary element in the development of violence, it is usually not sufficient in itself. Equal consideration must be given to the personal operating styles, strengths, and weaknesses of each family member (i.e., diathesis). It is only through the study of both diathesis and stress elements that the logic of the violence in the family may be understood. This is critical because *until the practitioner can understand why violence seemed a viable alternative for reducing perceived stress in the family,* intervention cannot begin. A view of the features common to all types of violent families will reveal their tenuous nature, even in the absence of additional stresses.

Assessing the Family's Commonalities with Other Violent Families

The exact relationship between the differing forms of family violence is unclear (i.e., mirror image? chance? unrelated?). What is clear is that there are common themes. *Discovery of these fundamental themes in a family and assessment of how these themes dictate family functioning are the goals of the initial assessment.*

Just how each set of marker variables come together in a given family will differ in every case. *There are no universal rules and patterns.* What is universal for the practitioner is the complexity of

TABLE 2.3
Marker Variables Correlated with Intra-Familial Violence

	Physical Maltreatment	Sexual Abuse	Conjugal Violence	Elder Mistreatment
Social Environment				
(1) Multiple environmental stressors	X	X	X	X
(2) Social isolation	X	X	X	X
(3) Inadequate survival skills	X	X	X	X
(4) Financial stress	X	X	X	X
(5) Employment/occupational difficulty	X	X	X	X
(6) Educational barriers	X	X	X	
(7) Racial/ethnic over-representation	X	X	X	
(8) Overcrowded living environment	X	X		X
Psychological Environment				
(1) Psychopathology and/or personality/ character disorders and distortions	X	X	X	X
(2) Confused dependencies and attachments	X	X	X	X
(3) Low self-esteem and poor self-image	X	X	X	X
(4) Feelings of helplessness, powerlessness, and worthlessness	X	X	X	X
(5) Immaturity	X	X	X	X
(6) Depression	X	X	X	X

Characteristic				
(7) Failure to control aggression and anger	X	X	X	X
(8) Anhedonia (inability to experience pleasure)	X	X	X	
(9) Defensiveness	X	X	X	
(10) Low physiological stimulus threshold	X			
(11) Hypersensitivity	X	X	X	

Family Process

Characteristic				
(1) Pervasive family/marital stress and dysfunction	X	X	X	X
(2) Poor/distorted family communication patterns	X	X	X	X
(3) Distorted/elevated expectations of victim	X	X	X	X
(4) Deprivation and hostility in family of origin	X	X	X	X
(5) Power imbalances generated from rigid, domineering, and controlling family style	X			
(6) Role confusions, reversals, and disturbances	X	X	X	X
(7) Competitiveness and jealousy	X	X	X	X
(8) Difficulty in trusting	X	X	X	X
(9) Inadequate caregiving knowledge	X			X
(10) Religiousness	X	X	X	
(11) Non biological family relationships	X	X		
(12) Single parenthood	X	X		
(13) Over-valuation of physical punishment	X			
(14) Victim characteristics that contribute to the problem	X			X

NOTE: See Appendix A for references.

patterns that must be traced in each family before an understanding of the violent act can occur.

The Good Guys and the Bad Guys:
The Violent Family Matrix

A harsh history of failures in the child maltreatment area has provided many valuable lessons over the past 25 years. Among those lessons is the knowledge that single-factor theories do not begin to explore the dark side of families (Newberger, 1985a; Wolfe, 1985; Wolfe, Kaufman et al., 1981, p. 13). In any violent family, multiple factors are simultaneously in operation. Beyond the individual family member's personal characteristics a "socially impoverished environment" (Garbarino, & Gilliam, 1980, p. 188) contributes to the pathological adaptation of all family members. The practitioner is wise to adopt this ecological perspective when putting the pieces of the family jigsaw puzzle together.

In the ecological view, the family and its environment are seen as interdependent systems (Garbarino, 1977a, p. 722). Such models consider the cultural support for or aversion to violence, available social supports, external stresses, and deficiencies/strengths in all family members (Herrenkohl, Herrenkohl, Toedter, & Yanushefski, 1984, p. 647). The goal of such models is an understanding of the interplay between personal history, social structure, historical events, and processes that "generate and sustain" the violent behavior within the family (Belsky, 1980, 1984; Garbarino, 1977a, p. 725). It is only through a comprehensive assessment of the marker variables mentioned at the outset of this chapter and placement of these marker variables upon a matrix that captures all family contexts, that understanding of the violence in a given family will be reached. The chapters immediately following will provide some sense as to the family contexts that describe the greatest danger.

Part II

Capturing the Critical Environments

3

Critical Issues in the Violent Family's Social Environment

Partners in Crime:
Family Violence and Poverty

Garbarino (1977a) has said it best: "Being poor is bad for families." In a poor family, opportunities are closed, deprivation is increased, and the scarcity of resources may generate extreme competition between family members, which culminates in a violent act (Mulford & Cohen, 1967). This poverty, and the resultant competition, are major reasons why practitioners will find that the most crucial early role to play is the *stabilization of resources*. Only after that stabilization has been completed will the more familiar professional roles become useful. This will be true irrespective of the type of family violence encountered.

The Physically Maltreating Family

From the outset of child maltreatment research (Brody, 1968; Gil, 1970) to current study (Herrenkohl et al., 1984) it has been clear that socioeconomic status (SES) influences the interactions between parents and children. According to Brody (1968) lower SES mothers are found to be less stimulating to their children and to put a higher value upon control through punishment. Herrenkohl and colleagues (1984, p. 644) supported this thesis through their finding that the higher the family income, the more positive the overall tone of family interactions. Higher income was related to affectionate behavior, warmth, amount of speaking and overall positive interactions between parent and child. Obviously, it is easier for the parent under less stress to concentrate on luxuries such as worrying about their relationship with their child. But the Herrenkohl research team (1984, p. 642) also reminds the reader that physical and emotional health problems, as well as reduced academic performance of the lower SES child, negatively influences the parent-child relationship.

Gabinet (1983, p. 399) describes lower SES origin as the first step in the intergenerational transmission of inappropriate parenthood behaviors. In an atmosphere of pervasive poverty, it will be difficult for parents to teach their children to function more appropriately than they are functioning themselves. So the pressure upon the parent, negative influences from the child, and general difficulty in improving circumstances seem to combine to make family life more difficult. A comprehensive view indicates that lower SES families exhibit more coercion and control and may be less supportive, verbal, and/or stimulating with their children (Green, 1984a, p. 676). *If this is a single-parent family these effects of poverty are even more greatly exaggerated* (Kimball, Stewart, Conger, & Burgess, 1980, p. 58).

Being poor impinges on every aspect of family life. If families have few resources to cope with stress, even normal emergencies will increase the risk for family dysfunction (Garbarino & Gilliam, 1980; Giovannoni & Billingsley, 1970). Conflict over resources in the poor family is both internal and external (Burgess & Garbarino, 1983, p. 95). As Bourne notes (Bourne & Newberger, 1979a, p. 7), we live in a world where material success is a major goal. Too few resources exist for everyone to meet their needs; violence may be the natural consequence. The alert practitioner then will *assess not only the internal conflict related to poverty, but also the SES as a symbol to the parent of personal worth and value or its absence.*

A Summary View

A summary view would find the research on physical abuse somewhat ambivalent on the subject of poverty. Even as there is a suggestion that reported cases of family violence are biased toward lower SES groups, there are logical connections between poverty and such violence (Pelton, 1978). Most practitioners will be dealing predominantly with officially reported cases, those most subject to the over-reporting of poor families. It seems wise then to seek to understand the frustrations and internal competitions within the lower

SES family. It will be these frustrations and scarce resources upon which violent acts are constructed. The priorities of professional function, in light of these realities, is resource stabilization first, followed by concern over psychodynamics, at least in the physically maltreating family.

Child Sexual Abuse

The relationship between child sexual abuse and lower SES standing seem highly dependent upon the information source being used to examine the relationship. Officially reported samples of child sexual abuse cases are heavily weighted in the direction of the lower SES family (Brown & Holder, 1980; NCCAN, 1981). However, official reporting sources show a consistent bias toward reporting of lower SES families across all types of family violence. This lower SES presence is not found in representative community surveys (Finkelhor, 1986). In fact, one study has estimated that sexually abusive families in the community may have mean annual incomes as much as 10 percent higher than physically maltreating families (Brown, 1978). Studies of student populations reveal somewhat mixed results, but such samples are so highly selective that SES level is not accurately measured from such college populations (Finkelhor, 1986). Overall, it does not appear that child sexual abuse is highly correlated with growing up in a lower SES environment or in living in such an environment as an adult. Among those samples that do find such an association, the risk of reporting bias is sufficient to cloud the relationship found. This does not deny the possibility of an environmental/income interaction in the stresses that contribute to sexual abuse, but it does suggest that this relationship is not a significant one in most sexually abusive families.

Other Forms of Family Violence

The absence of economic resources stresses families, especially the primary adult provider. This remains true in *conjugal violence* and *elder mistreatment*. The effect of poverty is most direct in elder mistreatment in which a family that cannot afford an extra mouth is asked to house, feed, and provide medically for an infirm older person (Douglas, 1983, p. 396). Almost as direct is poverty's effect on the strapped wage earner who, already insecure, is constantly faced with an inability to provide sufficiently for a family. This violation of both the wage earner and the family's expectations can generate the potential for a violent response (Deschner, 1984, p. 29; Straus, Gelles, & Steinmetz, 1980).

The Violent Family: A Summary View

Family violence is not exclusively a lower SES situation. Other than officially reported cases, it may not even be predominantly a lower SES problem. Yet *most practitioners in the field will work with a majority of lower SES families.* In part, that is a function of the greater likelihood of being reported and in part a function of the chronicity and severity of the problems in lower SES environments. The impact of family violence is simply greater on lower SES families.

Families that are financially better prepared have more escapes which may be exercised earlier in the development of the violent pattern. Even if a significantly violent episode should occur, there are more resources and alternatives available to this family. These are not families necessarily trapped by recurrent violence. All families hold the potential for internalized destruction. But in the financially stable family, violence may more often be met by compensatory action than in the lower SES family in which the only possible reaction may be acceptance. Such acceptance is one element of the isolation of these families.

Social Isolation

Family violence is the most private form of violence. Violence feeds on family isolation for it prevents detection; ignores positive social values and monitoring that might inhibit the violence; and keeps resources, expertise, and the input of others from the family. All these are natural helping factors that might prevent the violence (Garbarino, 1977b, p. 569; 1977a, p. 727). No matter the form of violence in the family, isolation from support and detection can only serve to feed the on-going nature of such violence. *Isolation must be reduced before any hope for the elimination of the problem is realistic.*

The Physically Maltreating Family

Maltreating families are isolated both geographically and through their reluctance to use other persons for assistance in times of distress (Garbarino, 1977b). This isolation may be both purposeful and unintended in the same family at different times (Gaudin & Pollane, 1983). Bringing families to a point at which they are able to use existing resources is a basic element of work with violent families of every description (Wolfe, Kaufman et al., 1981, p. 16).

In child maltreatment particularly, the likelihood of violence toward children varies directly with the availability, adequacy, and the use of supportive services and kinship systems. Isolation from these sources of help has been described as the "extreme extension" of the concept of "privacy"; the type of privacy that allows child maltreatment to become a reality (Garbarino & Crouter, 1977b, p. 572, 1978, p. 604). Yet the privacy and isolation of the physically maltreating family pales in comparison to that of the sexually abusive family, which is hidden not only physically but psychologically.

The Sexually Abusive Family

Isolation contributes to the sexual abuse of children in many ways (Finkelhor, 1979; Justice & Justice, 1976; Tierney & Corwin, 1983). This isolation may be social or geographical (Tierney & Corwin, 1983, p. 107). For example, the isolation of a rural lifestyle has been understood to be one possible factor in the development of an intra-familial sexual orientation (Henderson, 1972). The isolation of the sexually abusive family may also be a double-edged sword, as its contributions to the loneliness of the victim may make them even more susceptible to the overtures of the perpetrator (Justice & Justice, 1976). Whether isolated within the family or isolated from outside sources of support, this predicts danger.

As families withdraw from the world around them, relationships between persons in the home become more critical (Finkelhor, 1979). As loneliness and the exaggerated importance of family members build together, the isolation limits the degree of scrutiny the family is subjected to; exempting parents from evaluation by friends, relatives, and neighbors (Finkelhor, 1979; Tierney & Corwin, 1983). Ultimately, the absence of extra- familial accountability and increase in intra-familial intensity offers the opportunity for uncontrolled experimentation and lapses in judgment. Importantly, *this is a pattern completely hidden from the outside world.*

The sexually abusive family is often outwardly stable, financially capable and has an adult male who is involved with the community. Isolation in this family is as much psychological as physical and is maintained through the cooperative acceptance of the family secret by family members (Kempe & Kempe, 1984, p. 53). Isolated, too, are the adults in this family—isolated from each other.

In the sexually abusive family the dominant paternal figure most often rules with an iron hand. He presents an unbalanced source of parental power in contrast to his passive-dependent or independent-critical spouse. Isolated from each other by fear or loathing, but dependent upon the relationships in the family as the sole source of human contact, these parents may turn to the children to reduce their sense of personal isolation. The result is often a secret set of psychological and physical alliances known only to the family members involved. This secret is held tightly until an awareness of its deviance or overt symptoms of its consequences no longer allow it. It is only after this dysfunctional pattern has become habitual that the practitioner will enter—a point at which success is often limited. A similar protectionistic and secretive relationship functioning is often found in the conjugal violence situation.

Conjugal Violence

Violent co-habitators are insulated from the eyes and ears of the community (Pagelow, 1984). They do not join (Gelles & Straus, 1980). They do not make friends (Dobash & Dobash, 1979). And, geographical mobility prevents the establishment of protective roots, that is, trusted friends or knowledge of community services (Pagelow, 1984). These are families isolated at the *community level.* For these families, there is nowhere to turn in crisis. But this may be of questionable import in that, were they aware, it is unlikely that the victim would be allowed to participate in any form of help (Deschner, 1984, p. 30).

The violent conjugal couple is isolated at the *individual level* as well. This is an isolation that forces them to be far too important to each other. In the absence of other supportive relationships, even destructive relationships become unrealistically vital (Ganley, 1981). In fact, as isolation builds, there is an increasing perception on the part of both victim and perpetrator that the world outside is a hostile place in which no one can be trusted.

If one member of this destructively attached relationship should gain the strength to venture into this dangerous world, violence is often viewed by their partner as the only way to keep them in their place (Kalmuss & Straus, 1983; Neidig et al., 1984, p. 5; Whitchurst, 1974). Since there is no one to tell the victim otherwise, and since the victim is cut off from official sources of support, that place is likely to be where he or she may stay. Such a lack of alternatives is characteristic of all family violence victims, particularly the frail elderly person being cared for in the home.

Mistreatment of the Elderly

Mistreatment of the elderly is a problem of hidden proportions largely because these older persons are maintained outside the community mainstream in homes or institutions (Luppens & Lau, 1983, p. 204). It is a product not only of victim isolation, but perpetrator isolation as well (Douglas, 1983, p. 146; Falcioni, 1982, p. 209). These caretakers are isolated from the support and knowledge that would be required to lighten their load. Victims, on the other hand, are isolated from sources of support by caretakers and by physical and/or mental impairments that impede movement (Falcioni, 1982, p. 209). Overall, isolation may be among the most critical features of the elder mistreatment situation for there is no treatment in the absence of reporting of cases (Cazenave, 1983, p. 200). The other side of the coin is presented by those elements of the family's social environment that make finding cases all too common, minority group membership, for example.

Racial Factors

Race is a dangerous variable in family violence work. It is among the weakest of the research variables as a result of the over-reliance upon official reporting—reporting which guarantees minority over-representation, (Cazenave, 1983, p. 189; Hampton, 1984, p. 2; Newberger, Newberger, & Hampton, 1983), confounding socioeconomic conditions (Friedrich & Einbender, 1983, p. 246; Hampton, 1984, p. 6) and wide-ranging ethnic variations in family operation (Friedrich & Einbender, 1983, p. 246; Giovannoni & Becerra, 1979). Racial stereotyping is also a common risk in practice.

Child Maltreatment

Racial stereotyping has resulted in an increased likelihood of being reported in both conjugal violence (Staples, 1976) and child maltreatment (Bourne & Newberger, 1979). It is a confusing element of the case. In the case of child maltreatment, for example, this high rate has been confirmed (Gil, 1970), denied (Billingsley, 1969), and found to be spurious overall (Young, 1964). Some writers describe racial differences as being related to poverty (Pelton, 1978), while others see the social distance between the minority family and the family violence practitioner to be a problem (Bourne & Newberger, 1979).

From the ecological perspective, Garbarino (1977a) writes that the social and kinship system that typify minority group members living in proximity should *reduce* the likelihood of family violence. Others write that family violence rates are predictably higher due to the generally oppressed and isolated circumstances described by that same ecology (Daniel, Hampton, & Newberger, 1983).

Ultimately, even if the research were more clear, there would be a strong sense in practice that the confounding effects of income level, employment status, social organization, cultural expectations, and in-group identity might prohibit minority group members from easy accessibility and willing use of outside sources of help in times of crisis (Cazenave, 1983, pp. 189, 199). This is especially true of the traditional clinical mental health setting, as will be discussed in a later chapter.

The conclusions must be that, empirically, racial differences in family violence have only been tentatively explored (Straus et al., 1980). Yet there remains a great propensity on the part of practitioners to accept allegations of violence as true when the family is a minority family; especially in child maltreatment cases (Gelles, 1982).

Child Sexual Abuse

The sexual abuse of children does not seem to demonstrate a strong relationship to ethnic group membership. There is some evidence that black women may be more frequent victims of general sexual assault than white women, but this research more commonly references rape than childhood sexual abuse (Wyatt, 1985, p. 507). Even in officially reported populations, populations that would be expected to reflect an ethnic group bias, the percentages of ethnic group participation for sexual abuse tends to mirror the percentage that exists in the community under study (Finkelhor, 1986). In both community and clinical samples the selectivity of sampling, definitions used, and failure to control for demographic variables limit generalizability and lead to less than firm conclusions.

Finkelhor (1986) has reviewed community studies and was unable to find an empirically valid work that demonstrated any real differences between black and white prevalence rates. The one study that did show a slightly greater black representation failed to hold that difference when demographic differences between black and white families were controlled. Two other studies (Peters, 1984; Pierce & Pierce, 1984) have implied, in fact, that the features of the white family that may contribute to the occurrence of sexual abuse are not as critical in the black family.

In the Pierce and Pierce (1984) work, it was determined that sexual abuse at the hands of an in-home perpetrator was somewhat less likely in the black family (p. 11). Detection was thought to be easier in the black home as well for the child seemed to have a stronger sense that he or she would be believed if they reported an assault than a white child facing a comparable dilemma. Since this study found the perpetrator in the black home much less likely to be living in the home than in the white family, the black mother was thought to be less dependent and thereby less tolerant of the sexual abuse (p. 12). Peters (1984) also found that vulnerability factors, which increase risk in the white home (e.g., paternal absence), were not as critical a risk in the black culture.

A study by Wyatt (1985) hints at the fact that the age of the child studied may influence the prevalence of sexual assault discovered. The conclusion of Wyatt's work was that the black female's risk of experiencing some form of abuse involving body contact was equal to or slightly higher than the white female. But these black women tended to be somewhat older at the time of the initial assault than the white women. Even in this study, the rates for blacks and whites are so similar as to negate any hint of preponderance for either group.

Although the work is extremely limited at this time, other ethnic groups may demonstrate some differential rates. In Finkelhor's reviews of both Russell's San Francisco study and the Kercher and McShane survey of Texas driver's license holders (Finkelhor, 1984, 1986) he reports these researchers to have found accelerated rates for Hispanic women. In his review of the Texas study, he reports a 21.7 percent sexual victimization rate for Hispanic women as opposed to a 9.8 percent white and 10.4 percent black rate. Similarly, Russell found Hispanic women to have higher general incestuous victimization and specifically father-daughter incest rates than the other ethnic groups in her sample. On the positive side, the Russell study found lower rates for Asian and Jewish women than the sample as a whole. So, there may be an interaction between ethnicity and sexual abuse in some population groups, but this is an effect that must be studied more carefully before conclusions are drawn.

Overall, it seems judicious to assume that sexual abuse of children is likely to be a risk shared across ethnic groups. It is not a risk that can be isolated in one group, nor can it be denied by any group. For the practitioner, it is wise to remember the frequent reluctance of some ethnic groups to become involved in outside sources of support for such problems. For sexual abuse, perhaps above all other family violence problems, a familiar source of help may be the only source of help approached.

Conjugal Violence

Walker (1979) notes the common belief that the lower SES minority woman is the most frequent victim of conjugal violence. Not only is this erroneous, but the lower SES woman is less dependent on the male perpetrator for survival in most cases, allowing her to be better prepared to fight back. This does not suggest that such violence does not occur in ethnic populations. However, it is likely that the most important features of the environment related to the occurrence of conjugal violence are found in demographic realities beyond ethnicity (i.e., financial stress). And, in some special cases, there is an ethnicity/environment interaction that does appear to increase frustrations.

Recently, Carrillo and Marrujo (1984) studied battering Hispanic couples based on the hypothesis that the strain of adaptation to a new culture (acculturation) might generate stresses that culminate in conjugal violence. This belief was confirmed. Psychological and personality variables in these couples were no different from other battering couples. When the sex role expectations, family obligations, and permissible amounts of contact with people varied from that of their male-dominated traditions, violence did erupt (Carrillo & Marrujo, 1984, pp. 4–5). The change in language, resulting in lowered self-esteem for some of the perpetrators, may have also played a role in the development of frustration and violence. Given these stresses, and the obvious risks represented by leaving all sources of personal and social support behind, newly acculturated minority couples are seen to be a special needs group.

For the practitioner, Carrillo and Marrujo suggest that any intervention be offered in the language of the couple. They go on to suggest that the focus of service must be on concrete needs (e.g., understanding immigration policy or financial aid), and that referrals be directed to their own community where social networks can be developed. As critical as these racial features seem in the conjugal violence situation, they seem more elusive in elder mistreatment.

Mistreatment of the Elderly

Elder mistreatment seems to be a white middle-class problem (Galbraith & Zdorkowski, 1984, p. 22). But this area of study is so new that it is unlikely that any true understanding of racial variables has been gained (Cazenave, 1983, p. 190). There is a general belief in the greater respect for older persons held by minority groups and the greater acceptance of common residence for extended families. These issues, however, are difficult to confirm. Similarly, inaccessibility to outside intervention and barriers to reporting may be providing a distorted view of racial issues in mistreatment of the elderly. Overall, it seems likely that no more accurate information will be available in this area until reporting systems have become more common and representative.

A Summary View

The minority family may be at greater risk for being reported for family violence. The nonminority family seems to be better insulated against official agencies or to have alternatives that are exercised earlier. Social, cultural, and economic differences do exist in poor minority families that not only increase risk but decrease environmental protection. These same risks face poor, nonminority families. Cultural differences impact the practitioner in both clinical and legal realms, and little has been done to test more effective differential approaches. Continuing failure to do so will result in a secondary victimization being placed upon the family by a well-intentioned, but under-informed, practitioner group.

A Summary View:
The Social Environment

A comprehensive view of the social environment of the violent family is of an environment that is hostile from several perspectives. Their resources are limited, isolation plays against any opportunity to become free of the environment, and practitioners seem to stereotype the minority group members among them as being at increased risk automatically. The point all too often forgotten is that enormous numbers of families face the stresses of such an environment without engaging in violence at any time. The assumption of violence in this environment is an assumption that must be tempered by a more thorough understanding of the additional critical environments of risk that are present in the violent family. One such critical environment is that of the family's psychological world, as will be described in the next chapter.

4

The Psychological Environment of the Violent Family

Psychological Issues

Whether a function of the medical model that defined early thinking, or the ongoing search for the characteristics of violent individuals that distinguish them from nonviolent individuals, much of the study of violent families has focused upon personality variables. There seems to be a pervasive need to view the perpetrator of family violence as psychologically impaired; such an impairment allows us to comfortably distance ourselves from the perpetrator. Not only have such single-factor views proven to be inadequate in the face of today's multiple-causation theories, the search for a violent personality pattern has been frustrated at virtually every turn.

Child Maltreatment

The psychiatric viewpoint defined initial exploration into the traits of the violent parent. In the earliest work, a search was initiated for a specific personality syndrome described by attributes that would lead to a characterological fault. This fundamental flaw would, it was hypothesized, lead to problems in cognition, motivation, and affective areas that could essentially prohibit the possibility of successful parenthood. To this end, personality profiles, early childhood experiences, and coping/defense mechanisms were scrutinized in the hope that a treatable pathology would reveal itself in these parents (Wolfe, 1985). It did not happen. In fact, overt psychopathology only revealed itself in 10 to 20 percent of the cases (Pollack & Steele, 1982; Wasserman, 1967). Ever optimistic that a treatable Achilles' heel would be found, clinical researchers moved from a hypothesis of pervasive impairment to one that speculated upon dysfunction in individual personality areas such as poor impulse control, poor self-image, and/or distortions in perceptions of and beliefs about children (Kempe & Helfer, 1972, p. xii).

In their search for treatment-worthy targets, clinicians explored virtually every clinical entity. Zalba (1967) described the parent as angry, depressed, passive-aggressive, compulsive, impulsive, and trapped in an identity/role crisis. Alexander (1972, p. 23) was more kind, viewing the parent as vulnerable to criticism and subject to feeling rejection more easily than other persons. Mulford and Cohen (1967) returned to the harsher perspective in which the parents were seen as hostile, aggressive, and self-defeating; persons who were sufficiently immature in their actions to suggest a character disorder. Elizabeth Elmer (1967) found "emotional disturbance." Johnson and Morse (1968) described "rigidity and dominance," and Spinetta and Rigler (1972) established a prominent and permanent place for low self-esteem in this parent that survives today. By the time Gelles (1973) successfully argued against a reliance upon psychopathology as a singular causal factor in child maltreatment, its place in theory was solidified. Echoes of these early studies will be found in research, clinical strategies, and statutory language to this day (Green, 1984a, p. 675).

For the practitioner, several realities have emerged since this early work. First, attempts to identify personality characteristics that distinguish maltreating parents have been inconsistent and difficult to translate into practice (Wolfe, Kaufman et al., 1981, p. 51), especially courtroom practice. Second, maltreating parents cannot be captured by a single diagnostic category or circumscribed set of personality traits (Caplan, Watters, White, Perry, & Bates, 1984, p. 349). This fact does not inhibit endless discussion of the nonexistent abusive profile. The reality, however, is that behavioral differences in maltreating parents are now known to be more a function of complex situationally specific variables than any personality element operating within the individual (Wolfe, 1985).

Lately, even some of the pioneering thinkers have moderated their views of psychopathology in this parent. Kempe and Kempe (1978, 1984) maintain that 10 percent will manifest severe symptoms, but that 60 to 75 percent of the nonsymptomatic can be helped. Steele

(1982, p. 486) has concluded that no psychiatric diagnosis is usefully applied to these parents, but that a "constellation of psychological traits are commonly seen." This is a pattern that includes a poorly developed sense of identity, which will be compensated for through exaggerated self-assurance and braggadocio. To accompany this, Steele posits a long-standing emptiness evident through neediness, dependency, and immaturity. This pervasive loneliness is furthered by having few friends, no ability to trust, and a fear of authority figures. There will be no joy in finding pleasure or allowing it in others. Satisfaction is limited to the compliant behavior of one's children. This compliance is reached through physical punishment and the immediate expectation of appropriate behavior, no matter the age of the child. For these individuals, unable to control themselves or their environment, it is the child that can and will be controlled. Other researchers describe pathological operating styles rather than psychopathology.

Milner and Wimberly (1979) have found a recurrence of inadequate child-rearing attitudes and expectations in these parents. There is anxiety, not only about the child, but other personal relationships. Feelings of inadequacy, isolation, and loneliness generate vulnerabilities, insecurities, and inappropriate dependencies upon those around them. An unhealthy level of immaturity, an impaired ability to cope with stress, and impulsivity usually follow. Over-reactions to problems lead to a rigid, fatalistic, and inappropriate affect, which may manifest itself in an inability to experience pleasure *(anhedonia)*. Seeking someone to blame for this empty existence, having lost the ability to cope with their own problems long ago, the defenseless child may be the only individual the maltreating parent can master (Bourne & Newberger, 1979b, p. 7; Rodriquez, 1977, p. 19).

Overall, it seems that, for the maltreating parent, it is the child who is the source of comfort for the narcissistic adult. The parent is the needy child, and the roles are reversed to allow the child to nurture. It is not necessarily the parent as an individual who is demonstrating pathology. It is more common that their relationship with the child and the world around them is where the pathology rests. The practitioner is likely to sense pathology in a large number of perpetrators. Gelles (1982) has noted that it is the rare practitioner who has not experienced the frustrating sense that "these people are crazy!" And if they are not imbalanced as individuals, their actions certainly are. Upon reflection, however, it is likely that what felt like psychopathology in the individual was the bizarre way in which the family related. *What provides the sense of psychopathology in many violent families is a pathological pattern of inappropriate relationships in interpersonal, social, and community exchanges* (Wolfe, Kaufman et al., 1981, p. 15). This is a pathological pattern that reaches its extremity in the sexual abuse situation.

Psychopathology and Child Sexual Abuse

It has been difficult to wrest the view of child sexual abusers as mental defectives away from public and professional opinion (Finkelhor, 1979). Yet there is no solid indication that persons involved in incest are uniformly influenced by psychotic thought processes. Nor are there other "easily diagnosed psychological disorders" present (Tierney & Corwin, 1983, p. 109); pedophilia notwithstanding. Groth and colleagues (1982, p. 130) find immaturity rather than psychopathology to be at the heart of the problem. But recent work on pedophilic pan-sexuality (the tendency to engage in multiple sexual aberrations) confirms the strong possibility of a maladaptive personality style in many areas (Abel, 1985).

Writing of the psychological basis of pedophilia, Groth and associates have identified recurrent feelings of inadequacy, immaturity, vulnerability, helplessness, and isolation (1982, p. 136). Adult sexuality, as a result, takes on a threatening character, which causes an avoidance or abandonment of it. According to the Groth research team, the sex offender relates to the child victim as a peer. Through fantasy, the "fixated" offender sees himself as a child and the "regressed" offender sees the child as a pseudo-adult (1982, p. 136). Sexual contact with a child is comforting for both.

Russell (1984, p. 223) cautions against accepting the psychological reports of incarcerated offenders. She reminds her reader that, in order to have been incarcerated, the offender must have behaved atypically in some way (e.g., bizarre acts). As such, Russell sees these offenders as different from the majority which are perpetrators too subtle to be apprehended.

In overview, both Ferracuti (1972) and Groth (1978) have described the sex offender as being prone to alcohol abuse. Earlier work had described socially deprived backgrounds (Kaufman, Peck, & Tanguri, 1954), emotional dependence and isolation (Gebhard,

Gagnon, Pomeroy, & Christenson, 1965), and a pervasive deficit in intimacy, affection, and attention (Giaretto, 1976). Recently, Bauman and colleagues (Bauman, Kaspar, & Alford, 1983) attempted to isolate specific characteristics of the offender. Although interesting, this review must be interpreted in a special light for not only was this an incarcerated population, it was drawn from a military prison. The impact of these two characteristics is difficult to assess.

The Bauman et al. study (1983, pp. 79–80) first describes the presence of dependency problems. The offender expects his wife and family to be totally dependent upon him. In other cases, the offender is dependent upon a wife as though she were his mother. The result is the adult male being treated as either a lord and master or a child. The response of this male may be passive-aggressive behavior, alcohol abuse, and occasional sexual dominance of the weaker family members: the children.

Related to dependency on the wife is the offender's idealization of women. Women are seen as pure and giving. This is a serious conflict for the hyper-sexual male offender who wants a responsive sexual partner, but remains incapable of seeing his wife in that "dirty" role. Children are somehow different—less frightening and easier to control. Sexual activity with them is not "dirty."

Control and anger play a central role. The offender feels that he must be in control of himself and others. He has spent the majority of his life feeling that his peers were superior to him. In seeking out a child, he discovers an individual he can control. This also demonstrates to his wife that he does not need her.

A comprehensive view of the incarcerated offender is one of social inadequacy. Relationships are uncomfortable. Masculinity is in question, especially in the offender's own mind. Passivity in social interchange is followed by resentment at not having been more assertive. And, through some form of "repetition compulsion" (a repetitive pattern of self-destructiveness growing out of early victimization), these men put themselves in a position to fail and then become angry and suspicious that others are out to get them (Bauman et al., 1983, p. 78).

There is the necessity of a warning to the practitioner at this point. The work on the psychological aspects of the sexual abuser has been conducted largely within incarcerated populations, a notoriously unreliable research source. There is also a schism in the practice literature between the in-home incest offender and the incarcerated child molester. As this gap begins to close, it is becoming less certain that these two offenders are widely different. There is strong suggestion from clinical samples at least, that many predatory pedophiles are operating out of what appear to be stable homes and families. They may assault only the children in the home, only children outside the home, or both. *The practitioner is cautioned against the view that the incest perpetrator is essentially harmless to children outside the home.* This conclusion requires individual study in each case.

To date, the psychological characteristics of the sexual abuse perpetrator closely mirror those of the physically abusive perpetrator. While that may be accurate, it may also reflect a reliance upon earlier (child maltreatment) models. Or it may reflect a reluctance to equate in-home perpetration to child molestation; evidencing the need to see the in-home perpetrator as less deviant than the child molester. In any case, there is a clear need to reach beyond traditional psychological typologies in describing these populations. That same need for new descriptions becomes evident in reviewing the current work on abusive co-habitors; another perpetrator who has perhaps been viewed too sympathetically for practical legal/clinical intervention.

Conjugal Violence and Psychopathology

The recurring psychological picture of the violent male co-habitor is that he has a low level of self-esteem and compensates for his sense of inadequacy through the use of violence (Boyd, 1978; Gayford, 1975a; Johnston, 1984). Somehow, in his mind, the violent behaviors are interpreted as an indication of masculinity.

LaViolette, Barnett, and Miller (1984, p. 13) describe the battering male as one who subscribes to the stereotypical view of masculinity even as he worries about his own ability to measure up in that area. The result is a conflict in which masculinity is over-valued, and a fear of not meeting this idealized view causes anxiety. At the core of this problem is low self-esteem.

Multiple sources describe low self-esteem in violent male co-habitors (Neidig et al., 1984, p. 21). There is insecurity, depression, and an extra sensitivity to criticism that may translate almost immediately into a violent act. This male feels himself to be, and demonstrates himself as, an inadequate individual. It seems that this male lacks the social skills and abilities necessary to develop relationships that might allow for an adequate self-image (Johnston,

1984, p. 7; LaViolette et al., 1984, p. 1). This male lacks the basic operating currency of relationships as a result of his lack of compassion, assertiveness, coping skills, and control over emotions. These are deficits that retard interpersonal success both within and outside his family.

The violent co-habitor's difficulty in getting along in the world not only provides debilitating stress, but creates problems in trust and even mood swings (LaViolette et al., 1984, p. 3). Lack of trust may lead him to excessive jealousy regarding all family members, especially the adult female, as well as a narcissistic belief that he, the man of the family, owns them (Boyd & Kingbell, 1979, Star, 1983). If violence should occur as a result of these accumulated frustrations and inabilities, the victims are expected to understand the stress he feels (Neidig et al., 1984, p. 6)—additional confirmation of the narcissism in this individual.

A summary view would find the violent male co-habitor locked into psychopathological patterns predominantly of his own making. Deficient in skills that he makes no effort to acquire, he attributes a series of stresses to his world that others cannot see, to justify his actions. A man's world is a difficult place in which to live, according to this perpetrator, and none but he can truly understand. If this man's world is difficult, the old man's world is impossible.

Psychopathology and Mistreatment of the Elderly

Psychological issues in mistreatment of the elderly cannot be approached without consideration of both victim and perpetrator as a violent unit. Victim psychopathology may be the most critical. Older persons are in the age group that suffers the greatest psychopathological morbidity, and its presence is a burden for all.

In a review of psychopathology and aging, Solomon (1983a, p. 150) reported that between 30 to 50 percent of all persons over the age of 65 will have a severe depressive episode. Irreversible dementia such as Alzeheimer's Disease and some organic brain syndromes are endemic to this group. Milder forms of neurological and neurotic anxiety-related disorders also abound. If these disorders occur in the home of an over-anxious or psychopathologically unstable caretaker, problems can quickly arise.

Perpetrators of elder mistreatment are often seen as reacting to situational stress. In addition, many will be found to present with some personality or character difficulty. The most common of these presentations is the immature personality, in which a domineering nature, high level of anxiety and excitability, and low level of tolerance clash with the needs of the older person in the home (Chen, Bell, Dolinsky, Doyle, & Dunn, 1981, p. 10). There are simply too many stresses implied in caring for an older person to allow an unstable caretaker to survive the experience without acting out the stress in some way. If the caretaker also fails to understand the limited capacities of the older person, it is common for them to perceive the resultant dependency as a deliberate intrusion into their life (Chen et al., 1981, p. 10). This interaction pattern is often found to be present in younger parents and children, but the result is the same: violence.

Psychopathology in the elder mistreatment situation may be in the older victim, younger caretaker, or both. When the stress of the situation (e.g., depression, feelings of loss, health problems, and economic pressures) becomes overwhelming, dysfunction may be triggered. If there is no outside source to intervene and help reduce the noxious effects of the accumulated stresses, assaultive or neglecting behaviors may result.

Psychopathology and the Violent Family:
A Summary View

Psychopathology does play some role in the development of violence in the family; however, psychotic processes that distort reality do not predominate. More common are the deficiencies in personality that cause individuals to distort their world in a vain attempt to find comfort and/or security. Also common are personalities that cannot find equilibrium in the face of stress or contradiction of their needs. In the extreme, these immature, dependent, narcissistic, and antisocial tendencies become full-scale personality and character disorders; a familiar presence to the practitioner in family violence.

A Special View of Violent Family Psychopathology: The Personality Disorders

Personality/Character Disorders: An Introduction

The diagnosis of personality disorder has always been problematic. Many personality disordered persons have no major complaint about themselves. The usual reason for seeking (or being forced into) clinical attention is the effect that their behavior has had on others (e.g., violence in the family). As a result, some fear that this label is more a judgment than a diagnosis (Penna, 1981, p. 12).

It is difficult to determine the difference between what is abnormal from what is normal in some situations. Additionally, it is difficult to separate the situationally specific action from the enduring. The questions of what is abnormally aggressive and what constitutes seriously irresponsible conduct plague the practitioner trying to place this diagnostic label within the framework of family violence.

Million (1981a, p. 8) describes *normality* and *pathology* as relative concepts, as essentially arbitrary points on a continuum. They may operate together in one person; some features of that person's personality being normal, others distorted. Or the environment may change, making an old behavior no longer adaptive. And since there are few definitions of normal for most behaviors, particularly in the family, any attempt at determining what is sufficiently abnormal to be called *disordered* is a difficult charge (Penna, 1981, p. 13).

Clinicians have attempted to describe the requirements of normal functioning. In doing so, Million (1981a, p. 8) calls first for the capacity to function autonomously and competently. Second, the normal person must adjust to their environment effectively and efficiently. Third, there must be some subjective sense of contentment and satisfaction. Finally, there must be evidence of the person's ability to satisfy their potentials. *The practitioner in the family violence situation must be prepared to defend the presence of each of these features in their client/patient.* Similarly, *the legal practitioner seeking to protect the victim should demand evidence of these abilities in the perpetrator's functioning.*

The individual manifesting a seriously abnormal behavioral style will engage in self- and other-destructive behaviors. First, according to Million (1981a, pp. 9–10), there is likely to be evidence of an "adaptive inflexibility," in which interpersonal skills and coping abilities will be found to be limited and rigid in presentation. These are skills applied in every situation whether appropriate or not. Stress is perceived where there is no stress and is unsuccessfully responded to in every case. And learning from failure seems an impossible task. Next, these individuals are also found to be in a vicious circle. The needs of these individuals, as well as their perceptions and behaviors, not only make current problems worse, but cause them to persist. Finally, these individuals are unstable. They are fragile and lack resilience, especially when under stress. They are vulnerable to events that reactivate old feelings as well as susceptible to new crises on a daily basis. Since they are not competent at the acquisition of new coping strategies, they repeat old strategies that failed in the past. The resultant failure increases the pressure they feel and generates a sense within them that the world is an impossible place in which to survive. In many ways, Million's conceptualization describes the relationship that many persons in violent families hold with their environment.

Personality disordered individuals typically conduct themselves inappropriately from adolescence. They will be found to have had disruptive home settings as children. As adolescents, destructive and antisocial behaviors may have been reported. Failure, conflict, and substance abuse were often a part of their teenage years. Their tendency as adults is to blame their parents or community for these problems (Leaff, 1981, pp. 341–342). Also as adults, these individuals have limited means for meeting their needs. Immediate satisfaction of their needs and desires drives their behavior without thought as to the conditions of consequences of the behavior. This constant drive toward meeting immediate needs, irrespective of the needs of others, is accompanied by an inflexibility and intolerance of others (Albert, 1981, pp. 362–364). It is not difficult to ascertain that violence in the family is one possible product of this behavioral style.

Common Personality Disorders in the Violent Family

The Antisocial Personality

The antisocial personality, previously referred to as the sociopath or psychopath, is a common diagnosis across all violent behavior. In violent families, it is most familiar in child maltreatment (Kempe & Helfer, 1972) and sexual abuse through perpetrators who sexually abuse and inflict physical injury at the same time. The presence of an antisocial personality also plays a frequent role in the attorney's decision to seek termination of parental rights in the physical maltreatment or sexual abuse case.

When describing a psychopath (prior to 1980), the McCords (1956) and Clecky (1964) were the most frequently cited experts. The McCords described this individual as an aggressive and impulsive person who feels little guilt and is unable to form lasting bonds with other human beings. In his pioneering work, Clecky (1964) notes 16 now-famous characteristics that typify this personality:

(1) superficial charm and high intelligence,
(2) the absence of delusion and irrational thinking,
(3) the absence of neurosis or nervousness,
(4) unreliability,
(5) untruthfulness and insincerity,
(6) lack of remorse or shame,
(7) inadequately motivated antisocial behavior,
(8) poor judgment and failure to learn from experience,
(9) pathological egocentricity and incapacity for love,
(10) a general impoverishment of major affective reactions,
(11) lack of insight,
(12) unresponsiveness in interpersonal relations,
(13) fantastic and uninviting behavior with drink and sometimes without,
(14) suicide rarely carried out,
(15) trivial, impersonal, and poorly integrated sex life,
(16) a failure to follow a life plan.

Million (1981a, p. 181) describes these individuals as driven by their need to prove their superiority. This is built more on mistrust of others than belief in themselves and, consequently, any authority (legal or clinical) becomes a threat.

Reid (1981, p. 137) employs behavioral descriptions of the antisocial personality. He notes a continuous history of chronic antisocial behavior in which the rights of others have been violated. This style has been present since childhood and results not only in an inability to find and keep a job, but a generalized incompetence in most life areas over a period of years. Most important for the family violence practitioner is this individual's virtual inability to form a true human relationship. This is often more critical than any aggressiveness that might be found.

Reid (1981, p. 152) indicates that the aggressiveness of the antisocial personality has been overestimated. It is not so much aggression as it is evidence of living in a world so egocentric that all others are insignificant. This individual also perceives many threats from the outside world as well as being somewhat self-destructive and punishing. Since the majority of antisocial personalities originated in grossly disorganized families, living under adverse social conditions, they learned to distrust parental and family safety early on. Aggressive acts against family members may actually be symbolic acts against "providers" they wrongly trusted in childhood (Reid, 1981, p. 152). This is sometimes interpreted as a manifestation of the intergenerational transmission of violence in the family.

The family of the antisocial personality is inadequate at best and destructive at worst. There is frequent mention of parental psychopathology and inconsistent operating style (Reid, 1981, p. 148). There may also have been the additional burden of brutality and a mother who was so impoverished in personality that she was completely reliant upon the child (Leaff, 1981, p. 343). Stubblefield (1975) describes the parental figures as overstimulating and inconsistent and confirms that the child was the source of satisfaction to the parents rather than the reverse. These negative parental characteristics, reminiscent of previous descriptions of the maltreating family, have been captured by Million (1981a, pp. 209–210) through a triad that encompasses parental rejection, discontent and hostility.

Million (1981a) describes the childhood of the antisocial personality as having been one of cruelty and domination by the parent(s). This caused the child to distrust his or her environment. Consequently, as adults, they do not rely upon others at all. There is a determination to reject all guidance from others and a resultant reduced ability to learn techniques for controlling their own impulses. Protecting themselves from others, providing their own pleasure and pain, handling emotions in their own ways, and being almost totally self-reliant or autonomous are all elements of their style. This is a style that tends to be consistent from adolescence forward, although some moderation is sometimes found in middle age.

Some antisocial characteristics can be found in children although the diagnosis is better left until late adolescence. To do otherwise may create a self-fulfilling prophecy (Wolff, 1984, p. 5). In addition, a variety of experiences may modify this style before it becomes entrenched. For example, the presence of at least one healthy parent who is not only loving but consistent and firm in discipline may help overcome this developing pattern (Reid, 1981, p. 151).

The Borderline Personality

Family violence clinicians are most accustomed to finding the borderline personality in children who have been victimized, especially sexually abused adolescent females. Current research into parental psychopathology reveals that the abusive and maltreating parent may also reveal borderline symptoms (Prodgers, 1984).

Borderline personality refers to intense fluctuations in interpersonal relations, mood, and self-image (Gallahorn, 1981, p. 74). With regard to behavioral characteristics, Gallahorn reviewed the DSM-III (American Psychiatric Association, 1980) as follows:

(1) impulsivity or unpredictability in at least two areas that are potentially self-damaging (e.g., spending, gambling, substance abuse, sex, or over-eating),

(2) pattern of unstable and intense interpersonal relationships marked by shifts in attitude, idealization, devaluation, or manipulation,

(3) inappropriately intense anger or lack of anger control,

(4) identity disturbances manifested by uncertainty about identity issues (e.g., self-image, gender, goals, career, friendship, values, or loyalty),

(5) affective instability with marked shifts from normal mood to depression, irritability, or anxiety usually lasting a few hours and only rarely more than a few days,

(6) intolerance of being alone,

(7) physically self-damaging acts,

(8) chronic feelings of emptiness or boredom (Gallahorn, 1981, p. 75).

Prodgers (1984, pp. 414–416) found five major personality elements that maltreating parents and borderlines hold in common:

(1) an *arrested emotional development*, describing the immaturity and dependency of both individuals,

(2) a *poor self-image*, referring to the identity conflicts, self-devaluation, and low self-esteem present,

(3) an *emotional isolation* based on the difficulty both these individuals have in creating and sustaining relationships or in realistically evaluating others so as to gain empathy,

(4) a *depressive loneliness* relating to the pervasive sadness, loneliness, and futility in the life of both individuals; and, finally,

(5) *poorly suppressed aggression*, which is tautological in maltreating parents and a consequence of deep-seated anger sometimes present in

borderlines; a major problem when interacting with the borderline's poor impulse control.

The mother of the borderline personality is typified by her own borderline nature (Masterson, 1976) and by her inability to tolerate separation from her child (Bradley, 1979, p. 426). When the child makes any attempt to separate from the mother, the mother withdraws expressions of love. The emotionally abandoned child responds with feelings of depression, rage, guilt, fear, and helplessness. To compensate, the child develops defense mechanisms such as splitting, denial, and projection (Gallahorn, 1981, p. 81; Prodgers, 1984, p. 419). This is a child who must suppress his or her need for independence in the family, an aspect of childhood which carries over to adulthood.

As an adult, the child who experienced the borderline parent is not only affected by the immaturity, poor self-image, isolation, loneliness, and poorly controlled aggression already described, they are also intolerant and fearful of separation. Any attempt on the part of their children to take part in normal separation or exploration results in the emotional abandonment or aggression previously mentioned (Gallahorn, 1981, pp 76–77). Since their splitting defense is so practiced, after this aggression or abandonment, they are able to dissociate themselves from it and go forward as if nothing unusual had occurred. This is obviously an unpredictable parental style that is intolerable for the developing child. One consequence of these mixed messages may be passive-aggressiveness.

The Passive/Aggressive Personality

The passive-aggressive personality is destructive from two perspectives. First, the family containing this personality is in constant upheaval. Second, the practitioners working with the family are constantly having their tolerance limits tested as this individual challenges, rechallenges, and fails to comply. This is a personality disorder common to the child and elder mistreatment situations and is seen more in neglectful behaviors than outright violence.

Malinow (1981b, p. 127) has paraphrased the DSM-III description of the passive-aggressive personality as one built upon hostility that the individual is afraid to express. There is a resistance to social and occupation (as well as clinical and legal) demands, usually manifested in two or more of the following: procrastination, dawdling, stubbornness, intentional inefficiency, and/or forgetfulness. These are the actions of an angry individual who does not harm by action but in-action.

Million (1981, p. 267) suggests that the passive-aggressive individual was subject to too much inconsistency in his/her family. Parental attitudes about and behaviors toward them as children vacillated enormously. Beyond the facade of caring, there were double messages. They were never exactly certain what their parents wanted, as nothing they did was the correct response to the initially perceived parental need. As a result, there was constant conflict in this family accompanied by an ever-present threat of dissolution. During childhood, these individuals were forced to take sides, switch sides, and repetitively divide loyalties in parental conflicts; obviously, a strong contributor to their equivocal thinking as adults.

The passive-aggressive individual does not know whether to trust and turn to others (a dangerous choice given how untrustworthy their own family was) or to keep to themselves. As Million states, "They behave in fits and starts, shifting capriciously down a path that leads nowhere" (1981a, p. 257)—nowhere except to confusion and disappointment for themselves and others (pp. 244–257).

Being totally unpredictable, demanding and dissatisfied, seductive and rejecting, dependent and independent has value to this person (Million, 1981a, p. 258). First, it keeps people away from you when you wish and draws them to you when you wish. Second, it allows you to avoid a direct course on all issues, a self-protective device for a person who has difficulty becoming committed to any course. Third, it allows for both affection and support even as it allows for the subtle discharge of hostility. And, finally, it allows for the control of events and persons by forcing them to adapt a course that is consistent with the individual's needs at the time (Million, 1981a, p. 258).

Obviously, for the victimized child seeking consistency, the spouse who fears that disappointing her husband may result in an assault, and the elderly person who must try not to be inconvenient for the martyred caretaker, the passive-aggressive personality promises to be a devastatingly difficult behavior pattern to adapt to comfortably.

Other Critical Personality Disorders/Styles

The Narcissistic Personality Disorder. This individual is a shallow creature who, as the name implies, is exclusively interested in the self. Superficially, at least, these individuals are often capable of a competent front of impulse control, but soon enough, the self-absorption will be evident. They become restless and irritable in the absence of someone to reinforce their grandiose view of themselves. They maintain their inflated perception of self by devaluing those around them. In short, these egocentric individuals are only interested in what others can do for them and what they feel to be justifiably theirs—almost everything (Phillips, 1981, p. 69). Should these individuals become parents, marital partners, or face the sudden need to provide caretaking for the elderly parent, the outcome could be disastrous.

The Dependent Personality. This personality style allows others to assume total responsibility for major areas of an individual's life. Self-confidence is virtually nonexistent, and virtually any need will be subordinated if it guarantees that someone will take care of them (Malinow, 1981b, p. 98).

There is a hostile character to this behavior. The behavior may initially be perceived as rewarding. Over time it becomes irritating in its repetitiveness and through the failure of this individual to learn how to do anything for himself or herself. As such, the dependent personality may be an initially attractive mate to the highly dependent individuals who populate violent families. But the level of dependency found to be attractive initially will quickly exceed the tolerance of the perpetrator and an aggressive act may occur.

The Avoidant Personality. The avoidant personality is extraordinarily susceptible to criticism and rejection. There is a struggle between needs for affection and the fear of rejection; inertia is the result. The anticipatory anxiety that grows out of this conflict may prevent them from embarking on any social activity. And, when in the midst of others, they are constantly scanning for potential threat. The most innocent remark or action may be perceived as being directed against them (Million, 1981, pp. 103–104).

There are two major problems with this style in violent families. First, it plays into the paranoia that exists in some perpetrators (e.g., conjugal violence). Second, the practitioner will find great difficulty in gaining their trust and confidence. The only apparent answer to gaining cooperation is to remain the sole source of support and avoid the introduction of the large number of collateral professionals and agencies, which are typically applied to the family violence case.

Episodic Dyscontrol Syndrome. Although not a personality disorder per se, the episodic dyscontrol syndrome (EDS) must be considered to be a troubling and dangerous behavioral style. Monroe (1982, p. 372) describes the actions of the EDS as "impulsive expressions of primitive fear-rage that are usually socially or self-destructive." Many family violence perpetrators describe their experience during the violence in the same way as do individuals afflicted with this syndrome.

In most family violence cases, the perpetrator's description as being out of control (as a result of a mysterious force) is nothing more than an attempt to deny responsibility. But, in some small, and unknown, number of cases it may be EDS. The EDS individual will report, "I just did it—I don't know why." There is no sense of motivation, no ability to remember when or why the decision to attack was made. It does not seem to the perpetrator that it was either deliberate or intentional, but something must have been operating at the time to allow it to occur (Monroe, 1981, p. 373).

EDS actions are undertaken without concern for the effect on the environment or long-term consequences. There is no time to reflect on the past or look toward the future. If, in retrospect, the individual is stunned by their behavior, EDS is possible. If on the other hand, the individual is less concerned or their shock does not seem genuine, the possibility of an antisocial personality disorder may be considered.

In the case involving the antisocial personality disorder, the intensity was nothing more than a mask for the intended action (Monroe, 1982, p. 376). This individual wanted to give the appearance of being out of control. It is also possible that this violence grew out of chronic neurotic, psychotic, or other psychological problems not immediately evident. In addition, neurological etiologies have been implicated in such violence (Monroe, 1982, p. 376).

The Newcomers: Diagnoses for the Future

Post-Traumatic Stress Disorders

Although post-traumatic stress disorder (PTSD) has become most familiar through its application to the behaviors of Vietnam veterans, it is being increasingly recognized in family violence work in the courtroom. The most frequently occurring mention of this disorder is in children who have been abused as all DSM-III criteria for this disorder have been described and validated in physical child abuse victims (Green, 1983).

PTSD occurs when an individual is exposed to an overwhelming event(s) resulting in helplessness in the face of intolerable danger or anxiety (Horowitz, 1983). Several issues will discriminate the child who is vulnerable to this disabling psychological state. Susceptibility seems to be related to constitutional and personality make-up, developmental status at the time of the traumatizing event, and prior life experiences. The content and intensity of the event also pertain.

When confronted with the same or similar situations to the traumatic one, the child is likely to respond with immobilization, disorganized thinking and behavior, physical symptoms, and regression. More subtly, this insidious trauma may have a deleterious effect on cognition (i.e., memory, school performance, and learning) as well as affect, interpersonal relations, and self-control. The themes mentioned by children in this circumstance are familiar to those working with both physically and sexually abused children. Among them are fear of repetition of the trauma-inducing event, shame, rage (at the source and at those exempted), survivor guilt, and pervasive sadness (Horowitz, 1983). It would seem wise for the family violence practitioner to become familiar with this syndrome.

DSM-III, R

A revision of DSM-III is in process at this writing that will affect categories of personality disorders available to the family violence practitioner. These proposed categories have not met with uniform acceptance among family violence practitioners, but are likely to become an accepted part of the nosological scheme in short order.

In the area of child sexual abuse, a disorder first entitled "paraphilic rapism" has now come to be called "paraphilic coercive behavior." That change was due to the feelings of many that such a descriptive label could allow perpetrators to escape criminal charges based on an insanity defense. The new title reduces that possibility.

Using a title that was greatly offensive to many in the conjugal violence situation ("masochistic personality disorder"), the authors of this nosology sought to describe many victims; predominantly female. Family violence experts argued that this was a term built upon clinical observation rather than a data base and won their argument. This will now be entitled "self-defeating personality disorder," a label that is thought to blame the victim somewhat less, but that will probably be applied in the case of the conjugal violence victim to elects to stay in the relationship.

Another predominantly female label, following on the heels of great interest in pre-menstrual syndrome, is "premenstrual dysphoric disorder." This remains somewhat offensive to many female practitioners for it singles out women as a special group. However, it seeks to describe a biological basic for the dysphoric states that can sometimes occur with that disorder. Finally, "ego dystonic homosexuality" has raised the ire of homosexual advocates in placing homosexuality again in a nosology of mental disorders. However, this may some day have application in the male sexual abuse victim whose homosexual behavior is a maladaptation to his early victimization and not a sexual lifestyle that he might have otherwise chosen.

While unclear just how these terms will be applied in family violence practice in the future, it seems certain that the presence of these new views will make themselves felt both in the courtroom and in the clinic.

The Personality Disorder: A Summary View

The personality disorder and its array of aberrant behaviors have long been an underappreciated element of the violent family. These disorders fall between the neurotic and psychotic disorders and help to explain the family violence practitioner's struggle to describe why so many perpetrators were not crazy, but were also not normal. The anger, unhappiness, and rigidity that are part of these disorders are a frequent presence in clinical reports on the adults in a violent family (Milner & Wimberly, 1980; Spinetta, 1978). So common are these elements that the American Psychiatric Association has recently held discussions of the inclusion of specific perpetrator and victim personalities in DSM-III's nosology. This proposal has met with anger from women's groups based on a concern that a "syndrome" will allow perpetrators to escape responsibility. In addition, the mention of female masochism in victim syndromes has also generated some anger. Yet most practitioners will find that the traditionally recognized personality disorders describe a necessary middle ground in clinical descriptions of violent families. These distortions in personality will be found to be some of the most dangerous operating styles within families; particularly as they affect children. It is time that the personality disorder was recognized as the problem it can be for some families. The same might well be said for the affective disorder.

The Affective Disorder

Affective disorders are also know as "mood" disorders. Mood here refers to an emotional tone that is at the extreme: highs or lows. In some persons one or the other of these extremes will predominate (a uni-polar disorder) and in others the individual will swing back and forth (a bi-polar disorder).

Depression is the most consistently identified affective disorder in violent families. When depression is both long-term and influential across multiple areas of the individual's functioning, the clinician may speak of a *major* depressive episode. The individual suffering from a major depressive episode need not look sad, but is likely to evidence a near-total withdrawal from social, occupational, and family activities. It is as if they have simply given up; which may be true in the repetitively victimized child or adult, and/or the caretaker who is overwhelmed with responsibilities (Deschner, 1984; Estroff et al., 1984; Morrison, 1983).

When the depressive episode is a major one there may be observable physiological affects. All appetites (e.g., eating or sexual activity) may decline and sleep problems often occur. At times, the affected person may have difficulty being still (psychomotor agitation) or moving with any speed (psychomotor retardation). Both thinking and memory are sometimes impaired and feelings of worthlessness and hopelessness can be strong enough to distort perceptions (Val, Gaviria, & Flaherty, 1982, p. 13). If these feelings are worst in the morning, the clinician may speak of *melancholia.*

A depression of shorter duration, with a less comprehensive impact on the individual's life and only intermittent occurrence, may be described as a "dysthymic disorder." While still a problem, this condition is more likely to result in a low energy level, pessimism, low self-esteem, and feelings of inadequacy than a near total inability to function (Val et al., 1982, p. 16).

In any depression, the clinician is concerned with the possibility of suicide. Child maltreatment researchers have found that the *suicidal parent* also tends to be the *homicidal parent* (Mohr & McKnight, 1971; Rodenberg, 1971). The practitioner should not be fearful of exploring the possibility of suicide with a parent who seems seriously depressed. Key features of the discussion include whether this person has a plan, whether the plan is possible, whether they will have the opportunity to carry out the plan (usually due to isolation), and any persons who can be contacted to stay with them until such an urge as passed (Fairborough & Litman, 1975). Other signals are their telling someone that they intend to kill themselves, a sudden and unexplainable "getting things in order" (e.g., making a will), giving valued possessions away, or a sudden brightening following a long depression for no apparent reason (this may indicate the relief felt at finally having made the decision to escape from tension through suicide). Importantly, it is not only depression but sometimes anxiety that motivates a successful suicide (Mehrabian & Weinstein, 1985, p. 545).

When suicidal parents become overwhelmed and incapable of dealing with responsibility, they may begin to think obsessively about how worthless and inadequate they feel. If this rumination persists, it can sometimes incorporate the children (e.g., "I wouldn't feel this way if they weren't so hard to deal with.") (Deschner, 1984, p. 203), and the suicide will be accompanied by a child homicide. This does not occur often and is much more likely in the psychotic individual who is told by internal voices to kill the children. But in any case, if parental suicide is suspected, the children must be protected.

Some theorists (Lewishon, 1984) trace depression to the absence of social reinforcement. The mother overwhelmed by child care, terrified by a domineering and sexually abusive mate, the woman battered by her husband, and the caretaker with sole responsibility for an elderly person *all* suffer from a critical absence of social reinforcement. These roles are restricted, rigid, and isolating. As sources of gratification are choked off by jealousy, embarrassment, or fear of disclosure of the family secret, reinforcement, recognition, and support disappear. In these situations, the downward spiral of depression is almost inevitable. *The practitioner's intervention in this downward spiral and provision of opportunities for personal gratification may be lifesaving.*

Theorists frequently apply Seligman's (1975) description of "learned helplessness" to the development of depression in violent families (Walker, 1979). Feeling helpless is the result of being trapped in situations in which you cannot control the factors that relieve suffering or provide gratification. It is the perception of being out of control that is as disabling as actually being out of control. And the battered wife, oppressed parent, and caretaker of dependent children or older persons have all learned that *someone else is in control of their life*. The result is a psychological mind set that not only reduces efforts to escape, but slowly eliminates the motivation to attempt to regain control (Val et al., 1982, p. 209). Common companions to this feeling are a belief in one's incompetence and a resultant loss of self-esteem (Gordon & Ledray, 1985, p. 31). So, once in place, this is a negative mind set that perpetuates itself. Both of these theories play heavily on the development of depression in violent families.

Common Factors in the Environments of Depressed Persons and Violent Families

Characteristics of the population from which most reportedly violent families are drawn may predispose them to depression. For example, while there is a greater tendency toward all mental disorders in lower income groups, this is particularly true of depression due to the futility, hopelessness, and self-hatred present (Val et al., 1982, p. 103). Racial differences also compound the depression issue. For example, while the rates for both whites and blacks are similar, whites tend to experience a milder degree of depression. Sex differences may also play a role.

Women outnumber men in depressions of all types. The rate of depression in women is twice that of men across age groups, countries, and types of depression (Gordon & Ledray, 1985, p. 26). This difference has been tied to feminine differences in endocrinology, birth control medications, the effect of giving birth, socialization, and genetics (Val et al., 1982, pp. 99–100). However, after controlling for all affects, the major contributor to depression in women is marriage (Gordon and Ledray, 1985, p. 26).

Married women have consistently higher rates of depression than single or divorced men and widowed women. After age 65, the male rate does approach the female rate, a finding that may bear upon depression's contribution to elder mistreatment. This is a real difference and unrelated to women's greater willingness to seek care (Weissman & Klerman, 1977). It has been suggested that such high rates of depression in married women are related to the lack of reinforcement and recognition in the woman's role in the family (Fleming, 1979; Walker, 1979).

In the view of one depression expert (Beck, 1979) depression is a direct result of the feelings of powerlessness that grow out of a lack of reinforcement. These feelings become translated into cognitions that suggest to the sufferers that nothing they do will matter in obtaining reward. The combination of hopelessness, lack of motivation, and the feeling that options have been exhausted provides an erroneous sense of inevitability to the negative circumstances. Following this sense of inevitability, there may be a depressive episode that results in the giving up of all family responsibility. It is clear that this occurs in violent families. It is certain to result in neglect in some cases of child (Polansky, DeSaix, & Sharlin, 1972) and elder (Kosberg, 1983a) mistreatment. It is certain to raise the ire of the angry and abusive males whose dominance may have brought about the woman's feelings of helplessness in the first place, placing her at increased risk. Should this cycle begin, the child is also at risk.

The Child and the Violent Family

The child in the depressed family is at risk. The depressed parent may manifest violent or inadequate behavior or the child may become seriously depressed. The child of the mentally ill parent holds a much greater risk for developing a psychopathological disorder than the child of functional parents (Garmezy, 1974).

Reid and Morrison (1983) have reviewed children's responses to growing up in families with mentally ill parents. They found significant effects. Parenthood is extremely difficult for some mentally ill adults. They may show a decreased capacity for forming need-gratifying relationships, a lack of satisfaction with parenthood activities, and a generalized sense of inadequacy. If the condition is chronic and subject to repetitive and unpredictable parental mood swings/personality changes, the effect on the child is magnified. On the other hand, if the parent's condition is consistent and recognizable in its symptoms and if there are other adults available who support the child in the child's belief that something is wrong, the child may develop adequate coping capacity. If the parent's condition is more subtle or unpredictable, and if adults do not see what the child sees, the child is at extreme risk. An inconsistent and unpredictable parental response can be troublesome for the child of the moderately functional parent. A similarly inconsistent response from a parent who is mentally ill can be devastating (Reid & Morrison, 1983, pp. 37–38).

Parenthood

Depression interferes with successful parenthood (Susman, Trickett, Iannotti, Hollenbeck, & Zahn-Waxler, 1985). The sadness, withdrawal, rumination, and confusion that characterize the depressed adult are negative influences on the parent-child relationship. The moodiness of this depressed parent may result in caution in the child as they approach the parent. Fatigue and social withdrawal in the parent reminds the child that their parent is not like others, and this also conflicts with the high energy level of the child (Susman et al., 1985, p. 238). The inability of depressed parents to regulate their emotions and the mis-match between parental lethargy and child energy may result in expressions of anger, hostility, and abuse (Kadushin & Martin, 1981). The child of the depressed parent is then at dual risk—for neglect due to inadequacy and for abuse due to hostility.

The Child's Depression

Depression in children is considered to be a clinical entity of its own. It has two possible presentations: the first is a condition that resembles adult depression; the alternative is one in which symptoms are masked and the depression is inferred from behavior through the use of depressive equivalents, for example, school problems, somatic complaints, or attention deficits (Val et al., 1982, p. 98).

Since it has long been believed that the depressed person reacts to pervasive internalized guilt and self-hatred, and that children do not develop this capacity until adolescence, childhood depression was thought to be rare (Derdeyn, 1983, p. 16). However, the 1970s found acceptance of the fact that children simply have a more difficult time identifying feelings of prolonged sadness and deep-seated fears or angers (Poznanski, 1982, p. 375). The result was the discovery of depressive equivalents through which children could act out affective states and indirectly express the feelings that adults were capable of confronting directly. One of the most common findings of children who demonstrate depressive equivalents is that there is also parental depression in their family (Poznanski, 1982).

Just how parental depression influences childhood depression is uncertain. Theories range from a genetic vulnerability to over-identification with the parent, and the child's depression being the result of inappropriate parent-child relationships. No matter the etiology, the outcome seems similar. The attitude most commonly evidenced by depressed parents toward their child is one of rejection. This rejection may be overt or a function of the apathy, withdrawal, and fatigue of the depressive state (Poznanski, 1982). And to assess the impact of this apparent rejection upon the child, consideration must be given to the child's developmental level, the family environment excluding the depressed parent, and the strength of the child's own personality (Bemporad & Lee, 1984, p. 147).

Depressed children seem to hold one of two characteristic relationships with their families; both of which are familiar to the family violence practitioner. In one presentation, the child is both overly tied to the parent(s) and overwhelmed by parental expectations. In the other, the child is scapegoated and rejected by the parents or the entire family. In either case, the child is overly stressed most of the time. Family relations as well as most other social interactions generate frustrations and deprivations. The parents of the child in either relationship are clearly overwhelmed by the prospect of having to rear this child. As a result one or both parents find it difficult to expect anything other than "adult" behavior from the child (Bemporad & Lee, 1984, p. 151). The children react to these pressures in predictably erratic ways.

A generally dysphoric (sad) mood is a central part of the child's reaction to pressure, scapegoating, or rejection by the family. The child may attempt to compensate for these feelings of pressure with braggadocio, aggression, and impulsiveness. Or there may be a more definable problem such as school performance, loss of energy level or weight, and the absence of appetite and poor sleep habits (Derdeyn, 1983, p. 19). A slowness of speech, poverty of language, dragging physical pace, and lethargy may also alert the clinician to depression (Poznanski, 1982, p. 375). These are characteristics that occur somewhat differently depending upon the age of the child.

Identifying depression in the pre-schooler is almost impossible. There may be some transitory sadness in response to a given situation, but there is too much for pre-schoolers to attend to in the world to become preoccupied with individual events for too long.

From 7 to 10 years of age, according to Bemporad and Lee (1984, p. 148) sadness, dissatisfaction and social isolation become more evident. Suicide may be a frequent thought, and some self-destructive behavior does occur. When children reach the ages of 11 to 13, the low self-esteem that often accompanies adult depression begins to show itself in both speech and action. Relationship problems become important, and feelings of rejection and of being unloved lead to dysphoria. At this age the child is developing an ability to deal with abstraction and is seeking deeper reasons for their negative feelings. These feelings are no longer automatically related to immediate events in the environment.

Upon reaching adolescence, the greater freedom and feelings of not being understood by adults generates a more secretive atmosphere in which depressive feelings are acted out rather than discussed. Many adolescents react to feelings of depression with aggressive and antisocial behavior. These are essentially self-destructive acts that do little to relieve the emotional distress in the adolescent. When there is no relief the adolescent begins to fear that the negative feelings will carry over into adulthood, and they adopt a somewhat fatalistic air (Bemporad & Lee, 1984, pp. 148–150). In many cases, this negative behavior and attitude is hard to distinguish from normal adolescent turmoil. The key is giving consideration to depression even when the referral described otherwise (e.g., if the child is a runaway).

The study of depression has always included the concept of depression as a response to loss (Poznanski, 1982, p. 383). The identification of the lost object in childhood depression is somewhat more difficult than in adult depression (Bemporad & Lee, 1984, p. 146). For children, loss tends to focus about their parents. There may be loss by death, divorce, or by other family disruption (i.e., violence), which steals parental attention from the child. No matter the cause of the parental preoccupation or anger, the child is likely to perceive it as having something to do with them and become depressed in response (Derdeyn, 1983, p. 21).

The maltreating parent creates an environment that is conducive to the development of depression in the child. It is important to understand that a parent's anger exerts a very powerful effect on a child, perhaps the greatest of all emotions that the parent could demonstrate. Derdeyn (1983, p. 23) notes that it does not even have to be directed at the child to have its corrosive effect on the child's sense of security and self-esteem. Similarly, the parental incapacity from illness, substance abuse, or even marital conflict (all elements of the maltreating environment) can bind the child to the parent in an anxious way that forces the child to fear abandonment. There is nothing in this environment to shield the child from the weight of the parent's problems; problems the child does not understand, but must try to resolve (in their own mind). The parent also projects problems on to the child, and the resultant scapegoating eliminates what little self-esteem and security the child may have been able to retain (Derdeyn, 1983, p. 24). If the maltreating does not promise depression in the child, it certainly promises its risk.

A Summary View of Child Depression

Children of depressed parents are at risk for depression. Children in maltreating situations are at risk for depression. The children of the depressed parent live with the sense of failure that comes not only from a failure to please the parent, but from a sense that they are the cause of the problem. This is a reflection of their parent's view of them.

Children of depressed parents are not reinforced for reaching out. Their attachment to that parent is an anxious one that promises only abandonment. In this circumstance, the children are prohibited from seeing themself as anything but a failure, perhaps a failure that can be compensated for by having children of their own. If there is a cycle of violence, perhaps this is one mechanism through which it occurs. Numerous other mechanisms have been posited, as will be described in the following section.

Intergenerational Transmission

Current indications are that the case for a cycle of violence or the intergenerational transmission of violence in the family has been over-stated (Pedrick-Cornell & Gelles, 1982), or that at least, empirical support for this conventional wisdom is less than convincing (Burgess & Youngblade, 1985). Not only are current works finding a lower prevalence of early violence in currently violent families (Caplan et al., 1984, p. 349), reviews of older studies have found the conclusions in this area to be somewhat over-enthusiastic (Bavolek, 1981, p. 40; Bourne & Newberger, 1979a, p. 82; Miller & Challas,

1981). These findings have ramifications across all forms of family violence.

Child Maltreatment

No area has held as tightly to the belief in intergenerational transmission as child maltreatment. It was described in the earliest works (Elmer, 1967) and continues to be discussed (Herrenkohl et al., 1984, p. 647). Pagelow has offered three reasons why intergenerational transmission has been such a treasured element of child maltreatment lore.

First, intergenerational transmission has a ring of common sense to it. Attachment research has suggested that the insecure attachment between maltreating parent and child places the child at risk for maltreatment (Lamb, Teti, Lewkowicz, & Malkin, 1985). Social learning research has suggested that the child will parent as his or her parent parented him or her—the maltreating parent teaching the child to be abusive. Feshback (1980) also suggests that right and wrong and the role of retribution and punishment are also lessons carried forward by the child. In fact, there are numerous supports for the transmission of child care patterns and learning of the use of aggression being a function of parent-to-child transmission (Bandura, 1973; Pagelow, 1984; Steele, 1975). It does make some sense and is probably true to a degree. However, the positing of a total acceptance and replication of this aggression does not allow for this learning to be mediated by other influences as is more likely the case.

A second feature of the long life of the intergenerational transmission notion, according to Pagelow (1984) is that it is so widely accepted that clinicians often seek to find it in their assessments. Practitioners, then, may automatically question early experiences with violence and discover the expected answer. This is true for the perpetrator of family violence is likely to be as aware of this belief as the practitioner. As such blaming his or her actions upon the family of origin provides a ready means for reducing his/her own responsibility in the act.

Finally, Pagelow points out the "emotion-evoking theme" that plays within intergenerational transmission. This "we must stop this or our children will become like their parents" message offers simplicity and is an effective fund raising and program development tool (1984, pp. 254–255). This common-sense appeal, however, is not borne out empirically.

Burgess and Youngblade (1985) reviewed the literature on intergenerational transmission in child maltreatment and found it wanting. They note that the most commonly cited studies are largely selected case histories and in some cases, the data have been misinterpreted or misrepresented. In what they consider the best study in the area, fewer than 15 percent of the abused parents were found to be abusive toward their own children. They note a possible connection between generational patterns that replicates the social class level of a family of origin and its lifestyle. They also offer that inappropriate interpersonal interactions or social incompetencies may be passed on from one generation to the next. But they agree with a review of this literature by Cicchetti and Rizley (1981), which concluded that the transmission of abusive patterns across generations is by no means an inevitable consequence of having been maltreated. It seems that the most that can be said is that the practitioner must be alert to the possibility that partial learning has taken place and that violence-mediating strategies may not be available to an individual based upon learned or observed patterns in their childhood.

Child Sexual Abuse

Practitioners in the child sexual abuse area (Groth et al., 1982) have begun to suspect that child molesters were victimized during their childhood. Their subsequent assaults are seen to be a result of the male victim's efforts to control the pain of the earlier experience (Finkelhor, 1981). Russell (1984, p. 241) suggests that this reaction to early victimization is typical of the male propensity for acting out pain and anger by moving against another. This stands in contrast to the female's internalization of pain and acceptance of responsibility for the victimization. Both are aberrant responses, but the male response results in victimization of another while the female response results in victimization of self, both of which are familiar patterns to the practitioner in the sexual abuse area.

The work of Groth and his colleagues, finding sexual molestation to be the "aftermath of physical and/or psychological abuse, neglect, exploitation, and/or abandonment during the offender's formative years" (1982, p. 130) does represent something of an intergenerational transmission. However, both Finkelhor (1984, 1986) and

Russell (1984, p. 223) offer warnings about this perception. Russell reminds her readers that, while victims are at greater risk for perpetration than those never victimized, not all victims become perpetrators. This may hint at a qualitative difference in the victimization experience for those who later become perpetrators. Finkelhor (1986) questions whether this finding can be generalized from incarcerated child molesters to all sexual abuse perpetrators. He also cautions that while the amount of sexual abuse in the backgrounds of molesters may seem high, it has not been conclusively demonstrated that it is higher than among similar men who did not become molesters. He calls for more rigorous definitions, a more representative spectrum of offenders, and better control groups before accepting this research. His general conclusion is that it is quite clear that being molested itself is not enough to create a molester. Importantly, he warns against the belief that we now understand this problem (as a result of the intergenerational theory), and, he offers sympathy for the victims and their parents who may now hold an "unrealistic and unnecessary" fear that their victimized children (especially male victims) are on the road to molestation themselves.

Overall, it would appear that the previously sexually victimized individual (particularly males) may have some small likelihood of increased risk of perpetration. This is by no means certain. Finkelhor (1986) notes that even the broadest generalization from studies of incarcerated offenders would suggest only a 30 to 60 percent perpetration rate. As a result, the practitioner may be alert to the possibility, but must recall that prior victimization is neither conclusive nor immediately condemning.

Conjugal Violence

Recent clinical examination of battering males reveals early exposure to a deprivational childhood environment that may have contained a paternal model who physically assaulted the mother (Walker, 1979, p. 39). Deschner and colleagues (1980) found about half the battering males in their work to have had fathers who abused their mothers. From such work, it is suggested that men who observe or experience violence in the home as children are more likely to physically abuse their female partner (Johnston, 1984, p. 1). The absence of universal support for this belief should be noted as at least one study of males who observed maternal beatings found these now-adult males to be strongly opposed to violence (Ulbrich & Huber, 1981).

Overall, there does appear to be some association between males who witness paternal violence toward females and later perpetration of violence in their own family (Pagelow, 1984). The most critical note being struck here for the practitioner is that violence in childhood need only be observed and not necessarily experienced for it to be duplicated.

A Summary View

Intergenerational transmission of family violence is unconfirmed through empirical study. Anecdotal reports of it abound. In both child maltreatment and sexual abuse, there is a likelihood of some form of prior victimization (Conte, 1984b, p. 259; Steele, 1982), but it is far from a certainty. It seems that the presence of childhood victimization does not mandate adult perpetration. In like fashion, the absence of childhood victimization does not insulate against possible family violence perpetration; especially if inadequate learning of social skills or controls against violence describe the childhood experience.

The perpetrator of conjugal violence may have observed violence in their family of origin. It seems probable that the father was aggressive toward the mother, the current perpetrator as a child, or both. And angry, abusive interchanges between an adult and an elderly parent may well be a part of a life-long pattern of miscommunication and resentment (Fulmer & Cahill, 1984, p. 18).

Learning does take place in the family. The practitioner must assess the patterns that such learning has imprinted. Supplemental information must be offered where the learning has been inadequate and correction offered where misconceptions exist. It is valuable in every case to help to develop new strategies to be used in times of stress that do not incorporate violence. It is equally important to provide some understanding of the conditions under which assertiveness is employed. In some cases, however, outside forces (i.e., alcohol or controlled substances) are brought voluntarily into the family behavioral equation; an addition that makes the practitioner's interventions in the psychological environment of the family all the more difficult.

Alcohol Abuse/Misuse

Few beliefs regarding causal factors in family violence are as enduring as the view that alcohol and violence in the family are intimate partners. This is an attractive view for the victim for it explains why it happened. It is similarly attractive to the perpetrator for it provides an escape from responsibility (McGaghy, 1968). Finally, it is attractive to the treatment provider for it provides a clear problem upon which to focus interventions. *To this point, however, empirical research does not support a causal relationship between alcohol and the development of a violent relationship* (Coleman & Straus, 1979). *At least, alcohol abuse does not have the strength to stand alone as a causal factor.*

Pagelow (1984, p. 89) suggests that the main supporters of the alcohol-family violence linkage are battered women and public opinion. This allows both groups to understand the violence and its perpetrator and to distance themselves from it. This is due largely to the near-universal acceptance of alcohol's incorrectly reputed ability to generate behavior that would not occur under other (i.e., sober) conditions.

In writing of child molesters specifically, McGaghy (1968) described the use of alcohol as an explanation for deviant behaviors as an attempt to sustain a "normal" identity. Common, and erroneous, beliefs about alcohol allow the perpetrator to disavow responsibility through the claim that they were "under the influence." People then evaluate the alcohol-influenced behavior differently. By maintaining that the behavior was alcohol-induced (deviance disavowal) or at least related to the reduction of inhibitions and loss of control (disinhibition theory), the family can continue to see the perpetrator as normal except when under the influence. The period of being under the influence can provide a time out during which the perpetrator can engage in a desired behavior and explain it away (Coleman & Straus, 1979; Gelles, 1974; MacAndrew & Edgerton, 1969; Pagelow, 1984).

Following from this argument, Gelles offers that individuals do not become violent because they are drunk; they get drunk to become violent. The degree of drunkenness seems dependent upon the degree of violence anticipated (Coleman & Straus, 1979). This varies somewhat across the various manifestations of family violence.

Child Maltreatment

The problems facing children whose parents are alcohol dependent are legion. Emotional, physical, and sexual abuse have been correlated with alcohol misuse (Matlins, 1981). So too have fetal alcohol syndrome, hyperactivity, enuresis, and delinquency. The child of the alcohol abusing parent has been described as having limited roles open to them: the *family hero* who holds the group together, the *scapegoat* who gets all the blame, the *lost child* who is ignored or assaulted, and the *family pet* who is shown to the world as a demonstration of the family's adequacy (Matlins, 1981). Black (1979) describes the variations within these roles as the responsible one, the adjuster, and the placater. These roles develop to hide the scars of living in such a family. Even with adaptive roles available, children living with such parents incorporate a sense of rejection and react with a pseudo-parental role reversal in which they care not only for their younger siblings, but the parents as well (Pagelow, 1984, p. 92). While it is clear that the child-rearing atmosphere in the alcohol-abusive family is tenuous (Hindman, 1977, 1979) it remains unclear as to how direct the link is between the drinking and overt violence toward the child.

About 19 percent of the population presents with some degree of alcohol dependence, while "heavy drinking" may be twice that common (Calahan & Room, 1974). Alcohol problems in maltreating families are more frequent, suggesting the presence of alcohol problems beyond the level of chance (Deschner, 1984, p. 90). However, this fails to control for the fact that child maltreatment is most frequently reported in populations in which not only the environmental stresses but the drinking is heaviest (Ebeling & Hills, 1975, p. 43; Gil, 1970; McCord, 1983; Young, 1964). These numbers are also distorted by the fact that some studies of maltreatment originate in populations drawn from substance abuse treatment programs (Pagelow, 1984, p. 90).

The summary perspective for the practitioner in the maltreatment area must be that families will very likely present with alcohol or substance abuse problems (Densen-Gerber, 1978; Deschner, 1984). However, the etiological complexities of the problem make substance abuse only one element which makes it difficult for this family to establish and maintain a relationship (Ainsworth, 1980, p. 44). This perspective is replicated in the sexual abuse of children.

Child Sexual Abuse

Lewis-Herman (1982, p. 40) describes alcohol abuse in the sexually abusive family as a "common but not distinguishing factor." Groth and colleagues (1982, p. 131) view the role of alcohol as a minor one in child molestation. Alford and colleagues (1984, p. 40) have found alcohol abuse to be a more significant clinical variable in the family of origin of the child molester than in the family that experiences the molestation. Practically speaking, however, the practitioner will find alcohol and deviance disavowal in the preponderance of families confronting the problem of incest (Russell, 1984, p. 257).

Alcohol is frequently blamed for the perpetrator's loss of control in the incestuous family. The thought that such behavior was either knowing or purposeful is beyond the coping capacity of most adults and children. *With very few exceptions, the practitioner is safe in viewing the alcohol-based disclaimers of the sexually abusive family as just that. Causal variables will be found elsewhere.*

The fact that alcohol is a disclaimer does not suggest immediate confrontation of that fact. Family support and crisis intervention must be initiated for a period before that learning takes place (Harrison & Lumry, 1984, p. 9). Practitioners should not fall into the trap set by the belief in alcohol as the reason why these families now sit in their offices.

Conjugal Violence

Alcohol has long been described as a primary factor in the development of violence between co-habitors (Coleman & Straus, 1979). In part, this may be a function of the role of Al-Anon in the development of early programs for battered women (Johnson, 1981). In part, this is a function of the need that victims have to see the violence as being out of the perpetrator's control; something perpetrators are only too quick to confirm.

Research finds substance use/misuse in this population to be mixed. Some perpetrators do not involve themselves with alcohol at all. Some have difficulty with substances, but are violent whether or not they are under the influence. Still others restrict their assaults to those periods when under the influence (Ganley & Harris, 1978). Alcohol and substance abuse, then, is *related* to but not necessarily *predictive* of conjugal violence. Ganley and Harris (1978) recommend that the practitioner facing the dual problem family (violence and substance problems) treat the substance problem first, assuming they cannot be treated together, to eliminate the perpetrator's rationalization for the violent behavior.

Roberts (1984, p. 30) suggests that the chemical variables do not predict battering. Heavy drinkers do, however, begin drinking in most cases to alleviate perceived stress or as a form of self-medication (Deschner, 1984, p. 31; Fleming, 1979, p. 290). Whether that need for self-medication originates in an effort to cope with environmental stress, or to suppress the anxieties and anger held within (Fleming, 1979, p. 290), is a point of clinical importance. In neither case is the effect of the alcohol that which was intended. Rather than a reduction in feelings of inadequacy, the alcohol exaggerates them. This inadequacy combines with what the perpetrator knows will be disappointment on the part of the family members who fear the drinking or view it as a broken promise. The almost inevitable result is a joint escalation of anger toward the self and family as well as the drinking behavior, an escalation that holds the probability of an explosive response to almost any interaction. The same is true of the perpetrator caring for an older person.

Mistreatment of the Elderly

According to the House Select Committee on Aging, the factors used to describe the generation of a violent event in other forms of family violence can also be found in mistreatment of the elderly; including excessive use of alcohol (Langley, 1981, p. 15). Alcoholism and alcohol abuse has been proposed as one of the psychopathological links between elder mistreatment and the other forms of family violence (Falcioni, 1982, p. 208). The interesting twist to alcohol use in this family is that it may be occurring in both perpetrator and victim (Douglas, 1983; Douglas & Hickey, 1983). The alcohol abuse in elder mistreatment is seen as not only a feature of the perpetrator's response to stress, but as a joint perpetrator/victim response to their being forced to live together (Chen et al., 1981; Douglas, 1983; Falcioni, 1982; Rathbone-McCuan & Hashimi, 1982).

Alcohol abuse in the perpetrator of elder mistreatment has been described as both an historic/chronic problem (Falcioni, 1982, p. 209) and as an expression of acute stress (Douglas & Hickey, 1983, p. 19). This stress is exacerbated by the drinking in a self-perpetuating spiral

(Douglas, 1983, p. 137). It has also been noted that some perpetrators not only abuse the older person's prescription drugs to keep the older person under control, but abuse the drugs themselves (Rathbone-McCuan & Voyles, 1982, p. 192). This may be due to nothing more than the tedium of enforced time alone with nothing to do but care for the older person (Anderson, 1981).

A Summary View

There is no question that alcohol and drug use/misuse will be a feature of the practitioner's work with violent families. The environment of the violent family trains it to use alcohol. It is used by those around them. It reduces stress in a way virtually nothing else can. It allows them to engage in deviant behaviors they wish to engage in without holding them responsible for outcomes. For the practitioner, it is something that presents a dangerous smokescreen, which can be used to explain too many behaviors, mask too many critical variables, and impede treatment and general progress. Before any work can be done with the family, this is something that must be removed or reduced to controllable levels, for if it is not; it will always be escaped to when the practitioner gets too close to the *real* issues in the family.

Part III

Violent Family Personalities and Processes

5

The Family Violence Victim:
Common Points of Practitioner
Study and Intervention

A s Table 5.1 indicates, the array of possible effects on the victim of family violence is vast. There are, however, a number of common features of this unique form of victimization. The results of the victimization experience across all forms of family violence seem to rest within the following: poor self-concept and low self-esteem, dependency problems, difficulty in trusting, revictimization, denial-defensiveness-withdrawal-isolation, emotional trauma and psychological difficulty, subsequent deviance, behavior problems and sexual maladjustment, and social and interpersonal problems. The specifics of these practitioner targets will be discussed here.

Poor Self-Concept and Low Self-Esteem

Child Maltreatment

The self-esteem of the victimized child has been a clinical concern for some time (Helfer, 1975). Whether this issue is described as low self-esteem (Egeland, Sroufe, & Erickson, 1983, p. 460; Martin & Beezley, 1977), poor self-concept (Kinard, 1980a, p. 453), poor self-image (Hjorth & Ostrow, 1982), or self-devaluation (Elmer, 1979, p. 69) the process is the same. These children have developed an

TABLE 5.1
Commonalities in Victims of Family Violence

	Child Maltreat- ment	Sexual Abuse	Conjugal Conjugal Violence	Elder Mistreat- ment
(1) Poor self-concept and low self-esteem	X	X	X	X
(2) Confused dependencies	X	X	X	X
(3) Difficulty in trusting	X	X	X	
(4) Revictimization	X	X	X	X
(5) Denial-defensiveness- withdrawal-isolation	X	X	X	X
(6) Emotional trauma and psychological difficulty	X	X	X	X
(7) Subsequent deviance, behavior problems, and sexual maladjustment	X	X		
(8) Social and interpersonal problems	X	X	X	

NOTE: See Appendix B for references.

understanding that they deserved the victimization and have accepted a negative view of themselves (Bourne, 1979, p. 9).

These children's sense of self is far too weak to accept the irrationality of having a parent who victimizes them for no apparent reason. They have no choice but to accept the "badness" that causes the victimization as something they cannot see in themselves but that the adult perpetrator can. What follows this acceptance is a series of repeated trial and error efforts at trying to remove the badness and do something to please the adult. What is also demanded is a hypervigilance to those around them in an effort to avoid the eventuality of the badness upsetting others.

These children are not only slow to develop confidence (Friedrich & Einbender, 1983, p. 248), they simply stop trying. After all, a bad self-image is better than none at all. But this leads them to see themselves as somehow different from others: not as good and not as deserving. There is no reason why anyone would love them save their own child; the answer to this lost caring. For the time being, prior to having their own children, there is a self-induced exclusion from peers. This becomes a circular process that not only confirms their differentness, but leads them further into isolation and continued self-deprecation (Kinard, 1980a, p. 458). This is a paradoxical pattern that must be interrupted not only for these children but for their children in the future.

Child Sexual Abuse

It is not surprising that the incest experience dimishes self-esteem (Kilpatrick & Amick, 1982, p. 2; Stone, Tyler, & Mead, 1984, p. 78; Tsai & Wagner, 1979). What is surprising is the strength of the negative feeling the child directs against him or herself (James & Nasjleti, 1983, p. 7). This is not a simple matter of feeling oneself to be less worthy than others. This is a pervasive self-blame and self-hatred that not only creates later vulnerability (Finkelhor, 1984, p. 194) but may cause self-mutilation or even suicide (Summit, 1984, p. 2). If this victim is male, he is not believed by his family or he is ridiculed for putting "yourself into that situation," the maximal effects will be felt (MacFarlane & Korbin, 1983).

Conjugal Violence

The victimized co-habitor is placed in an emotional quandry not unlike the child victim. If the irrationality of the perpetrator is accepted, continuing danger must be admitted and there is no choice but for the co-habitor to leave. If there is no place to go, however, this alternative is unacceptable. As a consequence, the victim may be left with little emotional choice but to accept the blame for the violence.

This victim is left feeling not only inferior but helpless to change the situation (Pagelow, 1984, p. 309). Once these feelings are adopted, it is a short path to a self-perception of being someone who is incompetent, unworthy, and unloveable. These feelings, taken in total, result in victims believing that they deserve whatever abuse they receive (Hilberman, 1980, p. 1342; Rosewater, 1984, p. 4). It will be only a brief time before the victims automatically underestimates their abilities and competencies. Any successes that might occur are quickly downplayed or attributed to forces outside herself (Walker, 1979, p. 31). This is the zero sum result of victimization; no victim can ever win.

Mistreatment of the Elderly

The loss of self-esteem experienced by the elderly victim is a double-edged sword. The initial loss comes with aging itself and the impairments that may disrupt interests and activities that were previously esteem-building (Pfeiffer & Busse, 1973). There is a decline in the ability to influence the environment and an accompanying loss of persons and property (Anderson, 1981, p. 81). If this is an individual whose physical frailty leads to dependence on another family member, there may be an accompanying guilt at causing problems (Kosberg, 1983a, p. 286). As these negative feelings converge in anxiety and guilt, this victim experiences the additional shame and embarrassment, not to mention helplessness, of being trapped in a home in which they are harmed by someone they thought loved them. At the very least, this is a set of perceptions that causes them to question their self-worth (Luppens & Lau, 1983, p. 209; Solomon, 1983, p. 161). The problem is dependency; the effect is feeling bad about oneself. The dependency issue will be found to be a key to the practitioner's understanding of the violent family.

Dependency

The Child Maltreatment Victim

Victims of family violence are in weakened, powerless, and dependent positions relative to the perpetrators (Olivira, 1981; Pagelow, 1984, pp. 358-360). Never is this more true than in the child victim (Egeland et al., 1983). There is no reason for child victims to perceive themselves as being anything but externally controlled (Galambos & Dixon, 1984, p. 286). The entire life-support system and resultant safety is at the whim of the adults around them; adults who show an overt unwillingness to allow the child normal environmental manipulation and exploration. The child in this family serves the parent; not the reverse. Departures from this role are severely punished.

The result of this unbalanced dependency is a child who is overly compliant to all adults, ineffective in tenuous and anxious efforts to please adults, and hypervigilant to cues in the environment that dictate what should be done, thought, or said. For this child, there is none of the spontaneous joy that should describe childhood (Friedrich & Einbender, 1983, p. 248). In fact, this is not childhood at all, but an immediate introduction to the problems of emotional survival usually confronted much later in life.

Child Sexual Abuse

The sexually abused child is one whose dependency needs are overpowered by the needs of the adults in the environment. These adult needs take precedence over all other issues in the environment: friends, siblings, and the nonabusive parent (Mitkus, 1982, p. 10). This is one of the narrowest childhoods imaginable.

For this child, needs for reasonable affection are ignored or distorted. Protection is only offered through the child's willingness to participate in physical intimacy. Security is something that is re-earned daily (James & Nasjleti, 1983, p. 6). Living in a family environment where destruction and abandonment are a constant threat, unless the victim is compliant (Prentkey, 1984; Mitkus, 1982, p. 13), fosters a child with no time or energy for meeting his or her own dependency needs. The fusion and enmeshment of adult and child roles—caretaker, confidante, or lover (Stone et al., 1984, p. 78)—result in childhood dependencies being ignored. The result is a childhood, and an adulthood, characterized by a "dependency hunger" (Summit, 1984, p. 2). This hunger places this victim in a position of being preoccupied with obtaining the nurture and affection missing during childhood (Browne & Finkelhor, 1984, p. 2). This will be true whether the victim is male or female (Rossman, 1980, p. 346).

Dependency and Conjugal Violence

Like the child sexual abuse victim, the victim of conjugal violence is a "keeper of the peace": keeping things as the perpetrator would have them (Walker, 1979, p. 34). The victim is submissive in this way, accepting the perpetrator's definition of the relationship (Ferraro, 1984, p. 4). This victim may well have entered this relationship preprogrammed to play it in this dependent way through a traditional view of sex role relationships.

For the victim of conjugal violence, the traditional view of the male as head of the household not only provides for rigid family roles (Fleming, 1979, p. 10), it may also lead to a general powerlessness in having critical needs met (Straus, 1980b, p. 702). If these victims enter the relationship with the view that marriage is sacred and that their role is to make difficult things in life better for husband or wife and children, they may be emotionally consumed by the perpetrator. This is a total self-sacrifice described as "altruistic madness" (Richardson, 1977). In this madness the victim becomes totally involved in providing nurturance to family members, worries excessively about perpetrator and child well-being, and feels sorry, not about their own victimization, but for the deprivation and abuse the perpetrator faced in childhood; the perceived cause of the violence (Deschner, 1984, p. 32; Hilberman, 1980, p. 1339; Pagelow, 1984, p. 309). The perpetrator, having confused dependencies as well, is only too happy to support this analysis and use it to manipulate the overly dependent victim even further.

Mistreatment of the Elderly

There are normal dependencies that come with old age. Blenker (1979) finds these in economic, physical, mental, and social realms. However, Luppens and Lau (1983, p. 208) point out that these normal dependencies can be exaggerated by physical or mental incapacity. Increased dependency means increased vulnerability. *The more the victim needs the perpetrator, the greater the risk.*

The individual at risk for mistreatment in old age is that frail elderly individual who has both mental and physical impairments, is housebound or limited in ambulation, and dependent for essential needs (Luppens & Lau, 1983). These victims are described by incompetence, frailty, senility, and/or multiple health problems. There is likely to be at least one major physical or mental impairment (Falcioni, 1982, p. 209) and the individual's feelings of helplessness are reinforced by the psychological losses of widowhood, retirement, and major life roles (Douglas & Hickey, 1983, p. 174). They are essentially at the mercy of the perpetrator. To make matters worse, they do not all handle this dependency with grace. To the contrary, they have been described as demanding, needy, provocative, antagonizing, and inappropriate in their demands (Chen et al., 1981, p. 11). Irrespective of their means for attempting to meet their dependencies, their search for understanding and responsiveness in the perpetrator is often in vain. It is from the vain search for adequate meeting of dependency needs that victims of family violence learn not to trust.

Difficulty in Trusting

Trusting in Child and Conjugal Violence Victims

It is obvious that the victim of child maltreatment will have difficulty in trusting (Kinard, 1980a, p. 453; Martin, 1976). If you cannot trust your parents, those individuals who are supposed to offer unconditional protection and caring, there are few persons who will gain your trust easily. Similarly, victims of conjugal violence, victims who walked blindly into a violent situation believing that this relationship (a marriage) may be the first place where love and trust could be found, will lose the ability to trust (Arndt, 1984; Walker, 1979). Quite simply, following their victimization, these victims must learn, through repetitive and frequent trial-and-error testing that there *are* people who do what they say and *will not hurt you*. And they must relearn what "family" means and their role within it. The sexual abuse victim, however, presents an extra measure of difficulty in regaining trust.

Trust and the Sexual Abuse Victim

There is no greater betrayal of trust than that experienced by sexually abused children (Stone et al., 1984, p. 78). The parental promise of protection has been betrayed by the perpetrator who emotionally abandoned them (Lewis-Herman, 1981, p. 31). The other parent, an adult who failed to protect, abandoned in yet another way (Browne & Finkelhor, 1984, p. 2). As such, despite the fact that the victims may maintain warm feelings toward the perpetrators (Pagelow, 1984, p. 386) a basic distrust becomes an element of their operating style (Summit, 1984, p. 2). An on-going difficulty in forming trusting relationships becomes a critical difficulty in their life (Browne & Finkelhor, 1984, p. 4; Lewis-Herman, 1981), as is a curious mix of trusting those who would hurt them and finding difficulty in being able to trust those who might help.

As time goes on, the inability to trust clashes with the inappropriate dependencies that grew out of the maltreating relationship. What results are needy, lonely, and passive individuals, who only know how to gain attention in one way: sexually. These are individuals who fail not only in learning who to trust, but in learning from whom to protect themselves in close relationships (Finkelhor, 1979, pp. 23–25). Revictimization quickly and repetitively follows.

Revictimization

The notion "once a victim always a victim" need not be true. However, a great deal of early victimization is found in the lives of adult victims (Steele, 1982). This may be the product of inappropriate learning of protective mechanisms or failed judgment. This may have a more psychodynamic origin in which a "repetition compulsion" is created through which the victims cannot accept success in themselves, and they place themselves in situations, in which failure is guaranteed. Both these etiologies may be at work in the revictimization of the family violence victim.

Child Maltreatment

Re-abuse is common in child maltreatment (Herrenkohl, Herrenkohl, Egolf, & Secch, 1979). This may be due to inappropriate learning, failed interventions, lack of discovery, or as a result of an on-going pattern. Some children, for example, are seen as having characteristics and behaviors (e.g., harassing of parents) that promote tension and subsequent explosion (Friedrich & Boriskin, 1976, p. 581). It is much more likely, however, that the child victim's poor self-image and distorted dependencies will lead to repetitive victimization not only in childhood, but as an adult (Bourne, 1979, p. 9).

Sexual Abuse

No area of family violence involves revictimization to a greater degree than sexual abuse (Alford, Bauman, & Kaspar, 1984, p. 41;

Summit, 1984, p. 2). There is clearly an expectation of abuse and disappointment in later relationships (Lewis-Herman, 1981). The victims are most likely to experience the compulsive repetition of failure (consistent with their self-image) in which they set themselves up for failure due not only to impaired protective mechanisms (Lewis-Herman, 1981, p. 29), but self-hatred. These victims seem to *want* to see themselves as the disgusting persons they feel they were in their childhood.

The male sexual abuse victim may reveal the clearest path to revictimization. The revictimization in the male victim is directed not toward themselves, but others. It appears that male sexual victimization predicts a greater likelihood of sexual abuse perpetration in the future, particularly child molestation (Groth et al., 1982). This does not mean that all males so victimized will become child molesters; only that it may increase the risk. Yet this is a bilateral risk, for the male once-victim-now-perpetrator not only victimizes a child, but continues his own victimization in this way.

Conjugal Violence

Victims of conjugal violence often face a secondary victimization through the assumption of "intrapsychic liability" (Hilberman, 1980, p. 1336). Quite simply, others may think there is something wrong with *them*. These are victims who are first punished by the perpetrator and then by the system, which sees something wrong with them or this violence would not have occurred. This victimization is compounded by the belief that such victimization is isolated (Hilberman, 1980, p. 1336) or that the perpetrator is not as dangerous as the victim makes him or her out to be.

Two obvious examples of secondary or revictimization can be found in (1) the belief that battered women are masochistic, and (2) the battered woman who, having been repetitively beaten for years, is on trial for killing her husband, and must go to great lengths to prove why she felt he was dangerous (Walker, 1985). In the first case, the woman who cannot handle the anticipatory anxiety of waiting for a violent confrontation, and causes such a confrontation to occur, is not being masochistic (Fleming, 1979). In the second situation, the woman who has accepted physical punishment for years and finally acts may be just as likely to kill herself to escape the terror (Martin, 1976). So these victims are not only harmed in their homes, but outside the home by helping persons who see them as sick or at the heart of the problem. Just as in the victim of conjugal violence, the victim of elder mistreatment is likely to experience revictimization from sources outside the violent home.

Mistreatment of the Elderly

Older persons are stereotyped not only by service providers but by older persons themselves. Within that stereotype is the sense that older persons are incapable of making decisions for themselves or taking care of themselves. Being treated in that way confirms the fears of older persons about their own dependency, and the result is a sense of hopelessness that increases the sense of helplessness already in existence due to the initial mistreatment (Solomon, 1983, p. 161). This is particularly problematic in this situation, for the victim of elder mistreatment, although physically dependent, may be quite capable of making realistic decisions about his or her situation, but if denied that opportunity may cease to try.

Overall, in many cases it seems the wisest course of action for the victim of elder mistreatment to avoid the service delivery system. Contact with that system seems to promise little more than revictimization in many cases from well-meaning providers. Under these conditions, the denial and withdrawal that typically describe the victim's response to disclosure of previously hidden family violence seems to be a relatively wise course of action.

Denial-Defensiveness-Withdrawal-Isolation

For the practitioner, a major frustration in working with the family violence victim is the apparent acceptance of the victim role. Even in the presence of absolute evidence that severe victimization is occurring, it is not uncommon for the victim to deny its existence. This is a factor in both physical and sexual abuse of children (Bourne & Newberger, 1979; James & Nasjleti, 1983), conjugal violence (Hilberman, 1980, p. 1345) and particularly in mistreatment of the elderly (Anderson, 1981, p. 78) where fear of abandonment, isolation, institutionalization, or retaliation looms large (Falcioni, 1982, p. 209). They may also believe that they are being paid back for the way they treated the child, now-adult perpetrator, or they may not recognize the behavior as mistreatment (Galbraith & Zdorkowski, 1984, p. 231).

Most frequently, the elder victims may feel the behavior to be a family matter. It is a source of shame. They do not want criminal attention directed toward the perpetrator nor the loss of pride it would take to admit that they are the recipient of such embarrassing treatment; withdrawal and isolation seem the better course (Kosberg, 1983a, p. 286).

The victims of *child maltreatment* are widely recognized as isolated children. They are withdrawn, emotionally unresponsive (Egeland et al., 1983, p. 460; Martin & Beezley, 1977), and avoidant of peers in situations in which interaction would have been expected (Kinard, 1980a, p. 459). Given the fears, lack of trust, expectation of revictimization, and low self-esteem already described, this can hardly be surprising.

The victim of *child sexual abuse* is often isolated by the family (James & Nasjleti, 1983; Tsai & Wagner, 1979), and self-isolated as well. Silence is not an uncommon reaction to sexual trauma (Burgess & Holstrom, 1979, p. 81). Fear of reprisal, shame, fear of parental anger, or fear of not being believed may keep this child silent and withdrawn (Finkelhor, 1979, p. 31; Summit, 1983). These are children alienated from their peers, owning knowledge of the world their peers do not share. They often feel that they are alone in this world in the victimization they have experienced (James & Nasjleti, 1983, p. 3). These children feel different from their peers and know that they can never again be normal (Lewis-Herman, 1981). To make their withdrawal complete, they may develop a communication disorder that allows them to keep their secret or as a response to the frustration of not having the words to describe what happened (Summit, 1985). Each of these is an effect that is exaggerated if the victim is a male.

Male sexual victimization is most often homosexual (Lewis-Herman, 1981, p. 14). The perpetrator was likely to be someone outside the family, there may have been physical abuse as well, and there may have been other victims present at the time (Burgess, 1984; Burgess, Groth, & McCausland, 1981; Finkelhor, 1984, pp. 164–166).

The result is a victim not likely to disclose the experience (Finkelhor, 1979; Kempe & Kempe, 1984; Landis, 1956; Nasjleti, 1980; Swift, 1980).

In general, it is less acceptable for males to express dependency, fear, vulnerability, or helplessness—all features of the sexual abuse experience. The result is silence (Nasjleti, 1980, p. 270). There are additional inhibitors. Finkelhor (1984, pp. 156–157) for example, notes that the male victim has more to lose than the female victim by disclosing.

First, he has not been prepared by his parents as to how to act in this situation (Landis, 1956). Second, people tend to see sexual activities with females as more serious and more abusive than those same activities with males. Females get a more protective response (Russell, 1984, p. 194). Third, the male victim may have a feeling that he is a sissy or unmanly for not protecting himself, and that this may result in ridicule or rejection. Fourth, the fears of not being believed or that this event means that he is homosexual may evoke a greater degree of shame than in the female. Finally, he may fear that the activity will not be stopped and the perpetrator will not only be sexually abusive but angry as well. Remember that threat or coercion may have been a part of the assault. The point is clear; disclosure is more dangerous, both physically and emotionally, than denial and withdrawal. This mixture of present shame and anticipated danger describes the reactions of other family violence victims as well.

The victims of *conjugal violence* may be purposefully isolated by the perpetrator. They are unlikely to participate in social activities, may have no close friends, are under the continuous control and monitoring of the perpetrator, and experience a change in residence as soon as any social contacts begin to build (Pagelow, 1984, pp. 320–321). In a complementary way, the shame and embarrassment felt at being treated this way, especially if it causes the victim to see herself as a failure, keeps the code of silence in operation; internal turmoil is preferable to abandonment and the unknown. It is better to be resigned and accept what this violent relationship may bring. Unfortunately, for many victims of family violence, what this relationship brings is on-going emotional trauma and psychological instability.

Emotional Trauma and Psychological Difficulty

Child Maltreatment

Of all family violence victims, the victim of child maltreatment seems the most psychologically resilient. Child victims endure seemingly impossible situations and continue to hold the potential to become productive adults. It is unclear whether this resilience is due to others in the environment or the relatively long recuperation period, and it does not negate the emotional trauma experienced.

Emotional maladjustment, instability, and overt psychopathology do sometimes originate from the experience of physical child maltreatment (Hjorth & Ostrow, 1982; Straker & Jacobson, 1981). These psychiatric problems are worsened by instability in the home, frequent moves, or living with a caretaker who has emotional problems (Kinard, 1980a, p. 459). The usual expression of these problems is a high level of anxiety or a depressive presentation of unhappiness and sadness (Elmer, 1979, p. 69; Kinard, 1980a, p. 457). There are also reports of extreme regression (Martinez-Roiz, Domingo-Salvany, Liorvas-Terol, & Ibanez-Cacho, 1983, p. 261) and character disorders (Blumberg, 1979). However the most severe pathology seems to occur in the sexually abused children.

Child Sexual Abuse

There are few psychological disorders that have not, in some study, been traced back to sexual abuse in childhood (Glasner, 1981). Some feel this to be the result of an over-reliance upon clinical samples in child sexual abuse research and others see it as an unwarranted hysterical reaction to the problem (Schultz, 1980a).

The argument that an over-reliance upon clinical samples distorts research is not as critical for this work as others as this work is intended to inform clinicians. And, for clinicians, sexual abuse of children seems to be a situation that predicts persistent psychological effects (Blumberg, 1979). These effects may be variable depending upon the developmental level of the victim and the nature of the abuse (Adams-Tucker, 1982a; Koch, 1980). They may be expressed in attitudinal as well as emotional changes (Silbert & Pines, 1981).

Some of the trauma is immediate and some long term (Blumberg, 1979; Byrne & Valdiserri, 1982). Key variables in the individual sexually abusive event have been described as predictive of major trauma although no uniquely trauma-producing elements have been empirically isolated (Browne & Finkelhor, 1986). A summary would find degree of trauma related to the relative maturity of the victim, the victim's emotional stability prior to the event, the nature of the incident, the relationship to the perpetrator, the parental response to the event, and pre-morbid family and child conditions (Burgess, & Holstrom, 1979, p. 74; Courtois, 1979; Leaman, 1980; MacFarlane & Korbin, 1983; Seider & Calhoun, 1984). The trauma induced by these variables has multiple manifestations.

At the extreme of responses to sexual abuse are the multiple personality reactions popularized by the media. Reactions of this type are very rare although they may occur through the victim's capacity to split a part of themselves off and assign to it the role of victim (Summit, 1984, p. 5). Major depressive episodes and excessive anxiety problems would be the more commonly observed among the most debilitating reactions (Browne & Finkelhor, 1984; Lewis-Herman, 1981; Tsai, Feldman-Summers & Edgar, 1979), with recurrent depressive effect the most common of all responses (DeJong, 1983; Kilpatrick & Amick, 1984, p. 2; Tsai & Wagner, 1979).

Personality and character disorders have been described among these victims (Blumberg, 1979; Pomeroy, Behar, & Steward, 1981) and their families. Anderson and Shafer (1979, p. 437) describe the entire sexually abusive family scene as "character disordered" and list the presence of poor impulse control, poor judgment, failure to learn from experience, inability to deal with authority, physical expression of needs, manipulativeness, irresponsibility, no expression of guilt, callousness and narcissism, dependency conflicts, and an inability to tolerate intimacy as features of this home. Obviously, this is a setting that provides immediate and long-term risk for emotional and personality problems (Lourie, 1984).

Among the more common reactions are generalized guilt, self-blame, and consequent depression (DeFrancis, 1969, p. 3; Tsai & Wagner, 1979). At the extreme this pattern has been posited to lead to hysterical seizures (LaBarbera & Dozier, 1980, pp. 902–903), but it is more likely to bring somatic complaints, sleep and appetite difficulties, anxiety and pervasive insecurity in social situations (Brown, 1980; Browne & Finkelhor, 1984; Kilpatrick & Amick,

1984). There may be evidence of feelings of hatred and betrayal regarding the mother who failed to protect (Stone et al., 1984; Tsai & Wagner, 1979), but the negativity is more likely to be self-directed, even if only in subtle ways (i.e., inability to hold a job). As with all depressed individuals, the practitioner must be alert to the possibility of suicide or other intensely self-destructive behaviors (Anderson, 1981). But even with this litany of possible negative effects, not all students of child sexual abuse accept damage as inevitable.

Since this work is directed toward practitioners whose work is with troubled individuals, intensive study of the "no damage" theorists will not be undertaken. It is important to be aware of them, however, and to be able to reassure the victim that they have been resilient enough to survive to this point and that the damage can be overcome.

Most of the "minimal effects" studies tend to be older works (Bender & Grugett, 1952; Gagnon, 1965; Landis, 1956). More recent work exists (Yorokoglu & Kemph, 1966) but have received criticism for the small samples employed. The most recent theorist who feels the negative effects view to be "alarmist" is Schultz, whose 1980 edited work provides several articles with a moderate view of victim effects. On the basis of these articles, Schultz suggests that there has been an overreliance on "victimogenic" descriptions (Schultz, 1980, p. 95). His view is that an iatrogenic situation is being created in which the *belief in* their victimization creates the negative effects. This is obviously the minority view in the child sexual abuse literature. A moderate position is offered by Lewis-Herman (1981, p.29) who indicates that while the majority of child sex victims find the experience disagreeable, they are not all permanently damaged. However, there are those who are made more vulnerable to significant problems as a result of the experience. Those are the victims most likely to be seen by the practitioner at some point.

It should be noted that the male sexual victimization experience is more likely to present the possibility of emotional/psychological disturbance (Guttmacher, 1962; Wahl, 1960). This is a male who has been forced into a passive role and failed to protect himself. He fears that his masculinity has been undercut in a way that may influence future behavior and may even fear homosexuality both as a consequence of the act and as a result of his ability to attract male sexual attention (Russell, 1984, p. 195). If he responded physically to the perpetrator's stimulation, this fear may be markedly increased (James & Nasjleti, 1983). Ultimately, whether reported or not, the male sexual victimization seems often to be an experience that the victim finds difficult to put behind himself.

Conjugal Violence

The description of victims of conjugal violence as emotionally sensitive, guilt prone, suspicious, and anxious (Arndt, 1984) is hardly surprising given the constant emotional tension in their lives. The victimization experience in conjugal violence is one of constant stress. To survive this experience, these individuals must remove themselves somewhat from an awareness of their own feelings and needs (Ferraro, 1984, p. 4) and become alienated and pessimistic about others.

The constant tension and feeling of imminent doom that marks the violent conjugal environment (Hilberman, 1980, p. 1341) results in hypervigilance, nightmares, sleep difficulty, and somatic complaints such as backache, headache and fatigue (Arndt, 1984; Hilberman, 1980, p. 1341; Walker, 1979, p. 35). The victims may feel trapped within this environment and even evidence the unique "Stockholm Syndrome" in which hostages develop an affinity and sympathy for their captors (Hilberman, 1980; Pagelow, 1984).

Psychologically, conjugal victims are under a constant struggle to contain aggressive responses to the situation (Hilberman, 1980, p. 1342). This may be done to protect the child or themselves. Eventually, the victim become inert. There is a sense of numbness, a total lack of energy, and an absence of self-motivation. Hopelessness, despair, and a sense of "learned helplessness" (Walker, 1979) at not being able to influence the environment pervade almost every interaction (Hilberman, 1980, p. 1342). Ultimately, as this victim reaches the breaking point, the practitioner must alter the possibility of self-destructive, suicidal, or even homicidal acts. This is critically true when working with the victim who has decided that nothing really matters any more other than escaping this intolerable anxiety and oppression (Hilberman, 1980, p. 1342). This is a point many victims eventually reach.

Mistreatment of the Elderly

In the elderly victim it is sometimes difficult to determine which psychological elements were present prior to the abusive event and which follow from it. It is known that this victim may have presented a picture that could have included frailty, incompetence, senility, pathological loneliness, fear, depression, long-term grief and despair, confusion, anger, and hopelessness even before entering the perpetrator's home (Chen et al., 1981, p. 11). The most that can be said is that these pre-existing conditions can be worsened by the victimization experience (Anderson, 1981, p. 81; Falcioni, 1982, p. 211). Also, if some organic condition pre-existed or appeared while in the perpetrator's home (e.g., organic brain syndrome), the prognosis for working with major psychological impacts declines (Luppens & Lau, 1983, p. 206). However, irrespective of the pre-existing or consequent nature of the condition, an impact on both behavior and the relationship with the environment is predicted for the mistreated older person.

Subsequent Deviance, Behavior Problems, and Sexual Maladjustment

Child Maltreatment

The list of behaviors that hide victimization in children includes delinquency, running away, prostitution, substance abuse, suicide attempts, and premature parenthood to name a few (Bolton, 1980; Bolton, Reich, & Gutierres, 1978; Garbarino, 1984b, McCord, 1983, p. 270). However, it is not the act itself that alerts the practitioner to the masked abuse, but the style in which it occurs.

Child maltreatment victims behave at the extremes. They are either very difficult and almost harassing toward adults (George & Main, 1979) or they are extraordinarily passive and show indiscriminate displays of affection and compliance (Helfer, 1975). The difficult child will reveal a pervasive hostility and aggressiveness (Egeland et al., 1983, p. 460; Kinard, 1980a; Martin & Beezley, 1977) matched with a difficulty in controlling these impulses (Hjorth & Ostrow, 1982; Kinard, 1980a, p. 460). This is especially evident in situations that test the child's attachment and separation responses (Ainsworth, 1980; Bolton, 1984; Kinard, 1980a).

When the child presents with a more passive or compliant style, there will be a notable inability to enjoy life (anhedonia). They are almost not children, appearing almost as pseudo-adults; a behavioral style rewarded by their parents. However, the undercurrent to this compliance is a great deal of emotional turmoil sometimes suggested by problems such as enuresis, tantrums, withdrawal, or sleep disturbances (Martin & Beezley, 1977).

To maintain the pseudo-mature and compliant behavior, the child is forced to be extraordinarily vigilant about their environment and painfully compulsive in making certain that all issues and problems are resolved. This is a child who is greatly anxious and will be described as a "worrier." The child who is sexually victimized may reveal an even more troubled pattern.

The Sexual Abuse Victim

Like their physically abused counterparts, sexually abused children have been known to become delinquent (Koch, 1980; Reich & Guiterres, 1979), become pregnant in adolescence (Bolton, 1984; Harrison & Lumry, 1984), and to run away (Brown, 1981; Weber, 1977). There is additional danger of drug addiction (Prentkey, 1984, p. 1) and admission to inpatient psychiatry units (Harrison & Lumry, 1984). However, few of the consequences of sexual abuse are as disturbing as the future sexual maladjustments that may be implied (Finkelhor, 1984, p. 15; Lewis-Herman, 1981; Rush, 1980; Russell, 1984, p. 248).

For the female sexual abuse victim, there is a promise of continuing problems in sexuality (Blumberg, 1974; Kilpatrick & Amick, 1984, p. 2; Pagelow, 1984, p. 386) and in relationships with men in general (Courtois, 1979). It must be remembered that this is a child who has developed within an oversexualized atmosphere that has given her not only inappropriate sexual models, but a distorted socialization experience.

As an outgrowth of this victimization and distortion in sexual socialization, there will frequently be precocious sexual activity (Glasner, 1981), early sexual experimentation (LaBarbera, Martin, & Dozier, 1980; Pomeroy et al., 1981), and excessive curiosity about, awareness of, and preoccupation with sexual issues (Browne & Finkelhor, 1984, p. 3; Kempe & Kempe, 1984, p. 55). The stigma that follows the victimization has been known to create an avoidance of as well as a compulsion toward sexual activity (Brown, 1981; Felman & Mitkus, 1983; Prentkey, 1984). Sometimes this victim is led to believe that she is good for little else but sex. The male victim may reveal even more difficult problems.

Two of the most common concerns regarding the male victim are that he will present an increased likelihood of perpetrating child molestation (Groth et al., 1982) and/or that homosexuality will result (Bell & Weinberg, 1978, 1981; Finkelhor, 1984; Herman, 1981). The male sexual abuse victim can also be found among the runaways, truants, incorrigibles, delinquents, prostitutes, and victims of physical abuse discussed earlier (James & Nasjleti, 1983). He may also replay the victimization experience (Nasjleti, 1980, p. 271; Swift, 1979).

The most common thesis regarding child molestation by a previously victimized male is that he becomes a victimizer in order to master the trauma he experienced. By taking on the power of the adult perpetrator, he somehow masters the powerlessness he felt as a victim (deYoung, 1982). This has also been related to the perpetration of rape with adult women (Nasjleti, 1980, p. 271). Even the mothers of sexual abuse victims have been described as having been victimized themselves (Goodwin, 1982). These second-generation effects may speak to the anger and helplessness that grows out of this experience in childhood.

Social and Interpersonal Problems

The child maltreatment victim shows a dearth of social skills. It is believed that these skills were unavailable to the child even before the victimization, perhaps causing some of the problem in his or her life (Burgess, 1985). It is not difficult to imagine these children as having impoverished communication and poor coping ability because that description also matches the operating style of the family in which they live (Egeland et al., 1983; Elmer, 1979, p. 69; Hjorth & Ostrow, 1982). These problems will reveal themselves in interactions with adults and peers at every level (Kinard, 1980, p. 453), but school may present the biggest challenge for this underprepared child (Summit, 1984).

Although it is not clear whether it preceded or followed victimization, the maltreated child demonstrates reduced intellectual ability (Egeland et al., 1983, p. 460) and impaired cognitive status (Friedrich & Boriskin, 1983, p. 248; Lynch, 1978; Martin & Rodeheffer, 1976; Perry, Doran, & Wells, 1983). Although these effects have been related as much to low social status and single parenthood as direct abuse (Burgess & Garbarino, 1983; Rosenfeld & Newberger, 1979, p. 83), the fact is that learning problems are demonstrated within this population (Martin & Beezley, 1977).

A school setting is not a comfortable place for the hyperactive (Kinard, 1980a, p. 459; Martin & Beezley, 1977) and distractable child victim. The poor self-control that grows out of the victimization experience clashes with the control needs of school personnel, and the child is seen as noncompliant (Egeland et al., 1983, pp. 468–469). The communication problems that burden this child do little to alter this view (Perry et al., 1983). These are difficulties mirrored by the sexual abuse victim.

The interpersonal skills of the sexual abuse victim are even more faulty than the physically abused child (Lourie, 1984). While they may or may not have the speech and language disorders that characterize the physical abuse victim (Blager, 1979; Summit, 1985) there is a great difficulty in intimacy (Kempe & Kempe, 1984, p. 54) and generally unsatisfying social relationships (Janas, 1983).

In a school setting the same learning difficulties (Brown, 1981), concentration difficulties (James & Nasjleti, 1983), and behavior problems (Browne & Finkelhor, 1983, p. 3) that marked the school's experience with the physical child abuse victim, will be found in the sexual abuse victim. In fact, poor attendance, truancy or lateness, scholastic changes, or sudden changes in conduct may, individually or in combination, be considered masked presentations of a sexually abusive situation (Pagelow, 1984, p. 396).

These are not problems demonstrated by the sexual abuse victim which end in childhood. The combination of pervasive self-hatred and difficulty with social, interpersonal, and sexual relations easily predicts difficulty as an adult (Blumberg, 1978). In fact the difficulty this individual has in finding a lover, mate, or marriage that can be trusted is almost paralyzing (Blumberg, 1978; Lewis-Herman, 1981). Even should this victim be among the lucky ones who find a way to tolerate the early life experience, they may continue to view themselves as different.

Initial and Enduring Differences

The victim of child maltreatment may have been viewed by their parents as different from the outset. They may have seemed hard to understand, difficult to manage, or difficult to relate to emotionally (i.e., they did not give the parents what they wanted). Somehow this was a child who not only deviated from the parent's expectation of what a child would be like; they were children who seemed to require some special care (Bolton, 1983, 1984; Frodi, 1981; Klein & Stern, 1971; Kotelchuck & Newberger, 1983; Lynch, 1977; Murphy, Jenkins, Newcombe, & Silbert, 1981; Stern, 1973).

In some cases, the child's differentness can be seen in something as obvious as prematurity, congenital anomalie (Friedrich & Einbender, 1983, p. 251; Herrenkohl & Herrenkohl, 1979; Sameroff & Chandler, 1975), neurological problems, and/or retardation (Buchanan & Oliver, 1977; Caffey, 1972; Green, Voeller, Gaines & Kubie, 1981; Sandgrund, Gaines, & Green, 1975). But, it is more likely that this problem is something much more evident to the parent than the practitioner; such as temperamental or behavioral differences that seem unresponsive or frustrating to the parent (Friedrich & Borishin, 1976, p. 587).

It is this type of temperamental or neurological mismatch between parent and child that may cause difficulty even in the well-prepared parent who has no difficulty in reading the child's cues. In an under-prepared parent it may be seen as purposeful behavior on the part of the child (Bourne, 1979, p. 9). Ultimately, the fit between perpetrator and victim is a poor one and the mechanisms that would ordinarily serve to protect the child from the destructive intrusion of parental needs are softened to the point that they are ineffective. As will be seen in the two following sections, it is the dangerous triad of victim characteristics, perpetrator characteristics, and family processes that come together in this family in the most destructive ways imaginable.

6

The Perpetrator in the Violent Family

No typology will ever capture all the critical features of the family violence perpetrator; the perpetrator-victim-environment interaction has too many possible combinations. But there is *one* feature that holds true: They are incapable of joining in a solidly attached, reciprocal, and protective relationship with other family members. There is a flaw. An analysis of the common flaws among perpetrators, as indicated by Table 6.1, finds the probable presence of psychopathology, unresolved interpersonal conflict, distorted dependencies, low self-esteem, role distortions, lack of preparation, dominance and control issues, approval of violence, lack of social interpersonal skills, and denial/defensiveness.

Practitioner Targets

Psychopathology

The Child Maltreatment Perpetrator

David Gil (1970), although most concerned with social inequity, also focused upon perpetrator psychopathology. His work describes the presence of paranoid schizophrenia, personality disorders, and depression (1970, p. 34). Steele has maintained his initial belief in the presence of psychopathology (1982) through recent discussion of "sociopathic" perpetrators who attack children in the family; attacks

TABLE 6.1
Commonalities Across Perpetrators of Family Violence

	Child Maltreatment	*Sexual Abuse*	*Conjugal Violence*	*Elder Mistreatment*
(1) Psychopathology	X	X	X	X
(2) Unresolved interpersonal conflict	X	X	X	X
(3) Inappropriate and distorted dependencies	X	X	X	X
(4) Immaturity	X	X	X	X
(5) Low self-esteem	X	X	X	X
(6) Lack of personal and experiential preparation for family role	X	X	X	X
(7) Need for dominance and control	X	X	X	X
(8) Approval of the use of violence	X		X	
(9) Lack of social and inter-personal skills	X	X	X	
(10) Denial and defensiveness	X	X	X	
(11) Distorted view of the victim	X	X	X	X

NOTE: See Appendix C for references.

that are unmotivated by stress (1982, p. 489). Sloan and Meier (1983, p. 445) have found psychopathology to be a supportable causal factor in child maltreatment through the presence of psychotic parents, ritualistic and unpredictable assaults unmotivated by outside forces and parental depression.

The Sexual Abuse Perpetrator

Some who study sexual abuse have seen the drive to find perpetrator psychopathology as being too strong, servicing the need to find the sex abuser to be "crazy" (Finkelhor, 1984). However, psychopathology does have a presence in sexual abuse and the time has come to re-examine the family systems view, which sees the perpetrator as a victim of circumstances.

Current study of the sexual abuse perpetrator describes psychopathology, at least in the case of the excessive hyper-sexuality of the predatory sex offender (Russell, 1984, p. 259). This is a perpetrator with hundreds of victims (Abel, 1985). This is a male who will develop an artificial relationship with a single parent, even marry, to gain access to the children (Summit, 1985). This is a male who will volunteer at child-focused agencies in order to develop his own sex ring in which to perpetrate sexual abuse (Burgess et al., 1981). This cannot be considered a functional individual. Rather, this is an individual so compulsively driven toward his victims that this obsession occupies all his thoughts and actions (James & Nasjleti, 1983, p. 18).

There may be perpetrators who are merely victims, but since no precise mechanism exists to differentiate them from those pathologically driven (Conte, 1982; Finkelhor, 1984; Summit, 1985), the practitioner is obligated to err on the side of the victim.

The Conjugal Violence Perpetrator

Walker (1978, p. 40) sees the perpetrator of conjugal violence as subject to significant psychological distress. Minor stresses incapacitate him, and he may present nearly dual personalities in and out of the home. He has an extreme sensitivity to others that becomes paranoia when under even marginal stress. These reactions have been described by Ferraro (1984, p. 3) as a paranoia that grows out of the perpetrator's belief that the victim is somehow a threat and by Fleming (1979, p. 304) as indications of the perpetrator's underlying depression.

The Mistreatment of the Elderly Perpetrator

Depression is a theme common in all forms of family violence, but none find it as familiar as persons in the situation that spawns mistreatment of the elderly. Depression and anxiety are more prevalent in the aged population, and in those who provide care for them, than other populations (Chen et al., 1981, p. 10; Falcioni, 1982, p. 208; Steinmetz, 1983). The practitioner will not need to search for psychopathology. It will be found on both sides of the family violence equation. The difficulty is in discriminating the psychopathology that is generated by the current situation from that which has been an unresolved element of this family's life for some time.

It has been noted that the influence of family experience in formative years on the development of family violence perpetration has been overstated. Yet, like psychopathology, the practitioner cannot afford to rule it out immediately.

Unresolved Conflict

The Child Maltreatment Perpetrator

Clarification of the effect of developmental experiences on maltreatment perpetration has recently been offered by Steele (1982). He now suggests that the maltreatment perpetrator has experienced early deprivation that inhibited separation and individuation. He has no complete sense of self, and his self identity is dangerously fluid. This individual may change identity as he feels it appropriate or, worse yet, may have no control over it. Behavior, then, is dictated by stresses and/or supports in the environment at a given moment (Cicchetti & Rizley, 1984; Herzberger, 1983). Despite these supports or stresses, most of the behaviors of these individuals will be immature and self-serving for, at their core, they remain children. Similar conflict exists in the life of the sexual abuse perpetrator.

The Sexual Abuse Perpetrator

The first hint of on-going conflict in sexual abuse perpetration may be found in sexual victimization in their own childhood (Gebhard & Gagnon, 1964; Groth, 1978; Pelto, 1981; Russell, 1984, p. 239; Swift, 1979). These were experiences that may have established patterns of inappropriate learning.

Perpetrators of sexual abuse have learned that adults could not, and cannot, be trusted for protection and care (James & Nasjleti, 1983, p. 17). In the absence of outright victimization, early loss of, separation from, and emotional distance/unavailability in their parents gave them an ambivalence about if not an avoidance of adults. This may be seen in their distorted identification with children and confused affiliation needs (Groth, 1979, p. 146; James & Nasjleti, 1983, p. 17). The cold, distant, and sexually abusive adult in these perpetrators' pasts (Alford et al., 1984, p. 40) may have helped to create individuals who are not only over-identified with the victimizer, but must now play that role to master their own pain. This relationship may, on the other hand, have created such dysfunctional adults that they may only gain caring through a romanticized relationship with a child (Groth et al., 1982, pp. 138–139). This distortion in attachment is one that can be found in all other forms of family violence (Carlson, 1977; Deschner et al., 1980).

Inappropriate and Distorted Dependencies

The Child Maltreatment Perpetrator

There is an emptiness and neediness in child maltreatment perpetrators that distorts relationships with their children (Oates, 1979; Steele, 1972, p. 32). One of the few clear clinical realities in family violence work is that the dependency needs of child maltreatment perpetrators are severely and dangerously frustrated. These needs will be a clinical target in virtually every case (Bavolek, 1981, p. 42). This is also true in other forms of family violence.

The Child Sexual Abuse Perpetrator

Sexual abuse perpetrators isolate their children and spouses. The family's importance is elevated beyond healthy levels as these individuals seek emotional support and nurturance of all types exclusively through family members. These families are simply too important; an importance growing out of confused dependencies in childhood (James & Nasjleti, 1983, p. 16).

These perpetrators are individuals who have never had the need for acceptance and affection met. As a result of pervasive mistrust, the answers to these deep-seated needs are only sought in the family setting (Alford et al., 1984; Bauman, Kaspar, & Alford, 1983, p. 80). In the family, the unfulfilled dependency needs and fear of abandonment are both protected, in the mind of these perpetrators, through the nurturance of the victim (Lewis-Herman, 1981, p. 87). A similarity can be found in the exclusive-source dependency of the perpetrator of conjugal violence.

The Conjugal Violence Perpetrator

Pathological jealousy and possessiveness are regularized features of the conjugal violence perpetrator's relationship to the victim. Continuous surveillance and obsession with the possibility of extramarital affairs is a normative presence (Walker, 1979, p. 38). Much of his seemingly "macho" behavior is nothing more than an artificial masking of his own deep dependence on his conjugal partner (Elbow, 1977; Fleming, 1979; Walker, 1979, p. 38).

This perpetrator's dependency needs are childlike. There is a need for constant approval and the going to extremes to please others (Elbow, 1977; Hilberman, 1980, p. 1339). This may appear to be passive, but there is a suspiciousness to it that generates violence (Faulk, 1974). Any association with others (children, family, friends) is seen as rivalry (Ferraro, 1984, p. 5). The need for allegiance and loyalty are fragile and any indication of threat brings about violence (Ferraro, 1984, p. 2).

Although marginally able to contend with persons outside the family, this perpetrator must have his own way in the family setting. By alternating between submissiveness and aggressiveness, he is able to manipulate victim responses to gain what is wanted (Deschner, 1984, p. 8). Whether his behavior is violent and aggressive or submissive and appealing, the victim tends to reinforce it through provision of what the perpetrator desires (Deschner, 1984; Hilberman, 1980, p. 1339) no matter how immature the need.

Immaturity

The Child Maltreatment Perpetrator

Emotional immaturity is a sine qua non in the child-maltreatment perpetrator (Shorkey, 1978). This personality style has been characterized by a lack of impulse control, neediness, low frustration tolerance, and an inability to delay gratification (Gil, 1970, Shorkey, 1978). Immaturity is so pervasive within this group of perpetrators that they have been referred to as "child parents" (Oates, 1979). This description of the perpetrator is appropriate for perpetrators in other areas as well.

The Child Sexual Abuse Perpetrator

The child sexual abuser has been subject to some arrest or fixation in psychosocial development (Groth et al., 1982, p. 133). This individual is not only sexually ignorant but socially immature (Alford et al., 1984, p. 40; Swift, 1979). There is an obvious lack of impulse control and virtual inability to delay gratification not only of sexual but nonsexual needs (Russell, 1984, p. 259; Summit & Kryso, 1978). For perpetrators of sexual abuse, the only important needs (as a result of the infantile character structure that rules their life) are their own.

The Conjugal Violence Perpetrator

The personality of the perpetrator of conjugal violence might be described as that of a "bully" (Faulk, 1984; Harper, 1979). The practitioner will often have this feeling about him. Unfortunately, the jealousy and inability to tolerate frustration that follows from this perpetrator's immaturity (Deschner, 1984, p. 21; Fleming, 1979, p. 295) extends well beyond that of the bully and may be life threatening.

The Mistreatment of the Elderly Perpetrator

The immaturity of the perpetrator of elder mistreatment may be sufficiently severe to qualify as a personality disorder (Chen et al., 1981, p. 10). This is an immaturity that is overly responsive to change; such as the change brought about by bringing an older person into the home (Falcioni, 1982, p. 268). When that happens, the impulsiveness of this perpetrator combines with a low tolerance level and easy excitability in the face of stress (Chen et al., 1981, p. 10) to create an explosive mixture. At the core, however, the pervasively low self-esteem of family violence perpetrators suggests individuals who understand that something is not right within themselves.

Low Self-Esteem

The Child Maltreatment Perpetrator

The perpetrator of child maltreatment exists without any cushion of self-esteem (Steele & Pollack, 1972, p. 5). Ostensibly, this sense of worthlessness and alienation is understood to have grown out of experiences with hostility, rejection, and abandonment in childhood (Helfer, 1975). Confused attachments have directed the perpetrators along a path in which they are nonpersons, responding only from the perspective of what those around them want them to be (Bolton, 1984). This is a life of multiple failures in self-image (Mulford & Cohen, 1967, p. 13). It seems that the violence itself may be either a rejection of that negative self-image or a confirmation of it. After all, living with a bad self-identity is better than the crisis of living with no self-identity at all (Sloan & Meier, 1983).

Perpetrators of child maltreatment lack a sense of identity, self-worth, or of ever having been loved and accepted for themselves (Mulford & Cohen, 1967; Steele & Pollack, 1972, p. 5). The behavioral outcome is individuals still seeking to please authority figures such as parents and living in constant need of reassurance. Should the victim's behavior fail to reinforce them adequately, or reinforce the inadequacy they feel, explosion toward or abandonment of the victim may result (Morris & Gould, 1974, p. 39; Restak, 1979, p. 19).

The Child Sexual Abuse Perpetrator

Child sexual abuse perpetrators feel that they have either lost, or have failed to ever find, a masculine identity (Alford et al., 1984, p. 40; James & Nasjleti, 1983, p. 16). No matter the rigidity, dominance, and control demonstrated in the man's-home-is-his-castle masculinity they portray, these perpetrators are weak, afraid and all too aware of their inadequate place in the world (James & Nasjleti, 1983, p. 16). The world is such a fear-producing place, in fact, that only a child can serve as a safe point of nurturance and caring.

The Conjugal Violence/Mistreatment of the Elderly Perpetrator

Personal insecurity and insidious low self-esteem are the hallmarks of the conjugal violence perpetrator. This hidden self-esteem crisis and over-concern about masculinity motivate almost all of his behaviors (Fleming, 1979). Responding to this fear with great bragadocio and bluster, this perpetrator is constantly alert to anything that might violate his fragile sense of self. Any deviation from this falsely competent facade, created to deny the inadequate individual within, is interpreted as a threat and acted against immediately (Ferraro, 1984, p. 2). It is when he feels most insecure, least worthy, and most likely to be found out that he will attack. If the threat of sharing a world with a dependent *child* or a submissive *wife* can draw such a reaction out of the child-maltreatment and conjugal-violence perpetrators, a similar threat can occur through an *older person* moving into the home (Chen et al., 1981, p. 10; Steinmetz, 1983). No matter the manifestation, personality inadequacies are magnified by the lack of preparation these perpetrators have for the roles to be played when a relationship is genuinely reciprocal.

Lack of Role Preparation

Family violence perpetrators are underprepared, in both predisposition and knowledge, to accept the logistical and emotional responsibilities of family membership. They are too rigidly accepting of traditional roles to be creative in problem solving. Personal inadequacies, early experiences, and inappropriate dependencies predispose them to role reversals and role rigidity. Their own inadequacy guarantees someone easily overwhelmed by family responsibilities. Each of these problems shows itself across the span of family violence.

The Child Maltreatment Perpetrator

Perpetrators of child maltreatment are educationally and personally underprepared for the role of parent. These individuals have unrealistic expectations of the child and a corresponding disregard for the child's needs, limits, and helplessness (Bavolek, 1981, p. 42; Feshback, 1980, p. 53). Not only do these individuals demonstrate minimal empathy for the child's developmental status (Bavolek, 1981, p. 42), their demands on the child are for activities that bring them, not the child, gratification (Steele, 1982, p. 489).

There is a near certainty that child maltreatment perpetrators are over-identified with their children. They wish to be the best parents and hold a fear that any misbehavior on the part of the child will reflect poorly on them (Straus, 1979, p. 5). They are anxious about potential misbehavior and frustrated when it does occur. The child pays the price for that frustration.

Many perpetrators of child maltreatment see themselves too clearly in their children (Steele, 1970, p. 32). This may be the result of the child's passing through developmental stages that were difficult for the parent, unique characteristics of the child they see as bad, or a defect in the child that the parent misinterprets as a defect in themselves, such as a congenital anomalie (Bolton, 1984; Gil, 1970, p. 30; Hill, 1975, p. 20). Sometimes the problem with the child may come to them through their own insecure and poorly integrated sense of self; a sense that defines all child behavior as a reflection of them (Steele, 1982, p. 488).

Child maltreatment perpetrators are ambivalent about their role as parents. They are both over-identified with and rejecting of the child (Morris & Gould, 1974, p. 39). The drive to be the perfect parent conflicts with the isolation, alienation, and frustration that accompanies the occasional feelings of incompetence known to every parent (Mulford & Cohen, 1967). The result is an over-reaction to the child's behavior whether stressful or nonstressful (Bauer, & Twentyman, 1985; Frodi & Lamb, 1981; Wolfe et al., 1983). This isolates the perpetrator in a competitive/survival posture relative to the child instead of the cooperative/advancement position that is more desirable. In the most severe cases the perpetrator sees the child not only as difficult but wrongly attributes motives to the child that suggest intentional misbehavior (Feshback, 1980, p. 53; Trowell, 1983, p. 392). This same pattern may be seen in other perpetrators.

The Sexually Abusive Perpetrator

The parental perpetrator of child sexual abuse is as role incompetent as the physically maltreating parent (Morris & Gould, 1974, p. 31) and they are inappropriately socialized to conduct the few roles with which they are familiar. Finkelhor (1983, p. 13) and Russell (1984, p. 238) have described the inappropriate socialization patterns in these perpetrators.

First, this individual finds it difficult to discriminate between sexual and nonsexual affection. Second, if male, this perpetrator's identity is closely tied to success at sexual conquest. Third, if male, sexual activity may be thought of as independent of relationship status. Fourth, again if male, this person has been taught to seek younger and smaller persons as sexual partners. Finally, if male, this perpetrator has been socialized to be the aggressor, seducer, and initiator in sexual activity. If this perpetrator reverses roles with the child and seeks nurturance, care, and protection from them; the nurturance may be sought through sexual activity.

Role reversal is common to the physically abusive and sexually abusive perpetrator alike. Both are still longing for the type of caring and nurturance they believe should have originated in their own childhood and did not (Morris & Gould, 1974; Steele, 1975). When feelings of personal deprivation, low self-esteem, helplessness, or rage occur, both will turn to the child. Failure to meet this demand, the lack of proper respect and obedience, or any resistance may well be met by abuse from the childlike perpetrator (Steele, 1982, p. 489). As inappropriate as this may seem, such behavior extends across the family violence map.

The Conjugal Violence Perpetrator

Perpetrators of conjugal violence have a dual victim/perpetrator role identification. Through watching violence in their own home they may have identified with the aggressive perpetrator model their father supplied. At the same time, having been powerless to stop the violence, they may have identified with the maternal victim and now, as adults, are uncertain about their ability to influence their environment (Fleming, 1979, pp. 288–289). The only solution seems to be the adoption of exaggeratedly stereotypical roles for themselves as adults.

The dominance and rigid control found in the sexual abuse perpetrator is mimicked in the perpetrator of conjugal violence. There is a rigid belief in both male dominance and female submission (Ferraro, 1984, p. 3; Walker, 1979, p. 36). The victim must meet the inflexible expectations of the perpetrator (Elbow, 1977); the inevitable strife to follow is solved through violence. A similar spiral may occur in mistreatment of the elderly.

The Mistreatment of the Elderly Perpetrator

Elder mistreatment perpetrators are caught (in their view) in an ambivalent role. They are resigned, to a degree, but feel that they have been asked to make a sacrifice that can never (and will never) be repaid (Anderson, 1981, p. 80). Such emotional and physical confinement can only lead to anger, hostility, and confusion from both perpetrator and victim (Chen et al., 1981, p. 11). Just as life had begun to level out for this middle generation (between child and grandparent) perpetrator, the demand for giving began all over again, and there is nothing left for them (Steinmetz, 1983, p. 141). In fact, this only reminds them of their own impending dependency.

Caught in what Steinmetz (1983, p. 141) has termed a "generational inversion," the perpetrator of elder mistreatment has not only lost a role (i.e., child) relative to this frail parent (now-child), they have also lost many of the rights and expectations that their own age had promised, for example, an unencumbered pre-retirement period (Steinmetz, 1983, p. 136).

In the same way that the child-maltreatment perpetrator did not understand the developmental needs of the child, the perpetrator of elder mistreatment does not understand the developmental changes implied by the aging process (Chen et al., 1981, p. 10). They have known this person as a competent individual and may see current behavior, despite obvious handicaps and the effects of aging, as deliberately disruptive. Their expectations of the victim are well beyond the victim's current capacities, and problem solving within the relationship becomes practically impossible (Chen et al., 1981, p. 10; Silverstone, Hyman, & Kirschner, 1979). This is a new set of role demands not only unexpected and unfamiliar, they are also inescapable (Anderson, 1981, p. 80).

There are too many roles for elder mistreatment perpetrators. They are being asked to care for children, for their aging parent, and for themselves even as the first hints of aging and dependency creep into their own lives (Anderson, 1981, p. 80; Kosberg, 1983, p. 268; Steinmetz, 1983, p. 141). This is not just a frightening sense of their own aging; its magnitude brings about a sense of what can only be described as hopelessness (Luppins & Lau, 1983, p. 125). Having nowhere to hide, this perpetrator is trapped on a treadmill of guilt, anger, and hostility that, in some cases, results in violence or neglect (Chen et al., 1981, p. 11).

Dominance and Control

The Child Maltreatment Perpetrator

Behavior control is an all-important issue to the perpetrator of child maltreatment. A great premium is placed upon the child's obedience. Unfortunately, what constitutes "good behavior" fluctuates by situation and point in time—that is, the rules are inconsistent—and it is not rewarded when it occurs; only not punished when it does not (Bavolek, 1981, p. 42). Also present is a certain self-righteous attitude toward the child built upon "knowing what is good" for them and seeing the child as a self-serving creature who will take advantage "if you let them." This constant surveillance of the child to prevent them from "putting something over on me" is accompanied by a concern over "spoiling" the child; spoiling that might be seen in a more functional home as normal love and affection (Alexander, 1972, p. 28; Bavolek, 1981, p. 42).

The Sexual Abuse Perpetrator

Power and dominance of a weak adult over a weaker victim is never so clear as it is in child sexual abuse (Lewis-Herman, 1981, p. 87). The perpetrator of child sexual abuse may well be engaged in this activity as a direct result of fear of failure in controlling sexual situations with adults (Russell, 1984, p. 258). However, to assure compliance from victims, the sexually abusive perpetrator must keep a tight rein, not only on the victim(s), but any sources of potential support, such as other family members as well. This is accomplished through severe parental dominance and restrictiveness (Brandt & Tisza, 1978).

Intimidation within the family is a commonly reported feature of the family rule system in the sexually abusive family (James & Nasjleti, 1983, p. 16). Outside contacts are restricted, dating is prohibited, extracurricular school activities are not permitted and general family isolation is the norm. This perpetrator is at the dictatorial helm of a family that has a secret he wishes it to maintain (Kempe & Kempe, 1984). However, this perpetrator knows that this is merely a pseudo-power that will eventually be lost, and the anticipation of that loss wears on him constantly. This only serves to increase his hostility and aggressiveness. This perpetrator will seek to regain this control at every opportunity; the practitioner cannot trust protestations to the contrary.

The Conjugal Violence Perpetrator

The need to control pervades the conjugal violence perpetrator's behavioral style. Although capable of controlling very little outside the home, his control in the home is absolute, extending through financial decisions, child care, sexual relationships, leisure time activities, and even menu (Ferraro, 1984, p. 6). Domineering and hostile, this perpetrator acts out his dislike for authority figures through those who cannot exert authority over him: the weaker members of the family (Fleming, 1979, p. 304).

There are sympathetic writers who suggest that this perpetrator is acting out this dominance as a result of depression that accompanies his powerlessness in other areas of his world (Faulk, 1984). Most are not so kind, suggesting only that this is a weak and interpersonally incompetent tyrant.

The Mistreatment of the Elderly Perpetrator

Descriptions of the irrational dominance of the perpetrator of conjugal violence are matched in descriptions of elder mistreatment. Whether as a result of the pressures of caring for a frail elderly person in the home, or as enduring personality traits, these perpetrators are found to be domineering, controlling, demanding, and aggressive with their victim and others (Chen et al., 1981, pp. 10–11).

Approval of Violence

For many perpetrators of family violence the use of violence as a problem-solving technique was acquired early. They may well have grown up in what amounts to a subculture that reinforced its use (Harper, 1979). It is a short intellectual distance from rationalizing the use of violence in general to rationalizing its use in the family. It is also possible to believe, if early modeling supported its use, that violence is situationally specific. That is, you do it and it is over; no consequences beyond the immediate behavior change that it brought about will occur (Walker, 1979).

Both *child* and *conjugal* violence perpetrators see the victim of their violence as being responsible agents who must suffer the consequences of their actions; especially if their actions were seen to be purposefully directed against the perpetrator (Feshback, 1980, p. 53). This self-righteous and inflexible individual will perpetrate violence against a spouse, a child, or both under the guise of it being his right to do so. This is behavior that is believed to be normal, not problematic, and outside intervention is not warranted (Fleming, 1979, p. 296; Walker, 1979, p. 36). This is also a strategy that backfires for, although short-term compliance is gained, the long-term consequences are antagonistic to what the perpetrator desired. Violence gains perpetrators little save alienation from and mistrust of their victim. Rather than gaining loyalty and protection from this family member (now victim), perpetrators lose a great deal of loyalty through their own betrayal of the victim's trust (Ferraro, 1984; p. 8). This is in keeping with perpetrators' typical incompetence in human interactions.

Social/Interpersonal Skills

The Child Maltreatment Perpetrator

The perpetrator of child maltreatment finds authority easier to manage than warmth (Kaufman, 1962, p. 21). The absence of rules and structure governing interpersonal interactions leaves these perpetrators unarmed and anxious. There are so many reminders of their interpersonal incompetence that there is little pleasure in living (Restak, 1979, p. 19). This causes an over-focusing on their own problems followed by withdrawal and inertia. In other situations, this self-centeredness, when combined with a lack of appreciation of others' rights, may lead to aggression and exposure to law enforcement contact (Morris & Gould, 1974, p. 39). These individuals rapidly and incompetently attack a problem, then just as quickly disengage as they sense failure; allowing them to blame the failure on others, most likely their children (Minuchin, 1968). In this way, the victims of their violence not only is used to gratify their needs through manipulation and deprivation, they also serve as a convenient point of blame for virtually all of the interpersonal failures they experience (Mulford & Cohen, 1967, p. 9).

The Sexual Abuse Perpetrator

The sexual abuse perpetrator's incompetence tends to focus in the area of adult sexuality. Although these people provide a good external appearance (educationally, careerwise, and community service), adult relationships that include sexuality range from intimidating (Groth et al., 1982, p. 137) to terrifying (James & Nasjleti, 1983, p. 17). Adult relationships have meant nothing to these individuals beyond failure and rejection (Bauman et al., 1983, p. 80) The nonthreatening and nondemanding caring of the child is the perfect retreat from the anxieties brought about by these previously failed adult relationships.

The Conjugal Violence Perpetrator

Perpetrators of conjugal violence are incapable of genuinely intimate behavior but can offer warmth and protection of a sort on their best days (Elbow, 1977). This mixture of occasional warmth and intermittent violence is what locks the victim into the relationship.

The perpetrators of conjugal violence find difficulty in much of their world. There are employment problems, relationship difficulties, a lack of recreational activities, and a withdrawal from other people (Fleming, 1979, pp 295–304). Their poor verbal skills tend to keep them feeling "one-down" in social situations or cause them to over-do in an effort to impress those around them (Deschner, 1984, p. 21; Walker, 1979, p. 37). Not only does this effort to impress tend to fall flat, the expectations they hold for their own success are rarely met, leading to dissatisfaction and disappointment (Elbow, 1977).

These individuals are not well aware of themselves and others. They are unreflective about their own feelings and needs; the failure to recognize stress and anger until it becomes out of control being one example (Ferraro, 1984, pp 2–3). The lack of empathy for others and fear of close relationships tends to keep them at a distant and superficial level in their interactions (Fleming, 1979, p. 320; Shapiro, 1982; Walker, 1979, p. 40). The only form of compensation for this superficiality and lack of influence on others is to exert a major influence in the lives of family members (Pagelow, 1984, p. 99). This influence is frequently exercised in a violent manner, which begins as far back as courtship (Pagelow, 1984) but is denied even to the present.

Denial/Defensiveness

The perpetrator of a violent act in the family is capable of denying or rationalizing the violence. The act may be denied outright, intention may be minimized, or blame projected on the victim. Somehow, the perpetrators distance themselves from the obvious consequences of their violence (Pagelow, 1984, pp 324– 325).

As a result, it is unwise to wait for a violent perpetrator to seek help (Hill, 1975, p. 20). This rarely occurs directly. It is more likely that there will be avoidance on their part. After all, acknowledgement implies parallel acknowledgement of their own disturbance and lack of control (Kaufman, 1962, p. 21).

The Child Maltreatment Perpetrator

It is common for child maltreatment perpetrators to be more concerned with themselves than their victims. It seems as if, to them, the injury was something that the child perpetrated; the perpetrator really had no choice (Morris & Gould, 1974). Their demands were completely reasonable, the child failed to carry them out, and violence was the only remaining course (Feshback, 1980, p. 53). This is the ultimate role-reversal; from perpetrator to victim in one strangely rationalized step.

The Sexual Abuse Perpetrator

The child sexual abuser has a complex intellectualization and defense structure. The application of minimization, denial, and projection of blame reaches levels at which the entire family is cooperating (for example, they excuse his behavior by saying "he was drunk"). There are many techniques for this removal of guilt, shame, and remorse. Some of the most familiar include the perpetrator rationalizing that (1) "there's no problem because we didn't have intercourse," (2) "it's better to have me introduce her to sex than someone who doesn't love her," or (3) "she wanted it to happen, I was seduced." Fortunately, there is almost no place today where such rationalizations are accepted.

The Conjugal Violence Perpetrator

The perpetrator of conjugal violence not only denies the existence of violence, he becomes enraged if the victim discloses it to an outside source. Even following disclosure, the blame is projected elsewhere, for example, the perpetrator rationalizes that, "if you had my boss, you'd hit things too," (Walker, 1979, p. 36). If there are two common features in every conjugal violence situation, they would be found in the perpetrators' repetitive belief that it was not their fault and the accompanying feeling that whatever happened was justified (Fleming, 1979).

These individuals not only deny their role in the violent act, they externalize blame for all problems, refuse to acknowledge the presence of a problem beyond the precursor to the violence, and may even scapegoat the victims into a genuine belief that they deserved what was done to them (Fleming, 1979; Pagelow, 1984, p. 99). Even when the act is an undeniable reality, the absence of remorse may be accompanied by continued verbal batterings of the victim (Dobash & Dobash, 1979). This is a pattern of denial that persists until absolute disclosure, followed by projection of blame on to the victim, that will also be found in the perpetrator of elder mistreatment (Steinmetz, 1983). What remains is to describe how characteristics of victims and characteristics of perpetrators come together in an explosive way. But first, some consideration should be given to special victims and perpetrators.

7

Special People in the Violent Family

Special Victims and Perpetrators
in Child Maltreatment

The Adolescent

The adolescent is not an attractive victim. The overloaded child protection system may have tried to help at an earlier point and failed. It may be presumed that this victim can protect himself or herself or will be leaving home soon. Finally, the behaviors that follow the victim's experience, for example, delinquency, drug use, promiscuity, suicide attempts and pregnancy (Elmer, 1977; Lindberg & Distad, 1985; Newberger, Reed, & Kotelchuck, 1977) further isolate the victim from a sympathetic and protective response. The results of inadequate protection are adolescents who feel frightened, abandoned, and left to their own devices to escape continued victimization. Isolated and abandoned by a world more sympathetic to the younger victim, adolescents have little left but rage.

The adolescent victims are young persons who have been hurt (Garbarino, 1980, p. 124). In adolescent maltreatment victims, hurt masquerades as acting out, typically through aggressive behavior that drives these children more quickly to court than therapy (Galambos & Dixon, 1984; Hoekstra, 1984, p. 286). *It is wise for the practitioner to consider the possibility of prior maltreatment in virtually every out-of-control adolescent* especially the aggressive delinquent (Mouzakitis, 1984; Tarter, Hegedus, Winsten, & Alterman, 1984, p. 668).

Garbarino (1984) has reviewed the literature on adolescent maltreatment and has developed several empirically based hypotheses. First, Garbarino feels that the incidence of adolescent maltreatment equals or exceeds that of child maltreatment. This includes all forms of maltreatment although psychological (terrorizing, rejecting, and isolating) and sexual abuse predominate. Consequently, females are the most likely adolescent victims. Garbarino goes on to note that some cases of adolescent maltreatment are a continuation of childhood maltreatment while others represent a decline of family behavior that culminates in maltreatment during adolescence. The families in which this occurs are most likely to contain step-parents and not as likely to be suffering from economic stress as families who mistreat younger children. Finally, both the maltreated adolescents and their families are less socially competent than most, revealing large gaps in adaptability, cohesion, support, discipline, and interparental conflict.

Malin (1981, p. 487) described the parents of maltreated adolescents as continuing to seek resolution of their own adolescent identity crisis and on a search for personal identity and self-fulfillment. Lourie (1979) also noted that the "middlesence" stage of life, which describes most parents of adolescents, and which is a time of reassessment of life course, accomplishments, and future, finds increased depression and decreased tolerance for adolescent behavior. So, whether the mistreatment is a continuation, begins at puberty, or is simply a qualitative change with intensified disciplinary activity in adolescence (Zeifert, 1981, p. 164), the adolescent and parental stages of development are mismatched.

Lourie (1979) delineated the points of explosion in this family as behavior control versus separation, poor self-esteem, poor identity formation, and poor peer relationships. Garbarino (1984, p. 3) sets forth the central issue as *power* in that the increased ability of the adolescent to think, argue, and act brings them into conflict with parents not yet ready to release the adolescent to their growing sense of self-control. Separation, individuation, control, and autonomy are fundamental clinical issues disabling this family (Zeifert, 1981, p. 165). Both overindulgence and authoritarianism predict problems (Garbarino, 1984).

As a rule, practitioners find adolescents, whether through anger, mistrust, or ambivalence, to be difficult to work with in the best of circumstances. When the adolescent has been victimized, this work is even more difficult. If the victimization is doubled, as in the case of the adolescent parent, the difficulty sometimes runs to impossibility.

The Adolescent Parent: Bilateral Victimization

It has been assumed that the adolescent parent was a high-risk parent, largely due to similarities between adolescent parents and maltreating parents (Bolton, 1980). It now seems that the risk of perpetration has been overstated and the risk of victimization understated. The practitioner must give serious consideration to the possibility that this "premature parenthood" was at least an indirect result of childhood victimization.

As Perpetrator

Adolescent parents can be high-risk parents. A review of Table 7.1, reveals a great number of commonalities between the adolescent and maltreating parent and their respective children.

An overview would find an over-representation of lower SES families in both groups (Gil, 1970). This is to be anticipated from the relative youth of both groups (Smith, Hanson, & Noble, 1973), the accompanying unemployment (Holmes, 1978), underemployment (Straus et al., 1980), and general relationship stress (Helfer, 1975), which increases the risk for single parenthood.

Both groups of parents tend to involve themselves in relationships that lack communication (Helfer, 1975). There is an inability to resolve conflict and crisis (Straus et al., 1980), and evidence of a dangerous triad of unrealistic expectations, ignorance of childcare/child development, and low tolerance for frustration (deLissovoy, 1973; Steele, 1975).

Personal history does play a role as both groups of parents seem to have experienced emotional deprivation, rejection, and/or violent behavior in childhood (Straus et al., 1980). This sometimes is tied to the psychological immaturity that characterizes these parental groups (Blumberg, 1974). Unresolved dependencies may lead to over-dependence on a child (Daniels, 1969). As is evident from what has gone before in this work, this combination of factors leads to a serious diathesis, which needs very little environmental stress to generate a destructive event.

Despite early studies that predicted high rates of child maltreatment among adolescent parents (Bolton, Laner, & Kane,

TABLE 7.1
Shared Characteristics of Adolescent Parents,
Maltreating Parents, and Their Children

Demographic Characteristics

(1) Over-representation of lower socio-economic status groups.

(2) High unemployment and low occupational level.

(3) Reduced education levels and premature education termination.

(4) Large numbers of children born in close succession.

(5) Over-representation of single parent, female-head-of-household.

(6) Youthfulness at first birth.

(7) High rates of relationship disruption.

Dynamic Characteristics

(1) Unrealistic expectations of the child.

(2) Ignorance of child-care techniques.

(3) Unfulfilled dependency needs and role reversals.

(4) An environment in which the child is unwanted, a parental-competitor, or perceived as being different.

(5) Lack of knowledge of child development and a view of the child based upon parental needs.

(6) Deprivation, indifference, rejection, and hostility experienced in childhood.

(7) Low self-esteem and poor self-concept.

(8) Fear of rejection.

(9) Low frustration tolerance and poor impulse control.

(10) Isolation.

Child Characteristics

(1) Complications in pregnancy likely.

(2) Prematurity, low birth weight, and handicapping conditions.

(3) Early childhood ill health and poor nutrition.

(4) School and behavior problems.

NOTE: See Appendix D for references.

1980; Kinard & Klerman, 1980) the suggestion now is that officially reported populations over-represent this group. A recent review of the National Study of the Incidence and Severity of Child Abuse and Neglect (Miller, 1983) revealed that adolescents were "only slightly over-represented" in maltreating populations. Longitudinal research on this issue (Bolton, Charlton, Gai, Laner & Shumway, 1985) suggests that adolescent parents who maltreat not only have special characteristics, but tend to be very abusive (i.e., greater frequency of reports than older parents).

It seems that the adolescent mother who uses pregnancy to escape victimization (i.e., sexual abuse) may be the adolescent parent at risk for maltreatment perpetration. This adolescent leaves the home prematurely and becomes immediately burdened by the stress of being a single parent in a low-income environment. These young parents cannot return to the home of their parents for the support and extra set of hands that makes the difference between an adolescent parent who copes and one who fails (Furstenberg, 1982). Since these adolescents are isolated from their own family and from the father of the child (Bolton & Belsky, 1985), they are alone with the unanticipated problems of parenthood. The potential for maltreatment under these circumstances increases as the adolescent becomes successively more entrapped, moving from one environment of victimization to another.

As Victim

Far too little work as been done with the possibility that adolescent pregnancy is the young female's response to victimization in her own family. The pregnancy may be a constructive response to a negative family situation if it allows her to escape (Friedman, 1971). This response gives her the illusion that she has power and control (Paulker, 1969; Klein, 1978), that she can replace the tenderness she feels she missed in her childhood (Hertz, 1977), and may seem as though it is the answer to independence/dependence struggles of adolescence (Daniels, 1969). In most cases, it is little more than a displacement of her victimization from her family to her new environment.

That the previously victimized adolescent views parenthood as an adaptive response to her dysfunctional family environment can be inferred from what is known about the thoughts of maltreated children. The maltreated child cannot tolerate the anxiety of having a parent, an adult who is supposed to offer protection and nurturance, mistreat them for no apparent reason. Consequently, the child ignores the parental role in the maltreatment and accepts wrong-doing as their own. In the absence of overt actions that caused the problem, the child adopts a negative sense of self that implies that they deserved the maltreatment. This negative self-definition may lead to avoidance of all genuine sources of love and affection during childhood (i.e., those that might be offered outside the family); people were once trusted in this area, and they failed. Being dependent upon herself, then, to create the love and affection she missed early on, there is no choice but to provide herself with "someone of my own to belong to" (Daniels, 1969). So, for the previously victimized adolescent, the act of having a child is an egocentric and narcissistic act that allows her to begin life again. Unfortunately, these are needs that conflict directly with the demands of the care-giving relationship implied by parenthood (Sadler & Catrone, 1983). Obviously this is a relationship at risk for the same type of breakdown as her relationship with her own parents.

In sum, the practitioner cannot consider the adolescent pregnancy an isolated problem. This may be a physically maltreated adolescent using the pregnancy as a constructive solution for getting out of a dangerous home. This may be the attention-getting device employed by the neglected or emotionally deprived adolescent. Or this may be the sexually abused adolescent seeking escape or relief from the sexual overtures in her home. *Previous victimization must always be considered in adolescent pregnancy.* This may be a solution to a problem, a form of "repetition compulsion," and/or a pattern of self-victimization and negative identity seeking. To perceive an adolescent pregnancy as deviant in every case, to view the adolescent parent as an automatic parenting failure, and to label the life of the child of the adolescent parent as being doomed to failure is an error given current knowledge. In the same fashion, failure to see the potential for victimization in the child involved in divorce is an equally great oversight.

The Victimization of
the Child Through Divorce

Divorce implies change for all family members. These changes may include, but are not limited to, social/financial status change, geographic change, changes in schools and friends, changes in social networks, and changes in family procedures; especially now that one parent is being asked to cope with responsibilities previously shared (Bane, 1979; Longfellow, 1979). Divorce is not just pressure on the parent-child relationship, it is a crisis. Almost every aspect of the parent-child world will change, all without the buffer previously offered by another adult in the family (Hetherington, 1979).

Increasing numbers of single parent-child relationships are being implicated in the child maltreatment literature (Friedman, 1976). The origin of maltreatment risk in single-parent families has been *speculatively* attached to styles of parent-child interaction, absence of positive affect, and high levels of coercive behavior (Burgess, Anderson, Schellenbach, & Conger, 1981). Complementary stresses in the parent adjusting to divorce include life changes, crisis, changes in social class, and social isolation (Burgess & Garbarino, 1983; Conger, Burgess & Barrett, 1979; Daly & Wilson, 1980; Garbarino & Gilliam, 1980). Some of these risk factors even carry over in remarriages (Duberman, 1975). As such, there is a great deal of appropriate concern regarding child maltreatment risk in the divorced single-parent home.

The Psychological Environment of the Divorced Single Parent

As Table 7.2 indicates, examination of the psychological resources of the recently divorced parent reveals an uncomfortable similarity to that of the maltreating parent. Table 7.3 reveals that same similarity in the contextual stresses and lack of support between recently divorced parents and maltreating parents. And Table 7.4 demonstrates that the child's reaction to the divorce greatly parallels the child in the family at risk for maltreatment. Fortunately, the presence of risk factors do not indicate absolute occurrence of maltreatment. There are warning signals, however, that are useful to the practitioner.

Assessing Risk

Even assuming the absence of psychiatric difficulties following divorce (Bloom, White & Asher, 1979) observation of the intensity of the response to the divorce and accompanying events is important. Two critical features are the parent's ability to cope with stress/crisis and the parent's reactions to the loss of the marital attachment.

TABLE 7.2
Psychological Resources in the Divorced Single Parent and Parent at Risk for Child Maltreatment

(1) Immaturity.	(10) Poor impulse control and impulsiveness.
(2) Unrealistic expectations.	
(3) Low self-esteem.	(11) Less verbal interaction with the children.
(4) Fear of continued rejection.	
(5) Unfulfilled dependency needs.	(12) High levels of disapproval of child(ren)'s behavior.
(6) Feelings of being out of control or overwhelming.	
	(13) Previous negative family experience.
(7) Depression.	(14) Attachment difficulty.
(8) Reduced responsiveness to their children.	(15) Role reversals with child.
(9) Difficulty in trusting.	

NOTE: See Appendix E for references.

TABLE 7.3
The Recently Divorced Parent and the Parent at High Risk for Child Maltreatment: Contextual Stress and Support

(1) Absence of intrafamilial and extrafamilial support systems.	(4) The responsibilities of single parenthood.
(2) Employment difficulty or dissatisfaction.	(5) Disruptive emotional relationships.
(3) Pervasive financial stress.	(6) Generalized isolation.

NOTE: See Appendix F for references.

TABLE 7.4
The Recently Divorced Parent and the Parent at Risk for Maltreatment: Stress-Producing Child Behaviors and Characteristics

(1) Difficult temperament.	(5) Discipline problems.
(2) Being perceived by parent as difficult	(6) Seen as competitor by parent.
	(7) Lack of "fit" with parental expectations.
(3) Problems in school.	
(4) Behavior problems.	

NOTE: See Appendix G for references.

The presence of crisis in divorce (a presence that lasts for at least two years) demands new mechanisms for coping. The need to find new means of coping with unanticipated crisis provides a sense of helplessness in parent and child. Disequilibrium is constant for both parent and child as are depression, anger, anxiety, panic, and loss (Hetherington et al., 1977). The parent's ability to handle crisis, cope with depression, and constructively reduce anger deserves practitioner attention.

During the early postdivorce period, custodial parents have been found to be less supportive, less nurturant, and more tense and anxious in their relationships with their children (Wallerstein & Kelly, 1975). In most parents, this reaction is no more damaging than becoming temporarily less attentive, somewhat more punitive, and less consistent in their behaviors (Hetherington et al., 1977). In some cases, particularly those in which the parent is inadequate and the environment nonsupportive, parents may react to their own feelings by over-reaching for control in at least one area—the children. At this point normal parenthood behaviors may turn into an abusive encounter (Conger et al., 1979). Unfortunately, the child holds the same capacity to push the relationship beyond tolerable limits.

Children who are disturbed by parental separation may be a dangerous source of stress for the parent trying to find stability after divorce (Bloom, White, & Asher, 1979). In the most dangerous situation, the parent's newly rigid and aggressive response to the child conflicts with the child's needs for understanding. The result is a competitiveness between child and parent to determine who is in control. This is a battle the child will eventually lose one way or the other.

Clive and Westman (1971) encourage assessment of five sources of crisis in the newly divorced parent-child relationship. They begin with an assessment of the competition for control. They also seek any source of hostile conflict not involving the children, the possible presence of a special alliance between one parent and the children, and the possibility that the stress between the parents is being promoted by extended family (i.e., grandparents). The breakdown in these dysfunctional situations manifests itself in the relationship between custodial parent and child. The intense anger and ambivalence through which the child views divorce in some cases, can cause them to try to hurt in any way they can (Weiss, 1979). The person most often hurt, however, is the child. Anger is a dangerous commodity in this parent-child relationship when it originates on either side.

Loss of attachment in divorce situations creates not only separation distress but anger. In most cases this is directed toward the ex-spouse. The parent may recognize some of their own contributions to the relationship failure, but a sense of guilt and failure may prohibit full acceptance of their part (Jacobson, 1983). If the parent is particularly underprepared to cope with the stresses of divorce, they may psychologically defend against even their spouse's contribution to the divorce, and direct the anger they have toward the child. Such displacement of aggression predicts risk in any situation, but in that situation where the child's reactions to divorce prove that they are a difficult child, the risk is magnified.

Some parents, and some children, are not competent to handle divorce. According to Jacobson (1983), adjustment to divorce is a two-part psychological process. First, there must be psychological resolution in which both positive and negative aspects of the prior relationship, and both parents' contributions to them, are acknowledged. The consequence of this, if successful, is normal sadness and guilt. Second, there must be a recognition by both parents that the other does not meet their current needs. The consequence of this, if successful, is increasing comfort in their new way of living. If either of these mandatory psychological processes fail, the child living with the "stalled" parent may be at risk.

A summary would find that all the players in a divorce situation may generate risk for maltreatment. Each new crisis in the postdivorce period, for perhaps as long a five years (Wallerstein, 1985) is a test of the parent's coping capacity, the environmental flexibility and support, and the child's ability to accept or modify the perception of the event. There is a constant likelihood of depletion of parental, child, and environmental resources. There is a real possibility that the parent will be overwhelmed. There is a real possibility that the child will contribute negatively, perhaps pushing the parent beyond tolerance levels. If the parent is incompetent to begin with, inappropriate reactions to all crises will be adopted and the resultant failure blamed on the child. If the parent has no other source of support, their eventual failure in coping will only drive them from their child. Finally, if the child's reactions are sufficiently aversive to overwhelm both parental capacities and environmental supports, outside help is mandatory before this fragile relationship collapses entirely. In this way the recently divorced mother may find herself as either perpetrator or victim, a position not unfamiliar to the mother in many violent families.

The Mother

As a result of early work that described mothers as perpetrating abuse as frequently or more frequently than fathers (Gil, 1970; Resnick, 1969; Steele & Pollack, 1972; Zalba, 1971), the mother has been assumed to be the most physically aggressive parent. Many reasons have been offered for this departure from the traditional protective role of the mother. Simple time-of-exposure to the children may make some difference. Others find the mother carrying a disproportionate share of the parenting role (Straus, 1979), and still others find her role in maltreatment not overt but merely cooperative.

Reavelky and Gilbert (1978) describe four ways in which the parent who does not directly perpetrate maltreatment may contribute to it. First, they may fail to recognize that their partner has a problem. Second, they may be hyper-critical of the perpetrator, further frustrating him or her. Third, they may attempt to isolate the children, pointing out the perpetrator's problem and making him or her angry. Finally, they may be so afraid that they withdraw completely and refuse to communicate with anyone. Recent conceptualizations suggest that a re-examination of who perpetrates is in order.

Martin (1983, 1984) closely examined the issue of maternal perpetration and concluded that fathers are more frequently involved in mistreatment of adolescents than mothers (p. 388). They are at least equal in their maltreatment of younger children. According to Martin, there were three mistakes made in the study of perpetration prior to her work.

First, some only studied maternal perpetration. Second, some report maltreating *parents* leaving it up to the reader to determine gender. Third, some study both parents, but emphasize the absence of "mothering" in their descriptions. For example, it is rare for an author to describe the perpetrator of neglect as anything except a mother, since nurturance and childcare roles fall disproportionately in her direction (p. 295).

As a consequence of this bias in the research, treatment programs are maternally directed (Gabinet, 1979). This not only fails to respond to the whole issue, it serves to inflate the number of mothers in "known" populations. The fact of the matter is that it is often difficult to determine who actually perpetrated the maltreatment in a family. Martin suggests that it was simply the path of least resistance to focus on what a sexist society considers the primary parent: the mother (p. 391). In part this thinking is built on the assumption that, if a child was injured, it was partially the mother's fault because she failed to protect the child. In answer to that notion, Russell (1984) counters, "Why should the mother *have to protect* children in their own family?" Considering this mother to have "failed" is seen as just another way of protecting society's all-powerful male, a male not unwilling to use this power in the family in physical and sexual ways.

Special Victims and Perpetrators in Sexual Abuse

The Mother in the Sexually Abusive Family: Victim or Perpetrator?

No mother is seen to have failed more in her maternal role than the mother in the sexually abusive family. There are statutory provisions in some states to punish mothers who allowed sexual abuse in their home. While these statutes are appropriate for clearly cooperative mothers, and mothers remain important in the insulation of children from maltreatment (Finkelhor, 1984, p. 58), it is not always reasonable to expect this protection from the mother (Lewis-Herman, 1981, p. 47). In spite of that, the mother in the sexually abusive family has been variously described as sick, powerless, alienated from her children, and sexually rejecting of her husband (Russell, 1984, pp. 259–263). In practice, these assumptions are not supported.

Mothers who are strong, healthy, and competent (i.e., having some power and control in their families) do not tolerate sexually abusive acts toward their children (Lewis-Herman, 1981, p. 47). Strong and capable mothers do not tend to show up in the family violence practitioner's office. The mother who is incapacitated increases environmental risk to the children (Finkelhor, 1984, p. 58). The mother in the violent family is also more vulnerable to personal and social incapacitation than mothers in more functional families.

The mother in the violent family is oppressed (Lewis-Herman, 1981, p. 49). This mother is known to be extremely dependent upon and subservient to the male adult (Ferraro, 1984), subject to increased risk for physical or mental illness (Harrer, 1981), more poorly educated in protecting herself from her husband's temper and assaultiveness (Justice & Justice, 1979, p. 147), and likely to have been a family violence victim herself (Finkelhor, 1984, p. 59; Goodwin, McCarthy, & DiVasto, 1981; Pagelow, 1982). Such oppression inhibits a strongly protective response; the mother has learned the role of victim too well.

A common aspect of discussion of mothers in sexually abusive families is that she has sexually rejected the perpetrator, somehow indicating tacit acceptance of his sexual involvement with a child. This belief, according to Lewis-Herman (1981, p. 43) is bolstered by the assumption that the wife is required to service the male upon command. Failure to do so gives the male entitlement to find whatever replacement is convenient. This in some way forces the endogamous male to become involved with the children. There is no rational way for the practitioner to accept such reasoning. The mother in the sexually abusive family may well provide an unsatisfactory sex life (Pierce & Pierce, 1984, p. 43) or even abdicate the role entirely (Tierney & Corwin, 1983, p. 108). This does not provide license for sexual contact with a child.

There is current suggestion that the failed relationship between mother and daughter may play a role in the sexually abusive family. This mother may well have been a victim and may tend to sexualize relationships (Kempe & Kempe, 1984). Consequently, she may have no ability to empathize with the daughter's victimization. She may even be competitive or jealous. On the other hand, she may be so over-identified with the victim role that she is fearful of saying anything or else her insecure marriage might dissolve (Kempe & Kempe, 1984, p. 58). In this way, a role reversal takes place in which the daughter is protecting her mother's interests. This mother is genuinely underprotective.

The more common mother-daughter relationship in sexually abusive families is one in which the mother is not emotionally available to the daughter. This type of mother has been described as infantile, dependent, cold, and rejecting toward her children, and panicky in the face of responsibility (Alford et al., 1984, p. 40). This is not an individual who will stand up to a perpetrator upon whom she is dependent for survival, particularly to protect a daughter she feels somewhat cool toward (Finkelhor, 1984, pp. 26–27; Herman & Hirschman, 1977; Tierney & Corwin, 1983, p. 108).

James & Nasjleti (1983, p. 30) have encountered four types of mothers in sexually abusive families. First, there is the passive child-woman. This mother, a victim in childhood herself, is dependent and immature. She hates her own mother and learned that victimization is the female's "lot in life." Her own helplessness leaves her unaffected when seeing it in others, even her children. Second, there is the intelligent, competent, distant mother. The daughter of a highly achieving but cold and distant mother, this woman finds her worth in career achievements. The father is the nurturant parent and the primary child care provider. Intellectualization and absence (for career reasons) serve to insulate her from discovery or acceptance of sexual abuse in her charming and efficient home (p. 27). Third, there is the rejecting-vindictive mother. Bright, but hostile, she will do anything, including lose her children, before she will admit to sexual abuse in the home. Her wrath is limitless and her manipulative skills extensive. Children in this family need the utmost in protection (James & Nasjleti, 1983, p. 29). The final pattern is the psychotic or severely retarded mother. Treatment may be a possibility in some cases, but never forget to train the children to protect themselves against assault and to report each event, however minor, immediately (1983, p. 30).

In summary, the mother's role in the sexually abusive situation is overstated in some ways and underappreciated in others. If the mother fails to submit to the sexual overtures of the father, blame for subsequent sexual abuse of children should not follow. On the other hand, emotional distance from the daughter may increase risk. The failure of the mother to serve as a source of protection, information, and support for the daughter is a substantial protective loss.

The Female (Mother) as Perpetrator of Child Sexual Abuse

Russell (1984, p. 231) has noted that the current interest in the female perpetration of sexual abuse (Plummer, 1981; Sgroi, 1982) grows out of the previous assumption that females *never* perpetrate sexual abuse. Russell continues to view female perpetration as a minor phenomenon and agrees with Finkelhor (1986) that, in this area, there remains a "male monopoly." There is some current conflict about this.

Plummer (1981, p. 227) has described the connection between pedophilia and maleness as a "stereotype" that masks female perpetration. There has recently been some increased reporting of maternal perpetration of sexual abuse of children of both sexes (Goodwin & DiVasto, 1979; Pelto, 1981). Some writers (Justice & Justice, 1979) have also speculated upon masked sexual abuse in maternal child-caring activities for some time. Groth (1979, p. 192) not only agrees with the perception of sexual abuse in maternal care, he feels it occurs in other maternal-child activities as well, but is suppressed by the reluctance of children, especially males, to report such an event. Many see this as a particularly damaging form of incestuous relationship (Kempe & Kempe, 1984, p. 68). Some sexual abuse researchers simply discredit this thinking as pure speculation.

Finkelhor (1986) finds "practically no" evidence to support maternal perpetration. He notes that in 90 percent of reported cases the offenders are male. In self-report studies, 95 percent of the adult contact with girls and 80 percent of the adult contact with boys are made by men. Also, even in those situations where there is some contact by a female, it seems that it occurred at the urging of a male who also participated in some way. Finkelhor would "turn the tables" and suggest that the real question must be why are there so many male perpetrators? If victimization and perpetration were linked, it would seem that more females would later become perpetrators. There is some sense that female victims may become adult mothers of victims (Goodwin, McCarthy, & DiVasto, 1982). However, certainly not all victims later become mothers of victims.

James and Nasjleti (1983, p. 23) take a somewhat more moderate view and allow for the possibility of female perpetration. They describe the information on this issue as "sketchy," but suggest some common characteristics in such women. The shared pattern in female perpetrators seems to be described by infantile and extreme dependency needs, a dysfunctional spousal relationship, possessiveness of the child victim, and the use of alcohol as a support and disinhibitor. The child in this case is expected to fill the mother's emotional emptiness. Caretaking masks the event from the mother as well as from others in many cases. If the victim is male, he may well be playing the role of an absent father. He may be asked to be supportive of the mother and participate in adult roles well beyond his capacity for understanding. The mother's infantile relationship with the victim continues well beyond the time that people are typically comfortable with such treatment. In contrast, cases involving female victims seem to find the child to be an extension of the mother herself.

Awareness of female sexual abuse perpetration is increasing. As more cases become known, more information will be available. At this time it is unclear what the sex of the victim may be, whether the act is undertaken in isolation or in cooperation with another (perhaps male) perpetrator, or what the consequences may be to either victim or perpetrator. It seems wise to withhold judgment about such cases until more is known. The recognition that female perpetration is even possible is a relatively new view. It will be quite some time before our knowledge of the female perpetrator approaches that which is known of the male perpetrator, as evidenced by the following section.

The Child Molester

It is curious that, as evidenced by Table 7.5, theorists and clinicians alike have tended to ignore the sex crime within child sexual assault. Rather, there has been a strong bias toward viewing the in-home molester as different than the out-of-home. The crime itself has often been described in terms that suggest that it is the sexual expression of nonsexual needs. Current research (Conte, 1984) offers that it is time to put these beliefs and polarities behind us. The father who perpetrates incest in the home can, and does, perpetrate child molestation on the street in some cases. Sexual abuse of children is, at its core, an undeniably sexual act. No amount of denial, distortion, or minimization can alter these facts (Conte, 1984). Power, fantasy, pure physiological arousal, and the use of sexual pornography all may play a role in a given case. As Conte (1984) notes, inadequate personality is not an adequate theory of causation in sexual molestation. However, from the scarcity of knowledge available to date, we may not be prepared to describe an accurate mechanism of transmission. Table 7.5 describes some of the lengths researchers have gone to explain the development of the sex offender. This is an effort that must continue, for no clear answer is yet available (Finkelhor, 1986).

The Sex Offender:
Fact and Fiction

As a group, incarcerated sex offenders tend not to have been a stranger to the child, as is often believed. There is also nothing in their demographics that discriminates them from the general population, and the problem is one that occurs across all social and mental health/illness continuums (Groth et al., 1982, p. 130). As a rule, these are males who initiated sexual assaults against children during their adolescence, have had multiple victims, will engage in other forms of sexual deviance if denied access to children, and who will violate literally hundreds of victims if they are not apprehended prior to middle age (Abel, Becker, Murphy, & Flanagan, 1981).

The stereotypical sex offender maintains an exclusive interest in children and assaults them in an aggressive manner. He is the stranger that parents prepared their children to run from when they see him. In fact, the familiar person or relative presents a much larger risk.

In reality there are multiple offender types. Some are exclusive in their drive for children, others mixed as availability dictates. Some seek participation in child-care agencies. The more devious may seek out a single-parent female and prey upon her family to get at the children. This may include marriage. Whether homosexual, heterosexual, or pan-sexual, these individuals are sexually aroused by "childness." Some are so aroused by childness that their search becomes an obsession that overwhelms any other activity or selectivity by situation or age. The role of alcohol is overstated as a causal factor. However, pathology, organic damage, and even the loneliness and lack of touch experienced by older persons may play a role (Abel et al., 1981). Where there are children, there will be sex offenders, many of them. The sooner they are identified (adolescent versus adult offender), the better opportunity the practitioner holds for potential change.

The difficulty in detection of sex offenders is that their contact with children does not appear sexual. It is likely to be wrestling and rough-housing. The offender, stimulated by touch, may then seek isolation to masturbate. A short play period, disappearance, reappearance, play, and disappearance should be explained. So, too, should repetitive efforts to get children alone on field trips or at a residence. Special care must be taken with child-care from all males

TABLE 7.5

Author(s)	Descriptor	Etiology
Karpman (1954)	Preference offenders	Stable erotic attraction to children
	Surrogate offenders	Use of the child as a surrogate for adult partner
Mohr (1962)	Multiple perversion	The polymorphous perverse nature of man
Gebhard & Gagnon (1964)	Mental defective sociosexually underdeveloped	A fixating sexual experience in childhood
	Alcohol involved offender	Alcohol/substance abuse
Cohn (1969)	Fixated offender	Passive dependency/social immaturity
	Regressed offender	Life stress, inadequate masculinity, poor marital adjustment, confrontive sexual experiences in adolescence
Swanson (1971)	Fixated offender	Poor social, educational, and employment adaptation
	Situational offender	Response to life stresses
	Brain-damaged offender	Impairment in intelligence, perception, and/or judgement
	Inadequate sociopathic offender	Lack of regard for others, possibly confounded by alcohol dependency or mis-use.
McCaghy (1971)	Offender working with children	Seeking legitimate contact through occupational or volunteer roles
	Career molester	Sexual fixation upon children

	Incestuous molester	Marital instability
	Spontaneous molester	Response to life stress
	Aged molester	dementia
Summit & Kryso (1978)	Incidental offender	Erotic interest or dependency
	Idelogical offender	Belief in the benefit to the child
	Psychotic offender	Confusion in reality testing
	Rustic environment	Isolation
	Endogamous incest offender	Distorted family relationships
	Misogynous incest offender	Fear or hatred of women
	Imperious incest offender	Household emperors
	Pedophilic incest	Erotic fascination with children
	Child rapist	Masculinity vs. power confusion
	Perverse incest offender	Exploring that which is most forbidden
Groth & Birnbaum (1978)	Preference	Fixated on attraction to children through psychosexual experiences in development
	Situational	Sexual expression of extra-sexual needs brought about by current circumstance
Justice & Justice (1979)	Symbiotic offender	Dependency
	Introverted offender	Family fusion; shutting out the world
	Teacher/offender	In-Home sex education

(continued)

TABLE 7.5 (*continued*)

Author(s)	Descriptor	Etiology
	Protector/offender	Providing a "safe" introduction to sexuality
	Alcoholic offender	Alcohol/substance abuse
	Psychopathic personality/offender	Character disorder
American Psychiatric Association (1980) DSM-III	Pedophilic offender	Repetitive child preference or exclusive child preference in achievement of sexual excitement (excludes situational considerations)
Burgess (1981)	Group offender	Operating alone with a small group of children
	Solo ring offender	Using to exchange or sell pornography of children
	Transition ring offender	Organization used to recruit children, produce pornography, direct sexual services, and develop customer
	Syndicated ring offender	network
Howells (1981)	Preference offender	Primary sexual orientation to children
		Unplanned and compulsive assaults (usually of males)
		Not precipitated by stress
		Do not understand society's concern
	Situational offender	Normal heterosexual development and orientation
		Social skill deficits
		Significant life stresses

	Fixated offender Regressed offender	Both fixated (persistent) and regressed (sporatic) had perpetrators who were (a) seeking sexual gratification, and (b) seeking relief of agression within their classification
Groth, Hobson, & Gary (1982)	Fixated (classic) offender	Primary orientation to children from adolescence Compulsive/obsessional unresolved psychopathology
	Regressed offender	Conflict in adult roles impulsive responses to adult stress Alcohol use
	Child molester	Builds relationship with child; slow and patient seduction
	Child rapist	Aggressive act against child in which there is no personal investment
Bauman, Alford, & Kaspar (1983)	Aggressive offender	Dominance need incestuously directed
	Passive offender	Poor self-image Shallowness Awkwardness, socially inept
Conte (1984)	Cross-over offender	Sexually motivated in multiple paraphilias/offenses involving both children and adults

who conduct themselves in this way. Only vigilance on the part of knowing adults will serve to reduce risk to trusting children.

The Adolescent Sex Offender

It is difficult to categorize juveniles who commit sex crimes against other children. Within this group there are *hebephilic* offenders who prefer adolescent females, *ephebophilic* offenders with a homosexual preference, and still others who appears generally pedophilic (Costell, 1980, p. 30). No matter the category of offense, it must be dealt with at this time rather than waiting for it to become an entrenched behavior.

Adolescent sex offenders are usually isolated socially and have parents who minimize the seriousness of their acts (Costell, 1980, p. 29). There may be a history of physical, sexual or emotional abuse followed by the typical low self-esteem and sense of inadequacy. Poor anger management, low frustration tolerance, and a diffuse sense of sexual identity are all problems. Since fear of being powerless, controlled, or helpless is predominant in their thinking, children smaller and younger than they are selected.

James and Nasjleti (1983, p. 19) describe this offender as "the boy next door." He is typically a nice young man who keeps to himself and is seen as a loner. He is an average student liked by teachers, but not by peers, because of his quiet demeanor. In the absence of friends he has time to babysit, something he is only too happy to do. His victims are fond of him and are often willing, if unknowing, partners.

It is very likely that this offender was sexually abused. His own assaultiveness may serve not only learned sexual gratification but as an outlet for hostility and the provision of a sense of control. It may also validate heterosexuality in a nonthreatening manner. His lack of social skills and poorly controlled anger provide him little opportunity to test issues of power and control in other ways. His acts with children often mirror precisely the acts perpetrated against him as a child (James & Nasjleti, 1983, pp. 19–20).

The most important feature of the adolescent sex offender is that he may be more accessible and responsive to treatment at this point before the sexually abusive behavior has become ingrained. If not stopped, he will continue to molest children outside his family, children within his family as a father, and their children as a grandfather (Goodwin, Cormier, & Owen, 1983). The time to stop this behavior firmly is at the point of first detection.

Special Perpetrators in Physical and Sexual Maltreatment

The Stepparent

Living in a family as a stepchild provides increased risk for both physical (Burgess & Garbarino, 1983; Daly & Wilson, 1980; Gils-Sims, 1984) and sexual (Finkelhor, 1984; Lewis-Herman, 1981; Russell, 1984) abuse. This abuse may occur at the hands of a stepparent or it may occur at the hands of other persons known to the stepparent, especially the stepfather, and especially with child sexual abuse (Finkelhor, 1984, p. 25). If there is a mix of biological and stepchildren, the stepchildren present the most frequent target (Burgess, 1978). Multiple theories have been applied to describe this increased risk.

Giles-Sims and Finkelhor (1984) have reviewed several theoretical positions regarding stepparent perpetration and concentrate their probabilities in four areas. First, the sociobiological position seems to merit increased study. In this view, there is a reduced parental investment in the nonbiological child (Bolton, 1983; Burgess & Garbarino, 1983). Related to this reduced investment is reduced attachment in the stepparent-stepchild relationship. In sexual abuse this reduced attachment has been traced both to the stepparent's absence in the child's early life and the absence of that stepparent's participation in the child's early care, a process that may reduce the parent's protective feelings toward the child (Lewis-Herman, 1981; Van den Berghe, 1983).

The absence of a father figure in the child's early life may also increase his or her exposure to the predatory pedophile. The unsuspecting single-parent mother may be susceptible to the advances of the pedophile. He is good with children, more than willing to participate in child care, and comfortable having children around. He is the ideal man for the harrassed and overburdened single mother to bring home. If the child is starving for affection, particularly from a male in a quasi-paternal role, the risk is enhanced (Finkelhor, 1984, p. 26).

A second theoretical position is that of normative controls. As this applies to stepchildren, Giles-Sims and Finkelhor (1984) suggest that the normative controls against physical or sexual abuse are reduced below that which might be perceived in a biological child-parent relationship. Russell (1984, p. 20) concurs on this point and joins Finkelhor (1984, p. 25) in suggesting that the stepfather's friends are potential perpetrators due to the reduced constraint they feel when faced with potential sexual involvement with their friend's stepchild.

A third position spoken of in physical maltreatment is stress. Simply put, the stress of trying to establish a stable blended family is often overwhelming. A fourth theoretical predictor of risk described by resource theory, which explains that the authority structure of the stepfamily (particularly that with a stepfather at the helm) may reduce what the other family members feel to be the stepchild's legitimate access to family resources. Burgess and colleagues (1981) call this the "Cinderella Syndrome"; the stepparent may simply view this child in a less protective way than one of their own.

Ultimately, if the stepfather holds conservative family values that require obedient children at all costs, if there is an absence of physical affection in the family, and if the child has a great affection-hunger, both physical and sexual abuse are increased risks (Finkelhor, 1984, p. 26). It is important to remember that not every stepparent presents with increased risk (Caplan et al., 1984) and that just as great a risk may be present in brothers and sisters, biological or not.

The Sibling as Perpetrator

Sibling abuse implies an aggressive or violent act directed from one sibling to another. The greater the age distance between these two, the more likely the assault and its effects will approximate those that accompany family violence between adult and child. Sibling abuse is found in both physical and sexual maltreatment cases.

The family in which physical abuse between siblings occurs tends to be chaotic and disorganized. The balance of care and attention is inappropriate. The child perpetrator is often an only child who has had to accept the intrusion of new half-siblings. The sibling who perpetrates is often on the down side of the family equation. They are seen negatively by the parent(s). The parent is preoccupied with providing attention to the child victim while the perpetrating child suffers in silence. There is a great deal of crisis in the family particularly centered about the mother. When maternal resources are otherwise directed, the perpetrating child is often asked to serve as caretaker for the child victim. That is the point at which the assault occurs (Green, 1984, p. 316).

It seems obvious that family factors may influence the development of rivalry and assault. The discrepancy between the quality of care given the children is extreme, obvious, and painful for the perpetrating child. The abuse toward the seemingly "more loved" sibling may be an effort to "get even," a way to release hatred intended for the mother, a way to get attention, or a way to master their own victimization by adopting a perpetrator role (Green, 1984, pp. 312–314).

Sibling abuse is more likely to occur in a home that already knows child abuse at the hands of the parent. Exposure to this aggressive parent and a general lack of positive affect can result in difficulty in controlling aggressive impulses. If there are learning problems, organicity in the child, or any feature of his or her physical or psychological being that makes the child feel inferior, the chance of abuse increases (Green, 1984, pp. 312–316). Sexual abuse by siblings follows a similar pattern.

Sexual play in siblings has long been recognized and largely ignored. Kempe & Kempe (1984, p. 75) describe the most familiar variety as casual, exploratory, same-age sexual play, which, in the absence of extreme parental reactions, is relatively benign. Others have followed that thinking in suggesting that sibling sexual contact is the least damaging both physically and psychologically (Arndt & Ladd, 1976; James & Nasjleti, 1983, p. 15; Lukianowicz, 1972; Weeks, 1976). At most this was thought to be damaging only in its ability to limit normal peer group relationships and experiential learning. This is becoming an outmoded view.

There is increasing recognition that sibling abuse occurs most frequently in homes where there is sexual contact between parents and children (James & Nasjleti, 1983, p. 15). There may be incestuous intent or it may be a mechanism for transmission of love and nurturance in a family with parents who are otherwise preoccupied (James & Nasjleti, 1983, p. 16; Justice & Justice, 1976, pp. 104–106). This may also be an expression of nurturance in a family where the only expression of caring between parent and child is sexual contact.

The point is that sexual contact between siblings can be forced and coercive (Kempe & Kempe, 1984, p. 77). The greater the age differential between siblings, the more force or coercion is used and the closer the resemblance will be to adult-child sexual abuse. This will generate seriously negative outcomes, guilt in particular (Kempe & Kempe, 1984, p. 77). No longer considered a benign situation, sexual abuse between siblings (especially in this day of blended families(is now seen as another genuine threat to normal childhood development.

Special Perpetrators, Victims, and Maltreatment of Adults

The Marital Violence Perpetrator: Husband or Wife?

Violence between adult members of the family is bidirectional. Husbands are violent towards wives and, in some cases, wives are violent toward husbands. The most typical case of wife-perpetrated violence is one in which the violence is in response to repeated violent assaults by the husband. The result may be murder at the hands of a wife who has reached the end of her rope (Walker, 1984). Both husbands and wives murder each other. The wife is about seven times as likely to murder in self-defense (Gelles, 1979, p. 139). Whether in outright defense of self during an attack or a "protective reaction violence," striking first to prevent an anticipated attack, (Gelles, 1979, p. 139) the wife's violence most often occurs in response to that of the husband.

Straus (1979) has recognized the high rate of violence reported for female perpetrators, but he urges that the primary focus be given to female victims. This is urged as a result of the more serious outcomes for females. In most cases the injuries are more serious, as are the emotional consequences if the family should dissolve. Additionally, husbands have a higher rate of the most dangerous and injurious forms of violence, and when violent acts are committed by the husband, they seem to occur more frequently (Straus, 1979, pp. 448–449). Steinmetz (1977, 1978) would likely argue that the numbers are closer to being equal due to the husband's reduced likelihood of reporting, but could not argue that these cases are equal in the severity of their outcome (Pagelow, 1984, p. 272). The same atmosphere of fear and dependency that characterizes the female victim may embrace the male victim. The male victim presents the same reluctance to leave: the spouse is contrite and loving, the victim loves the abuser; the abuser has many positive features, and behavior is excused by circumstance (Pagelow, 1984, p. 275). Yet all things considered, violence between husband and wife must be considered a male-perpetrated act in most serious situations.

The Conjugal Violence Victim Who Stays for More: Why?

One of the practitioner's greatest frustrations in working with the conjugally violent family is the victim's seeming inability to escape the perpetrator. Many victims continue to expose themselves to violence despite practitioner efforts and obvious alternatives. But appearance may be deceiving.

Elbow (1977) has noted that the victim of conjugal violence has but three alternatives: She may leave; she may stay, hoping that the perpetrator will change; or she may stay knowing that he will not change. The third alternative, resignation to victimization is the most frustrating for the practitioner. The latter two alternatives are understandably those most frequently chosen.

Gelles (1976) collapsed the decision points in staying into three categories. First, the less severe and frequent the violence, the more likely the wife will stay. The perpetrator is not violent all the time and may be a solid mate periodically. This "variable-ratio reinforcement" schedule is most compelling. Second, the amount of violence experienced as a child plays a role. A great deal of experience predicts a higher tolerance. Third, educational and occupational realities are motivators to stay. This is especially true if a lack of either predicts financial entrapment in the relationship. A final factor, mentioned by some of the female victims in the Gelles study, was whether they felt any agency offering intervention could really understand their problems. They were not confident that they could trust the agency to understand and protect them; it might be better not to rock the boat. Other researchers (Fleming, 1979; Pagelow, 1982; Walker, 1979) have expanded this perspective. Many victims of conjugal violence stay for very concrete reasons; they have nowhere to go and no way to ensure physical survival when they find a place to hide. "Hiding" is correct here because the perpetrator of conjugal violence must be assumed to be capable of on-going and accelerated violence should the victim leave. This male is perfectly capable of forcing the victim's return or even murdering the victim out of anger at her leaving. The decision to leave, then, may be life threatening for the victim and/or her children. The safety of the victim must always be the practitioner's first consideration (Fleming, 1979, p. 21). Even should the victim find a place that offers safety, continued economic survival is almost always in question.

Many victims of conjugal violence have been subjected to economic dependence on the perpetrator. They are unfamiliar with the process of seeking/gaining employment and managing financial responsibilities. Child care requirements often exceed any expected salary due to premature educational termination and lack of occupational experience. There are few, if any, places where these women may go to change those facts in the short time they can support themselves and their children (Fleming, 1979). But these financial dependencies may be insignificant when compared to their psychological dependencies.

The victim of conjugal violence is often a very dependent individual. This is not universally true, but inappropriate dependencies are usually present. For this pathologically dependent victim to leave the conjugal relationship is to deny virtually every traditional value she holds. Ball and Wyman (1978) describe this victim as "over-socialized" into traditional roles. This is an individual who has learned to be docile, submissive, nonassertive, and sacrificing. Independence in decision making and personal responsibility are foreign concepts. To leave is to admit not to her co-habitor's failure, but her own. His violence is seen as little more than her failure to provide adequate nurturance. She must stay to help him. The children need a father. Instead of being angry at this assaultive male, she frequently internalizes the anger and directs it at herself. The result is an emotional paralysis that leads to the fatigue and depression that eventually becomes inertia (Fleming, 1979; Martin, 1976).

Without intervention to interpret the realities of her life, the conjugal victim has little realistic information upon which to base a decision. This is a victim who feel psychologically and physically powerless. Through her traditional views, she understands leaving to be a loss of identity, social approval, and love as well as the acquisition of stigma (Waites, 1978). She may only be able to describe this as "embarrassment," but it means a great deal more.

This victim may believe that this relationship is not only all she has; it is all she is. To leave it is to lose her identity. These thoughts are difficult to break through, particularly with an intervention not able to eliminate the practical problems as well (i.e., employment).

What the practitioner does have to offer is an opportunity for sorting out life plans and alternatives while the victim prepares to leave. The first step is getting a victim to see themselves as victimized, then watching a serious and feasible plan emerge from initially grandiose escape fantasies. It is wise to expect a rocky course that progresses in fits and starts.

Admitting to victimization is the keystone to solving the stay or leave dilemma. Ferraro (1983) has described a process of rationalization that prohibits this realization in the conjugal victim. Each point in this process must be dealt with before a rational stay-or-leave decision can be made and acted upon.

The steps taken by the victim to rationalize the violence are not sequential or independent. They occur and reoccur as needed. They are built upon a social and economic context that is unique to the situation in which the victim is living. The practitioner may see large social reality; the victim sees only the family situation. To expect more is to expect too much.

The first constant process is *denial of the victimization*. The violence is not attributed to the conjugal partner, but to some outside force (i.e., alcohol, employment problems, "nerves"). His violence is seen as a natural response to the problem he is facing and will end when the problem ends. This is related to the victim's *appeal to the salvation ethic*.

Basically, the perpetrator is perceived to be a good man who has specific problems. These problems are expected to be resolved with the victim's help. This is curious because even as they see themselves as perfectly capable of helping this man, their *denial of options* reveals a clear lack of belief in their ability to help themselves. They do not believe that survival is possible without this man. They believe that none but this man would ever love them. Leaving means permanent isolation; isolation that reactivates fears from their own inadequate childhood.

The only remaining option for this victim is *denial of injury* when it occurs and *appeal to higher loyalties*. In this final process they rely upon their fundamental valuing of the good in marriage and children to cope with the contradiction between the love and commitment they feel and the violence they receive (Ferraro, 1983, pp. 205–207). These are rationalizations almost impervious to the efforts of the practitioner.

For the practitioner to survive this type of work, it is critical to accept the victim's decision to stay. This may not be seen as the best decision, but it may be the only decision possible. The losses in leaving may be perceived as greater than the gains.

If leaving is ever to occur, it will not occur without a series of separations and reunions. Like any dependency, a periodic return to the addictive element is a frequent part of the rehabilitation process. Passing judgment of these reunions, pressuring the woman to leave by a certain time, or devaluing the perpetrator could backfire and result in termination of the practitioner's relationship with the victim (Fleming, 1979, p. 99; Geller & Walsh, 1977).

The practitioner may tire of the victim and her violent partner. It may appear as if no progress is being made. However, the practitioner must try to avoid, as much as possible, a personal commitment to the victim's staying or leaving. The practitioner must also have someone of his or her own to talk to in the event the victim returns to the violence. Even though the practitioner cannot deny the on-going violence to be faced by the victim, it remains the victim's choice to continue. This is a critical point in working in cases of family violence; adult victims have the option of defending themselves or not. One final perpetrator will be considered here, not typically thought of as someone the adult will have to defend themselves against.

The Child Perpetrator of Violence Toward Adults in the Family

Many parents are terrified of their children, especially adolescents, and some with good reason. In some cases the violence of the child against the adult is so extreme that the result is a parricide (parental murder). This tends to occur only in the most dysfunctional of families in which a single isolated and extremely violent episode has occurred (Harbin & Madden, 1979, p. 1288). But the fact remains that children do assault their parents (Straus et al., 1980).

The family that succumbs to assaults from the children is one that has abdicated responsibility and authority over the children. The child is the parent. The real parent is emotionally incompetent and over-taxed and the child has long been asked to accept responsibility beyond his or her capabilities. The eventual result is an explosion (Harbin & Maddin, 1979, p. 1289).

Since these children were forced to adopt parental roles before they were ready, they are trapped in a pseudo-independence. The parents may compete with each other for the child's attention. The child seeks the emotional dependence of the parent, but really wants it for him or her self. These children may develop a grandiose sense of self, feel omnipotent, and expect all to respond to them accordingly. These children are seeking some kind of structure in a family environment without boundaries. But they are not capable of providing those boundaries for themselves in any rational way. The result is a series of explosive responses to situations for which no prior family rules exist.

This is a difficult family to deal with due to their denial of the problem, minimization of the violence, and inability to admit to their failures in parenthood. They must, instead, sanction this violent behavior on the part of the child and continue along their helpless and anxiety-ridden path. For the practitioner there is little choice other than removal of the child perpetrator in an attempt to provide them an environment with limits as quickly as possible (Harbin & Madden, 1979). Yet, even for these special victims and perpetrators, there is a sharing of the processes that generate the dysfunctional behaviors in all violent families. These processes will be described in the chapter to follow.

8

The Family Violence Process

Translating family violence theory into clinical/practitioner target areas is a difficult task. Part of this difficulty originates in the complexity of variables that must be considered simultaneously. Early theoretical work was, perhaps, somehow kinder to the practitioner. Theoretical explanations were self-contained and hinted at their own treatment directions. In those early years, depending upon the orientation of the practitioner, only one of several schools of thought was applied. Consider that psychiatric/psychological practitioners could seek out unconscious drives, social learning (i.e., modeling effects), and cognitive-developmental inadequacy (i.e., poor preparation for parenting). Sociologists could lay claim to environmental stress, labeling, and social-interactional deficiencies as causal factors. Unfortunately, single process theory did not cover the necessary ground (Newberger, 1985a).

We have not come to understand the complexity of simultaneous factors in the process within which violence in the family develops. Gelles and Straus (1978) capture these many areas in three broad classes of process variable, intra-individual, social-psychological, and sociocultural. Others maneuver these many variables into an "ecological" process theory that seeks to examine every reciprocal interaction between individuals, families, and societies with the environment in which they must attempt to survive (Belsky, 1980, 1984; Garbarino & Gilliam, 1980). To paraphrase Newberger's perspective upon the process of child maltreatment (1985a), the processes that lead to violence in the family are best thought of as symptoms of a fundamental dysfunction in a complex ecosystem with many interacting variables. The clinical fact is, most families will

TABLE 8.1
Commonalities in Family Operations
Across Violent Families

	Child Maltreatment	*Sexual Abuse*	*Conjugal Violence*	*Elder Mistreatment*
(1) Confused and distorted attachments	X	X	X	X
(2) Unequal power and status distributions	X	X	X	X
(3) Frustration	X	X	X	X
(4) Distorted cognitions and attributions	X	X	X	X
(5) Role incompetence in the face of stress	X	X	X	X

NOTE: See Appendix H for references.

present with multiple points of causation; no single factor theory or academic perspective will satisfy the practitioner's need to capture a comprehensive view. However, there can be a translation from theory to practice of the more commonly occurring process elements in the violent family. Table 8.1 represents that translation. This table represents the major commonalities to be found in the dysfunctional processes affecting the violent family.

Distorted and Confused Attachments

The protective mechanisms that ordinarily insulate family members from the aggressiveness of other family members are reduced in the violent family. The reciprocity, care giving, altruism, and continuous emotional availability that marks the attached family are not available (Bolton, 1983).

The confused attachments between parent and child in the violent family have been referred to as psychopathologically deviant (Spinetta & Rigler, 1972), an intense, pervasive, and continuous demand from parent to child (Steele & Pollack, 1972), lack of "good enough mothering" (Steele, 1975), a poor mothering imprint (Helfer & Kempe, 1972), and a role-reversal (Morris & Gould, 1963; reviewed in Garbarino, 1977, p. 722). Justice and Justice (1976) note more simply that violent parents have inappropriate values about the relative legitimacy of their needs as compared to those of their children. These are not usually parents who intentionally harm a child. These are parents whose own inadequacies, fears, and needs inhibit their ability to nurture (Newberger, 1979, p. 15).

There are, of course, parents who interact violently with their children with knowledge that they are doing harm. The sexually abusive parent is one such parent. In the case of sexual abuse, however, the damage is not due so much to sexual activity as to the betrayal and abandonment of parental protectiveness that is implied (Summit & Kryso, 1978, 1980).

The confused attachments and dependencies in the sexually abusive family are brought forward by the parent. Stern and Meyer (1980) describe the perpetrator/victim relationship in this family as holding one of three forms. First, there may be a dependent/domineering relationship in which the father is dependent on a more capable daughter. This is the "little mother" situation in which the daughter takes over for an emotionally or physically absent parent and becomes responsible, in her mind, for the day-to-day survival of the family. Second, the possessive/passive situation is one in which a domineering and aggressive father simply consumes all aspects of the daughter's life and commands every action. Finally, there is the dependent/dependent relationship in which two emotionally insecure, isolated, and unsupported individuals turn to each other for identification and affection. This is a family that promises abandonment if the slightest error, such as disclosure, is made. If this tenuous attachment is additionally stressed by absence and unavailability of the other parent, a generally poor relationship with the parents, conflict between the parents themselves, or the presence of a stepparent (especially stepfather) the risk for sexual abuse is increased (Finkelhor, 1986).

While the confused attachment in the physically abusive family may lead to rejection, the child in the sexually abusive family may be over-attached (Kempe & Kempe, 1984, p. 49). Trapped in a family in which mother and daughter are estranged, dominated by an authoritative patriarch, and having the promise of a special relationship held out to them by the perpetrator, this child has no choice but cooperation (Finkelhor, 1979; Herman & Hirschman, 1980). In this attachment, the perpetrator promises protection from all others, but in exchange, the victim experiences the ultimate loss of protection. Power in the family, then, may operate both covertly and overtly, but in either case, when inappropriately distributed may result in victimization of family members. Such confused attachment effects in the conjugally violent and violent families in which elder mistreatment occurs are more easily seen through a description of other family processes as will be seen in the remainder of this chapter.

Unequal Power and Status Distribution

Feminist theorists have offered power imbalance as the basis upon which conjugal violence (Dobash & Dobash, 1979; Martin, 1976) and sexual abuse (Russell, 1984) are built. With the all-encompassing statement that all family violence gravitates toward the greatest power differential, that is, parent versus child, Finkelhor (1981) provides license to consider power imbalance as a common feature in all family violence situations.

The perpetrator in the *conjugal violence* situation has been repetitively described as attempting to compensate for perceived powerlessness elsewhere. The resultant infliction of compensatory violence on the family is nothing more than using the family as a scapegoat for the original powerlessness (Pagelow, 1984, p. 99). This is described as a predominantly masculine response to powerlessness and a means used to assert masculinity when there is an intra-familial power imbalance, for example, differential occupational or educational status in conjugal partners (Carlson, 1977; O'Brien, 1971).

Violence is a means by which the male perpetrator can gain an area of dominance; dominance that culture and society expect but do not offer to this inadequate male in any other way (Deschner, 1984, p. 28). If this male controlled greater resources, there would be less need for violence as a means to prove himself (Allen & Straus, 1980).

The opposite member of the conjugal power imbalance is the almost totally powerless female. She is described by Walker (1979) as experiencing a learned helplessness; the same learned helplessness exhibited by those who come to understand their situation as being completely out of their control and influence. In the case of conjugal violence, this victim could wrest some control away from the male perpetrator if only she could believe it possible. But the cognitive set guiding this victim is that she cannot control events. If that mental set is strong enough, it will be adhered to even in the face of contrary evidence; evidence that is rationalized away.

Perpetrators of *sexual abuse* hold the same need to rule over their victims as do the perpetrators of conjugal violence. Summit and Kryso (1978) have written of "imperious" incest in which the main need is for the perpetrator to elicit obedience from the family members. This is a pathological exaggeration of traditional father roles that occurs in a large number of sexually abusive families (Herman, 1981) as well as families that experience violence of different origin (Maisch, 1972; Tierney & Corwin, 1983, p. 108).

Control is critical to the incest perpetrator and child molester alike. Both feel more in control when involved with a child. There is less risk of a rebuff or rejection and the perpetrator's sense of competency is not threatened (Groth et al., 1982, p. 137). In this situation the adult has social authority, physical superiority, and virtually all the experience and knowledge (Groth et al., 1982, p. 137). Such power imbalance is found in the individual sexually abusive event as well as the sex initiation ring in which the adult capitalizes upon legitimate power roles (such as coach) to coerce children into sexual activity. Additional power against disclosure is offered through the peer group pressure associated with the event (Burgess et al., 1981). This is the same power that is found in sexually abusive situations involving siblings who perpetrate against younger siblings (Hunter, Kilstrom, & Loda, 1978, p. 24).

Like the conjugal violence perpetrator, the sexual abuse perpetrator creates an authoritarian role in the family in spite of inadequacy and immaturity (Cormier, Kennedy, & Sangowicz, 1962). The child victim cannot afford to complain, does not fight back, and does not tell as a result of this authority (Summit, 1984, p. 2). The perpetrator, whether out of a need to overcome feelings of inadequacy, or as retaliation against his too-powerful wife, sees this compliance as freedom to continue the sexual abuse of the children (Kempe & Kempe, 1984, p. 60; Tierney & Corwin, 1983, p. 108).

In the situation involving *mistreatment of the elderly,* the neglecting or abusive perpetrator is in total control. He or she holds all the power due to the elderly person's needs for assistance in the activities of daily living (O'Malley, O'Malley, Everitt, & Sarson, 1984, p. 362). In this family, as the need for assistance in the older person increased, the power relationships have shifted. The older person may retain some control through manipulation of financial resources (Pagelow, 1984, p. 78), but as this slips away they are virtually at the mercy of the caregiver (O'Malley et al., 1984, p. 368).

There are several points in the relationship between the elderly person and caregiver at which power struggles may emerge. There may be values and standards of behavior that differ. A long-standing personality conflict may be worsened or resurrected (Hickey & Douglas, 1981, p. 174; Kosberg, 1983a, p. 268; O'Malley et al., 1984, p. 366). Long-standing conflicts regarding control, responsibility, and dependence may be regenerated (Luppens & Lau, 1983, p. 212). If all these problems are exaggerated by the overwhelming need for care presented by the older person, disaster may result.

Several inappropriate reactions can occur in response to power shifts in families caring for older persons. First, the elderly parent may refuse to relinquish authority, treat the adult caregiver as a child, and intrude on family privacy. Second, the caregiver may push the elderly person into an inappropriate degree of dependency while still capable. Third, the caregiver may remain dependent too long. Finally, the elderly individual may elect to give up and become dependent long before it is necessary (Luppens & Lau, 1983, p. 210). The family relationship only tolerates a short period of dependency in an older person. If the victim lives too long, especially if they are infirm, they lose all power and are seen as a burden.

Being a burden is dangerous as there is nothing to offer the caregiver, no resource held by the victim that is wanted by the perpetrator, and no hope of a reciprocal relationship. It is only the perpetrator's altruism that offers protection (Luppens & Lau, 1983, p. 209). This is frustrating for both the older person and their younger caretaker.

Frustration

That aggression *can* occur in response to frustration has been firmly established since the 1930s (Dollard, Dobb, Miller, Mower, & Sears, 1939). Whether it will occur is another matter. As a result, the thought processes and attributions that move the perpetrator from the experience of frustration to a violent act are key assessment points.

Frustration must be cognitively interpreted. There must be some uniquely important meaning to the goal or expectation that was not met to merit violence (Feshback, 1980, p. 50). Additionally, aggression will not occur unless the setting in which it does occur is considered to be appropriate for the demonstration of violence

(Deschner, 1984, p. 70). Consequently *the practitioner must first determine why the home and family was considered appropriate for violence.* Then, some clarification must be given as to *why the issue was so critical to the perpetrator.*

After the practitioner has determined *how the perpetrator provided personal permission to be violent in the family setting* they must then assess (1) under what conditions aggression in response to frustration is thought to be appropriate, (2) where and how the perpetrator learned not only the behavior but its justification, and (3) whether the perpetrator is aware of any alternative responses to frustration (Giles-Sims, 1983, p. 27). Acquiring this knowledge about a family is important as frustration is a regularly occurring aspect of most violent families.

Two characteristics of the *child maltreatment* situation seem to involve a frustration-aggression linkage. First, if corporal punishment is accepted, as it is in most American families, it may get out of control at times. If this discipline strategy is combined with the anger that grows out of frustration, whether related to the victim or not, the danger is increased (Feshback, 1980, p. 57). Second, certain developmental stages in children are more difficult for some parents (Steele & Pollack, 1972, p. 11). A lack of understanding of or preparation for specific needs or behaviors may frustrate this parent. This is especially true if this is a parent whose self-esteem is built upon the child's responses to them (Bolton, 1984). This is the same pathological need for nurturance and reassurance from the child found in *sexual abuse.* Frustration of that need in that family may also result in increased aggressiveness (Groth et al., 1982).

The frustration encountered in *conjugal violence* is akin to that experienced in child maltreatment. In both there is an expectation that the victim will provide the perpetrator some sense of meaning and control in their life. In addition, the victim of conjugal violence is just as likely as the child victim to pay the price for frustrations that the perpetrator brings into the family from the outside world. This is a perpetrator who is not only personally inadequate but interpersonally incompetent. The victim is often assigned the impossible task of compensating for those two glaring inadequacies.

Psychological tension from repetitive failure in personal and interpersonal areas builds in the conjugal violence perpetrator. One mechanism for relieving this feeling is explosion; often toward one or all family members. The perpetrator may describe this as "I just had to let it out." This perpetrator finds psychological relief not only through the release of tension but through the sense of victory ("Now I'm in control.") and cessation of threat that results (Deschner, 1984, p. 64). There is also one other major violence producer that grows out of the perpetrator's personal insecurity: jealousy.

Jealousy is nothing more than anxiety that grows out of insecurity. It is usually related to another person, but it may be related to a situation or object. It can also become obsessional and occupy a great portion of its victim's life as the level of anxiety escalates as a result of internal cognitions (e.g., telling themselves increasingly exaggerated tales). This is an escalating spiral that can culminate in violence against another person.

Since this perpetrator is not a strong person, any violence that eventuates from this spiral effect is likely to be directed toward a weaker individual, usually spouse and/or child. Violence in this way is not only a means of isolating the conjugal partner and assuring on-going possession of him or her (Giles-Sims, 1983, p. 26; Hilberman, 1980, p. 1339), it also serves as a mechanism to reassure the perpetrator not only that he or she loves and is loved but that he or she is powerful as well.

Frustration related to an over-extended dependency period may be the most potent force in the *elder mistreatment* situation. The quality of the relationship between an elderly parent and their offspring is directly related to the juncture of the older person's health condition and the attitudes about aging demonstrated by the younger. If pushed beyond acceptable dependency, abuse or neglect may occur (Anderson, 1981, p. 79). Frustrations and resentment related to the excessive responsibilities of caring for a frail elderly person seem a regularized feature of the elder mistreatment situation (Hickey & Douglas, 1981, p. 504).

Obviously, not all families providing care for an elder member fall victim to violence. Even in those that do, it is only rarely intentional or premeditated. Rather, it is the product of frustration, stress, and exhaustion, which grows out of the care-giving burden (Pagelow, 1984, p. 369). This is a particular problem for the family in which the caretaker is approaching retirement age and was looking forward to the freedom to do some of the things they had been putting off due to time, financial, or parenthood constraints (Block, 1983, p. 224). Under this circumstance, the hard work of caring for the older person combined with the sense of loss over what this time was expected to be can cause extreme frustration. So great is this frustration in some cases that the perpetrators feel themselves to be martyrs caring for elderly victims who have purposefully ruined their lives. Such cognitions are the fuses that light the explosions in family violence.

Cognitions

Exactly what the perpetrator is telling himself or herself about the situation and family members is a necessary element in the assessment of the violent family. Perpetrator perceptions have a direct bearing on the likelihood of a violent act. Since any statement or act that violates their fragile sense of loyalty and/or self-image is perceived as a threat, family members are endangered by almost any statement or action (Ferraro, 1984, p. 2). What is perceived as dangerous varies from moment to moment. The result is paralyzed individuals who do not really know how to act. It is not just their own actions that may result in victimization, but the words and actions of others outside the family. There is no escape from this double bind.

The cognitions and attributions of perpetrators of violence hold a common theme: Somehow *there is always a threat to self implied.* The perpetrator's response to this perception of threat is some combination of anger, disproportionate emotion, and quickly aggressive action that is inappropriate (Deschner, 1984, p. 68). *The path traveled from distorted cognition to violent action* is one that must be understood by the practitioner working with this family for the *reshaping* of these cognitions plays a large role in treatment as will be seen later.

According to Deschner (1984, pp. 71–73) cognitions play several roles in violent families. Beginning with the conviction held by perpetrators that they are 100 percent right and the victim is 100 percent wrong, it is a short distance to the belief that their needs must be met or that they must get their way at any cost. Once having made this internal decision, they are typically able to attribute intent to the victims' actions. When they decide that the threat was purposeful, the question of whether there will be violence is moot. The only question is how much violence and how long. In other words, once deciding that the victim did something to them they need only determine how much punishment or retaliation is merited under the circumstances. This process is most clear in the *child maltreatment* situation.

Feshback writes of the interaction between the "cognitive attribution of intent" and the "cognitive parameter of responsibility" as they bear upon child maltreatment (1980, pp. 50–52). In brief, frustrations that are perceived to be intentional are likely to be responded to more quickly than those perceived to be accidental. And persons not expected to be responsible for their actions are less likely to be punished than those who should have known better. Maltreating parents do not make accurate interpretations of these aspects of their children's lives.

The inappropriate expectations of the child and lack of child development knowledge found in maltreating parents allows them to see children as being capable of actions that they are not. This further allows for the perception of intentionality in normal and random child behaviors. The problem is that this parent's need to be a good parent is so high, and their self-esteem so low, that even normal behaviors from the child may be interpreted as criticism or evidence of parental inadequacy (Steele & Pollack, 1972, p. 11).

Ultimately, based on their own sense of personal inadequacy, maltreating parents may see normal child behavior as threatening of rejection or abandonment (Ainsworth, 1980, pp. 42–43), or may attribute their own qualities to the child; particularly those they dislike (Steele, 1982, p. 488). In worst cases, this child will be thought of as a burden, source of irritation, and a taker whose behavior is "willful naughtiness" (Johnson & Morse, 1968, p. 151). In these cases, punishment is more an expression of agitation than a mechanism for teaching behavior (Johnson & Morse, 1968, p. 151). It is clear that this individual is not competent to play the parental role. This is a "role-incompetence" found across violent families.

The "Family-Role" Incompetent and the Family Violence Process

A repetitive sense provided regarding individuals involved in family violence is that *they are not competent at the roles family members play*. There are insufficient skills and no reciprocity. They are too needy and frightened to offer altruism. Supports for positive behavior as well as inhibitions against negative behaviors are unavailable to them. They are simply incompetent at family roles.

Garbarino has adapted Elder's perspective on role incompetence to the child maltreatment process. Elder (1977) suggests that, in order to be competent, one must have adequate preparation for and rehearsal of a role. They must also be aware of clear expectations within the role, and exist without too much change to allow the role to be incorporated. Not one of these features describes the violent family.

Child Maltreatment and Role Incompetence

In the maltreating family, the rehearsal for the parenthood role has usually been somewhat dysfunctional. Unrealistic expectations abound, and the limits and responsibilities within roles are usually blurted out in spur-of-the-moment fits of passion, rage, or despair (Johnson & Morse, 1968, p. 151; Parke & Colmer, 1975). The lack of practice and role clarity provides for unpredictability in the resulting family roles.

The child victim confronted by an unpredictable parent becomes incompetent in their role as child. They are trapped in an approach-avoidance conflict as they both try to avoid and yearn for the parent at the same time (George & Main, 1979). This creates a situation in which the few interactions that do occur do so out of desperation during those times when the child can no longer repress their need for the parent.

A second difficulty comes about when it is recognized that, even when approached by the child, these parents are not giving; they are taking. As the interactions become repetitively unsuccessful, the child is convinced that the parent does not want them. The parent then wonders why the child does not seek them out. This is the vicious cycle of the unprepared parent and the consequently needy child (Burgess et al., 1981; Herrenkohl et al., 1984, p. 642; Kadushin & Martin, 1984). A similar cyclical pattern emerges in some *conjugal violence* situations.

Giles-Sims (1983, p. 24) draws parallels between the development of violence in conjugal couples with the development of revolution. In the first stage there is a precompetitive situation in which cooperation and interdependence exists. As time goes by, competition builds and escalates into conflict. At some point this spiraling conflict reaches crisis proportions and there must be a decision made as to whether to resolve the competition or revolt. The role-incompetent conjugal violence perpetrator and their partner do not have the necessary skills to negotiate.

Walker (1979) and others (Hilberman, 1980, p. 1339) have identified a cycle in conjugal violence that begins with tension building. The mutual dependencies of this victim/perpetrator pair build until some noxious event creates a coercive situation. In this situation, threats are exchanged and the tensions that had been hidden find an avenue of expression. Internal and external stresses combine in an escalating spiral that results in violence (Patterson & Hops, 1972; Patterson, Reid, Jones, & Conger, 1975).

Over time the victim learns to submit to this violence in order to get it over and reduce the day-to-day tensions (Deschner, 1984, p. 18). In some cases the cycle is shortened to include only build-up and attack to enable the perpetrator/victim pair to reach the reconciliation phase more quickly. If this is seen as masochism, it should not be. Some question this similar lack of self-protection in the sexual abuse victim.

Finkelhor (1984, pp. 36–37) suggests that the practitioner ask several questions regarding the perpetrator's role competency in the sexual abuse situation. First, there is the question of *how sexual contact with a child can be emotionally congruent.* In answer, Finkelhor cites studies of arrested psychological development in child molesters as individuals who experience themselves as children. In addition, he points out that immaturity, low self-esteem, distorted control needs, and unresolved childhood trauma are mechanisms that inhibit the perpetrator from preparing competently for the parental role.

A second question revolves about *the ability of these individuals to be sexually aroused by a child* and their seeming inability to be gratified from a more normatively acceptable source. Blockage of normal sexual development may play a role here as might repressive sexual norms overall, according to Finkelhor. Situational blockage of sexual needs through crisis or loss of relationship must also be included here (Finkelhor, 1984, pp. 43–44).

Finally, it must be asked why this perpetrator *is capable of looking beyond conventional social inhibitions regarding sexual contact between adults and children.* Finkelhor (1984, p. 45) notes the common findings of impulse control problems, senility, substance abuse, mental illness, or some combination of these factors as partial answers. Situational stresses found in loss (e.g., death) may exacerbate these features of the perpetrator's life and push this undercontrolled and incompetent parent into a sexually abusive act.

Ultimately, according to Finkelhor (1981, pp. 3–8) the practitioner must determine why this perpetrator has sexual feelings toward children, how the individual overcame both internal and external restraints against this sort of behavior, and what the perpetrator was willing to do to overcome the child-victim's reluctance to participate. These are important for it is only when these four preconditions are met that sexual abuse occurs. No matter how they are answered, this adult is obviously far too incompetent to play the role of parent.

Many indications of incompetence and under-preparation have been related in the situation involving *mistreatment of the elderly.* The perpetrator may be underprepared for the role of caretaker. The victim may be underprepared for their role as dependent adult. Society is undeniably underprepared to provide the sorts of supports needed by the family caring for the elderly person in the home (Pedrick-Cornell & Gelles, 1982).

The decision to move an older person into the home is one made in haste. There may be no conceivable emotional alternative ("But he's my father!") and no realistic financial alternative (Anderson, 1981, p. 78; Steinmetz, 1983, p. 138). Unfortunately, however, this decision is frequently made in the absence of any recognition of how underprepared almost all persons are for the demands of this caregiving task. Adding this single variable to the family environment may move the whole family from a competent place of caregiving and security to a potentially explosive environment.

Ultimately, when the individuals in the family who must be competent for the family to be safe are not competent, external help is required. Some cases may present with such urgency that legal intervention, as described in the next section, is required.

Part IV

**Capturing the Family Violence
Practitioners' Environment (I):
Legal Work and the Violent Family**

9

The Legal Environment
of Child Maltreatment

A s in the other forms of family violence, alternative court structures and proceedings are available in cases of child maltreatment. Legal proceedings intended to protect children may be
brought in the juvenile court, and criminal prosecution of the perpetrator may also be available under state codes (Caulfield, 1978).
Other than capital cases, the usual forum for dealing with issues
associated with child maltreatment is the juvenile court. The proceedings of the juvenile court are often more informal than criminal
proceedings and have treatment and family reunification as goals
rather than punishment. The juvenile court's ostensible focus is the
welfare of the child and the rehabilitation of the family. However, a
review of concerns with both the intervention and disposition phases
of this court's operation will reveal that many are skeptical about the
court's benevolent results.

Juvenile court proceedings have two distinct phases: adjudication
and disposition. The adjudication phase is marked by the state's
responsibility to prove the facts that justify the exercise of jurisdiction
over the minor child. The state must prove, usually by a
preponderance of the evidence, that the child has been maltreated as
defined by state law. If jurisdiction is established, the court moves
forward to the dispositional phase and determines the steps necessary
to treat both child and family. Most critical in this decision process is
the determination of where the child's custody will rest (Fraser, 1978).

In making decisions, the "best interests of the child" is the standard applied. Using this standard, the juvenile court judge holds the

power to allow the child to remain with his/her parents under the supervision of a child protection specialist, to remove the child from the home and place him or her in an alternative living situation (for example, with relatives, foster parents, or a residential treatment facility), and in extreme cases, may move toward termination of parental rights with an eye toward adoption or permanent foster placement. Justifiably, the exercise of this degree of decision making over the entire life outcome of a child and family does not go unexamined or uncriticized.

Controversy surrounds both the intervention and disposition phases of the juvenile court process. Complex questions regarding unwarranted interference with family autonomy, deficiencies in definitional structures for child maltreatment, and parental or children's rights are raised regarding adjudication hearings. Equally complex questions regarding placement decisions, judicial discretion, right to treatment, and failures to review decisions are raised about disposition. These issues will be reviewed here.

The Intervention Decision

Davidson (1980, p. 4) has written,

> The rights of the family to privacy and integrity have been recognized as fundamental and of constitutional significance. Due process is therefore required before the state intervenes into the lives of children and parents.

There is a serious concern today as to whether such due process rights are being protected by the child protection system and the juvenile court. In the typical substantiated child maltreatment situation, dependency proceedings are initiated by a child being taken into some form of protective custody by a child protective services worker or law enforcement officer. Due process (notice and an opportunity to be heard) may well follow the taking of the child (Weinerman, 1981). The reason for this apparent reversal is over-riding concern for the safety of the child. State intrusion into the family without prior court approval is lawful when a person authorized by the state to act does so with knowledge of facts that would lead a person of ordinary prudence and caution to believe that there is an immediate danger to the physical health or safety of the child and there is insufficient time to obtain a court order (Sampson, 1978). Of parallel concern is that the parents of this child, whether the case is ultimately substantiated or not, often find themselves on a central registry of suspected abusive parents as a result of this initial (even if erroneous) intervention. Both of these actions, obviously, raise concern regarding family autonomy and degree of official intervention.

Family Autonomy and State Intrusion: The Call for Reform

The call for reform in the legal approach to child maltreatment begins with an examination of the emergency removal powers described earlier. Concern rests with the fact that this removal precedes any court involvement and only mandates a hearing within a brief period for the court to determine whether this emergency removal (without notice and a hearing) was justified. Of additional concern is the issue of whether the child should remain outside the home pending a full hearing on the issues brought forward by the dependency petition. The call for reform of emergency removal proceedings is based not only on the immediate disruption of the family, but the fact that the emergency placement often becomes the temporary (or longer) placement of the child pending adjudication.

The other common threads in the call for reform are the demand for more objective standards and an increased respect for and preservation of family autonomy. In reality, the present standards empowering the court to intervene in the lives of parents and children are little changed from the laws passed in the nineteenth century. They are vague, open-ended, require highly subjective determinations, and permit intervention not only when the child has been harmed or is endangered, but also when parental habits or attitudes conflict with societal values (Mnookin, 1974). Decision making in this area is far from reliable, and invalid choices are made daily. In fact, such decisions have been described as highly subjective and value-laden, which may result in intervention based solely on a judge's opinion on proper child-rearing practice or environment (Uviller, 1980).

The most frequently heard criticism of existing standards for intervention refers to the subjectivity in decision making; usually due to elusive definitions. The definitions in the law in this area simply do not provide child protection practitioners such as law enforcement officers, social workers, prosecutors, or judges objective measures for appropriate intervention. Poor and minority families, in particular, have suffered from the vague and imprecise statutory language in this area as any child rearing practice that is not in accord with those of state officials making the intervention decision may result in removal (Goldstein, Freud, & Solnit, 1979; Hampton, 1984).

Davidson (1981) echoes this position through criticism that child maltreatment statutes fail to define the bases for intervention and do not define the maltreatment itself either precisely or appropriately. He urges the removal of such phrases as "without proper care" and "injurious to the child's welfare" in favor of specific descriptions of maltreatment. Child maltreatment expert Michael Wald (1980, 1982) has called for similar clarification in definitions. Douglas Besharov, former director of the National Center on Child Abuse and Neglect, applies his years of legal study of this problem and concludes that existing law may be criticized in this area for it places too much responsibility on social workers and judges (1985). According to Besharov (1985), child maltreatment laws should make clear the inability to predict future maltreatment, eliminate preventive juris- diction, and authorize intervention only when parents have already maltreated their child(ren), except in very limited circumstances. Clearly, the emphasis is moving toward recognition of better defini- tions and family autonomy.

Family Autonomy

The preference for family autonomy is a point of agreement among the advocates for legislation limiting intervention. Goldstein and colleagues (1979) indicate that the break in family integrity is detrimental to the child's development. Wald (1982) characterizes parental autonomy as a basic tenet of our laws, as comporting with a value preference for diversity of lifestyles and as consistent with existing knowledge of child rearing. Children simply develop best when raised by their parents (Wald, 1980). Wald (1982) also suggests that family autonomy is to be preferred because of the growing fear that coercive intervention and the removal of children from their homes into foster care may do more harm than good. The authors of a recently completed ten-year view of children in alternative forms of placement following legal actions in child maltreatment situations note there is little evidence of the effectiveness of coercive interventions (Wald, Carlsmith, Leiderman, French, & Smith, 1985).

Proposals for Limiting Intervention

The most restrictive view of intervention has been urged by Goldstein and colleagues (1979). The exclusive grounds for intervention proposed by this dual discipline group (attorney and psychiatrist) as they relate to child maltreatment are; conviction of a sexual offense against one's child, serious bodily harm inflicted by parents upon their child(ren), an attempt to inflict such injury, the repeated failure to prevent their child(ren) from suffering such injury, and refusal by parents to authorize medical care when experts agree that treatment is (1) nonexperimental, (2) appropriate, and (3) anticipates a result that would provide a chance for normal healthy growth or a life worth living. Except in emergencies involving the risk of serious bodily injury to the child, these authors suggest that parents should be left free to continue care for the child.

The Juvenile Justice Standards Project of the Institute of Judicial Administration and the American Bar Association promulgated its *Standards Relating to Abuse and Neglect* in 1977. These standards favored a strong presumption for family autonomy. One of the stated goals of the *Standards* was to limit intervention to cases in which it is reasonably probable that coercive intervention will do more good than harm (Flannery, 1979). Intervention is also proposed to be limited to specific harms suffered or likely to be suffered. The proposed grounds for intervention are to be limited to serious nonaccidental bodily injury or the imminent threat of serious nonaccidental bodily injury, failure to protect the child from such injury, serious emotional damage and the parents unwilling to provide treatment, sexual abuse by a parent, failure to provide needed medical treatment, and the committing of delinquent acts by a child as a result of parental encouragement or approval. Finally, the court must also find that the intervention is necessary to protect this child from endangerment in the future (Flannery, 1979; American Bar Association, 1977, Sections 2.1, 2.2). Obviously, these *Standards* were influenced by issues similar to those brought forward by the Goldstein group. However, not all child maltreatment professionals are in agreement with the standards.

Criticism of the restrictions of these standards have been voiced by Bourne and Newberger (1979), who believe that any reform in statutory standards should reflect different degrees of intrusion upon family autonomy and less intrusive methods of intervention. Specifically, Bourne and Newberger disagree with the *Standards'* distrust of unrequested state intervention and oppose the ban upon intervention in cases of nonserious harm.

Bourne and Newberger (1979) believe that the jurisdiction of the court should be divided into two separate categories: to order services and to order removal. Their criticisms and this suggestion are based upon the *Standards'* jurisdictional limits without regard to the nature of the intervention sought. The same grave level of harm that would justify removal constitutes the exclusive occasion for all unrequested state intervention.

On the other side of their suggested scheme, Bourne and Newberger (1979, p. 100) propose that "to establish jurisdiction to order services, the petitioner should have to show by clear and convincing evidence that the child has suffered or will imminently suffer physical and emotional harm, serious or nonserious." Wald (1982) comments that less deference to family autonomy when the intervention is less intrusive is not valid. This is particularly true due to the paucity of evidence of the usefulness of coercive social services. Moreover, until state legislatures are willing to fund concrete services (e.g., day care, homemaker services), it is not reasonable to consider the type of divergence of jurisdiction suggested (Wald, 1982). According to Wald, current circumstances dictate the limitation of jurisdiction for intervention to serious harm.

Wald (1982), whose earlier work served as the basis for the *Juvenile Justice Standards* has concluded after five years of study and reflection that the *Standards'* restriction of jurisdiction of courts to intervene in cases of abuse and neglect should not be changed. The existing evidence, in his view, still justifies a cautious policy for intervention.

Wald (1982) urges that laws regulating state intervention be drafted as specifically as possible in order to limit the discretion of decision makers. He concludes that specific rules will produce better results than leaving decision making to the discretion of judges and social workers. In practice, this will also relieve social workers and law enforcement officers of some measure of the burden they carry personally. Judges in many jurisdictions, according to Wald, lack training relevant to making the intervention and disposition decision, and current statutes have been applied in an arbitrary and discriminatory manner. Specific standards are more likely to be applied in an even-handed way without economic or cultural discrimination. Finally, he notes that funding questions cannot be ignored in evaluating standards for intervention. The most efficient use of resources is to intervene well in serious cases rather than poorly in larger numbers of cases (Wald, 1982).

After more than fifteen years of being closely involved in legal reforms in child maltreatment, Besharov has formulated a current call for reforms in this area. Besharov (1985) proposes that laws be redrafted so that child protective intervention is authorized only when the parents have already engaged in maltreating behaviors. Limiting state action to situations of past wrongful conduct is the criminal law's posture, and it has equal validity for protective intervention for children in Besharov's view. The only two exceptions proposed by Besharov are where the parents are suffering from demonstrable and severe mental disabilities and where parents of infants or very young children report that they feel themselves slipping out of control and fear they may hurt or kill the children.

In this scheme, Besharov (1985) does not advocate that parents must seriously injure their child(ren) for the behavior to be considered abusive or for it to be the subject of child protective proceedings. He proposes that intervention be authorized if the parent did something that could have caused serious injury. By having engaged in seriously harmful behavior once, Besharov sees the parents as having demonstrated that they are a continuing threat to their children. Child protective intervention should also be authorized if the parent's behavior was capable of seriously injuring the child.

Besharov further proposes that the law should recognize two categories of seriously harmful behavior: immediately harmful behavior and cumulatively harmful behavior. Laws defining seriously harmful behavior could provide judges and social agencies all the preventive jurisdiction they require. Such laws would authorize intervention to prevent a child from being seriously injured, but only after clear evidence of the need is established. Child protective intervention in response to the past seriously harmful behavior of parents is based on the reasonable assumption that they will do it again. This approach to standards for state intervention would minimize unreasonable expectations about what protective workers and judges can accomplish, helping to relieve the unfairness under which they are working, both personally and professionally. It must be remembered that the person forced to make decisions under a law that provides little guidance may suffer as well.

Issues in Disposition

Following the finding of the court that the child victim has been maltreated, the court assumes jurisdiction over the child and is empowered to determine a remedy or disposition. The remedies or dispositions usually available to the juvenile court judge include permitting the child to remain in the home under supervision, placement outside the home, and in the most extreme cases, termination of parent rights, thus permitting the child to be established in another permanent placement. In arriving at these decisions, the juvenile court judge is statutorily bound to apply the "best interests of the child" standard.

The first controversy to be faced in the dispositional phase of juvenile court proceedings concerns this standard that has long been applied. The simple question is, what is the best interest of a particular child and how does the court go about determining it? This is a standard that has been roundly criticized in recent years, not only as a result of its subjectivity, but because the outcome for children who have been placed pursuant to this standard has not been uniformly positive. There is additional concern that judges applying this standard may be applying their personal values (Mnookin, 1981) or merely rubber stamping agency recommendations (Hoekstra, 1984). As a result of these concerns, there are an abundance of alternative suggested standards.

The initial publication of Goldstein, Freud, and Solnit (1973) proposed that, in the place of the "best interest" standard, a more reasonable approach might be the "least detrimental alternative." Following that offering, Mnookin (1974) also advocated replacing the standard. His rejection of the "best interests" approach was based on its need for "individualized determinations based on discretionary assessment of the best interest of the child," which, according to Mnookin, cannot be make objectively and fairly (1974, pp. 160–161).

Mnookin believes that the "best interest" test makes it too easy for a judge to remove a child from parental custody. Judicial discretion to remove children should be more limited and more objective (e.g., the state should remove only in the presence of immediate and substantial danger to the child's health and no alternative means of protection). Mnookin also suggests that the court be required to articulate its reasons for concluding that removal was necessary as well as a description of its consideration and rejection of less drastic alternatives.

Mnookin (1974) proposes that removal from the home be a last resort and used only when the child cannot be protected in the home. He further proposes that the decision to use foster care be based on legal standards that can be applied consistently and fairly; not subject to the influence of the values of a particular judge. Finally, when removal does prove necessary, according to Mnookin (1974), the state should be required to help the child's parents to overcome the problems that led to removal as a first step toward family reunification. In a related issue, he notes the need for a maximum period of foster placement at the end of which termination of parental rights would occur if the home remained unsafe.

The *Juvenile Justice Standards* (1977) also call for reduced discretion in placement decisions once the grounds for intervention have been established. The *Standards* permit removal only if the child has been physically abused or endangered and cannot be protected without being removed. Removal must also be conditioned on the court's finding that a suitable placement is available. If removal has been ordered, the *Standards* require that efforts be made to facilitate return of the child as soon as possible (Flannery, 1979).

If the disposition in the maltreatment case is other than removal, the *Standards* propose services that least interfere with parental autonomy, yet protect the child, be chosen. Consistent with the *Standards'* policy of least interference, periodic reviews of possible termination of services should be undertaken. The *Standards* would require that the court review whether conditions still exist requiring intervention every six months. Jurisdiction over the child would automatically terminate after eighteen months unless, pursuant to a hearing, clear and convincing evidence were presented that the child would still be endangered if services were withdrawn (*Standards*, 1977, Section 7.4). For children placed outside the home, return would be considered by the court every six months and the child returned upon showing by a preponderance of evidence that the child will not be endangered (Section 7.5). The *Standards* also provide time- and age-related guidelines for termination of parental rights assuming a child cannot be returned (Section 8).

On these issues, Wald (1982) continues to urge caution in removal of the child and urges no modification of the *Standards* in this regard. Wald also proposes that parental rights should be terminated after 12 months if the child is under the age of three and after 18 months if older than three and cannot be returned home. Wald also continues to reject the "best interests" test as a basis for removal.

Wald notes that, under current state laws, children are permitted to remain in foster care as long as it is in their best interests. However, laws regarding termination do not allow it solely on the basis of the child's best interests. As a result, children may become legally locked into foster care. The standards proposed by Wald (1982) alter both the law on return and termination; the court must review all cases within six months of placement and every six months thereafter to determine whether the child should be returned or parental rights terminated. Return would be ordered unless the child is likely to suffer one of the harms justifying initial removal or unless there is clear and convincing evidence that return of the child would create a substantial risk of detriment to the physical or emotional well-being of the child. The focus of the inquiry is harm to the child, not the child's best interests.

Besharov (1985) relates the increase in the number of children in foster placement to the states' failures to establish long-term treatment services for maltreating parents. In his opinion, up to half of the children in foster care could have safely been left with their parents had proper and limited standards for removal existed. Foster care should only be permitted for children whose parents have engaged in "immediately harmful behavior" and services short of removal cannot adequately protect the child. Removal for "cumulatively harmful behavior" would be prohibited unless (1) the parents refuse to cooperate with the services needed to protect the child, (2) the child needs services only available in residential care, (3) there are irreconcilable conflicts between parent and adolescent child, or (4) as an interim step to a planned termination of parental rights (Besharov, 1985). There are, obviously, some situations that do require emergency removal.

Emergency Removal Reforms

For family conditions that may require emergency removal, several standards have been proposed. The *Juvenile Justice Standards* (1977) limit emergency temporary custody of children pending adjudication to situations where the person authorized by state law to remove the child has probable cause to believe that the emergency is necessary to prevent the child's "imminent death or serious bodily injury" (*Standards*, 1977, Section 4.1). Wald (1980) concurs in noting that removal pending adjudication be limited to cases of "extreme physical danger." Besharov (1985) also applies his scheme of immediately harmful behavior and cumulatively harmful behavior by proposing that emergency removal be authorized in the former situation, noting that a victim of cumulatively harmful behavior does not need immediate rescue.

The overall view of current work in both intervention and disposition seems to be that the juvenile courts have been too enthusiastic in their approach to these cases. Definitions that are not sufficiently restrictive permitted child protection specialists of all types to make decisions. These decisions have not been subject to monitoring and have all too often proven less than helpful to the on-going development of the child. Legal authorities are currently calling for a moderating in legal approaches and a great emphasis on the family's right to rear a child as they deem appropriate, assuming no physical harm will result. The problem for the practitioner becomes one of working within a legal environment that must be manipulated in such a way to benefit both child and family. The suggestion here, as in other sections of the work, err in the direction of the victim.

The Practitioner in the Legal Environment of Physical Child Maltreatment

Representing the Parents

In representing the parent(s) in the child maltreatment case, the role of the parent's attorney is clear; he or she must represent the interest of the client zealously within the bounds of the law. Fulfilling that role, when representing parents in a juvenile court proceeding, may take different forms. It may mean conceding jurisdiction. It may mean negotiating a dismissal in exchange for the acceptance of voluntary services. It may mean developing a treatment plan for the entire family to be offered as an alternative to the social service agency's plan. It may mean monitoring the agency after disposition to ensure that services are provided. Or, it may mean using an expert witness to counter the expert opinion offered by the state regarding the best interest of the child. It may mean all of those things. What must remain paramount in the attorney's mind, however, is that he or she represents the parents, not the child or the social services agency, and the parent's decision regarding the desired goals of the proceeding must guide the attorney's actions. As in any other case, the attorney's view of what is best is not controlling; the parents' view is. (Davidson, 1980; Duquette, 1981; Weinerman, 1981).

Representing the Child

The role of the child's attorney is less clear than that of representing the parents. The lawyer is often charged with representing the child and the best interest of the child. If the child client is too young to articulate his or her views or is old enough to state a position, but it is one with which the attorney disagrees, the question arises as to what the attorney should advocate. Duquette (1981) notes that if the attorney for the child is to decide what is in the child's best interest, nothing in his or her training has equipped the attorney (1) to assess parental conduct, (2) to appraise harms to the child, (3) to recognize strengths in the parent-child relationship, or (4) to evaluate the soundness of an intervention strategy proposed by the social services agency. Duquette (1981) suggests that the attorney for the child should come to an independent judgment as to what will be best for the child and then advocate for that position. Obviously, one must question why this author stated all the reasons why the attorney is unprepared to draw independent judgment and then recommends exactly that. It is easily anticipated that this view is a controversial one.

There is a great deal of disagreement with the view that the attorney become an advocate for the best interests of the child. Davidson (1980) notes that the child's lawyer is bound to the same standards of professional responsibility as lawyers for adults. If the child can express his or her wishes to an attorney, Davidson feels the attorney must represent the child's desires. When the child is mature enough to have a clear understanding of his or her interests, the attorney must unequivocally advocate for what the child wants. Davidson suggests that when the child is very young, the attorney is really functioning as a guardian ad litem whether or not he or she has been specifically appointed as such. A guardian ad litem is specifically charged with representing the child's best interests (Fraser, 1978; Long, 1982).

In further consideration of whether the attorney should represent the child's view, other experts also advocate for listening to the child. Long (1982) suggests that the guardian ad litem issue, the questions of differential age, and changing roles in specific cases are not relevant. She suggests, instead, that the attorney for the child represent the child's view whenever possible. Ramsey (1983) likewise recommends advocacy of the child's viewpoint and proposes a standard for lawyers to assist in the child's decision-making abilities. She recommends that a child with the mental and emotional capability to make a decision that has a "reasonable possibility of accuracy" should be able to have his or her view advocated (Ramsey, 1983, p. 306). She further suggests that the attorney judge the child's decision-making ability by assessing the child's ability to understand, reason, and communicate. Finally, she offers that lawyers use presumptions of capacity based on the child's age; children under seven would be presumed to be without capacity. This is a presumption that has been discussed by others.

Guggenheim (1984) agrees that children seven years of age and older be permitted to direct their counsel in protection proceedings. For children under age seven, he believes that courts should re-examine the need for appointed counsel. He is in accord with the view of Goldstein and colleagues (1973) that the lawyer for a child under seven years of age should side with the parents until jurisdiction is established and the parents are disqualified as the exclusive voice in how the child is raised. Once jurisdiction is established Guggenheim (1984) suggests that the lawyer alter his or her role and oversee enforcement of visitation, implementation of the treatment plan, and guarantee the periodic review of placement. For children under seven, he sees the role of either investigator or advocate as being inappropriate.

A Summary View

The summary view of the juvenile court in the maltreatment situation is a somewhat confusing one. The decisions of the court make promises of help that are not fulfilled. The rights of the family may be over-ridden by the protection of the child, but that protection is sometimes not forthcoming. The role of the attorney is one that guarantees this protection. Expert opinions, intervention strategies, and dispositional alternatives inclusive, the attorney must come out of the case feeling that the child has been protected or the conduct of their role has not been complete. Like many other professional roles with violent families, this is not one that ends with a judicial decision for the promises of agencies following disposition decisions are rarely kept in full. Only the legal practitioner can monitor such promises with authority. These are the burdens of the legal practitioner in the family violence case and are burdens that are carried across each manifestation of violence in the family, as the following chapters will confirm.

10

The Legal Environment of the Child Sexual Abuse Situation

The child sexual abuse situation provides both personal and professional dilemmas for most legal practitioners. In addition to the personal and legal position to be established regarding punishment versus rehabilitation, that is control versus compassion (Newberger & Bourne, 1979a), there is one more difficult problem: the protection of the child victim from secondary victimization sometimes suffered through the vagaries of a legal system ostensibly designed to prevent such victimization. What is required is a balancing of the needs of the legal system against the needs of the child. The legal environments in which this balance must occur are precariously narrow in their construction.

Establishing a Protective Environment: The Use of Criminal Versus Juvenile Procedures and Settings

The professional view of child sexual abuse is currently undergoing some alteration. The humanistic "family systems" or "psychiatrically ill perpetrator" views that have marked the past two decades of system response are finding their place within a larger perspective that the sexual abuse of children is a crime. The public is generally resistant to the impersonality of judicial decisions in family problems (Finkelhor, 1984). However, in the case of child sexual abuse, public and professional groups alike seem to be moving toward increasing amounts of judicial control in such situations. There is room for compassion, but only with the assurance that the victim will be protected.

The major elements of victim protection and perpetrator control today are the authority of the criminal court and the strength of its prosecutorial decisions. The application of these two powerful elements are being applauded in all forms of family violence. For example, the *Final Report of the Attorney General's Task Force on Family Violence* (1984, p. 5) noted that

> the first indispensable step in preventing family violence is to ensure that abusers and victims alike recognize that a crime is involved and that, when appropriate, the legal system will intervene on the victim's behalf.

In essence, this report echoed the sentiment being offered through many public groups and state legislatures that the legal system must convey a message to family violence perpetrators that their behavior is a crime and will not be tolerated. Practical application of this message, according to the Attorney General's Task Force, means the exercise of flexibility at the point of disposition, not prosecution.

Criminal prosecution is not without therapeutic value. Kempe and Kempe (1984, p. 85) applaud the increasing use of criminal sanctions as a result of their superior ability to protect the victim and provide that victim a sense of security. That is a protectiveness sometimes unavailable in previous approaches to the problem, which found their control in the therapeutic rather than the legal setting. In addition, Kempe and Kempe (1984) find value in the necessity of admission of guilt in criminal prosecution. Until guilt has been admitted, in their view, therapeutic efforts can always be undermined through the projection of responsibility on an amorphous illness. This projection is detrimental to successful therapy in that the perpetrator will believe that they successfully manipulated the system (1984, p. 90). This escape from the recognition of responsibility, according to Armstrong (1983), provides the green light to become sexually involved with a child victim again. Therapeutic benefits aside, the criminal prosecution position reveals other strengths.

First, criminal prosecution does serve the traditional function of protecting not only the victim but society at large. This is a critical feature in child sexual abuse, especially given recent suggestion

(Conte, 1984a) that the in-home perpetrator may also be a child molester in some cases. Second, this is a mechanism by which practitioners can assure themselves that the victim will be safe, the goal of intervention in all cases. The criminal court retains discretion over such potentially volatile perpetrator-victim issues as pretrial release, vacation of the home, and probationary conditions (Bulkley & Davidson, 1981). And, very importantly, this court can provide for court-ordered treatment through the leverage of diversion or incarceration (Kocen & Bulkley, 1984). This is the type of lever, as mentioned in later clinical sections, that provides a near guarantee of attendance at treatment, thereby increasing the possibility of success. Yet the criminal courts do have some distance to travel in protecting the victim, particularly when the victim is within the courtroom itself.

A major historical complaint against criminal prosecution and one that persists today, is the focus of the criminal courts on the prosecution of the offender. This is a focus that may lead to the needs of the child victim being overlooked or at least subordinated (DeFrancis, 1969). As early as 1969, in a preview of what has become a major issue today, DeFrancis advocated against criminal prosecution as a result of his belief that the prosecution itself often caused more serious emotional damage to the child than the sexually abusive event itself. The current frame for this problem is that of *iatrogenic* or secondary victimization which comes from being involved in the protection system itself. This is a system-induced trauma that is seen by some as anti-therapeutic and discouraging for the family involved (Wulkan & Bulkley, 1984) to this day. This trauma will be discussed at length in a later section of this chapter.

The movement from the juvenile court to the criminal court has been a shift that is worrisome to many legal and clinical practitioners. The juvenile court, with good reason, has been seen as a humane and flexible court, particularly as a result of the judge's ultimate concern for the best interests of the child rather than the prosecution of the perpetrator (Bulkley & Davidson, 1981). With respect to the child sexual abuse situation specifically, it has been suggested that the parents may be less likely to contest the charge of sexual abuse in a juvenile court and that they will more readily seek treatment in the absence of the threat of criminal prosecution (Bulkley & Davidson, 1981). Unfortunately, these are hopes that have not been borne out in practice.

The indirect powers of the juvenile court in most jurisdictions reveal themselves as not equal to the task of dealing with the repetitively abusive family. The indirect control over the parents or perpetrator does not seem adequate to arrive at the logistical necessities in many of these cases, such as having the perpetrator eliminate all contact with the child. This may lead to a need for the child to be removed, seemingly placing the wrong-doing on the victim instead of the perpetrator. If the perpetrator is not a parent, his or her distance from this court is even greater. In some cases, the intractable and judicially experienced family may simply not take these proceedings as seriously as they do those of a criminal nature (Bulkley & Davidson, 1981). The answer seems to be a greater use of the criminal court with the addition of successful juvenile court experiences such as diversion programs.

In summary, the trend today is the criminal prosecution of sexually abusive perpetrators whether in the family or external to the family. This provides a great sense of control, compliance, and security to the child victim. There is assurance in the criminal process that the perpetrator recognizes his or her commission of a crime, accepts responsibility for its occurrence, and is committed to some course of action that may be monitored and observed in outcome. It is a less than perfect system as it exists today as children remain traumatized in some circumstances. Overall, however, given the lack of certainty that safety for the victim can be gained through therapeutic endeavors exclusively, the partnership of criminal courts, juvenile courts, and the clinicians/legal professionals who carry out their mandates seems to be our most effective response to date. Unfortunately, for all that we have learned in these two courts, the appearance of sexual abuse allegations in yet another court, the domestic relations or family court, is revealing, once again, how little is certain in working with these families.

Child Sexual Abuse in the Domestic Relations Court: Discovery or Destructiveness?

Sexual abuse allegations may occur unexpectedly in the course of the legal practitioner's work. Such an allegation in the midst of a domestic relations matter, such as divorce or custody modification is one such possibility. In fact, the increasing numbers of such allegations in the domestic relations setting is becoming not only a growing reality but a serious concern. This concern settles in several specific areas.

Credibility of Reporting Source

All practitioners familiar with the domestic relations case are familiar with irrational anger. The sexual abuse allegation may be a manifestation of that anger. Quite simply, the pain that is engendered in being the subject of a sexual abuse investigation (Stone et al., 1984) may serve as punishment at the hands of an ex-spouse with unfinished anger eating away at their rationality. In some cases the pain experienced by the child is ignored. In the worst cases, in the authors' experience, the injury is inflicted upon the child simply to provide the opportunity to punish the ex-spouse in this way.

Credibility of the Victim

The general perception of child specialists is that children neither manufacture nor fantasize sexual assaults (Summit, 1985). While comfortable with this belief in juvenile and criminal matters, clinicians are somewhat less sanguine in the domestic courts where children are possibly influenced by parental urgings. There is a particular problem with the younger preschool child whose verbal abilities do not lend themselves to certainty in confirmation. In the absence of clear physical evidence, there is a quandry especially in determining the identity of the perpetrator.

Practitioners are encouraged to avail their clients of all possible tests of credibility in these cases. For the child who is not verbally proficient such projective techniques as drawings, doll play, or anatomically correct doll examinations should not be accepted unchallenged. All data regarding the family must be synthesized to arrive at a credible conclusion, practitioners should not simply rely on the child's report. Currently, an addition to traditional investigation is the stipulated polygraph of both parents. A technique drawn from German courts entitled "Statement Reality Analysis" is currently being researched as a possible addition to the clinician's arsenal of techniques for determining truth in these cases.

Hyper-Vigilance in the Reporting Source

Current media and professional fascination with the sexually abused child has set the stage for problems. Parents of all types are ever vigilant for "stranger danger" in their neighborhoods, school, and their child's entertainment or recreational settings. The home of the ex-spouse is not above suspicion. When this is an ex-spouse who harbors a great deal of animosity toward the other, vigilance is increased. In some cases, it is not difficult for a custodial parent (joint or otherwise) to believe that a hated ex-spouse, the ex-spouse's new conjugal partner(s), or their friends could be involved in an act of this sort.

Under-Responsiveness of Protective Agencies

Although empirically elusive, there is a belief that parents in joint custody of children are seen as less credible when making a report of suspected assault against the other parent (ex-spouse) or persons in their environment. If a situation is perceived as a "custody beef" or "harrassment," the reality is that skepticism may greet the reporter. In such cases, a call directly from the parent's attorney usually gains immediate attention.

Underappreciation of the Child's Suffering

Despite the adversarial nature of the relationship between the parents' respective legal counsel in a domestic relations case, both attorneys should temper that adversariness at the time of a sexual abuse allegation and consider the child. When a sexual abuse allegation is made, the child must be protected. To facilitate the protection of the child, Bulkley (1985) suggests that domestic violence statutes, although originally designed for victims of conjugal violence, are often written broadly enough to allow the practitioner to petition the court for a protective order. That protective order may prohibit the alleged perpetrator from contact with the child.

In the domestic relations situation both parents may be suspected. When a sexual abuse allegation is made, the question may arise as to whether the complaining parent concocted the allegation, or in extreme cases, was the actual perpetrator, using the allegation as a weapon against the other parent. There may be no physical evidence that sexual abuse occurred, and the child may be too young to confirm or deny the allegation.

The attorneys must inform their clients of their statutory duty to report suspected abuse to the child protection agency. Placement of the child in some setting that guarantees first safety then neutrality may facilitate reaching the truth. Since both parents ostensibly want to learn the truth and protect the child from future abuse, the attorneys should be able to convince their respective clients that reporting and even temporary placement is the best course of action.

A Summary View

A summary view would find the sexual abuse allegation to be a possibility across the span of the practitioner's contact with families. No court is immune from such an allegation. The key to adequate responsiveness is to understand that the child requires the protection of the practitioner first, even when the client is the adult. The hatred and bile that may exist in the domestic relations dispute is a fertile medium for the generation of pain and punishment through such an allegation. Once in motion, the secondary victimization that may result from the investigation of a sexual abuse allegation may occur. The practitioner must first protect the child alleged-victim as much as possible, then facilitate the investigation through the protection of their client's rights. Unfortunately, owing to the huge definitional gaps that exist between clinical and legal approaches to the problem of sexual abuse of children, this is often a difficult task.

Clinical Versus Legal Definitions of Sexual Abuse: Never the Twain Shall Meet

That which is considered a "sexual assault" by clinicians and that which constitutes "incest" under the law is quite different in many respects. However, the distance between these definitions can be understood from a historical perspective.

Incest was not a crime at common law. Rather, it originated as a religious offense (Wulkan & Bulkley, 1984). As such, the focus of incest law has been to prohibit marriage between close relatives and somewhat secondarily deal with the sexual matters implied (Bratt, 1984). Even when sexual assault is given consideration, it tends to be limited to sexual intercourse. This can be cumbersome for it demands the inclusion of such issues as proof of penetration as well as other specific and narrow definitions of sexual contact. Sexual abuse can be prosecuted under these statutes, but the practitioner will find much more flexible assistance available.

Most older incest statutes are definitionally inadequate for prosecution of much sexual abuse. This is particularly true as the legal practitioner and clinical practitioner work in tandem. The clinician's view of sexual assault upon a child extends from intercourse (sexual abuse) to much less obvious sexualized behavior such as inappropriate wrestling or exposure to adult sexuality (sexual misuse) (Brandt & Tisza, 1978). Any adequate definitional structure must reach beyond sexual intercourse and include all the forms of sexual behavior and exploitation to which a child may be subjected (Bratt, 1984). Fortunately, this is a recognition that is becoming shared across the nation.

Reform legislation that better defines the sexual acts occurring between adults and children have been adopted in many jurisdictions. New descriptions of sex crimes against children are replacing older perspectives on varying degrees of statutory rape. The age of both victim and perpetrator, as well as their relationship, is considered in establishing the severity of the offense. The adult being in a position of parent or in an authoritarian role that might encourage the child to submit removes any defense of consentual sexual contact between that adult and child (Kocen & Bulkley, 1984). New approaches to the child molester and sexual psychopath not only better define circumstances but increase the probability of treatment in some cases (Bulkley, 1984).

Yet even in the absence of such new legal weapons, the practitioner is reminded of the utility of criminal statutes of general applicability in such cases. Those statutes that concentrate upon such acts as assault, battery, contributing to the delinquency of a minor, rape, and sodomy may also have application in the child sexual abuse case (Sloan, 1983a). Some more specifically approaching sexual contact with the intent to sexually arouse the child or perpetrator, those in the child molestation area, and those which prohibit lewd and lascivious acts and indecent liberties with children have also proven useful (Kocen & Bulkley, 1984).

Ultimately, all states will provide usable statutes that define child sexual abuse in the scope of their respective child maltreatment statutes. Most states, have reasonably productive and useful perspectives now. These child abuse statutes are clearly the most useful alternative across most situations (Bratt, 1984). The point is they were not generated overnight, and mistakes were made in their development. This should serve as a warning signal to those who would rush to develop new techniques to protect the child sexual abuse victim in the courtroom. As the next section will illustrate, it is beginning to appear that seemingly logical protections for the child victim, such as video technology may not be the panacea that was promised.

Process-Induced Trauma in the Child Victim of Sexual Abuse: Secondary Victimization

As has been mentioned elsewhere in this work, a child's involvement in the protection system is often a traumatic experience in itself. Both critics and advocates of criminal prosecution of child sexual abuse perpetrators recognize this potential for trauma to the child victim and both are concerned. In some cases this concern is related to the degree of emotional distress experienced by the child victim. In other cases the concern is that a traumatized victim may reduce the likelihood of conviction. Both remain factors in case planning (Rogers, 1982).

From the clinical side, it is well known that the degree of psychic trauma experienced by the child victim is directly related to the way the child is treated after discovery (Libai, 1980). *Legal process trauma* is one feature of this disruptive experience. While clinicians admit to difficulty in the measurement of legal process trauma in the midst of the other disruptions in the victim's life at this time, there are characteristics of the legal process predicted to be troublesome. Libai (1980) suggests that each of the following hold the capacity to subject the child to prolonged mental stress: repeated interrogation and cross-examination, facing the accused, the official atmosphere of the court, the acquittal of the accused, and the conviction of the accused who is the child's parent or relative.

Investigative Trauma

It is clear that involvement in the investigation of a child sexual abuse situation is traumatic for all concerned (Stone et al., 1984). For the child, in particular, the repetitive relating of the initially traumatic event in all of its upsetting detail can be abusive in itself. Beginning with the police officer or child protection specialist and moving through a long line of emergency medical personnel, grand jury members, prosecutors, and even relatives, the child is asked to recall vividly an event he or she wishes only to forget (Schultz, 1980a). As a measure of how far this has gone, Summit (1985) notes that the average child sexual abuse case, in his experience, finds the child victim involved in nine to nineteen interviews. This is obviously unnecessary.

Perhaps the most radical reform proposed to deal with this problem is that offered by Schultz (1980a) who suggests that child victims have a right to remain silent, a right to have this option explained to them, and a right to have their choice respected. More common would be that solution described by Libai (1980), who finds utility in a comprehensive first interview. Such an interview would be undertaken by an individual who is trained to reconcile the counter-vailing considerations found in the need for effective interrogation and the desire to protect child sexual abuse victims from possible ill effects of such interrogation. A mid-range position is represented by those who would have an initial team interview with law enforcement and child protective personnel present. In any case, a reduction in the amount of repetitive questioning will be found productive both in reducing stress upon the child and in building a cleaner case not subject to multiple answers to similar questions. Recent technological advances seem to offer some hopeful applications in this area.

Avoidance of Repetitive Questioning

One seemingly logical suggestion that persists in the literature, and is appearing with great frequency in statutory reform, is the use of videotaping of the child witness. The utility of this strategy is that the initial account of the event may be captured by a skilled interviewer and later shared with the multiple professionals holding an interest in the case (Lloyd, 1985). While logical and seemingly more humane than the typical approach, this application of videotechnology has not proven to be without problems.

Practical use of this procedure has been found to provide the defense with a tool not previously available (MacFarlane, 1985). If a criminal complaint is filed, the defense attorney and the defendant will have the right to see all existing evidence in the case, and the videotaped interview becomes a courtroom target. MacFarlane finds that the videotaped interview may be later used to discredit the child witness, the interviewer, and the techniques used to interview the child. The most common defense tactic, according to MacFarlane, is the claim that the interviewer, "lead, coached, or played upon the suggestibility of the child who then alleged child sexual abuse in order to please the questioning adult" (1985, p. 134).

The young child in particular is subject to recall errors over a period of time. There may well be discrepancies between initial videotaped interviews and later reports. Clinical interviewing styles differ, and the sexual abuse victim is a difficult interviewee. The initial interview rarely appears as a neat, clean, and well-organized piece of work that moves the child directly to the point. Finally, it must be remembered that there are many ways to ask a child a question based on age, the proximity in time to the event, and the trauma experienced. Each of these features, and more, is subject to defense scrutiny in the courtroom setting. To date it is uncertain that video technology, at least in its wide-open application, is the blessing it was promised to be by child advocates.

Changes in Courtroom Practices

When a child victim is a necessary witness at trial, the right of the accused to a fair trial may create a clear conflict with the need to guard the child victim's mental health (Libai, 1980). Although legal practitioners are more than familiar with it, the clinical practitioner must be aware that the Sixth Amendment to the U.S. Constitution guarantees the accused the right to confront witnesses against him or her and to cross-examine them in the presence of the jury. In our criminal courts, at least traditionally, the child witness has been treated no differently than the adult witness on this point. As a result, in today's increasing number of child-centered cases, the trauma of this confrontation and the limited abilities of the child may contribute to an unsuccessful prosecution (Stevens & Berliner, 1980).

Given these realities, Stevens and Berliner (1980) argue that if there is an insistence upon criminal prosecution of sexual abuse perpetrators, special legal techniques must be adopted. These techniques within the criminal justice system would not only encourage cooperation of the child witness but also improve their performance. However, any new technique adopted must satisfy the Sixth Amendment rights of the accused to confrontation, cross-examination, and a public trial as well as First Amendment rights of the press and the public to access to the judicial process (Melton, 1984). To date, the satisfaction of both sides of this legal fence have been elusive.

Melton (1984) has reviewed the use of video technology in the child sexual abuse case. The use of videotaped deposition in lieu of trial testimony of a child victim is statutorily permitted in several states. To be admissible under these statutes, these depositions must be taken in the presence of the defendant (sometimes behind a one-way mirror), his or her counsel, and the prosecutor. Such a strategy has been recommended by the Attorney General's Task Force on Family Violence (1984) if the technique is undertaken with consent of the defendant. However, legal writers in the field caution that the constitutionality of statutes that permit such a technique without the defendant's consent remain in question (Bulkley, 1985; Graham, 1985; Melton, 1984). It seems that the videotaping of the initial interview is more likely to stand the test of time than this videotaping of the child's deposition for later use as testimony in the case.

As an alternative strategy, Libai (1980) has proposed a "child courtroom." Libai is one among many who feel that the right of confrontation and a policy of child protection are not immediately reconcilable. Any means of preventing the child victim from meeting the accused face to face at trial, limiting the scope of effective cross-examination, having someone else conduct the questioning of the child, or permitting the introduction of evidence given earlier must be closely scrutinized for constitutionality. The concept of the child courtroom would answer such concerns according to its major proponent.

The child courtroom would be a facility where the child's testimony could be taken in a relaxed and informal setting. The child would see only the judge, the prosecutor, and defense counsel, and a child examiner. The accused, the jury, and the audience would be seated behind one-way glass, enabling complete observation of the testimony. The accused would have access to a microphone and earphones to provide confidential communication with the defense counsel. On the surface, this appears to answer many problems.

The concept of a child courtroom has many who defend it as well as a host of critics. Constitutional issues abound in its design, which will be discussed later. As a preview, one of the significant and unresolved issues related to confrontation and such a facility is whether confrontation means face to face confrontation. If it does, the design of this facility violates the Sixth Amendment (Melton, 1984).

A summary view of these issues finds Lloyd (1985) calling for more research and study in the area. Lloyd suggests that the literature, which concludes that the child's participation in court as a complaining witness is psychologically damaging, is conclusory and/or anecdotal rather than built upon controlled research. He describes a need for research in how testifying in court affects both children and adults, research testing alternative models, such as testimony in chambers, videotape, or closed circuit television, research that examines the impact of confrontation on truth telling, and research in the moral development of children as it influences truth telling. In addition, Lloyd sees the areas of loyalty to caregivers, secrecy, and the impact of violence and sexual victimization on moral development as under-researched areas. Given the difficulties, questions, and unresolved issues in this area, it seem that Lloyd's view that we have much to learn regarding innovations necessary for more effective child witnessing has merit.

Evidentiary Issues

Evidentiary Issues in Conflict

A review of evidentiary issues as they affect the child sexual abuse case reveals increasing innovation and creativity. Issues involved in hearsay (that is, prior out-of-court statements), admission, expert testimony, competency, credibility, and the minimization of trauma to the child witness have created a labyrinth of evidentiary issues and innovations in criminal cases involving child witnesses (Whitcomb, 1985). Some of these creative applications pass constitutional muster, others remain questionable.

Competency

To provide adequate testimony, a witness must be competent. Although it seems a simple concept, the witness being a child complicates the issues. Under traditional practice, the judge was required to conduct a hearing to determine whether a child was competent to testify. The judge would examine the child to determine whether the child had a present understanding of the difference between truth and falsity as well as an appreciation of the obligation or responsibility to speak the truth. Also included was an evaluation as to whether the child had the mental capacity at the time of the occurrence to observe or receive accurate impressions of the occurrence, whether the child possessed memory sufficient to retain an independent recollection of the observation, and whether the child had a capacity to truly communicate or translate into words the memory of such observation. Finally, the judge had to determine whether the child had the capacity to understand simple questions about the occurrence (Bulkley & Wulkan, 1984). This complex process has been modified significantly in recent years.

The Federal Rules of Evidence enacted in 1974 have removed the competency examination and the common law presumptions of competency based on age (Whitcomb, 1985). By 1985 almost half the states had eliminated competency qualifications for child witnesses (Bulkley, 1985). The implication of this elimination is that the child's testimony can be offered and the finder of fact (the jury) decides how much weight to give the testimony by direct evaluation of the testimony itself (Berliner & Roe, 1985). This is the same presumption of competency for child witnesses suggested by the Attorney General's Task Force on Family Violence (1984). Similar changes have come about in the credibility of child witnesses.

Credibility

There has been a great deal of concern regarding whether children can be effective witnesses. Will the jury believe them? There has been a concern that children cannot testify reliably in court, but that concern seems unnecessary (Berliner & Roe, 1985). Historically children have been seen as "distorters of reality," "fantasy weavers," and "intellectual liars" (Schultz, 1980a). There is a tendency to think of children as being suggestible and as having memories not comparable to that of adults (Goodman & Helgeson, 1985). This view of children seems to be inappropriate.

Goodman and Helgeson (1985) note that while children recall less than adults, what they do recall may be quite accurate. Their errors seem to be in omission not in commission. Children as young as five are able to answer questions about simple concrete events as well as adults. On a parallel issue, while children are not necessarily more suggestible than adults, they can be in those situations in which their memory is weaker or the questioner is of relatively high status to the child. In such situations, Goodman and Helgeson (1985) caution strongly against suggestive questioning. As regards the last concern about the child witness being prone to fabrication, Goodman and Helgeson (1985) note that there are no modern studies suggesting that children can be led to fabricate an entire event although there is suggestion that children can be manipulated into making false reports (a warning signal in the domestic relations allegation). Even in this case, Lloyd (1985) suggests that, overall, children are not a great deal more suggestive than adults. The attorney and clinician must both be aware, however, that a high status model (e.g., parent) holds some capacity to influence a child's report.

The notion that a child may be a credible witness does not indicate that there is no need to support that child witness in order to increase credibility. Berliner and Roe (1985) have suggested several mechanisms through which the credibility of the child witness may be enhanced. In the opinion of these child experts, the child will be most credible and effective as a witness when there are specifically trained personnel involved in the investigation and prosecution of the case. Added to this are the requirements that the number of interviews be kept to a minimum, that devices such as anatomically correct dolls are used to assist the child victim while testifying, and that the child victim be properly prepared for the courtroom experience. Accurate testimony is also achieved by making certain that the child is permitted to recount the events in his or her own words and in the absence of leading questions (Goodman, 1984). It is Goodman's position that inaccurate child response results not from the child's limitations, but from inaccurate questioning by adults (1984, pp. 187–188). In any case, there is the clear suggestion that corroborating evidence might serve to strengthen the child's testimony.

Corroborating Evidence

Although virtually no jurisdictions require corroboration of the child's testimony as part of the government's case in chief (Berliner & Roe, 1985), practical results are achieved from the introduction of corroborative or supportive evidence in many cases. There is frequently a subtle need to overcome public perceptions of sexually victimized children as being less than credible witnesses (Lloyd, 1984).

When corroboration does become necessary, the use of hearsay and expert testimony are probably the most available and frequently chosen alternatives.

Hearsay

Most practitioners find the "excited utterance" to be a useful hearsay exception in the child sexual abuse case. For a statement to quality as an excited utterance, there must be "a sufficiently startling experience suspending reflective thought" and "a spontaneous reaction, not one resulting from reflection or fabrication" (Bulkley, 1984, p. 155), such as "Mom! A man just pulled down his pants in front of me!"

In the child sexual abuse case the courts have frequently stretched the spontaneity requirement and have considered only whether the delay between event and utterance provided the opportunity to fabricate. This relaxation is particularly characteristic of cases involving young children. In some cases, even when a child's statement was in response to inquiries, the courts have continued to accept them as excited utterances. In extreme situations, some jurisdictions have admitted the excited utterance of a child so young that she was not competent to testify (Bulkley, 1984). This clearly is a useful mechanism for gaining admission of hearsay evidence to corroborate the fact of sexual abuse.

Statements made to a physician regarding a medical condition are also considered admissible hearsay. Statements made to a physician about bodily feelings, symptoms, and conditions may be admissible, particular if they were made by the child for purposes of diagnosis and treatment. Such admissible statements may even include the child's statement about the cause of the problem (Lloyd, 1984). The rationale behind the acceptance of these statements can be found in the belief that a person would not usually be motivated to fabricate symptoms and conditions when going to a physician for treatment (Graham, 1985).

The "complaint of rape" exception to the hearsay rule may also be available as corroborative evidence in the sexual abuse case. In this situation, if the complaint of rape was made without a delay that cannot be explained, it is likely to be admitted without difficulty (Lloyd, 1984).

Finally, in jurisdictions where the Federal Rules of Evidence have been adopted, prosecutors have looked to the "other hearsay exception" found in Rules 803(24) and 804(b)(5) where the declarant is unavailable. This residual hearsay exception allows certain statements into evidence despite the fact that they do not fit established exceptions. However, there are several specific criteria of acceptance. The statement(s) must have circumstantial guarantees of trustworthiness equivalent to the traditional hearsay exceptions. The introduction of the statement(s) must be necessary, that is, more probative on the point for which offered than any other evidence that may be reasonably procured. The fact to be proved must be of substantial importance in determining the outcome of the litigation. The interests of justice must be served by the admission. Finally, notice must be given to the opponent of the intended use of the hearsay (Graham, 1985). However, it is wise to note that this "other hearsay exception" approach should be a sparingly used strategy. The committee notes to this exception stated that it should be used rarely and only in exceptional circumstances. The committee had no intention of giving broad license to judges to admit hearsay (Bulkley, 1984).

Rather than relying upon this residual hearsay exception for child sexual abuse victims, a special hearsay exception is advocated by some writers (and has been adopted in some jurisdictions) solely for the victims of child sexual abuse (Bulkley, 1985). These statutes, applicable only to child sexual abuse, permit the admission of out-of-court statements of child victims when the guarantees of trustworthiness equivalent to the traditional categorical hearsay exceptions can be shown (Graham, 1985). This proposed exception covers both the available and unavailable declarant, usually requiring corroboration if the statements of an unavailable declarant are offered (Bulkley, 1985).

Prior Bad Acts

Evidence of prior bad acts or bad character of the defendant is generally inadmissible to show that the defendant committed the crime for which he or she is on trial. Most jurisdictions recognize an exception to this in sexual assault. Evidence of prior sexual offenses is admissible to show a "passion or propensity for illicit sexual relations," and such an admission is also justified to "dispel the notion that the present charge or accusation is fabricated or the product of the child's fantasy" (Liles & Bulkley, 1984, pp. 199–200). Other sexual misbehavior by the defendant with the victim or similar crimes against others may be admissible to show design, motive, plan, scheme, or modus operandi (Liles & Bulkley, 1984). Given the repetitive nature of the predatory pedophile's sexual contact with children, the child sexual abuse case finds this introduction to be a common one.

Experts

Expert testimony as corroborative evidence in the child sexual abuse case has many roles. It has been offered by the prosecution to dispel notions about children fantasizing such occurrences. It is used to educate the jury about the memories and credibility of child witnesses. It is frequently used to explain and illuminate the behavioral characteristics of the child that are indicative of sexual abuse victimization. And, it is used to explain reluctance in reporting, recantation, and other critical elements in the child's development (Roe, 1985).

Experts, as indicated in one of the concluding "special issues" of this work, are permitted to draw inferences from facts which a jury would not be competent to draw. But the expert is not permitted to usurp the province of the jury by drawing conclusions about ultimate facts (Berliner, Blick, & Bulkley, 1984). Rather, they are to use their expertise to shed light upon the issues in such a way as to aid the jury. The expert is an individual who has expertise on the subject, can assist the jury on matters about which the average layperson cannot reasonably be expected to have knowledge, and working from a framework (state of the art or scientific knowledge) through which a reasonable opinion can be offered.

The rules used to examine the admissibility of expert testimony in the child sexual abuse case are the same as those that are applied to all expert opinion evidence. These standards include: Does the probative value of the evidence outweigh its prejudice? Will the introduction of the testimony aid the trier of fact in evaluating and understanding matters that are not within the common experience of the jurors? Is the expert qualified? And is the state of the art or science such as will permit a reasonable opinion? (Roe, 1985) It is generally accepted that child sexual abuse is an area "about which most jurors do not have general knowledge" (Berliner et al., 1984).

One unique aspect of expert opinion testimony in the child sexual abuse case is that of the presence of a belief in "syndromes." In other words, is there a clear set of characteristics and consequences that occur often enough in perpetrator or victim to qualify as a syndrome? Experts in the family violence area are fond of adopting this quasi-scientific stance, and it is ambivalently supported by the research literature in most areas. Syndrome testimony in child sexual abuse cases describes characteristics that sexually abused children exhibit generally and attempts to match those characteristics with the child victim in an effort to demonstrate the likelihood that the child in question was sexually abused (Roe, 1985; Lloyd, 1984). Syndrome testimony tends to bolster the credibility of the child witness' complaint that sexual abuse occurred. However, it is often criticized for attempting to demonstrate a level of scientific knowledge that is beyond empirical validation; and thus subject to assault upon cross-examination.

Courts that have rejected this type of testimony have been known to note that the bolstering of the credibility of the child witness invades the province of the jury and that syndrome testimony is unreliable (due to the lack of empirical validation). Roe (1985) suggests that neither of these reasons is sufficient for rejection of child sexual abuse syndrome evidence. It is her belief that while the evidence may have the indirect effect of bolstering the credibility, "so does most testimony in a trial or it wouldn't be offered" (Roe, 1985, pp. 13–17). Roe (1985) also finds the jury free to reject the expert evidence and finds this type of expert testimony no less reliable than other types of expert testimony commonly accepted. The subjective interpretation of information supplied by victim or defendant has been routinely admitted in other contexts. Roe does admit, however, that admission of this syndrome testimony (due to its somewhat subjective basis) may lead to a "battle of the experts."

As a comprehensive summary statement of this issue, the Attorney General's Task Force on Family Violence (1984, p. 42) has recommended that expert testimony be admitted in all family violence cases. This is seen as an effort to educate the judge and jury about the "dynamics and complexities" of family violence. With regard to child sexual abuse, it was the conclusion of the task force that courts should allow testimony that explains "the characteristics and effects of child sexual abuse" (1984, p. 42).

The Expert's Provision of
Information to the Attorney

Of special consideration in working with the expert witness in the child sexual abuse case is the type of information that should be available following the expert's review of the case. There are critical features that the expert cannot ignore. Assuming that the expert is a clinician who has been working with the family, the attorney should expect the following information to be available:

(1) the range of sexual activity that has taken place in the family since the initiation of sexual contact between adult and child;
(2) the age of the child;
(3) relationship to the perpetrator;
(4) duration of all sexual activity;
(5) frequency of sexual activity;
(6) method(s) of coercion used with the child;
(7) method of concealment (how the family secret was kept);
(8) physical symptoms and indicators;
(9) behavioral symptoms and indicators;
(10) precipitating factors in the family history and process;
(11) timing and place of sexual contact;
(12) involvement of other children in-home or out-of-home;
(13) disclosures to other persons;
(14) sexual history of all family members;
(15) family and individual family members' responses to disclosure; and
(16) prognosis, including recommendations regarding reunification of the family.

Treatment goals for the individual victim, perpetrator, and all other family members as well as suggested interventions should also be available.

Constitutional Limits in Criminal Prosecution:
Confrontation and Cross-Examination

As has been made clear, reform and innovation designed to protect the child victim during prosecution of the child sexual abuse case will be unacceptable and ineffective unless they satisfy the criminal defendant's constitutional rights. Those reforms revolve in large measure around proposals which permit the child's testimony to be taken other than in the courtroom. The constitutional rights implicated by proposed reforms, as mentioned earlier in this chapter, are those guaranteed to the defendant by the Sixth Amendment, the right to confront and cross-examine witnesses in the presence of the jury.

Face-to-Face Confrontation and Technological Innovations

A key issue to the adoption of logistical reforms (e.g., videotape, closed-circuit television, or a child's courtroom) is whether the Sixth Amendment's confrontation clause requires face-to-face exposure or is only intended to permit cross-examination within the observation of the defendant and the jury. The alternatives that have been suggested hold the common feature of allowing the prosecution to elicit testimony from the child under circumstances in which the child would be shielded from face-to-face confrontation with the defendant.

The underlying rationale for confrontation is that cross-examination in the presence of the accused and in the presence of the fact-finder is the best method of judging credibility. It cannot be doubted that there is a clear preference for face-to-face confrontation based on this belief (Bulkley, 1985). However, there are those who suggest that this belief is not correct when applied to children. Goodman and Helgeson (1985), for example, note that the delay in testimony makes it likely that the child's memory will fade. Also, the stressful nature of the court appearance may reduce the chances of obtaining accurate reports and eyewitness identification.

Libai (1980) describes child experts as believing that children should put thoughts of sexually abusive episodes behind them as soon as possible. He therefore urges that the child be permitted to testify in advance of the criminal trial. With respect to the constitutionality challenge to his proposals, Libai (1980) argues that the essence of confrontation is the right to effective cross-examination. Therefore, in his thinking, a pretrial examination with the defendant fully advised of the charges against him or her and given the opportunity for full cross-examination through counsel should be found to meet the essence of confrontation and be held constitutional.

Mlyniec (1985) advocates for a position that would not find logistical innovation violative of constitutional rights when the procedure chosen (1) does not deny the defendant a meaningful opportunity to confront accusers, (2) the defendant can still assist in cross-examination and otherwise assist in the defense, and (3) when there is a particularized showing of need to protect the child witness based on a showing of potential trauma or intimidation.

But even if face-to-face confrontation is not required to meet the Sixth Amendment, the proposals to utilize pretrial or closed-circuit television examination of the child in lieu of live testimony at trial must clear a second constitutional hurdle, the requirement of unavailability.

The Requirement of Unavailability

The Sixth Amendment also has been interpreted to require a showing that the witness is unavailable to testify before prior testimony (hearsay) can be admitted in lieu of that witness' testimony at trial.

For any prior out-of-court statements of the child victim to be admitted at a criminal trial, they must satisfy both a hearsay exception (as described earlier in this chapter) and the confrontation clause. The Supreme Court has held that for a statement to satisfy the confrontation clause it must (1) provide the opportunity for cross-examination, (2) it must be made under oath, and (3) it must allow the jury to assess the demeanor of the witness. Despite these general requirements, if the victim testifies at trial, the confrontation clause is not implicated, and the hearsay statement need only meet one of the recognized exceptions. This is true because while the prior statement may not have met these requirements, at trial the witness must affirm, deny, or qualify the truth of the prior statement under oath. The inability to cross-examine at the time the statement was made is not relevant because the defendant can have full and effective cross-examination at the time of trial. The jury also has the chance to observe and evaluate the demeanor of the witness as he or she affirms, disavows or qualifies the earlier statement (Graham, 1985).

The confrontation clause also requires the production at trial of a complaining witness as a condition for admissibility of the witness's out-of-court statements. The available complaining witness must be called by the prosecution and examined in open court and then subjected to cross-examination. Under the compulsory process clause of the Sixth Amendment, it is clear that the accused is not required to present and examine witnesses against him or her. The available complaining witness must be produced by the prosecution, examined by the prosecution, and presented for cross-examination to the defendant. The prosecution will not be permitted to offer hearsay statements of the complaining witness merely on the grounds that the complaining witness is available to be called by the defendant (Graham, 1985).

The Sixth Amendment requirements are lessened upon a showing that the declarant is unavailable to testify. Hearsay can be admitted in the place of the unavailable witness' live testimony (Lloyd, 1985) if the hearsay satisfies the requirements of oath, cross-examination and ability to observe demeanor as noted above. But what must be shown to demonstrate unavailability so that a videotaped deposition or other than live courtroom testimony may be constitutionally admitted in evidence?

Graham (1985, p. 199) has noted that finding that a child witness, if required to testify in open court, would suffer "severe emotional or mental distress, substantial emotional or psychological impairment, or substantial trauma" is probably not sufficient to constitute unavailability under the confrontation clause. In Graham's view, unavailability requires more than showing the possibility or even the likelihood of emotional distress or trauma.

Graham notes that unavailability based upon mental illness or infirmity was held in *People v. Stritzinger*, 34 Cal.3d 505, 194 Cal. Rptr. 431, 668 P.2d 738 (1983) to require a finding that the present or likely to be incurred mental illness or infirmity renders the witness' testimony "relatively impossible" (Graham, 1985). He concludes that if the "relatively impossible" standard is met and the child is therefore declared unavailable to testify, that a perpetuation deposition or other technological innovation may be admitted without violating the Sixth Amendment. In order to establish such unavailability, Graham suggests that current statutes and rules be amended to provide specifically for unavailability based upon the potential of severe psychological injury to the child witness if forced to face the defendant in open court. He also believes that supporting commentary must make clear that the appropriate standard is "relatively impossible." Bulkley (1985) tempers Graham's view suggesting that a showing of "severe psychological trauma" may be sufficient for the establishment of unavailability.

The use of the "relatively impossible" standard or some less stringent standard to establish unavailability will most likely have to be proven through expert testimony (Bulkley, 1985). The mere claim that the child is frightened to testify or will be traumatized is insufficient for a determination of unavailability. Expert testimony will be required to prove that the child is truly unavailable due to the adverse effect that testifying will have on the child's psychological well-being (Graham, 1985; Lloyd, 1985).

Reliability

Before a hearsay statement of an unavailable declarant can be admitted, the confrontation clause and the general requirements for admission of hearsay require that the testimony bear adequate indicia of reliability (Graham, 1985). Reliability is established when the hearsay evidence falls within a firmly rooted traditional hearsay exception. Otherwise, the evidence must possess "particularized guarantees of trustworthiness" equivalent to the traditional exceptions (Bulkley, 1985; Graham, 1985). Videotape, closed-circuit television, and testimony in a child's courtroom are all characterized by oath, cross-examination, and the ability to observe the witness' demeanor. These are all strong indicia of reliability and therefore should be sufficient for the admissibility of such testimony under the reliability requirement (Graham, 1985).

Limitations on Use of Technological Innovations

All commentators, except perhaps Libai (1980), caution extremely sparse use of innovations that follow from witness unavailability because the impact of these innovations on the testimony of the witness and the perception of the jury remains unknown (Bulkley, 1985; Graham, 1985; Mlyniec, 1985; Whitcomb, 1985). Mlyniec (1985) notes that the impact of these innovations on the perceptions of reliability of the testimony is unknown. Graham introduces questions regarding distortion, exclusion of evidence, and status conferral variations in credibility. Another concern is whether the presumption of innocence will be affected by the jury's evaluation of the circumstances that merited (i.e., demanded) such a dramatic alteration in procedure (Graham, 1985). Graham's concern is that the jury will give weight to the innovative logistical procedure itself in determining guilt or innocence.

A Summary View

Criminal prosecution of perpetrators of child sexual abuse can be successful with the child victim as the chief prosecution witness. Attention to minimizing the investigatory and testimonial trauma, use of specially trained personnel, and sensitivity to the limited capacities of child witnesses will enhance child credibility. The use of corroborating admissible hearsay and expert testimony will also assist in obtaining convictions of these perpetrators. The adoption of a special hearsay exception for prior statements by the young child victim about the abuse is a promising addition to corroboration in states where it has been adopted.

A cautious view of the evidentiary reform proposals that would keep the child out of the courtroom altogether is suggested. The protection of the child's emotional well-being can only be balanced against, not preferred over, the defendant's constitutional rights. Strict requirements should be established for unavailability before the child's testimony is presented in a non-conventional way. The requirements of the confrontation clause require this. Moreover, the lack of data of the effects of testifying on children and the effect of the proposed innovations on jury and witness perceptions dictate restrictive use of these new procedures.

New procedures and innovations on old procedures dominate the concern of those who prosecute child sexual abuse and are concerned about secondary victimization resulting from participation in the court process. While the rights of the defendant must be protected in criminal prosecutions so must the psychological well-being of the child victim of sexual abuse. The accommodation of the interests in the protection of both victim and accused is still developing and with increased prosecution of child sexual abuse the constitutional questions raised by the proposed innovations should soon be settled by the appellate courts. As will be seen in the following chapter, those concerned with the plight of the victim of conjugal violence are not so concerned about innovations and new prosecutorial methods as trying to get the law enforcement community to enforce the laws which already exist.

11

The Legal Environment
of Conjugal Violence

The Police Response

Recognition of the fact that husbands batter their wives is not new. What is new is recognition of such battering as a crime and as a matter about which the courts, civil and criminal, should provide a remedy. Traditionally, conjugal violence has been considered to be a private family matter, not one that concerns law enforcement (Fields, 1978). Domestic assault complaints have not been viewed by the police as criminal matters (Martin, 1976), complaints have been ignored or treated as a low priority, and arrests were rare (Lerman, 1983, 1984; U.S. Commission on Civil Rights, 1978). When police did respond to a domestic call, the only action taken was usually an admonishment to the husband to cool off, assistance to the wife in leaving, or perhaps an attempt at reconciliation (U.S. Commission on Civil Rights, 1978). Police training manuals and curricula specified a nonarrest policy. Arrest was seen as counter-productive, to be used only as a last resort and only after attempts to mediate the conflict between the spouses had failed (Fields, 1978; U.S. Commission on Civil Rights, 1982). Often there was not even a report filed (Lerman, 1984).

The refusal of police officers in New York City to afford protection to women who were victims of domestic assault resulted in the filing of a lawsuit against the police department and others by a group of victims of spousal assault in 1976. The case resulted in a settlement with the police whereby the department agreed (1) to respond promptly to domestic calls, (2) to arrest as in other criminal matters, (3) to remain at the scene to prevent further violence, (4) to provide assistance to the wife, and (5) to revise department regulations to conform with these agreements (*Bruno v. Codd*, 393 N.E. 2d 976, 1979).

The initial response of the police in the case of conjugal assault has been seen as the "most crucial" for the battered co-habitor (Fields, 1978). The call for improved police response, elevating the priority of domestic calls, implementing arrest policies, and affording protection to the victim are but some of the reforms in police response that have been urged (Attorney General's Task Force, 1984; Lerman, 1984; U.S. Commission on Civil Rights, 1979, 1982).

The Response of the Court

Historically, the response of prosecutors and the courts was no better than that of the police. Prior to the legislative reforms of the past decade, peace bonds, the violation of which resulted in a monetary forfeiture, were the only injunctive-type relief available through the courts unless a divorce action was pending (Lerman, 1984). Divorce was often viewed by judges and prosecutors as the solution to the problem of spouse assault (Fields, 1978). Even when arrests were made, prosecution was rare (Fields, 1978; Lerman, 1984). Prosecutors discouraged women from filing complaints and often used deferral mechanisms rather than go to trial on those complaints that were filed (Fields, 1978). A U.S. Civil Rights Commission Report published in 1982 stated that in some cases prosecutors refused to proceed with criminal charges unless the women agreed to institute divorce proceedings.

Reform in Police and Court Practices: The Law Enforcement Model

Within the past ten years, most states have adopted legislation authorizing the issuance of an order of protection for an abused spouse that may bar the abuser from the home. This legislation makes the violation of the order of protection a criminal offense. Arrest procedures have been liberalized in many jurisdictions permitting arrest even in cases where there are no visible injuries to the victim and the offense took place outside of the officer's presence. The courts and prosecutors' offices in many jurisdictions have adopted new policies for prosecution of the wife batterer (Lerman, Landis, & Goldzweig, 1983; Laszlo & McKean, 1978).

The Attorney General's Task Force on Family Violence (1984) takes the position that the legal response to family violence should be guided by the nature of the abusive act and not by the relationship between the victim and the abuser. The task force recommended that the legal system treat assaults within the family as seriously as it treats the same assault if it occurred between strangers. Among its *Recommendations for Law Enforcement* were (1) that law enforcement agencies make family violence calls a priority response, (2) that a report be required on all such calls, (3) that arrest be the preferred response, (4) that police officers order the abuser from the premises when no arrest is made, (5) that police officers inform the victim about shelter and victim assistance programs available in the community, and (6) that violations of orders of protection be a priority response with a current file of such orders maintained within the department's jurisdiction (1984, pp. 16–17). The task force's *Recommendations for Prosecutors* included vigorous prosecution of all domestic violence complaints and pretrial release orders restricting access to the victim.

Recommendations for arrest and prosecution of perpetrators of conjugal violence represent a radical change. The recognition of conjugal violence as criminal activity and of the victim's right to be protected by the criminal justice system from further violence is a departure from the traditional view of conjugal violence as a private family matter. This *law enforcement model* can be characterized as advocating formal legal action against perpetrators followed by punishment or rehabilitation programs. Law enforcement model proponents place their priorities on protection of the victim and broadcasting a societal message that this type of violence will not be tolerated (Lerman, 1984).

The effectiveness of the law enforcement model, at least with respect to a strong arrest policy has support in the data. Sherman and Berk (1984) in a controlled experiment conducted with the Minneapolis Police Department in 1981 and 1982 found arrest to be the most effective method in reducing domestic violence as compared with counseling or ordering the abuser out to cool down. Despite this data and the recommendations of many advocates for victims of conjugal violence, there is another model for response to conjugal violence that enjoys widespread support across the country, the *conciliation model*.

Conciliation and Mediation

The conciliation model relies on informal dispute resolution devices, especially mediation. The majority of police agencies in this country use a conciliation model in dealing with problems of spousal assault (Lerman, 1984). Police officers have been trained in crisis intervention techniques for dealing with domestic calls. Police are trained to diffuse the violent situation and attempt on-the-scene mediation rather than take formal action against the abuser (Lerman, 1984). Lerman (1984) reports that by 1977, 70 percent of the nations's police forces of 100 officers or more were trained to use crisis intervention techniques to mediate rather than arrest.

Mediation also takes place in the court system in lieu of the filing of any formal proceedings or as a diversion program from the criminal justice system. Generally the agreements reached are not enforceable and no resolution can be imposed on the parties by the mediator if the parties fail to agree (Lerman, 1984). Lerman credits the rapid growth of mediation to the economics of the court system. Backlogs plague both domestic and criminal courts and alternative forums for the diversion of substantial numbers of cases are attractive. Lerman also theorizes that the preference for conciliation is reflective of societal values that hold that conflicts between spouses are not appropriate matters for state intervention. She characterizes the diversion from prosecution to mediation as a "tacit decriminalization" of spousal violence (Lerman, 1984, p. 92).

Lerman is not alone in her criticism of mediation as an effective tool to prevent spouse abuse. Mediation, the Attorney General's Task Force (1984) notes, is most often an inappropriate law enforcement response in family violence because it assumes that the parties are of equal culpability. Lerman (1984) reports that the U.S. Civil Rights Commission recommended that mediation never be used as an alternative to prosecution in cases of physical violence.

Criticism of mediation for spouse abuse cases also centers on the presumption of the mediators that the parties are on equal footing and are able to negotiate as equals in reaching an agreement (Fields, 1978). Mediation assumes shared responsibility for the conduct and in effect requires the victim to agree to a modification of her behavior in exchange for the batterer's promise not to engage in further violence (Fields, 1978).

Most mediation agreements lack accountability. If the agreement is breached, it usually cannot be enforced. The mediation agreement most often results in the dismissal of any criminal charges that may have been pending or threatened (Lerman, 1984).

Mediation proponents agree with some of the criticisms including (1) that serious cases of violence should not be mediated, (2) mediation is most likely effective where the parties have relatively equal bargaining positions, and (3) mediation is likely to be ineffective if one party is very frightened of the other (Lerman, 1984).

Reform in Mediation

Although the popular thinking about the law enforcement model as a preferable alternative to mediation may be changing, mediation will continue to be used extensively. Societal values, budgetary constraints, court overcrowding, and the parties' wishes to avoid criminal prosecution all indicate a future for mediation of conjugal violence. How can mediation techniques and procedures be improved?

When a couple in a violent relationship is referred to mediation, there are often a wide variety of problems presented in addition to the violence. Mediators must be trained to deal with the issue of violence. The mediation agreement must deal specifically with the violence and not rest upon the assumption that dealing with those problems susceptible to compromise will resolve the violence (Lerman, 1984). Lerman urges that the process must lay clear responsibility for the violence on the abusive party. He or she must know that serious consequences will result if the mediation agreement is breached. Mediation should be coupled with criminal proceedings to provide effective deterrents to future violence.

Lerman (1984) advocates that when mediation is used, the primary focus of the hearing be to prevent subsequent abuse. The victim's safety should have a higher priority than keeping the couple together and resolving other problems. Mediators should place less emphasis on reaching an agreement and more on determining whether the arties need more formal legal action. Mediators should not push for reconciliation of the parties in a violent relationship unless the victim wants to maintain the relationship.

If mediation occurs only after criminal charges are filed, those harges should be deferred only as long as the abuser complies with he agreement. The appropriateness of domestic violence mediation depends on whether it is likely to offer effective protection for the victim against further abuse. To be enforceable, mediation agreements an be incorporated into a consensual protection order, be the condition for continued deferral of criminal prosecution, or become the erms of a sentence of probation after conviction (Lerman, 1984).

A Summary View

In the past decade, there have been many legislative and policy hanges that have improved the probabilities that the victim of onjugal violence can obtain protection. The probabilities that the erpetrator of the violence will be arrested and/or prosecuted have lso improved. This is not to say that there is widespread societal cceptance of conjugal violence as a criminal offense or a budgetary riority of an already overburdened criminal justice system. As chudson (1978) noted, there is nothing inherent in the structure of ur criminal justice system that would make it especially responsive o conjugal violence. These offenders limit their violence to the home nd are not believed to be a threat beyond the confines of the family.

Orders of protection, shelters, victim's assistance groups, and o-fault divorce legislation may represent improvements but are by o means solutions to the problem of conjugal violence. The solution o conjugal violence will only be found when there is a change in ocietal values. For unlike child maltreatment and child sexual abuse, t cannot be said that physical mistreatment of one's spouse is niversally condemned. Laws cannot change values or behaviors; hey can only provide remedies for their violation. Conjugal violence vill remain a common occurrence until it becomes morally repugnant n our society.

The ultimate act of conjugal violence, homicide, has not been the ocus of reform in criminal justice because this act of conjugal iolence has always been criminally prosecuted and has never been excused as a private family matter. Today, attention is focused on the victim turned aggressor; the battered wife who kills her husband.

Experts and Conjugal Homicide

Self-Defense

An emerging area of controversy in cases of spouse abuse concerns the criminal justice system's response when the battered wife kills her abuser and enters a plea of self-defense. Self-defense is established by the defendant proving that she reasonably believed she was in imminent danger of death or serious bodily injury and reacted with the force necessary to avoid the danger (Thar, 1982). Self-defense requires a reasonable and honest, though not necessarily correct, belief in the necessity of using force to avoid serious harm or death (*State v. Kelly*, 478 A.2d 364, N.J., 1984). The defendant must use the least amount of force necessary to prevent harm (Walker et al., 1982). Deadly force may be used in self-defense, defensively, and not in retribution for past assaults or in anticipation of future assaults that are not imminent (Acher & Toch, 1985).

In addition to an honest belief, the belief of imminent danger must also be a reasonable one in view of the circumstances at the time of the homicide (*State v. Kelly*). What is reasonable for a woman facing imminent attack by a man may be different than for a man facing attack from another man. A woman may not necessarily be held to the equal force or eye-for-an-eye traditional standard; she may be permitted to use a weapon in self-defense when no weapon is being used by her attacker (Walker et al., 1982; *State v. Wanrow*, 559 P.2d 548, Wash., 1977).

Justification for the Use of Experts
to Support Self-Defense

Experts on the subject of the battering relationship have been permitted to testify on the phenomenon and characteristics of that relationship when the woman has pled self-defense. The purpose for which this testimony has been offered is to provide the jury a framework for understanding the defendant's state of mind and her honest and reasonable perception of life-threatening danger at the time she killed her husband. The justification for the need of expert testimony to provide such a framework is that the average juror cannot understand the battered woman's state of mind without expert assistance. Advocates of the use of expert testimony claim that stereotypes and societal myths about battered women interfere with the jurors' ability to assess the facts of the case. The expert will help the jury understand that a battered woman can correctly perceive imminent danger from her husband and be unable to safely retreat under circumstances that might not appear either dangerous or inescapable to the average juror (Bochnak, 1981).

The justification for the admission of any expert testimony is that the expert has the ability to draw inferences from facts that a jury of lay people would not be competent to draw. To be admissible, expert testimony must be relevant and satisfy three special requirements. (1) It must be so distinctly related to some science, profession, business, or occupation as to be beyond the ken of the average juror. (2) The witness must have sufficient skill, knowledge, or experience in that field or calling as to make it appear that his or her opinion will probably aid the trier of fact, that is, the jury. (3) The state of the pertinent art or science must permit a reasonable opinion to be offered (*Dyas v. U.S.*, 376 A.2d 827, D.C., 1977). Finally, because expert testimony is viewed as highly reliable due to the status of the expert and the scientific nature of the testimony, the court must find that the testimony is more probative than prejudicial and neither confusing nor misleading (Thar, 1982).

Attacks on the admissibility of expert testimony in battered women self-defense cases can take many tacks. The judge may not believe that domestic violence is a subject outside the jurors' common knowledge and thus does not require expert testimony. Opponents also will argue that there is no unanimity in the social sciences about causes and characteristics of domestic violence making the testimony unreliable and therefore inadmissible (Sternberg, 1981). The defense must also be ready to establish that the testimony about domestic violence and about the defendant's life has probative value that is not outweighed by prejudice to the prosecution or risks of misleading or confusing the jury (Thar, 1982). The prosecutor may argue that expert testimony diagnosing the defendant as a battered woman will prejudice the jury because it labels the deceased as a batterer and the defendant, not the deceased, is on trial (Acher & Toch, 1985). But Sternberg (1981) points out that prior acts of violence by the deceased are admissible in all self-defense cases where the defendant claims the deceased was the aggressor.

Walker and colleagues (1982) assert that it is within the expertise of a psychologist to give an opinion about a battered woman's state of mind at the time she killed her husband. They claim that this opinion is necessary because without the admission of expert testimony, judges and juries will rely on common myths to explain the behavior and motivations of battered women. These common myths include

> the belief that battered women are masochistic, that they stay with their mates because they like the beatings, that the violence fulfills a deep-seated need within each partner, or that they are free to leave such relationships if that is what they really want [Walker et al., 1982, pp. 1-2].

An explanation of the psychology of the battered woman is necessary to refute these myths and allow the jury to understand why she believed she was in imminent danger and needed to use deadly force in self-defense (Walker et al., 1982). "Battered woman's syndrome" testimony describes the pattern of physical and psychological abuse inflicted upon the wife and attempts to explain why she fears her abuser and is psychologically unable to escape (Thar, 1982). Walker and colleagues (1982) argue that when a battered woman pleads self-defense, her state of mind at the time the homicide occurred is beyond the ken of the jury and thus requires an expert opinion.

The most widely cited case recognizing the admissibility of expert testimony on battered woman's syndrome in support of a claim of self-defense is *Ibn-Tamas v. United States*, 407 A.2d 626 (D.C., 1979). While not passing on the admissibility under the facts of the particular case before it, the court held that such testimony did not invade the province of the jury nor was it more prejudicial than probative. Dr. Lenore Walker had been called to describe wife battering and give her opinion about the extent to which the defendant's personality and behavior matched those of battered women Walker had studied. The court found that Dr. Walker's expert testimony would have given an interpretation to the facts different from ordinary lay perceptions and therefore the subject about which she offered her opinion was beyond the ken of the jury. Interestingly, upon remand to the trial judge, he ruled that the defendant had failed to establish the third element of the test for admissibility of expert testimony, that the state of the art or science was such as to allow a reliable opinion. The trial judge found that the defendant failed to show acceptance by the expert's colleagues of the methodology used by Walker in her study of battered women. This ruling was affirmed on appeal (*Ibn-Tamas v. United States*, 455 A.2d 893, D.C. App, 1983). As a result, a landmark case recognizing the admissibility of battered women's syndrome testimony is one where it was ultimately not admitted in support of the defendant's self-defense claims.

The use of expert testimony in support of a battered woman's plea of self-defense and specifically the need and appropriateness of such testimony has been highly criticized in a recent article by Acher and Toch (1985). In the article Acher and Toch analyze the New Jersey Supreme Court's decision in *State v. Kelly*, 478 A.2d 364 (N.J., 1984), which also held that the battered woman's syndrome is an appropriate subject for expert testimony, was relevant to both the honesty and reasonableness of a defendant's belief of imminent danger of death or serious bodily injury, and that the expert's conclusions are sufficiently reliable. The court found that it was "clear that this subject (the battering relationship) is beyond the ken of the average juror" (478 A2.d at 379).

Acher and Toch argue that the premise that battered women's syndrome testimony is appropriate for expert testimony because it involves matters beyond the ken of the average juror is faulty and unproven. They also believe that there are dangers attendant to the admission of the expert testimony that have not been considered and that militate against its admissibility. Battered woman's syndrome testimony, in their view, prejudicially shifts attention from the defendant's claim of self-defense and to the deceased battering husband's behavior (Acher & Toch, 1985).

One conclusion the jury was expected to draw from the expert testimony in *State v. Kelly* and in all other battered women's self-defense cases is that a person who has been severely and continuously beaten might very well reasonably fear that the imminent beating she was about to suffer could either be life threatening or pose a risk of serious injury. Assisted by a scientific interpretation of the history of violence, the jury would presumably be better qualified to evaluate the defendant's testimony about the events immediately surrounding the homicide (Acher & Toch, 1985). Acher and Toch (1985, p. 137) argue that the fact that "a history of abuse breeds familiarity with one's abuser and sharpens expectations of the risk of future cruelty" does not require expert testimony. The psychology involved in reaching this conclusion is neither complicated nor foreign to lay thinking; "no expert testimony is required to explain that prior harm breeds present fears" (Acher & Toch, 1985, p. 137). The layperson can draw this simple inference from the facts without expert assistance.

Another area where the court feared the jury may be mistaken was the failure of battered women to leave their abusive husbands. While a juror may ask him or herself this question, Acher and Toch (1985) argue that it does not necessarily follow that one can predict that most jurors would conclude she was free to leave. The court in *State v. Kelly* assumed that juror's would mistakenly conclude that the woman was free to leave. Their criticism of the use of expert testimony to explain the battered woman's failure to leave is that it was not based on documentation but on the judges' prediction that a common myth believed by the average lay person is that the battered woman is free to leave. Absent evidence to the contrary, Acher and Toch (1985) argue that the most reasonable assumption is that the public has more awareness and less prejudice than the court implied.

Acher and Toch (1985) suggest that due to the difficulty of resolving what we can presume juries believe, that they should be asked about their beliefs in the jury selection process (i.e., voir dire) rather than use expert testimony during trial. Questioning jurors about the viability of separation or divorce could be justified either as a prelude to resolving the issue of relevance of expert testimony, to disqualify biased jurors, or to educate the jury. Acher and Toch conclude that, at best, expert testimony in a battered woman's self-defense case has only limited probative value far outweighed by the possible prejudicial effects.

The dangers of prejudice and confusion to the jury must always be weighed against the probative value of the expert testimony. Acher and Toch (1985) argue that the expert's testimony threatens to expand the scope of self-defense beyond the bounds of lawful justification and invites the jury to consider the battered woman's homicide as lawfully excused. Thus they content that the prejudicial aspects of the offered testimony might easily outweigh its probative utility.

Acher and Toch (1985) believe that when expert testimony about the battered women's syndrome is admitted at trial, it is likely to affect the ways in which the jurors interpret and apply self-defense principles. The expert would be called to testify about prior acts of conjugal violence even years before the event that precipitated the homicide. The expert's emphasis on past behavior for evaluating the perceptions of the accused at the time of the homicide is likely, in their view, to divert the jury's attention from the homicide and refocus it on the battering relationship and specifically the deceased husband's violent behavior. The jury's attention would be deflected from the responses of the accused at the time of the homicide to the repeated acts of violence by the deceased that occurred in the past. Cognizant of the enhanced reliability ascribed to expert witnesses, the effect of the expert's testimony could be to distract the jury from the self-defense issues and refocus them on justifying the killing of a battering husband, not because it was necessary, but because it was a fitting act of retribution.

Acher and Toch (1985) assert that if battered woman's syndrome testimony is admitted on behalf of criminal defendants, a "just world syndrome" may lure jurors from the strict necessity of self-defense to the conclusion that the deceased battering husband got what he deserved. If this is the result of battered woman's syndrome testimony, it is clearly prejudicial and not of assistance in establishing the specific requirements of a claim of self-defense.

A Summary View of Expert Testimony

Both the proponents and opponents of expert testimony in battered women's self-defense cases suffer from gaps in knowledge. While the experts may not have data confirming the societal myths and common perceptions shared by average jurors about the battered woman's failure to leave; neither do the opponents know if the juror will ignore the strict requirements of self-defense instructions and excuse the defendant's behavior as fitting retribution. Battered woman's syndrome testimony and its use defensively in homicide cases has some distance to travel before its general admissibility is established or disproved. Until then, defense attorneys should consider the possibilities of self-defense and expert testimony on battered woman's syndrome whenever conjugal homicide follows a history of conjugal violence. If admitted, the expert testimony can be a powerful tool in bolstering the defendant's claim of a reasonable belief in imminent danger and the necessity of the use of lethal force to protect herself.

A lack of sufficient data is part of the problem in analyzing the use of expert testimony on battered woman's syndrome. In the area of elder mistreatment, however, a lack of data, knowledge, and information form the most significant problem in coming to terms with the appropriate way for the legal system to attempt to remedy or alleviate the problem. As will be seen in the next chapter, remedies have already been implemented without enough consideration being given to whether the victim of elder mistreatment will truly benefit.

12

Mistreatment of the Elderly: Disproportion in Knowledge and Response

That elderly persons may suffer as a consequence of their own mental, physical, or financial difficulties is well known. The focus of study on the growing aged population has also demonstrated that older persons may suffer mistreatment at the hands of institutional staff (Caznave & Woodburn, 1981). The most recent realization in this area is that mistreatment of older persons may occur at the hands of familial caretakers. And, to the extent that this is a problem, it appears to be one that will grow in proportion to the increasing number of older persons being cared for in familial homes during their declining years. Unfortunately, at this time the mistreatment of the elderly remains a problem without clear definition.

The proper legal or clinical approach to the problem of mistreatment of the elderly remains elusive as a result of lack of knowledge about the problem itself. The incidence and prevalence are unclear, and uniform definitions (legal, practical, and research) have not yet been established (Gelles & Pedrick-Cornell, 1985; Katz, 1980). This lack of knowledge has not deterred a zealous campaign of state legislative enactments and the establishment of state protective agencies to do something about elder mistreatment. As with other seminal efforts dealing with newly acknowledged manifestations of violence within families, most of the early models for response, both legal and clinical, are patterned after the child protection system. That model, as applied to mistreatment of the elderly, is a controversial one. A review of the three most common elements of that response, (1) adult protective services, (2) the use of guardianship, and (3) mandatory reporting statutes will reveal the origin of the controversy.

Adult Protective Services

Adult protective service legislation has been adopted by many states both with and without accompanying reporting statutes. Adult protective services specialists function under this legislation in much the same manner as do the more familiar child protective services specialists. The goals of such laws are typically the provision and/or coordination of service delivery to persons eighteen years of age and older who are at risk for some reason. The services usually include a wide variety of health, housing, and social services, which are coordinated by a case-worker who is responsible for assessing the individual in question and delivering or arranging for the requisite services (Regan, 1983). Most of the states that have adopted adult protective services legislation also include a component that gives the social agency the right to intervene if the client refuses services. This form of intervention involves a guardianship proceeding or other statutorily authorized protective proceeding (Regan, 1983). This is one point of controversy because many of the adult protective clients are not dependent as are clients in the child protective services system, which served as the model for the adult system.

Adult protective services legislation is directed toward incapacitated adults who are being mistreated (i.e., abused, neglected, and/or exploited). This legislation typically allows access by social workers to investigate, requires professionals to report known mistreatment (and includes penalties for failure to report), and allows for both voluntary and involuntary provision of adult protection. The criteria for state intervention usually links the existence of some form of mistreatment of the adults and a functional, mental, or physical inability that prevents the adults from caring for or protecting themselves (Sloan, 1983b).

With respect to the specific intervention strategy, much adult protective legislation provides for the use of guardianship by the protective agency. Some of the states with adult protective legislation have created special court proceedings for authorized intervention apart from guardianship. These new proceedings may authorize such things as orders for protective services, for protective placement, or for emergency services. In some cases, the "least restrictive alternative," best known in mental health applications, is the statutory standard for determining the content of the order (Sloan, 1983b).

Whether the authorized proceedings under the adult protective legislation is the traditional guardianship or special protective proceedings, this is a feature that is designed to ensure that the adult in question obtains the assistance that the caseworker believes is necessary (Regan, 1981). These provisions place great responsibility on the case-workers' decision making. This degree of responsibility, in making decisions for adults, is one significant point of controversy.

Regan (1981) views the trend toward special proceedings that bypass guardianship as posing a threat to personal and property rights of the adults who are the subject of these proceedings. For example, the definition of "protective services" in many statutes is very broadly defined. It may include virtually any social or health service. Consequently, once the court enters an order for protective services, the agency might well assume authority equivalent to a guardianship but in the absence of the findings such as incompetency traditionally required for the imposition of a guardianship (Regan, 1981).

The purpose behind the creation of special court proceedings for protective services is ostensibly to provide limited involuntary assistance to the abused or neglected elder. A guardianship requires a finding of legal incompetence; the involuntary provision of protective services does not. Under some statutory schemes an order for protective services can be entered upon a showing that the elder person "is suffering the infirmities of old age" and is abused or neglected or exploited; competency or lack of it is not implicated (Sloan, 1983b, p. 37). While the purpose of limited intervention may be a laudable one, the reality is that intervention is not necessarily limited. Sloan (1983b) criticizes much of this new legislation as being "vague and conclusory" regarding the standards for intervention, an argument familiar to child protective legislation (Besharov, 1985; Bourne & Newberger, 1979; Wald, 1982). Sloan goes on to describe a concern that such all-inclusive standards for intervention and the court's failure to limit intervention or require periodic accountings from the agency may well create a "total dominion" by the public agency over the elderly client. And this client is one who has never been found to be legally incompetent. A question that remains is whether the older and more traditional guardianship approach is preferable or offers more protection of the elderly person from unwanted intervention.

Guardianship and Civil Commitment of the Elderly

Caring for those who cannot care for themselves is a recognized responsibility and power of the state. Through its power as sovereign (parens patriae), the state has long asserted its authority and duty to protect those who cannot protect themselves. Most often, the state fulfills this duty through the appointment of a guardian for the incapacitated person or through the civil commitment of the mentally ill person.

As designed and intended, civil commitment to a state mental hospital is an option for providing care and treatment to a person suffering from a mental illness. This has been an alternative that has been over-used in the case of elderly persons who were without family willing or able to care for them (Regan, 1983). Recognizing the restrictiveness of this alternative, not to mention the inhumaneness, there have been increasing efforts in recent years to establish public guardianships to provide community-based services (Schmidt et al., 1981). That has brought about change. Elderly persons unable to care for themselves and who are no danger to themselves, but whose only sin is being without family or friends willing to care for them or serve as guardians, are no longer being subjected to inappropriate confinement in mental hospitals through civil commitment. The most frequent alternative has been the appointment of a guardian.

Establishing the Need for a Guardian

Guardianship proceedings, whether public or private, are initiated by the filing of a petition by an interested person asking that an individual be declared incompetent and that a guardian be appointed. Notice of the hearing must be sent to the alleged incompetent and, depending upon state law, to his or her relatives. At the hearing, evidence is presented to prove the claim of incompetence. At this time the alleged incompetent is entitled to be present, and to provide evidence and/or witnesses in opposition to the petition. The alleged incompetent also has the right to be represented by counsel and in some states, counsel will be appointed if private counsel has not been retained (Regan, 1983).

For the allegation of incompetence to be upheld, the individual or public agency filing the petition must prove and the court must find, that the individual in question, "by reason of mental illness, drunkenness, drug addiction, or old age is incapable of caring for himself and/or providing for his family or is liable to dissipate his property or become the victim of designing persons" (Regan, 1983, p. 283). Once incompetency has been found, the court will appoint a guardian of the person and/or the estate (sometimes called a conservator). This guardian assumes complete control over the incompetent. The guardian serves as the legal representative, may make medical care decisions, and may even decide where the incompetent will reside (Regan, 1983). According to Horstman (1975), upon being found in need of guardianship, the person is reduced to the "status of a child in the eyes of the law."

Issues in Guardianship as a Protective Measure: Procedural Irregularities

The power of the state to appoint a guardian (over the person and property) has been characterized by Horstman (1975) as its "most devastating and far-reaching power." Regan (1983) agrees, describing the consequences of guardianship as "drastic"; the person is suddenly rendered incapable of performing any act of legal consequence. Yet, the evidence suggests that the proceedings that establish this extensive control over an individual are often conducted in a less than thorough manner.

In practice, the guardianship proceedings is often perfunctory and characterized by "unseemly informality" (Regan, 1983). In many such proceedings, the alleged incompetent is not present. A 1975 Los Angeles study of over 1000 guardianship/conservatorship proceedings found that in 84 percent of the cases, only the judge, the petitioner, and the petitioner's attorney were present (Schmidt et al., 1975).

Inadequate notice, lack of representation (or perfunctory representation) by counsel, procedural informality, absence of appellate court review, and vague legal standards set out by state statute are also seen as typical of most guardianship proceedings (Regan, 1983; Schmidt et al., 1975). Some writers argue that there is a need for full adversary proceedings in establishing guardianship as a result of the

serious deprivations of liberty that may result. However, the traditional informality of such proceedings and indeed the state's exercise of
its parens patriae power generally, has been justified by the fact that
these proceedings are nonadversarial in nature. The sole preoccupation of the court is to be the individual's best interests (Horstman,
1975; Schmidt et al., 1975), an argument reminiscent of child protection proceedings.

Guardianship and the Elderly

In examining the application of guardianship procedures for the
protection of the elderly, Regan (1983) predicts a great potential for
abuse. In theory, according to Regan, the application may hold some
logic. In practice, guardianship laws may be inappropriate and repressive instruments despite their intent to assist the elderly person. As is
noted in the clinical section of this work, it is easy to misinterpret the
functional disabilities of many older persons (Daiches, 1982). Regan
sees the potential for the court's overemphasizing mental incapacity
and ignoring evidence of functional ability as a contributor to the perceived need for protection. It is far too easy, in Regan's view, to label
some of the behavioral aberrations sometimes associated with aging,
such as forgetfulness or careless habits, as evidence of incompetence
requiring guardianship. The many elderly persons who experience
only a partial or gradual deterioration in functional capacity are not
the persons who require full guardianship or for whom it was
designed. The need in these cases, as suggested by Regan (1983), is
for legislation authorizing flexible guardianships tailored to the individual's capacities. Such flexibility would allow that person to retain
control over the decisions they retain the capacity to make; a more
humane approach which would aid in sustaining self-esteem as well.
The special intervention legislation contained in some adult protective
legislation as earlier discussed, was intended to provide this type of
flexible and limited intervention.

Horstman (1975) has reflected upon the reduced involvement of
older persons in society. In fact, his notion is that increasing reliance
upon guardianship with older persons may contribute to this
disenfranchisement. Horstman (1975) believes that protection of the
elderly under the guise of guardianship contributes to the proliferation
of elderly persons unable to provide for their own welfare. He cites
evidence that this elderly person may be little better off after such a

drastic measure as guardianship than prior to it. This is particularly true when the guardianship appears to be more a medical than legal decision (Horstman, 1975; Schmidt et al., 1975).

Horstman (1975) has commented that guardianship seems to focus more on the sanity of the individual than upon their self-reliance. In his view, the courts and legislatures have been only too willing to rely upon psychiatric/psychological labels in the determination of what constitutes acceptable behavior. As a result, a medical opinion regarding mental competency is often dispositive of the ultimate legal question. Instead of concentrating on questions about functional abilities of the proposed ward, the courts concentrate on the condition of the mind, to the virtual exclusion of all else. Since the medical condition often fails to connect its label with any operational definition or behavior, the proposed ward is merely categorized through the use of a conclusory diagnostic label. The consequence is that medical disability has become confused with legal disability (Horstman, 1975). Legal incompetency is not the same as mental illness. Mental illness can, but does not necessarily, result in legal incompetence (Regan, 1983).

Guardianship and a Therapeutic Endeavor

Courts have generally recognized the state's power to require noncriminal involuntary confinement of nondangerous mentally ill persons for therapeutic purposes. Civil commitment proceedings are characterized by the requirement of a finding that involuntary confinement is the least restrictive alternative necessary for the protection, care, and treatment of the mentally ill person (Krauskopf, 1983). The results of a guardianship may be quite similar to the results of a civil commitment, yet the same restrictions are not required. The question that must be asked is whether there should be limits on the state's power to impose protective services upon those persons who do not want them. In adult protective services situations, the benevolent intentions of the state should not negate the requirements of substantive due process. Horstman (1975) argues that guardianship actions affect the same fundamental liberties as criminal laws. The state interest to be served therefore must be compelling and the means adopted to accomplish the state's interest the least restrictive. Horstman (1975) believes that the reason these constitutional standards have not yet been judicially applied to guardianship is because there is little litigation concerning declarations of incompetency in guardianship matters.

A Summary View:
Protection Against Those Who
Would Save Us From Ourselves

Horstman (1975) suggests that a full adversary proceeding, the only time-tested protection for the rights and interests of the individual, be required for guardianship proceedings. Regan (1983) and Krauskopf (1983) suggest statutory reform authorizing limited guardianships tied to specific functional disabilities and requiring the use of the "least restrictive alternative." Both the protections offered as well as the potential abuses should be carefully considered before taking reflexive action in the case of elder mistreatment. One such reflexive action that has occurred is the adoption of mandatory reporting statutes for elder mistreatment.

Mandatory Reporting

The Practical Issue of Available Services

No single element of the adult protective services legislation has been debated more than the issue of whether or not to require mandatory reporting of suspected mistreatment of the elderly. When it is adopted, it tends to follow the reporting legislation found in child maltreatment laws (Faulkner, 1982).

Typically, mandatory reporting statutes in the adult protective area require professionals of varying description to report. These statutes require or permit reporting based upon reasonable cause for suspicion that the elder person has been abused or neglected. The agency receiving the report is generally required to investigate within a fixed time period and procedures for gaining access in order to investigate the report are often included within the legislation (Sloan, 1983b). Each of these elements is held in common with mandatory child maltreatment reporting laws that have been in place since the early 1970s.

The rationale for the commonalities between adult and child protection statutes that mandate reporting is that these two problems are seen as parallel. Both victims are seen as being dependent upon others for their needs. Both victim groups are seen as "politically weak" and without "adequate legal protection" (Katz, 1980, p. 716). It is also feared that without mandatory reporting, the victims will be unable to obtain protection (Katz, 1980). The problem with mandatory reporting of elder mistreatment is that far too little study went into answering the question as to whether the child and adult problems were analogous before reporting was mandated. It is not clear that mandatory reporting is positively generalized from child to elder mistreatment. Even if effective, there is the policy question as to whether it should be applied to adults.

Mandatory reporting is a case finding tool implicitly promising a remedy. It should be unthinkable to screen for a problem and have either an inadequate remedy or no remedy available. Yet the statutes that require reporting of elder mistreatment are premised on the desire of the state to protect those who cannot protect themselves; a premise that also implies the availability of services (Faulkner, 1982). Many states entered into mandatory reporting prior to appropriate allocation of treatment resources. The result is an unkept promise for elder mistreatment victims. In response to this reality, Faulkner (1982) argues that even if mandatory reporting can be justified, it is prematurely adopted in the absence of the services which fulfill its promise; a compelling argument.

The Fundamental Issue:
Can This Intrusion Be Justified?

Beyond the issue of the case finding outstripping available resources, there is the fundamental issue of the justification for the state's intrusion into the lives of its older persons. "Our laws are predicated upon the assumption that adults should have the freedom to live as they choose so long as others are not harmed" (Faulkner, 1982, p. 79). Parens patriae, the state's duty to protect those who cannot protect themselves, is an exception. Adult protective services legislation has been designed to assist the impaired adult residing in the community without unnecessary involuntary intervention into that person's life. Protection from mistreatment by a caretaker and the mandated reporting of suspected cases of such mistreatment are an element of that protective service in many states. Using the standard of "no unnecessary involuntary intervention," before mandatory reporting is enacted (an involuntary intervention into the elder person's life) there must be a justifiable need demonstrated. At this time, there is no clear notion as to whether the older person would seek out help in such situations if it were readily available; whether mistreated elders generally have the capacity to seek help; or whether they want third persons to be mandated to report (Faulkner, 1982; Katz, 1980). To date, mandatory reporting legislation is long on good intentions and short on scientific study providing justification. In fact, if mandatory reporting is not bolstered by service availability, it may well be detrimental.

Faulkner (1982, p. 81) sees mandatory reporting statutes as having a "severely negative impact upon individual elders and the aged as a group." The solutions found commonly following mandatory case finding, according to Faulkner, such as guardianship or institutionalization, may be worse than the mistreatment reported. If a reported victim of elder mistreatment refuses the proffered services, an incompetency proceeding may be brought which ultimately results in the elder person's loss of freedom and autonomy (Katz, 1980). For many elder persons living in a home where some mistreatment occurs can sometimes be infinitely preferable to an institutional placement. Every adult protective services specialist has had the experience of an older person saying, "If you move me I will die," and often it is true. Institutionalization of the elderly has been found to hasten death (Katz, 1980).

That the older person prefers to stay where they are has been addressed elsewhere in this work. The most frequently occurring reaction to an allegation of mistreatment will be denial. In some cases, resignation, psychological acquiescence, and passive acceptance will be the victim's response. There is good reason to deny. Fear of retaliation, the paucity of alternative shelter, fear of the unknown, and the shame and stigma of admitting their own victimization by family members all inhibit admission (Katz, 1980). Even when a resigned admission does occur, it is not necessarily positive for it may signal a giving up on life in general. Recognition of this pattern in those victims who are known brings up the question of respect for the victim's wishes and whether the mandate to report to authorities should persist.

Voluntary Intervention and Services

The solution to this difficult question may rest with voluntary intervention and treatment services. These services would stand in contrast to mandatory reporting that may trigger an unwelcome intrusion into the lives of elder abuse victims who do not wish to be protected by outside sources (Katz, 1980). In those situations where the individual cannot make a conscious decision, all traditional protections should apply. But for the older person capable of making the conscious choice to refuse assistance, at least one author (Faulkner, 1982) advocates for respecting the victim's choice. Perhaps such a strategy would also encourage the development of services which could aid families who care for older persons before the mistreatment occurs, as called for in other sections of this work. Consideration of this issue brings back the question of program and legislative planners drawing too close an analogy of this problem to child maltreatment.

The Analogy to Conjugal Violence

As Katz (1980) reminds her readers, to be a child is to be dependent and without capacity to decide what is best for oneself. But to be an adult is to be independent with the capacity and authority to decide and act upon what the adult decides is best. The law acts to protect children due to their dependency and lack of decision-making ability. Upon reaching majority, the decision-making capacity belongs to the individual and aging should not rob the individual of this capacity. Aging is not equivalent to incompetence or the need for protection from oneself or others as is youth.

Both Katz (1980) and Faulkner (1982) suggest that the response to suspected mistreatment of the elderly should be more closely modeled to the response to conjugal violence than the response to child maltreatment. The victims of elder mistreatment and conjugal violence are adults, persons who have options, not mandates, in choosing protection. Like families involved in conjugal violence, older persons and their families require support, not involuntary intervention and mandatory reporting (Faulkner, 1982). Katz (1980) agrees stating that it is the lack of meaningful programs which define the barriers to the prevention of mistreatment of the elderly, not the lack of a reporting mechanism. These are both positions that are supported by the Attorney General's Task Force on Family Violence (1984) as well.

A Summary View of Intervention

The state justifies intervention into the lives of adults based on alleged mental incapacity. As this intervention plays upon the lives of suspected victims of elder mistreatment, it describes troubling questions of self-determination. If, as a society, the belief is held that the aging enjoy the same fundamental rights of privacy, personal autonomy, and freedom as other adults, we must respect their choices, even if they hasten death (Faulkner, 1982). We can not continue to model our approach to this problem as if it were a program built for dependent children. The elderly are not children and in many cases they are not dependent. We cannot continue to remove them from their chosen environment, against their will, and place them in one we have chosen for them. To do so is not our right for unlike the children we analogize these adult victims to, the older person has the right to make his or her own choices.

The Attorney's Role

As was described in the section on legal issues in child maltreatment, the attorney for the elderly person facing guardianship or other protection hearings often faces a personal quandary. This attorney may have a strong temptation to substitute decisions that he or she has made for those more properly made by the client. There is a decision to be made at the outset as to whether the attorney will be a strong advocate without qualification for the legal rights of the client or will be offering representation within the attorney's personal view of the best interests of the elder client. The latter representation may be in direct conflict with the client's wishes and rights (Krauskopf, 1983). The attorney representing the elderly person with limited capacity but who is strongly objecting to the proposed guardianship knows this professional and personal quandary only too well.

The conflict between legal rights and best interests is potentially present in every situation involving guardianship, limited guardianship, residential placement or other protective services (Krauskopf, 1983). Krauskopf asserts that the possibility of the drastically detrimental effects of the state intervention into the life of the elderly person demands that counsel occupy a traditional adversarial role and respect the expressed wishes of the client. It is only this role that will assure the client of due process, and prevent unwarranted loss of liberty. Any stated desire to contest, and even in those situations when meaningful communication is impaired, Krauskopf believes that professional responsibility rests on the side of presenting the best possible case for limited intervention.

At a minimum in every protective proceeding the attorney for the elder person should (1) present any evidence that the client is not mentally ill or legally incompetent, (2) present alternative plans (such as voluntary treatment if the client is willing to accept it, (3) assure that only proper evidence is admitted at the hearing, (4) cross-examine the expert to reveal the basis upon which the opinions of incompetence were derived, and (5) strenuously object to commitment or institutionalization if there are less restrictive alternatives (Krauskopf, 1983).

A Summary View

Legal interventions in the case of suspected elder mistreatment is tenuous. Clinical support and research evidence is currently unavailable. Expert opinion is largely based upon research that has little empirical validity (Gelles & Pedrick-Cornell, 1982). Apparently inappropriate analogies are being drawn between this and the child maltreatment problem. Yet, the practitioner's clients in these two forms of family violence are quite different. At this time, the key seems to be the understanding that these aging clients are not who they appear to be. They should not be stereotyped as an "old" person as discussed in later chapters. They should not be treated as children. They should be listened to and heard even if rapport is difficult due to infirmity. They should not be considered incompetent simply because rapport or communication is difficult. The elder mistreatment client is frequently a capable adult who is being intruded upon by an official agency that does not realize that it has nothing to offer that would be superior to the elder person's current situation. It is the role of the legal practitioner to gain that understanding on the part of the state if that is the wish of the client. It is the role of the legal practitioner to persuade the state that it is intruding upon the life of an individual who has made a decision, not upon the least restrictive alternative but upon the lesser of two evils. Like many other victims of family violence, it is not the attorney's role to determine what is right for the victim. Rather it is the attorney's role to interpret this victim's wishes to the court and to assure that the victim's rights are protected. To do otherwise would to be part of the victimization of this aging individual. The following section will provide both legal and clinical practitioners some practical suggestions in how best to arrive at a comfortable and communicative relationship with the victims of all forms of family violence.

Part V

Capturing the Family Violence
Practitioners' Environment (II):
Clinical Work and the Violent
Family

13

The Clinician and the Violent Family: Basic Skills

Working with the violent family is often personally uncomfortable. *Many of these families are difficult to like.* The chaotic nature of these families, their failure to learn from experience, dependencies, and the expenditure of clinician's time make for a grueling experience (D'Agnostino, 1975, p. 44). Whether the family is abrasive and belligerent or submissive and helpless, the clinician's emotional resources will be drained. This family demands unfamiliar roles from the clinician, such as community advocate. They may be suspicious of each therapeutic suggestion. Through all this, the clinician must arrive at some personally neutral position regarding their violent acts. For it is only when a nonblaming attitude is reached that the atmosphere necessary for defining and resolving specific problems is created (Newberger & Bourne, 1979a, p. 16; Wells, 1981, p. 117). In the final analysis, the clinician must be honest with themselves about their willingness to work 24 hours a day trying to accomplish tasks for which their professional training has left them largely unprepared. A view of specific family types may aid in making that decision.

The Clinical Process

The Maltreating Family

The maltreating family has been described as unmotivated, unfamiliar with, and fearful of the clinical process, and presenting with a difficulty in forming a therapeutic relationship (Wolfe et al., 1981, p. 35). Others have written of the lack of motivation, passive-aggressiveness, denial, and sabotage that exists in both nuclear and extended family members (Alexander, 1972, p. 25; D'Agnostino, 1975, p. 43). Even when the appearance of cooperation is given by the family, the clinician must be alert to the possibility that this family is exercising its ability to give an authority figure what it wants. Another possibility is that this is a demonstration of pseudo-normality, which disappears upon return of the child (Alexander, 1972, p. 25; Rodriquez, 1977, p. 83). *This manipulative and artificial presentation is one of the strong recommendations for the inclusion of the extra motivation provided by court-ordered and monitored clinical work.*

These families assume an artificiality in initial presentation. It is not planned or purposeful; this response is built on a fear of the clinician. These families assume that they will be used, attacked, and thought of as bad by authority figures, clinicians among them (Avery, 1975, p. 88). This results in a layer of distrust that is difficult to penetrate.

Clinicians must assume the presence of distrust in these families. Repeated testings of and experiences with the reliable clinician are the only means of breaking this down. Laying a foundation of honesty is important. From the outset, the clinician must be honest with the family and explain obligations in detail, such as reporting (Newberger & Hyde, 1979, p. 34). Some clinical ground may be lost initially but regained as the family realizes it needs the support of the clinician. Persistence and dependability will be among the clinician's strongest weapons across the entire course of treatment. *Be honest and be there when needed* (Rodriquez, 1977, p. 110; Wells, 1981, p. 117).

There is a fear in this family that if the clinician really knew them, their inherent worthlessness would cause the support to cease (Alexander, 1972, p. 26). The mere anticipation of this abandonment may cause the family to terminate treatment prematurely (Avery,

1975, p. 88). The members of these families cannot tolerate the anxiety of awaiting yet another rejection in their lives. They are in such need of caring that demonstrations of caring are fear-producing. After all, the caring demonstrated may not be real. As a result, clinical disclosure will be slow. The clinician's key skill is patience.

This is not a family comprised of verbal individuals. Rather, they have an extra measure of "verbal inaccessibility" (Wells, 1981). In the beginning, issues will remain superficial, present-oriented, filled with denial, and focused upon the outrage they feel at how others, such as child protective agencies, are treating them. Clinical roles at this time include the building of a noncritical atmosphere that allows for frightened ventilation, helping to label emotions being experienced, and taking the rarely presented opportunity to focus on a key issue within the family (Wells, 1981, p. 116).

This is a family which needs and wants direction and information. If it is available in this early crisis period, it should be offered. The clinician must not be nondirective at this time. It is wise to provide sympathetic understanding regarding the family's struggles (Steele & Pollack, 1972, p. 7). It is unwise to assume that the family will find their own path out of this morass.

There is frequently a deep dependency upon the clinician in these families. This may be uncomfortable. But dependency is not as contra-indicated in work with maltreating families as it may be with others. Dependency is a problem for the individuals in this family as they have never successfully negotiated a relationship. To do so with the clinician serves as a model for later efforts with others. Initially, this will mean that the clinician is doing a great deal more for and with the maltreating family than is customary, such as personally introducing them to collateral service providers (Holmes, 1978, p. 83). It may seem, at first, that this family believes that they are the clinician's only patients. They will demand attention accordingly. Emotional support from colleagues familiar with such families may be useful to avoid exploding at the family and its demands.

In order to keep both clinician and maltreating family in balance during the early phase of clinical contact, Schmitt (1978) has offered the following suggestions:

(1) Let the family know, right away, that you are interested in them and what they are going through.
(2) Let the family tell you what they feel their problems to be.

(3) Try and determine if there was *anyone* in their past who gave to them spontaneously (i.e., they did not have to earn the attention).

(4) Determine how individuals use and misuse other family members to meet their needs.

(5) Identify the defenses most frequently used by all family members.

(6) Show confidence in them and use their ideas whenever possible in formulating solutions to problems.

(7) Be alert to rigid interpretations of the world.

(8) Give them hope that change can occur.

(9) Let them know immediately about the healthy aspects of their functioning and reward it.

Among the elements Schmitt saw as leading to a more positive prognosis were (1) a previous experience with a person in a warm, "parent-like" role, (2) a good work history, (3) the ability to use outside help, and (4) the ability to say "I need help." Ultimately, each family member must be viewed first independently then as part of a family system. To develop a treatment plan, the clinician must be able to answer "(what) treatment, by whom is most effective for this individual with that specific problem?" (Blythe, 1983, p. 333) Unfortunately, even as the hope for the positive prognosis in the maltreating family is improving, that same hope for the sexually abusive family is fading as more is learned.

The Sexually Abusive Family

The sexually abusive family may be the most distant and self-contained encountered by the clinician. This family is held together by knowledge (of the sexually abusive acts and environment) inaccessible to others. The extremes to which all family members may go to protect this knowledge may border on a secondary victimization.

It is unwise to expect the sexually abusive family to protect the victim following an allegation. Fear in the perpetrator and disbelief in the nonperpetrating parent can combine to discredit the victim's disclosure. If the evidence is undeniable, the anger of the nonperpetrating parent and siblings may still contribute to a nonprotective or abusive response to the victim. When this failure of protection follows disclosure, it is likely that the child victim will demonstrate Summit's "child sexual abuse accommodation syndrome" (1983).

The sexual abuse victim may test the protective response of the family through a minimal disclosure of a sexually abusive event. If they find protection in the family or those in authority to be lacking, predictable steps occur. They first feel the continuing need to withhold the family secret. This is followed by an overwhelming sense of helplessness, entrapment, and attempted self-adjustment (accommodation) to the situation. When this becomes unbearable, there may be a tentative disclosure outside the family that is so unconvincing that it may not be believed. As this skepticism on the part of hoped-for sources of support is encountered, the child may retract the disclosure and the sexual abuse continues.

Summit (1985) states unequivocally that children do not distort the truth in the disclosure of sexual abuse. If they disclose, according to Summit, they should be believed. Others are not as certain, particularly with regard to allegations made in the midst of a child custody battle. *However, if an allegation has been made and then retracted, the clinician must give serious consideration to the possibility that the initial allegation was, indeed, genuine.*

A parent or protective agency labeling a disclosure of sexual abuse as nonsubstantiated must not distract the clinician from proceeding with the family. The rigidity, denial, projection, and fear within this family are all capable of forcing such a retraction (Adams-Tucker, 1984, p. 664). This will only be one of many sexual abuse situations in which the clinician is not certain whether or not the event actually occurred. In all such cases, it is wise to err in the direction of the alleged child victim and work with the family as though the situation was genuine (Brandt & Tizsa, 1980, p. 46). In these, and in substantiated cases, several ground rules apply.

Collaboration with legal professionals is mandated in the sexual abuse situation (Conte, 1982; Conte, Berliner & Nolan, 1980; Furniss, 1983; MacFarlane & Bulkley, 1982). Clinical work in the sexual abuse situation is critical, but so too is the recognition of the criminal nature of the act (Finkelhor, 1984, p. 96). Cooperative involvement of the legal system makes for a dramatic difference in at least attendance, if not total cooperation in the clinical process.

It is wise not to lose sight of the trauma associated with involvement in a sexual abuse investigation (Stone et al., 1984; Tyler & Brassard, 1984, p. 51). Even in the out-of-home molestation, support should be offered the victim's family if only to help them understand the attack (Mrazek, 1980). In addition, the nonabused children involved require reassurance and answer to their many questions. Beyond the circumstances of the mysterious events, the reactions of the adults surrounding the children may frighten them. The child's interpretation of the event is largely a matter of how important adults around them respond (Lewis-Herman, 1981, p. 121). A calm clinician may go a long way toward reassurance. Allow the parent(s) to be angry in the presence of the clinician, not the child. *Do not expect the family to play this role without some help.*

It is the victim of the assault who requires the lion's share of clinical intervention immediately following discovery/disclosure. Immediate reassurance is necessary. Summit (1984, p. 7) suggests that the problem be approached without any skepticism or revulsion and that constant reinforcement of the child's normalcy be given. For example, Summit suggests that the medical professional conducting the examination might indicate:

> I've examined your body very carefully inside and out and everything is perfectly normal. There's nothing that shows or will ever show anybody else what has happened to you (1984, p. 7).

Above all things, do not compound the insult of the investigation process by repeated interviews with the victim (Kempe & Kempe, 1984, p. 99). A single interview can serve the purposes of both clinical and legal professionals who are cooperating.

Even when questioned, the child sexual abuse victim may not reveal anything of major importance. They should not be expected to *talk.* They may play it out, draw it out, or symbolically represent sexual situations through anatomically correct dolls. But it may be that quiet time initially   will open later doors to more revealing questions and discussion (Kempe & Kempe, 1984, p. 103).

Finally, as with the maltreating family, the clinician may find themselves in conflict with the family over values and expectations, have difficulty in identifying anything positive about the family or its members, feel frustration at the slowness and inconsistency of organizational responses to the problem, and find rapport to be a struggle (Chapman, 1984). These are problems that plague the clinician in every form of family violence.

The Conjugally Violent Family

As in other violent families, secrecy has been used to protect the conjugal violence perpetrator (Hilberman, 1980, p. 1344). Both perpetrator and victim will deny or minimize the frequency and severity of violent events (Walker, 1979). The perpetrator will often avoid help, claim that there is no problem, and/or fail to follow through on appointments (Fleming, 1979). A triad of hostility, lack of motivation, and confused dependencies will interfere with the clinical process (Star, 1983, pp. 49–51). Yet the two greatest clinical confusions may be (1) difficulty in understanding the victim's reluctance to accept the label of victim, and (2) the resultant reluctance to view the conjugal partner as a perpetrator.

No matter how distasteful the conjugal partner seems to be to the clinician, it is predictable that the victim merely wants the violence, not the relationship to stop (Roberts, 1984, p. 88). The goal of working with this family is, consequently, a behavioral one: *stopping the violence*. The focus is on skills, not psychodynamics. If the objective of stopping the violence is not met, the next goal is helping the victim gain enough strength and independence to leave the relationship (Fleming, 1979, p. 8). To initiate this process, there are several mandates according to Deschner (1984, p. 97).

(1) The perp: trator must want to change even if entry to the clinical process i. not voluntary.
(2) Intervention must be immediate. There must be no opportunity to rationalize or deny the behavior and/or its consequences.
(3) The victim should not stay with the perpetrator and should be absent until treatment is complete.
(4) Mutual dependency must be replaced by mutual respect, increased flexibility, and more realistic expectations.
(5) New techniques for the expression of anger and dealing with conflict must be learned and adopted.

Following from the call for new techniques, the literature in conjugal violence suggests that, in general, insight therapies tend not to be found effective in this problem. Neither coercion, rescuing, rumination, nor emotive/ventilationistic activities will prove effective either (Star, 1983, pp. 46–47). What does seem to apply is supportive confrontation, enhancement of self esteem through reinforced activities, improved problem solving, structured exercises/practice, and honesty on the part of the clinician (Neidig et al., 1985; Star, 1983, p. 43).

Traditional marital therapy does not seem to fit this situation. If conducted, the victim may support the perpetrator and accept too large a personal role in the development of a problem which rests with the perpetrator (Fleming, 1979, p. 126; Ganley & Harris, 1978). The clinician must be able to identify with the perpetrator's problems, but it must never be forgotten that this is a situation in which an essentially defenseless victim is being assaulted. He or she is a victim and should be labeled so from the outset. This avoids the victim's propensity for denial of that fact (Walker, 1979). If the victim rejects this label, or the perpetrator will not share in the clinical process, the treatment program is going to effect little behavioral change. A temporary shifting of dependencies from perpetrator to clinician and back again will do little to establish a new way of relating (Hilberman, 1980, p. 1344).

A Summary View

A summary view of the basic clinical process is simple. New treatment strategies directed toward active behavior change are required. This will demand creativity and flexibility on the part of the clinician. The roles of perpetrator and victim must be clearly labeled and accepted before any change can take place. Finally, this family will drain the clinician unlike any other, asking the clinician to make up for all of the emptiness that has described their life in the past. To the extent that the clinician holds the tools to accomplish this demanding task, a description of these tools follows.

14

Therapies and the Violent Family

Psychotherapies

Today there is what has been described as an "awkward tension" (Newberger, 1985a) between the clinical side of family violence and the legal side of the problem. The clinician is wary of the court's somewhat unpredictable nature. The legal practitioner is equally fearful of the apparently minimal impact of traditional therapeutic strategies upon the violent family. Both sides of this issue are justified in their concern.

That traditional therapeutic strategies are effective across family violence types remains to be empirically proven. It is not clear whether the therapeutic target should be victim, perpetrator, family observer, or the family as a unit. What is clear is that the range of problems facing most violent families and the uniqueness of variables in each family/environment interaction make it certain that no universally ideal intervention is likely to be discovered (Conte, 1985; Lamb et al., 1985).

What is clear from the work in this area is that the primary therapeutic target in the family violence situation is the violent behavior, not the psyche of the persons involved. Most persons in these families want the *behavior* not the *family* to cease. The second target in family violence situations is the environment of the family or the misinformation that sustains the violence. Only after the violence has been reduced and the environment stabilized are insight-oriented therapies used to affect intrapersonal stressors. Viewing traditional therapies as the third step in the therapeutic process is too much for many helping professionals. Consequently, the record of success in this area has been a poor one at best. It is not the application of psychotherapies in violent families that has been in error. The error has been in the timing of that application and a history of too many inflated promises to legal professionals. The time has come to admit just how long and arduous the task of rehabilitating a violent family may be for all concerned.

The Maltreating Family

Ann Cohn authored the first major evaluation of child maltreatment success in 1979. The news was not good. Cohn (1979) found that 30 percent of the maltreating parents repeated the maltreatment, *while in treatment*. The workers in the programs being evaluated, when pressed, admitted to an expectation that only about 42 percent of the parents were less likely to maltreat their children at the end of treatment than prior to the treatment. In most cases, the child victims were not receiving treatment. Taitz (1980) has determined that fewer than one-third of maltreated children who are reliant upon parental treatment only to change their lives for the better show any positive growth. Many question why these tried-and-true methods are not as functional with the violent family as with other problems.

Bourne (1979, p. 11) offers several reasons why insight therapies are not the strongest weapon in the clinician's arsenal when working with the violent family. He notes that such therapies require a great deal of time, cost too much, require a near-immediate capacity to develop a trusting relationship, and not only demand a commitment to a process, but the ability to be personally introspective. These are not assets uniformly held by maltreating families. Bourne also notes that individual insight therapy elevates the belief in individual psychopathology in the violent family. This, in his opinion, detracts from attention that should first be directed to social and environmental contributors.

Wells (1981, p. 113) echoes some of Bourne's concern in describing maltreating families as having a low level of "verbal accessibility." He also describes a concomitantly low intellectual capacity and psychological immaturity in some families. Wells sees these families as not valuing "talking" in solving problems, are not introspective, expect help to be in the form of concrete goods and advice, and are not good at conceptualizing problems. After agreeing to this assessment of the maltreating family, Holmes (1978, p. 186) prescribes the problem-focused and goal-oriented therapies that are addressed to specific behavior changes as the solution to reaching such families. The exploration of feelings and attitudes are seen as too abstract for a family facing genuine danger from within. This is a position that is gaining increasing currency as behavior and cognitive therapies are being examined for application with violent families (Feshback, 1980; pp. 49–50; Rivara, 1985; p. 85).

Beyond verbal capacity, attitudinal, educational, and value differences between these families and those which respond well to insight therapies may be a problem. Wolfe and colleagues, (1981) after attempting insight programs, have returned to goal-oriented behavioral programs. This change was largely brought about by the road blocks they encountered from the families themselves. The litany of barriers includes such family features as anger, denial, cultural differences, passive-aggressiveness, poor attendance, and unrealistic expectations of the therapeutic process. Personal variables such as poor comprehension, slow learning, the absence of social support, and intra-familial disagreements also played a role. Some of these are barriers to behavioral therapies as well, but practice suggests that they are less debilitating in those approaches (Goldstein, 1973).

Following a major review of treatment strategies, Holmes (1978; p. 188) concluded simply that traditional mental health services do not work with maltreating families. Fixed appointments in out-of-home locations, and techniques that de-emphasize concrete services hold little interest for this family. The short-term prognosis of such an approach is poor. Its effectiveness in the long term may be negligible. At least one writer (Rivara, 1985; p. 86) is taking a strong stance against referral of violent families to such traditional services. If for no other reason, traditional services do not effect change in the violent family because of missed appointments, although court-ordered services may help this problem. All this does not mean that insight therapies have no place with the maltreating family. It means that insight therapies must take their place in a multi-model (Lazarus, 1981) strategy. Insight therapies, at least with the maltreating family, should not be the primary or the exclusive form of treatment.

Putting aside the issue of "which therapy first," Wolfe and colleagues (1981) have identified common points of attack for every clinician, regardless of discipline or therapeutic orientation. First, these child maltreatment specialists recommend providing more appropriate child management skills for everyday as well as unique child behaviors and problems. This implies skills in problem solving and alternatives to the parent's currently dysfunctional disciplinary style such as reliance on punishment. It is hoped that increased anger control and a reduction in impulsivity will follow this learning.

These experts, as did Steele and Pollack before them (1972; p. 14), seek to reduce the isolation of this family and to break down destructive patterns. This is accomplished through an increase in skill level as well as the development of a greater sensitivity to anger and the persons/situations that stimulate that anger (Feshback, 1980; pp. 53–54). It is hoped that this combination of increased skills and knowledge will reduce the excessive need for control the parents feel (Mulford & Cohen, 1967; p. 12). It is further hoped that an increase in the number of positive experiences will generalize to an improvement in self-image, an increased capacity for enjoyment, and a better ability to cope with the natural stresses of childrearing (Rodriguez, 1977; p. 80; Wolfe et al., 1981). The parent who finds greater gratification in their world may be able to offer some to their children (Steele & Pollack, 1972; p. 14).

The strictly behavioral clinician may suggest the need to identify all stimuli in the parent-child relationship that reinforce assaultiveness (Feshback, 1980; p. 55). This strategy presents the same time and money limitations as the extensive course of insight therapy. The more feasible behavioral goals for this family are limited. Some of the initial targets are better problem solving, tension relief, and improvements in coping skills (Steele & Pollack, 1972; p. 16). Family competition, rigidity, and the feeling that good punishment solves all problems (Rodriguez, 1977; p. 85) can not be ignored if present. Anger management, self-control training, assertiveness, and increased knowledge of community resources must be added to the family's repertoire of responses to problems (Wolfe et al., 1981). Most important, however, is the clinician's ability to help the parent separate the child's behavior from his or her own self-concept, begin to see the child as a separate individual, and help to separate the parent's self-esteem from the child's performance (Steele & Pollack, 1972).

If the clinician is able to demonstrate that they value the members of this family as individuals, that there is hope for success in the therapeutic process, and that the rewards for changing behaviors are greater than those in not changing, progress may be made (Deschner, 1984; p. 197). Once troublesome behaviors are identified and altered, skills brought into the family where once there were none, and applications for these skills have been learned, practiced, and reinforced, the time will come for identification of insight issues.

Until that time, the fundamental goal is bringing that family to a level of behavior which guarantees a reduction in physical risk.

The Sexually Abusive Family

In spite of the family-systems therapies currently being applied in sexual abuse cases, the individual perpetrator predominates as the therapeutic target. Current success in this area is less than encouraging. However, this may be, at least in part, a function of difficulties in researching this area. The primary question in this research is recidivism (Finkelhor, 1986). The measure of success is whether the sexual abuse perpetrator replicates his or her act in the future. As a result of differences between populations studied, length of follow-up period, and differing research criteria, current research cannot answer this pivotal question.

Finkelhor (1986) is as quick to offer hope for treatment success as he is to condemn current research (especially upon incarcerated offenders). He notes the number of studies claiming "successful" results. However, his feeling is that outcome measures such as attitude change, physiological arousal measures, and short-term self-reports of self-control beg the question. The question of whether re-abuse will occur in the long run remains. However, he closes his argument with the caveat that some of the best treatment programs remain to be evaluated. Others are less kind in reviewing this research.

At what might be considered the extreme of failure, a study of 39 German sex offenders who had been voluntarily castrated revealed that even this did not eliminate sexual assault entirely (Heim, 1981). In the hopeful range of this research area, various combinations of convert sensitization to deviant responses, aversive deconditioning, social skills training, and antiandrogenic drug treatments are being tried (Josiassen, Fantuzzo, & Rosen, 1980). These strategies have not been tested longitudinally. Neither have they been tested adequately in a nonincarcerated environment in which temptations are greatest. Those described as pedophiles appear somewhat resistant to most known psychotherapeutic and behavior modification techniques; however, some impulse control/suppression strategies offer hope (Costell, 1980; Lanyon, 1985). The label of "pedophile," through its lack of uniformity, confounds this research as well. The overall conclusion must be that no single psychotherapeutic strategy with the perpetrator seems totally effective. What does seem necessary in every case is the involvement of the court to assure compliance and completion and a probable array of psychotherapeutic interventions rather than a reliance upon a single strategy (Giaretto, 1982). As in the physically maltreating family, a cessation of behavior and stabilization in environment must precede insight, but all three are necessary to effect long-term change (Dixen & Jenkins, 1981).

Conte (1984), although a clinician who believes in treatment for the sex offender and victim, offers warning to those who approach the sex offender from a humanistic bent. First, Conte notes the absence of empirically supported psychodynamic causes for sexual abuse. He views the introduction of such elements as allowing the perpetrator room for denial of responsibility and rationalization (p. 261). He views manipulation and force as clear elements of the sexual abuse situation. This is not the sexual expression of nonsexual needs. This is sexual assault (pp. 259–260). The perpetrator may be remorseful and regret events, but he has still committed a sex crime and must both recognize and admit it.

The fundamental clinical issue with this perpetrator is control; either he develops internal controls for this behavior or he must be externally controlled (Groth et al., 1982; p. 139). It may require chemotherapy, behavior modification, psychotherapy, psychosocial education, or a combination of all these strategies. Targets for treatment include interpersonal deficiencies, aggression, and self confidence (Brodsky, 1980) as well as internal predispositions and living conditions/strategies (Groth et al., 1982; p. 139). The initial treatment is often most effectively offered in a controlled environment (Groth et al., 1982; p. 139). No matter the treatment setting, control over the urge to assault is a battle that the perpetrator must continue to fight each day of the remainder of his life. Cure is not at issue. Cure will not occur, control might (Bauman et al., 1983; p. 80).

The father in the sexually abusive home, if a perpetrator, must be confronted. That may take place directly, although suicide can be a concern in the midst of the crisis of disclosure. Or he may be ordered to pay for the treatment of the victim if disclosure comes later (MacFarlane & Korbin, 1983; pp. 232–233). The mother must be allowed to clarify her feelings. She may feel criticized by professional and friend alike for not wanting to leave her husband immediately. It must be remembered that this is the man she married, believing in such a thing is not easy. Even in the face of evidence, loyalty conflicts are difficult. There may be anger, guilt, and empathy toward both perpetrator and victim at once. These are feelings that are played upon by problems in her own background. This is the trap of family violence. There are never any easy answers as a review of the therapeutic targets in conjugal violence will reveal.

The Conjugally Violent Family

As has been discussed in other forms of family violence, insight-oriented therapies do not seem the therapy of choice in conjugal violence either (Fleming, 1979; p. 304). In that conjugal violence seems to be responsive to self-generated anger, it seems more therapeutically productive to identify critical points in family interaction and introduce new mechanisms for dealing with them (Deschner, 1984; p. 79; Edleson, 1984). Some form of cognitive restructuring combined with a skills training procedure seems, currently, to offer the best hope for working with this family (Deschner, 1984; Novaco, 1975, 1979). The goal here is gaining control over the type of stress which helps to bring problems about.

Star (1983, pp. 13–14) has described treatment goals in the conjugal violence situation as (1) the development of self-awareness, (2) learning to identify feelings, (3) assertiveness training, (4) anger management, and (5) relaxation training. Behavioral alternatives are needed by this couple. A comprehensive attack upon these goals demands a combination of psychodynamic, family, cognitive, and behavioral therapies. The result must be an individual who has improved self-monitoring skills, is capable of relaxation, and has behavioral alternatives which reach beyond violent responses (Edleson, 1984; p. 237).

In addition to the familiar behavior modification and skills training models, some form of cognitive restructuring seems to be critical in work with the violent co-habitor. Three of the most influential cognitive therapies in use are Ellis's Rational Emotive Therapy (RET) (1962), Meichenbaum's Self-Instructional Training (1977), and Beck's Cognitive Therapy (1976).

RET indentifies irrational thoughts that are confronted and reinterpreted by the clinician. With rehearsal and practice in a real life setting, the individual comes to understand his destructiveness. In the conjugal violence setting, it appears that the perpetrator says (1) I must have control, (2) I cannot control emotions, (3) since I feel out of control, and it could not be my fault, it must be her fault, (4) I am now so upset that I can't help but hit the person who upset me like this (Edleson, 1984; p. 238). This is a combination of denial, blaming the victim, justifying the violence, and externalization that will be used across all forms of family violence (Edleson, 1984; p. 239).

Meichenbaum's strategy is to ask the individual to identify maladaptive thoughts and self-statements that occur prior to, during, and after an event. The clinician then describes more appropriate thoughts and behaviors as well as mechanisms for self-reinforcement while thinking these more appropriate thoughts. This is practiced by the patient. Changing the self-messages that operate in violent situations will curtail not only frequency but degree of rage and explosiveness (Deschner, 1984; p. 69). The perpetrator may have previously convinced himself that his rages were too great for him to control. This strategy provides an alternative.

Novaco (1975, 1979) writes of a "stress innoculation" procedure whereby the individual becomes better prepared to meet known stresses, that is, situations in which he becomes violent. The patient undertakes mental rehearsal of the situation in which he finds new and better "self-talk." Skills are also provided that are practiced and combined with self-talk. With the increase in both assertive and relaxation skills, problem solving can take place in an atmosphere that was only explosive before. One useful addition to this technique is an "anger log" in which the anger-provoking situation, self-talk, feelings aroused by recalling the situation, and identification of the false beliefs that justify actions are all incorporated into a journal (Edleson, 1984; p. 238) later reviewed by the clinician and discussed.

In Beck's procedure, the patient identifies inaccuracies and distortions in thinking, replaces these with thoughts seen as more accurate by the patient and clinician, and is reinforced for those changes (Latimer & Sweet, 1984; p. 12). This, and the other cognitive therapies, seem to be attractive to the perpetrator of conjugal violence who is surprised by the here-and-now orientation and the empiricism (i.e., objectivity) of the process. They had expected an ambivalent look at past experiences in the clinical process; what actually occurred is a pleasant surprise (Latimer & Sweet, 1984, p. 13; Walker, 1979, p. 231).

Overall, a self-focused, problem-specific, and quantifiable treatment program will provide the perpetrator of conjugal violence fewer places to hide. The use of contracts, theme discussion, and skills training gives this individual something against which to use, manipulate, and measure progress. Most important, it gives them a skill to apply immediately in the violent situation (Star, 1983, p. 53).

The Victim

Working with the victim of conjugal violence is somewhat different than other victims of family violence. These individuals hold the capacity to make a difference in their situation. Working with this victim means strengthening them at the same time their partner is being given new skills. Together, these strategies can help build an affiliative relationship where there had been a competitive or destructive one.

Pinderhughes (1972, pp. 135–137) has looked at the threatening qualities of the conjugal violence situation and suggests the following strategy. Initially, define the violence according to the victim's experience. Seek to establish some superordinate goal between the couple that will demand that they work together toward a goal they both wish to achieve. Find a shared power base rather than the aggrandizement that has been directed toward the perpetrator in the past; a feature of the relationship that led to denigration of the victim. After the elimination of this omnipotence, balance the talking on one side with the listening on both sides and help them move forward together.

The victim of conjugal violence feels overwhelmed. This relationship is sufficiently violent to frighten almost anyone, much less this frequently dependent and nonassertive individual. It is necessary to seek the victim's barriers to her own protection by separating out problems, labeling feelings, identifying strengths and weaknesses as well as defining realistic goals (Fleming, 1979, pp. 145–146; Hilberman, 1980, p. 134). If this is followed by an achievable plan of action, the result can be a victim who can either end the violence or end the relationship.

The victim is also an angry person, but getting in touch with this rage too quickly can become a barrier to constructive action. If independence is pushed too quickly, the newly found independence, fanned by anger, will likely result in increased violence on the part of the perpetrator (Hilberman, 1980, p. 345).

Walker (1979, p. 231) finds several points of ambivalence in the conjugal violence victim that must be resolved before decision making can take place constructively. These include love/hate for the perpetrator, internalized rage/terror of the perpetrator, staying/leaving, and security/panic. If the choice is made to leave, there must also be continued support or the dependency and loneliness in their lives causes them to fall into another violent relationship (Fleming, 1979, p. 63).

The victim of conjugal violence, in the psychotherapeutic setting, is an individual who must overcome fear, self-hatred, and the paralyzing resentment that flows from a self-perception of helplessness. Even as the perpetrator must be given new skills and thoughts to aid in the negotiation of the violence producing event, the victim must also be led to the decision as to whether it is worth it to attempt to survive the time it will take the perpetrator to learn new ways of acting (Deschner, 1984, p. 74). Unfortunately, far too few either learn the necessary skills or elect to leave the violent perpetrator behind. However, it is worse for the family violence victim who finds self-motivated extraction from a violent situation not an option. The mistreated elder is such a person.

Mistreatment of the Elderly

The largest problem in psychotherapeutic work with the elder mistreatment case is the propensity to stereotype the patient. Solomon (1983, p. 155) has reviewed an extensive body of literature indicating that psychotherapists, in particular, are reluctant to work with older persons. When they do participate, all too often, stereotyping of the older person leads to services given automatically because they are "services for the elderly." This leaves no room for the needs of the individual or for those needs which extend beyond custodial or maintenance requirements (Hickey & Douglas, 1981, p. 506; Solomon, 1983).

Rather than focus on how much this older person is like others, there is a need to consider how the losses of aging such as identity, usefulness, productivity, status, independence, friends, peers, and family have affected them individually. The capacities of this older person currently hold little meaning in the absence of knowledge of who they once were. Helping to give some meaning to life and reducing the crippling nature of loss can help the older person feel more involved, and make them easier to live with, thus reducing stress on the caretaker.

Work must also be undertaken with the caretaking family. Earlier conflicts and dependencies must be surrendered and the view of the parent must change. There is a need to relate to the parent as an individual, recognize that they made mistakes as a parent, and accept past hurts as unintentional (Blenker, 1965, pp. 57–58). This is particularly important as the infirm parent drifts slowly into the role of child (Block & Sinnott, 1979, pp. 53–55; Steinmetz, 1978). It is not easy to learn to live with someone who suddenly has no energy, loses the intactness of their thinking process, has impairments in judgment, exhibits little control, and appears fearful most of the time. This is especially true if they were once the biggest and strongest person you knew (Luppens & Lau, 1983, p. 211). Psychotherapeutic support and psychoeducational work must be conducted regularly with the caretaker(s) to keep their spirits up and their caretaking skills growing. In this, and other areas of family violence, group therapy has shown itself to be valuable.

Group Therapies

Assuming that the individuals within the family are psychologically and intellectually competent, group therapies have been found to be successful with violent families. The involvement in the group setting helps to reduce the isolation felt by many of these families. Gaining an understanding that they are not alone in their tensions, fears, and frustrations is a positive result. Finally, the mutual support that may develop between group members provides a healthier dependency than has generally been available to these individuals previously.

The Maltreating Family

For the maltreating family, particularly the parents, a group setting furnishes more than a means for reducing tension and isolation; the group may also help reduce the dependency that this family has upon the clinician. The group provides a mutual support system in times of need and a mechanism by which the denial in these families can be confronted by peers.

Within the group setting, the maltreating parents gain a sense that they are being genuinely helpful to others, perhaps for the first time. Getting attention from someone they did not know prior to group membership also helps to reduce the sense that they must do something for someone before they are valued. If the group membership is able to value them simply because they are human beings, perhaps they can come to value their children more easily, reducing expectations. Last, but in no way least, the group setting provides a vehicle for the transmission of accurate child development, childrearing, and skills/information that can be rehearsed and reinforced. Such a goal-oriented group, or even a simple activity/leisure group, has proven to be helpful to maltreating parents generally and those with a limited fund of knowledge particularly (Holmes, 1978, p. 185; Rodriguez, 1977, p. 84).

The question as to whether maltreating parents can be mixed in a group setting with individuals who have common problems (marital discord, poor communication, or family stress), but who are not abusive, remains open. There are those who believe that the heterogeneous groups promote greater "universality" (i.e., the sense that they are not the only persons with those problems). It may also be valuable for these parents to understand that *all* parents experience intense anger at their children from time to time (Linnell, Zieman, Romano, 1984, p. 80). However, it does require a somewhat unusual perpetrator to be willing to disclose effectively in such a setting. There is a danger of the maltreating parent becoming involved in the group only to the point of acting out a changed facade or having the group support them in an artificial flight into health.

The Sexually Abusive Family

Group work seems to hold the same advantages with the sexually abusive family as with the maltreating family. Although each of the members of this family also require a one-on-one therapeutic relationship throughout the course of treatment. Importantly, anonymity is of increased concern in the sexual abuse case. If there has been no legal admission of responsibility, civil and legal rights are easily violated. Public recognition between group members can also be embarrassing (James & Nasjleti, 1983).

In the group setting sexually abusive parents learn how to listen and how to become familiar with and communicate genuine feelings. This should not be a freewheeling group, however. The clinician in this group must retain control at all times. The clinician must attend to the pace of the group, contain persons who tend to dominate, deal with discomfort, observe nonverbals, and confront ambiguous statements. Empathy from group members is important, but so too is confrontation from those who know the denial from personal experience (Kempe & Kempe, 1984, p. 154). Group members who are perpetrators will not tolerate manipulation and subterfuge.

Activity based and topically related groups are useful and help promote effective conversation and sharing. As a model, Groth's groups in residential treatment include such vital topics as sex education, relationships with women, personal victimization, understanding sexual assault, anger management, communication, and anxiety/depression (Groth et al., 1982, p. 140). Many of these topics will be found useful across varying types of family violence.

The Conjugally Violent Family

Ganely (1981) sees group work as the fastest method for dealing with alternative behavior development in the perpetrator of conjugal violence. In her view the group that is based on a clear goal (ending the battering) can work quickly with the help of constructive confrontation from group members, members who do not allow the perpetrator to ignore responsibility. In this way, an active membership and clinician can serve not only as a vehicle for the teaching and learning of new skills, but in the reduction of minimization and denial. In this group, too, the transfer of dependency from the clinician to group members can help lighten the clinician's load (Deschner, 1984, p. 98).

Victims of conjugal violence have benefitted from group experiences in the shelter setting (Fleming, 1979; Roberts, 1984). Meeting another victim and finding that they are equally frightened seems to have an immediate therapeutic effect. Learning takes place in this victims' group that cannot be duplicated in working exclusively with the couple.

The targets of victims' groups include assertiveness, anger, self-esteem, life-planning options, sex roles, independence, and problem solving. At a later time topics such as separation, divorce, child support, child care, property, public housing, welfare, and employment may prove critical to victims who have elected to leave their spouses (Fleming, 1979; p. 111).

In some cases, the group therapy that is conducted with violent family members confronts the family as a unit. Other styles separate victim and perpetrator and have separate sibling or noninvolved family member groups. The clinician must be alert to the dangers of excluding seemingly noninvolved family members or paramours.

These persons may not be directly involved nor hold a legal position in the family, but that does not negate their influence. These persons are often capable of destroying even the most elegant of treatment strategies. This point gives rise to an examination of the family therapies.

Family Therapies

Although a family problem, the clinical literature on the violent family reveals surprisingly little emphasis on the use of family therapy. This may reflect the relatively recent recognition of "family system" influences in these families. Since the early work focused on clinical pathology in the perpetrator and the emphasis in treatment was separation of victim and perpetrator, there has been an absence of attention in the family area. The more recent thrust toward in-home services and family skill building may predict a rapid growth of research in this area for all types of violent families.

The Maltreating Family

In family therapy with the maltreating family, clinicians have devoted the greatest attention to communication patterns. Communication in these families, families in which power imbalances dominate the system, seems to be action-oriented. This tendency to act immediately on feelings is combined with isolation, misperceptions, denial, and blaming. It is clear that communication must be at least confused or worse (Wells, 1981, p. 113).

Wells (1981, p. 115) has studied communication patterns in maltreating families and has found that they do not listen. In fact, attention is gained *only* through yelling. Conflicts go repeatedly unresolved, and the range of problems dealt with is small compared to the range that are present. The members of these families exist at two different poles at any given moment. They are either active and volatile toward or apathetic and oblivious of each other. Positive feelings are rarely expressed and negative messages clearly predominate.

In many families, this is a style that is constructed upon the parent's perceived inadequacy. Unresolved conflict, feelings of inadequacy, loneliness, and lack of confidence combine in the parent to create an individual who does not feel capable of performing competently in the family and is angry about it (Avery, 1975, p. 87). A reliance upon corporal punishment, when combined with the anger generated by feelings of inadequacy becomes difficult to control (Feshback, 1980, p. 57). The interruption of that incompetency cycle, as well as dealing with any child behavior that may accelerate the parents' feelings of inadequacy, is the role of the family therapist.

In the special case where problems from the marriage are displaced upon the child, more than communication needs to be approached. Here the goal is increasing the gratification that the parent finds in the marriage. If that cannot be accomplished, permission to separate should be given. *The clinician must be alert to the possibility that problems with the child are only masked marital problems.* If so, the goal is helping the parents to understand that the constant friction is more detrimental to the child than living with a single parent (Alexander, 1972, p. 37).

A summary view would find the meat of family therapy with the maltreating family to be found in the symbiosis between dysfunctional roles in the family, and the resultant isolation, marital problems, child management problems, confusion, temper, stress management issues, and anger management failures. A combination of behavior therapy and traditional family work seems to hold promise (Justice & Justice, 1982). If this family is somewhat intellectually limited or absolutely without resources, the addition of concrete resources or arts/crafts/games to the therapeutic process may increase its effectiveness. Through these multiple activities, the involvement of parents with their children can be increased, and there is a vehicle through which problems in the family can be introduced and resolved safely (Wells, 1981, p. 116).

The Sexually Abusive Family

James and Nasjleti (1983) have provided a review of the goals of family therapy as it exists in a multi-model treatment package for the sexually abusive family. This is somewhat different from a traditional family therapy perspective and includes the following goals:

(1) open confrontation of the sexual abuse as a family,
(2) a definition of the pattern of abuse agreed upon by the family,
(3) the development of both short- and long-term goals for individual family members and the family as a whole,
(4) the establishment of a visitation plan,

(5) monitoring of progress toward goals,

(6) adjustment strategies after re-unification, and

(7) arriving at a termination point for the court-ordered treatment.

In order to complete this process, the sexually abusive family must complete three phases of treatment: (1) the "disclosure-panic" phase of crisis intervention, which lasts three weeks to three months; (2) the "assessment-awareness" phase lasting up to a year and a half; and (3) a "restructuring" phase, which may continue over an additional two years. During this time, the family will also be involved in individual crisis therapy with each family member, peer group support, individual therapy with each family member, couples therapy, mother-child and father-child therapy, conjoint family therapy, and will have demonstrated an ability to reach out to other services (James & Nasjleti, 1983). This is not a simple process, but it is not a simple problem.

An important, and often missed, element of family treatment with the sexually abusive family is that of sibling work. The trauma experienced by siblings may parallel that of victims or parents. These children are subject to the same misperceptions that all family members with knowledge of the event(s) have: anger, disbelief, resentment and/or blame (Mitkus, 1982, pp. 8–9). They may fear consequent destruction of the family, abandonment, vulnerability, shame, stress, and "survivor guilt" ("Why wasn't it me?").

In response to these problems, siblings will be found to experience over-identification with the victim, denial or rejection of the victim, blame and anger, jealousy, symptomatic reactions, and negative identification with the perpetrator. Brothers have particular problems trying to decide whether to identify with the father or protect the victim(s) (Mitkus, 1982, p. 13). As treatment, Mitkus recommends that each sibling be evaluated independently, sibling meetings be held jointly to evoke support, and individual therapy be added to the family therapy regime where indicated.

James and Nasjleti (1983, p. 25) see the mother in the sexually abusive family as the key to therapeutic success. Her ability to protect, capacity to empathize with the children, and ability to place what has happened in perspective are the clinical features that should gain initial attention. Some reality-based treatment may first be necessary to break down the disbelief that she feels. Some reparenting may be necessary in addition to the family work to allow her to feel strong and independent enough to go forward on her own.

She must, however, ultimately be prepared to deal with the concrete and emotional stresses that come about through the maintenance of a single parent household, for separation of perpetrator from family is the most common family position in today's treatment programs.

The Conjugally Violent Family

Work with violent couples has undergone substantial change in recent years. Early writers in the field concentrated much of their work in conflict management, displacement of aggression, and ventilationist (tension-reduction) activities (Bach & Goldberg, 1974). More recent research has indicated that ventilationist strategies, which teach couples to be "better fighters," only provide practice for an already deviant behavior (Straus, 1974; Walker, 1979). The more recent innovations tend to center about structural realignment of the couple's interactions.

Structural family therapy maintains that all recurrent interactions between family members such as battering may have been initiated by one family member, that is, the perpetrator, but these interactions have become a functional part of the maintenance of the entire family system (Deschner, 1984, p. 36). To break this functional link, the clinician must first interrupt the escalating cycles of anger by teaching the couple how to reduce stress as much as possible, to modify aggressive communication between them. More realistic role and communication patterns between them must be established (Taylor, 1984, p. 11). At the individual level, this is accompanied by better self-management techniques, which facilitate coping with stress and the use of assertive, not aggressive, behavior.

In the structural family approach, the assumptions are made that (1) abusive behavior is a learned pattern, (2) the behavior begins with the perpetrator and slowly develops into a system of operation that is self-perpetuating, (3) this is a system of behavior that is intensified by self-dialogue and stress, and (4) this behavior is fundamentally related to low self-esteem, powerlessness, and poor problem-solving skills on the part of one or both members of the couple (Taylor, 1984, p. 12). It is not clear whether the living situation of the partners (separate or together) influences the outcome of the therapy, but it may take many failures, such as recurrent violence, and separations before recognition is gained by the victim that his or her fantasy of the relationship must die before it is replaced with something more useful. The victim generally spends far too much time lying to him or herself (Hilberman, 1980, p. 1344).

Before leaving the topic of conjugal violence, it is important to note supplemental procedures. Some of the techniques that have been used to augment the therapy process include a time out in which partners identify their own rising anger level and leave the scene (Deschner, 1984, p. 103), a special signal that allows one partner to withdraw from the other as they feel tension rising (Walker, 1979), scheduled problem-solving sessions (Stuart, 1974), and a combination of reinforcement for positive behavior and the recognition that you do not attempt to solve disagreements "at the scene of the crime" (Deschner, 1984, p. 115).

Mistreatment of the Elderly

Although the model that seems most useful for family treatment in elder mistreatment is more educational than therapeutic, it is no less necessary. Preparation of this family, especially if the decision to introduce the elderly person into the home came about suddenly, requires gaining of new knowledge of caregiving, expectations of older persons, financial responsibilities/alternatives, and an expanded familiarity with life span alternatives generally (Douglas, 1983, p. 147). Few families are trained for these responsibilities.

Both elderly and caretaker in homes where infirm older persons reside are trapped; trapped within family roles that are unfamiliar, unexpected, and overwhelming. Anything available to reduce that sense of being overwhelmed seems safely categorized as family therapy in its broadest sense. The biggest problem in this family is not abuse but neglect; neglect that comes from not knowing how to cope emotionally or functionally.

The goal of the clinician in a family of this nature is to find the degree of care that is reasonable to expect from this family and external support for all that is needed beyond that. Some of this support comes to the family from traditional insight-oriented and family systems work, but a greater amount flows from the judicious application of nursing home care, homemakers, home health aides, delivered meals, home repair, day care, respite, and transportation. These, as well as a directed effort to push the family toward "natural helpers," may be some of the most productive family "therapies" available (Giordano & Giordano, 1984, p. 235; Hooyman, 1983,

p. 377; O'Rourke, 1981). It is not glamorous to deal in concrete services, but it may be lifesaving.

Concrete Services as Therapy

The concept of concrete services as a therapeutic measure is unfamiliar to most clinicians. These elements have always been viewed as important, but also as the responsibility of other people. In most family violence situations, there are no other people. Once rapport and trust have been established, the family's therapeutic relationship is set as far as they are concerned. While most clinicians see their role in terms of psychodynamic, behavioral, or interpersonal problems, those who work with violent families learn quickly that their role reaches well beyond those limited avenues.

The elements that hold the potential to become immediately threatening to the violent family, as well as those most likely to motivate an explosive event, are related to resource lack and the competition within the family for those resources. This may be a concrete or an emotional resource that is being sought. An impoverished personality is a risk factor in the long run, but immediate crisis is generated by the lack of material support. The clinician who seeks to reduce the number of immediate crisis events provides greater flexibility to deal with the dynamic aspects of the family problems.

Clinicians working with the maltreating family must resign themselves to being available 24 hours a day. Whether supporting successful actions or preventing failure, these clinicians will find themselves out of their office, with and without the family, trying to get things done for the family. For most clinicians this means the "un-learning" of old strategies in addition to the adoption of new ones (Mulford & Cohen, 1967, p. 12). This person is no longer just clinician but clinician-advocate. Services are going to have to be discovered for this family and, even after making contact, follow up will be required (Newberger, 1979, p. 16).

Remember that the initial contact with the maltreating family is going to present individuals who are distrustful, suspicious, alienated from the mainstream, and fatalistic about the future. The sense of despair about the present and hopelessness regarding the future creates inertia. At this point, these persons are not likely to believe anyone who claims to be able to help. One means for combatting this presentation is the adoption of a pragmatic, personal, and helpful style that deals directly with concrete problems. These problems will be found to revolve about basic life maintenance rather than a psychodynamic crisis or lack of insight into a troubling emotional state. The clinician's response at this point must be problem specific and directly related to the fundamental issues being addressed by this family. *The past is no target until the present is stabilized.*

Stabilization of the concrete needs of the family is very difficult. Working with these problems will inform the clinician of something well known to the family; how many agencies make promises that are not fulfilled. Or at least how many agencies make families work terribly hard for services. The family will not fight these agencies. *The clinician must fight for them.*

Families who reject long-term counseling out of hand will be less likely to reject offers of concrete help, such as aid in seeking employment. Over time, a relationship that began in this way may move forward to dealing with emotional issues. The concrete services are not a panacea. Concrete service availability will not eliminate poor decision making, but concrete services are a hook that allows this family to come to understand the value of the relationship with this clinician. This is an understanding that is required if the psychodynamic roots of the family are ever to be reached.

The need for concrete services will also be found in the *sexually abusive family*, which may need to establish two households and/or find itself with an incarcerated parent. Both situations call for assistance payments, food stamps, and other entitlements (Berliner & Stevens, 1982; Tyler & Brassard, 1984, p. 51). This is also true in the family involved in *elder mistreatment* in which problems may be prevented through the use of family support services, meal preparation, homemaker, and transportation services (Douglas, 1983, p. 401). Also consider day care, visitor services, respite care, support groups for caregivers, Medicaid, supplemental security income, guardianship and drop in centers (Chen et al., 1981, p. 13; Steinmetz, 1983, p. 148) as possible concrete services for this family. Although the usual response is to move the victim of elder mistreatment, under some conditions moving concrete services into the home may be a viable alternative.

Irrespective of the specific need, the clinician working with the violent family will be asked to exceed normal expectations regarding empathy, availability, accessibility and range of services. This may be an overt or a covert demand used by the family to test limits, a testing that goes on constantly. This testing may well present one crisis after the next. The key is patience and the provision of concrete mechanisms to get from this crisis to the one that follows. Over time, the family will learn to acquire those services on their own, and clinical success, although atypically measured, will be at hand.

Parenthood Education

Parenthood education has been sold as a panacea in some forms of family violence. This is a promise that has not been upheld (Rivara, 1984). This is a particularly dangerous treatment technique because of the irrational faith that many hold in its value, even in the face of clearly contradictory empirical evidence. Over all, it seems that this educational programming is not ultimately effective, not due to a failure in the presentation of useful material, but because it is (1) often directed at an intellectual level beyond the violent family, (2) cannot be applied in the conflict-ridden world of the violent family, (3) a treatment that provides gains only in cognitive and attitudinal areas, and (4) holding differing beliefs about children does not imply automatic application of newly learned behaviors (George & Main, 1980; Martin & Beezley, 1977; Resnick, 1985; Rosenberg & Reppucci, 1985; Wolfe, 1985).

In 1983 Dumas and Wahler reported that violent mothers who received parent training behaved no better than untreated abusers one year later. Those who were socioeconomically depressed were the least likely to benefit. Recently (1985), Resnick's three-year study of two parent-training programs revealed no connection between short-term competency enhancement and long-term prevention of dysfunction. Even the modest attitudinal changes toward children that did occur disappeared almost immediately upon the mother's no longer being involved in the program. In this study, too, the economically depressed single-parent female found her world far too weighty to give a great deal of consideration to the abstract notions presented in parent training. After a review of such programs Rosenberg and Reppucci (1985) have concluded that "these programs have not yet demonstrated that those individuals whose parenting knowledge and skills are strengthened become less vulnerable to the likelihood of abusing their children" (p. 585). There is clearly an existing over-reliance today upon a treatment strategy that has yet to demonstrate effectiveness.

If education is ever to be a preventive measure for violent parents, it must be directed at a level of knowledge consistent with that of the individual parent. Parenthood programs have tended to overestimate the pre-existing level of parenthood knowledge available in the violent parent population (Bolton & Montagnini, 1975). The presentation of esoteric, abstract, or essentially foreign concepts, such as asking a nonempathetic mother to relate to her child's needs, falls flat. Presentation of this material in a too humanistic way guarantees that the overstressed and environmentally strapped parent will either terminate the classes or fail to incorporate the skills.

Neither of the parents in a violent family is likely to have a strong affective sense, and both struggle with the wide affective vocabulary that is used to describe parenting concepts. As a result, presentation of such concepts through the use of a strong feeling tone ("just share this with me for a moment") becomes essentially meaningless to this population.

The need for basic information cannot be ignored in the violent family. There are serious deficits in the knowledge of what is required of a parent. In these families, fantasies of parental responsibility are distorted, and basic childcare and child-rearing strategies are typically out of their reach. Educational efforts will not solve these problems in isolation. Parent education must be seen not as an answer but, at best, as a supplement to other treatment that is uniquely directed toward that family and its day-to-day problems. Information must relate to them, respite must be available when it does not seem to work, and someone must be accessible by telephone when the parenting skills make no difference in a child's behavior (Schmitt, 1978).

There is a presumption that violent parents uniformly have unreasonable expectations of their children. Many studies find such egocentrism to be present (Rivara, 1984, p. 86). In addition, there is near-unanimous research agreement that these parents do not have adequate sensitivity to their children's behavioral cues and that the majority of interactions between them are negative (Ainsworth, 1980). Yet these problems are not approached on an individual parent-child basis in most classes; classes that prefer to focus upon the abstract global elements of parenting. In some ways this is akin to asking an individual who must change his or her tire to take a course in physics to understand how.

To increase their effectiveness, parenthood classes need to be redirected toward the most basic of issues that allow an understanding of the child (Wolfe et al., 1981, p. 37). There is a need to understand not only appropriate behavior in children but inappropriate and misbehavior that should be anticipated (Feshback, 1980, p. 53). There is a need to eliminate the belief that the severity of physical punishment correlates with success and need to approach rigidity and righteousness in the parent's thinking as well as their inability to read their infant (Rodriquez, 1977, p. 99). This cannot be a one-time service. It must be on-going. It cannot be taught in a classroom alone but requires modeling and reinforcement (Wolfe et al., 1981, p. 37). The parent who is given a skill must be reminded again and again that this skill will not always work. A parent who knows they have no skill may be less dangerous than one who has learned one skill and expects it to apply across all situations.

If parenthood education is to be used by the clinician, it is most successful if (1) it is flexible enough to meet the needs demonstrated at a given point in family development, (2) it provides skill training in the most basic of child-rearing behaviors, (3) it provides skills in small doses that can be utilized successfully right away, (4) it is provided in a setting that allows for interchange with other persons in similarly frightening situations (e.g., other violent families), (5) it allows for realistic practice and social reinforcement in the training setting before taking it home, and (6) it is understood that it will not always work (Coolsen & Wechsler, 1984; Gabinet, 1984; Goldstein, 1973). These are parents desperate in their need to be perfect. A failure in the application of a skill is easily seen as the fault of the child. In this way, parenthood education can be more a burden than a gift.

Measurement of Progress in Therapy

If the clinician has adopted behavioral treatment goals and objectives, the measurement of treatment progress is no problem. The court and the legal practitioner will also appreciate the ease of understanding such needs and progress in the family. However, there are markers outside the objectives of treatment that remain subjective indications that progress is being made.

In the maltreating family, the measures of improvement cover the span of environmental, attitudinal, and interactionist variables. It is to be hoped that there will be a general reduction of the environmental stress being experienced by the family. At the same time, recognition that all stress will never be removed should lead the clinician to find progress in the family who reports that a crisis has been dealt with by the family without the clinician's help (Steele & Pollack, 1972, p. 18). In best case, they dealt with the situation themselves, but even if others' involvement was implied, that is an indication of an ability to use community resources and increased confidence in others.

The clinician should be alert to changes in the relationship between the parents as well as changes in the relationship between either or both parents and the child. There should be a reduction in the child's provocative behavior and a change in the attitude of the parents as they come to view the child as an individual. Increased freedom, exploration, and interaction both within and outside the family should be evident. An alteration in relationships with extended families toward actions that are more supportive and less destructive is mandatory.

There should be some sense that the parents are not as dependent upon the child. These parents should be finding more ways of getting satisfaction and pleasure in their lives other than through the child. But exercise caution as these parents are more than capable of giving the enthusiastic clinician what he/she wants to see. When the parents' self-images are improved, they see the child in a more positive light, and lifelines are used in times of crisis; there is progress in the parent (Kempe, 1975). When the health of the child, as well as behavioral (i.e., aggression, stealing, withdrawal) and developmental problems in the child are reduced, progress is being made. Similar measures of progress in the sexually abusive family are more critically assessed.

In the sexually abusive family there must be a *full acceptance of responsibility* on the part of the perpetrator. The nonperpetrating parent must acknowledge whatever role they played in the development of the situation and be able to describe necessary changes. The victim must be able to understand and forgive the parents, demonstrate an improved self-image/confidence level, and to verbalize problems. In the expression of problems, if they are problems common to the victim's age group, even that demonstrates some improvement over the prior secrecy and withdrawal (Kempe & Kempe, 1984, pp. 179–180). It is not just the cessation of the incestuous behavior that is critical, it is the total restructuring of the family (Anderson & Shafer, 1979, p. 440).

The conjugal violence perpetrator who is making progress should demonstrate an ability to identify the behavioral parameters of his situation, both his and his partner's feelings, solutions which benefit both of them, demonstrate an ability to remove himself from a tense situation, negotiate problem resolution, and compromise under stress (Edleson, 1984, p. 239).

The family involved in mistreatment of the elderly must demonstrate increased knowledge of, acceptance of, and response to the problems of the aging in general and their parent in particular. Knowing and using the community resources, slim though they may be, are both critical. Finding leisure time, arranging for respite, and gaining the cooperation of all age groups in the family are imperative. An admission of the difficulty in caring for this older person, and the ability to find relief from that pressure must be present. However, in each form of family violence, there should be some failure expected.

Permission to Surrender

The recognition of the impenetrable nature of the family is as important as the recognition of progress. *Some violent families will be intractable.* The clinician who is not willing to terminate treatment and recognize that no amount of caring will stop the violence in some families will spend 80 percent of their professional time on 20 percent of the families. This cannot be allowed to occur; there are too few clinicians to waste precious time. Only an accurate assessment of these families, as described in the section to follow, will allow the clinician to make an accurate choice when faced with such difficult treatment decisions.

15

Professional Assessment of the Violent Family

It is difficult to standardize an assessment protocol effective for all types of violent families. Psychometric instruments can serve as a-point-in time measure, but most are directed more toward the understanding of an existing condition than the more pressing question within family violence evaluation: *prediction of future behavior*. Unlike many other evaluations that focus on the *persons* involved, assessment of the violent family demands a much more intense analysis of the *environment* in which the problem flourished.

Assessment of Multiple Environmental Stressors

The context in which the violent act occurred is a critical point of analysis in the violent family situation. Garbarino (1977a, p. 730) calls this the *community context*. The contextual evaluation typically includes economic resources, housing, work patterns, and attitudes in the community/culture toward family life. The special needs of family members, ability to adapt to change, and the scope and timing of major developmental events in the family are also important. Any enduring institution, organization, or neighborhood affiliations must also be evaluated as to their potential support or destructiveness. This community context is sometimes called the *ecological* view.

Howze and Kotch (1984, p. 405) have also described assessment points through an ecological model. They first suggest that the practitioner consider the cultural milieu from which this family draws its norms and values. Within this area, consideration is given to attitudes toward violence, children, discipline, and the role of the family. A second point of analysis is the social environment of the family. This is the structure of the community and society with which this family most closely identifies. Pivotal elements include social networks (formal and informal) as well as economic, employment, agency, and shelter resources available to the family.

Cicchetti and Rizley (1984, p. 44) use the terms "challenges" and "buffers" to capture the strengths and weaknesses of the family environment. Challenges are the stresses of a family's world. Among them are loss, physical injury and illness, legal difficulties, marital and family problems, and problems in childcare and discipline. Buffers are loosely categorized as financial support, employment, and social support. If there are too many challenges and too few buffers for a family, the result may be a decline in function and possible violence. Once the understanding of the environment is complete, practitioners must turn their attention to gaining understanding of the interaction of perpetrator, victim, and family process as they work together (or against each other) in some systematic way.

A focus on the family as a system is vital to assessment of violence (Giles-Sims, 1983). The interactions between all family members are informative. Knowledge of the individual family member's perception of the family and their tolerance level for the behaviors within it must be gained. Each member's view of themselves, their ability to cope, and their emotional health play a role. Just how this family is connected and who is available to help in a crisis are key points of knowledge in understanding this family's ability to keep itself from a violent act. So it is not just the presence of individual family member characteristics which become critical, but how these individuals match or do not match that become predictive of danger.

Assessing Family Relationships

The Maltreating Family

Belsky (1984) sees the maltreating family relationship as being multifaceted. The parents' psychological predispositions and early experiences, elements of the social environment (such as work), and the temperamental and behavioral characteristics of the child join together in the development of functional or dysfunctional family operations. Fortunately, this is a "buffered" system (p. 91) in that a threat to any one area will not result in total collapse of the family. For example, Belsky cites Sameroff and Chandler (1975) in noting that the family that is financially stable has an easier time coping with problems in the child. The marital relationship is thought to be the major support for parents although other sources of support are also helpful, assuming the support received matches the support desired. Assessment of this ability to find support in the family system is vital. Finally, a good fit between parent and child (Lerner & Lerner, 1983) as well as all other family members is predictive of this family's ability to relate to each other and the world outside.

An element of assessment that cannot be ignored is the parents' experience in their family of origin. While intergenerational transmission of violence is not direct, child caring patterns can be replicated (Steele, 1982, p. 487). The parent who has had little exposure to appropriate models may not know how to reduce bad behavior and/or promote desired behavior (Wolfe et al., 1981, p. 17). A positive parental experience (in their own childhood) may mediate relationship stresses with their own child even as a negative one may lead to overreaction (Roberts, 1984, p. 159).

An often-reported feature of maltreating parents is their propensity to perceive inaccurately the skills and abilities of their children (Bavolek, 1981, p. 41). Having experienced failure in most other relationships, there is a tendency for these parents to seek relationships in which they can gain emotional support without reciprocating and in which someone else will solve the problems in living that press upon them. Sadly, they often turn to the child for this (Bavolek, 1981, p. 43). The practitioner must assess this propensity for such parental egocentricity and role reversal.

In this reversal of dependency roles, the parent turns to the child for nurturing and protection (Morris & Gould, 1974). The result is a relationship failure as parental need exceeds the child's capacity to perform. At best, the child's failure to compensate for the parent's needs leads to a belief that close relationships are disappointing and that people cannot be trusted (Bavolek, 1981, p. 43). At worst, the parent's disappointment and rage at the continuation of unmet needs lead to violent assault. If there are environmental pressures on this family (Miller & Challas, 1981, p. 7; Morris & Gould, 1963, p. 15) negative outcomes are likely.

The Sexually Abusive Family

Role confusion is as common to the sexually abusive family as it is to the maltreating family (Finkelhor, 1979; Summit & Kryso, 1978). The most obvious role reversal is that of mother and daughter. However, reversals also occur between both parents and the daughter (victim) who becomes the caretaker for the entire family. The power in this family is so unbalanced that the powerless child must do absolutely anything to gain some sense that survival is possible (Lewis-Herman, 1981, p. 4).

The sexual abuse victim faces strain between herself and her mother (Herman & Hirshman, 1977) and authoritarian father (Finkelhor, 1979); she also is not comfortable with her peers (Summit, 1984). This is an atmosphere that promises abandonment unless something is done to anchor her role, even participation in sexual relationships (Finkelhor, 1979, p. 27).

This is a child in limbo. She is not certain what role to play and where to go for protection. She will be found to play almost any role she feels necessary, even that of reducing the perpetrator's emotional distance through physical contact (Lewis-Herman, 1981, p. 44). The practitioner, then, must approach issues of closeness, empathy, spontaneity, and social skills in the assessment of this family relationship (Kempe & Kempe, 1984, p. 53). Many of these are the same issues that will be explored in the examination of the conjugally violent couple.

The Conjugally Violent Family

The pivotal point of relationship assessment in conjugal violence is that of power imbalance (Deschner, 1984; Walker, 1979). That will also be true in sexual abuse (Lewis-Herman, 1981; Russell, 1984) and elder mistreatment (Pagelow, 1984, p. 100). The general family violence relationship is one in which the stronger (either through size or ownership of resources) dominates the weaker (p. 75). The perpetrator of conjugal violence uses this differential to the fullest.

Males who assault co-habitors seem to have accepted the "macho" ideology and patriarchal nature of society and respond·

accordingly (LaViolette, 1984, p. 3). The excessive appearance of masculinity, the exertion of power, and the presence of extraordinary jealousy will often be present in the assessment of the violent act in an adult relationship (Allen & Straus, 1983). If these factors are present, the practitioner need not wonder whether violence will occur again, for in such a relationship, some form of violence is an inevitability.

Mistreatment of the Elderly

Persons who are caring for an infirm elderly person in their home are chronically frustrated (Douglas, 1983, p. 141). They are overwhelmed not only by the magnitude of their task, but by their lack of understanding as to how best to accomplish it, and the isolation that grows out of it (Douglas, 1983). This leads to stress in the family, in the family's relationship with the outside world, and between caretaker and victim (Anderson, 1981, p. 78; Falcioni, 1982, p. 208; Langley, 1981, p. 16; Renvoize, 1979). When any individual is trapped in such an angry and hopeless set of circumstances, he or she may turn the anger inward and generate a severe depressive reaction or may react explosively toward those in the environment he or she feels to be causing the problem, in this case, the infirm older person (Solomon, 1983, p. 160). That families who are housing elder persons are stretched to the breaking point is well understood. Evidence for this understanding can be found in the fact that neglect of these elderly persons is sometimes viewed as not only benign but normal (Hickey & Douglas, 1981, p. 506). It may even be seen as normal by the elder person who is experiencing it (Anderson, 1981). Obviously, this point of understanding is a key feature of general family relationship assessment and re-education. Once these general contextual and family relationship views have been established in the thinking of the practitioner, the time for individual assessment is at hand.

Using Tests in Assessment

There are no absolutes in selecting instrumentation for family violence evaluations. However, there are tests that are familiar to legal professionals that will be missed if not present in the evaluation.

These are tests that are used frequently in court and will not receive intense scrutiny by opposing counsel. The attorney should be aware of the availability of *The Mental Measurements Yearbook* (Buros, 1972) as a reference source for most tests that might be used in the evaluation of a client. The information in this yearbook describes not only the strengths and weaknesses of instruments but appropriate usage. It becomes a useful tool for both sides of an adversarial situation involving expert testimony.

The most commonly applied instrument in the family violence evaluation is the Minnesota Multiphasic Personality Inventory (MMPI; Butcher, 1987). This instrument may be used with adults or adolescents (using special adolescent norms) and provides a personality profile covering a range of categories. Special scales that look at specific behaviors such as alcohol use have also been developed.

The MMPI is the granddaddy of the paper-and-pencil personality instruments and has reliability and validity records in legal work that lend strength to its selection. Alternative instruments are sometimes found in the Cattell 16PF (Personality Factor) test (Cattell, Eber & Tatsuoka), the California Psychological Inventory (CPI; Crites, 1964), or in Lanyon's Psychological Screening Inventory. Recently, the Personality Inventory for Children (PIC) has come into use as a method of getting parents to answer questions about their children. Increasing interest in the relationship between child personality/temperament and child maltreatment may result in increased use of the PIC in family violence evaluations.

In addition to the use of objective tests, and only as a supplement, not a replacement, some evaluators use projective techniques. The Rorschach Test, which uses the familiar ink blot cards, is the most frequently used in the assessment of violence (Rapaport, Gill, & Shafer, 1975). In the child maltreatment situation, the Thematic Apperception Test (TAT) is more commonly used than the Rorschach. The TAT is a technique in which the evaluator presents a series of pictures and asks the individual to describe what the situation depicted may be. Responses can be standardized somewhat and inferences drawn (Rapaport et al., 1975).

The evaluator may use a test similar to the TAT to evaluate children entitled the Children's Apperception Test (CAT); (Bellack & Bellack, 1971) to identify themes and issues largely inaccessible through paper and pencil measures. The familiar House-Tree-Person Test is also used to elicit and assess feelings though artistic portrayals drawn by the child (Hammer, 1960). In sexual abuse work in particular, children may be evaluated using these techniques (Yates, Beutler, & Crago, 1985), or through anatomically correct dolls.

Projective techniques are subject to criticism as a result of the lack of objectivity in scoring. Scoring systems are available, but reliability across evaluators can be questioned. The training of the evaluator is pivotal. The attorney is advised to question the use of these instruments. Many clinicians use these techniques without having been specifically trained in their use and scoring. Drawing inferences from haphazard study of results is misleading and dangerous.

In a similar fashion, the anatomically correct dolls are difficult to use in assessment for several reasons. First, there is no standardization izationizationin interpreting responses. Second, many evaluators ask leading questions in their doll-based interviews, especially with preschool children. Third, the children are sometimes asked to identify anatomical parts using language they do not understand. Finally, there is limited empirical data on the reliability and validity of children's responses to the dolls. In general, the younger the child, the more tenuous the doll-based testimony. In practice many evaluators seem to be using the anatomically correct dolls to confirm their own suspicions. The conclusions drawn from the dolls are far too easily accepted as absolute corroboration of the sexually abusive event. Although not a "test" per se the use of the penile plethysmograph is becoming more common in sexual abuse litigation. This physiological instrument, when combined with other measures is giving increasing reliability in the evaluation of the sexual abuse perpetrator. The Abel and Becker scales (Abel, Becker, Cunningham-Rathner, Rouleau, Kaplan & Reich, 1984), Spence and Helmreich Attitudes Toward Women scale (Spence & Helmreich, 1978) and the Wilson Sex Fantasy Questionnaire (Wilson, 1978) are the type of paper and pencil measurements now coming into widespread and effective, courtroom use.

Measures of intellectual capacity are critical to the family violence evaluation. At this point, the Weschler series (1974) is the most familiar but the newer Kaufman and McCarthy Scales (1977) are beginning to be used in work with younger children especially. On rare occasions, sometimes through admission of school records, the Stanford-Binet Scales will appear (Terman & Merrill, 1973).

Psycho-education instruments have a good record with this population. They are most frequently found in assessments of the effect of maltreatment on the intellectual functioning of children. Some of the more common tests in use include the Wide Range

Achievement Test (WRAT, Kaufman & Kaufman, 1977), Peabody Picture Vocabulary Test (PPVT, Dunn, 1965), Illinois Test of Psycho-Linguistic Abilities (ITPA, Kirk, McCarthy, & Kirtz, 1968), and the Detroit Test of Learning Aptitude (Baker & LeLand, 1967). In the youngest children the Bayley Scales of Infant Development may be applied to demonstrate the presence of a developmental delay or as a special needs screening (Bayley, 1969). In each case the attorney is encouraged to confirm the evaluator's training in the use and interpretation of these instruments.

Since many injuries in family violence imply the possibility of head, brain, or neurological damage, neuropsychological batteries are often applied in the evaluation. The Halstead-Reitan series (Kaufman & Kaufman, 1977) is the most familiar total battery and the Bender-Gestalt Test of Motor Abilities is the most frequently used for a quick indication of functional or organic damage (Bender, 1946). The Bender also appears in a special children's version (Clawson, 1962; Koppotz, 1963). Other neurological batteries do exist but are not as widely applied.

Overall, the evaluator should be competent to select the appropriate test instruments. By way of caution, the attorney must be certain that the evaluator is aware of the scrutiny to be given to the instruments in court. It is not sufficient to understand interpretation. A familiarity with the development of the test, its norms, and other applications/failures is also required. Validity, reliability, norm groups, and the evaluator's previous training and utilization of the test are all subject to scrutiny and questioning in court. This may come as a surprise to the evaluator who has not previously undertaken court work.

Recently, checklist type paper and pencil measures have found their way into the court setting, especially in the social worker's case planning. Most are merely guidelines and do not claim statistical status as a test instrument. That, unfortunately, is not how protection specialists, hard pressed for decision-making tools, apply them in some cases. Propensity for violence checklists developed by Milner (1982) and Bavolek (1981) are now used by social workers in maltreatment situations as are stress checklists such as the Holmes/Rahe (1967). The attorney must be familiar with these instruments and their uses. As a rule they are merely planning devices although some have significant statistical development. The attorney should not allow admission of these checklists as last-word deterministic tools. In fact, it is best to view all psychometric measures, even those with decades of use, as devices that only service to confirm or deny impressions from direct personal exposure to the family. This direct exposure, as described in the following section, is the heart of the evaluation of the violent family.

Critical Issues in Clinical Assessment

The Maltreating Family

The keystone of the evaluation of the maltreating family is the child. The clinician is asked to determine the impact of the problem and the hope for the future. There are four broad areas that must be considered: cognitive functioning, behavioral responses to the stress they have experienced, communication skills, and adjustment to life outside the home, such as school behavior (Rodriquez, 1977, pp. 72–78). What is sought is an understanding of the child's capacity and the family's willingness/ability to help the child to move forward developmentally.

One of the more easily applied child development frameworks is that provided by Erickson (1963). Erickson first sees the necessity of *trust* (safety and predictability in relations with others) followed by the need for *autonomy* (independence, exploration, and self-control), *initiative* (goal striving and perseverance), *accomplishment, identity,* and finally, *intimacy.* This developmental trajectory is built upon a foundation of love, dominance, affiliation, mastery, recognition, rationality, interpersonal relationships, and the establishment of a conscience and moral standards (Mussen, Conger, & Kagan, 1963). It is not difficult to see how the maltreating family may interrupt this path. The questions for the evaluator are, at what point was this path interrupted? By whom? With what affect? How can we compensate for this interruption?

The evaluator is examining the ability of the child to protect himself or herself, the child's mental and physical capacities, the maturity level of both child and parent, and the caretaker's ability and willingness to protect (Medden, 1985, p. 60). Biological, situational, and learned response patterns must all be considered (Feshback, 1980, p. 48).

Bourne and Newberger (1979) have suggested points of discrimination that must occur at the outset of a child maltreatment evaluation.

The initial discrimination is whether this is a chronic pattern. If this violent action seems isolated and in response to situational circumstances, compassion might apply. If repetitive, the weight of the court's control is needed. If the maltreatment seems acceptable to the parent, as evidenced through an absence of guilt or concern, there is a need for control. This is especially important if there are other deviant behaviors present such as criminality in the parent. If the child is seen by the parent as an extension of the parent, there is a need to step between parent and child. This is a need which is increased if the parent views the child's behavior as intrinsically bad. Finally, if the parent does not seem to have sufficient control over their aggressive responses to the child's behavior, the time has come for direct protection through removal of the child. Schmitt (1978) suggests similar points of assessment to encompass all family members.

Schmitt (1978) finds critical assessment points in the maltreating family through the following: medical history (pregnancy, labor, delivery, neonatal course), parental history (family of origin, mother and father, relationships to all children), child care practices (safety of the environment, feeding, sleeping, play, discipline, and toilet training), physical problems of all family members, and crisis. There is also, of course, a mandate to assess the developmental history and current performance of the child-victim.

The victim's early development must be explored in detail. Any problem in the pregnancy or early developmental milestones must be noted. Special issues such as prematurity or congenital anomalie can be important as can tantrums, learning problems, or any feature of the victim that family members describe as special or different. Any child seen as difficult to understand may be assumed to be at some risk.

Individual parents must be examined closely. Any distorted attachment issues in their childhood should be given in-depth exploration. Early loss or separation should be noted and meanings sought. The meaning of each of their children to them is vital information as is how this parent was disciplined as a child and how they felt about it. Psychopathology, rigidity, dependency, and aggressiveness are obvious danger signals in the parent. Finally, the role played by the child in either relieving problems the parent feels or in generating new problems are topics that should be approached directly. This approach has some stylistic peculiarities.

Schneider and Pollack (1972, pp. 56–57) describe a specific interview process with maltreating parents. They suggest the need to establish three elements in the family: the potential for maltreatment, the presence of a special child, and the potential for crisis. These practitioners suggest that the interview be parent-centered, relaxed, short, and, above-all, honest. See the parents separately first followed by a joint session in which both parents are informed of progress in the case. Showing the family as much respect as possible during early contact may lessen the chance that they will leave the therapeutic setting prematurely.

In assessing the potential for maltreatment in the parents, the evaluator is seeking a sense that their family of origin did not value them, but that they feel this was justified. They may still be trying to gain acceptance from a parent who simply does not have the capacity to give it. The parents being evaluated are most accustomed to earning messages of personal worth through doing things for their parents, a habit acquired in childhood. Often there has been no one in their life who cared for them for no special reason. This is a critical absence that provides a negative prognosis.

Who these parents, especially the child's primary caretaker, turn to in times of crisis, is vital information. It is important to determine the emotional and geographical availability of sources of support. Within the crisis category, the parent's response to the child's crying is important. If it (1) makes them want to cry, (2) makes them angry, (3) makes them feel helpless, or (4) presents them with a child who will not allow himself or herself to be comforted, there is danger. If isolated, this parents needs one official and one unofficial source of support for the inevitable times of crisis during parenthood. Discover what these parents expect of themselves. Explore the reasons why they wished for parenthood at all. Evaluate the wantedness of the child. Child victims are not necessarily unwanted, but they may have been wanted for the wrong reasons. Never is this more true than in the sexual abuse situation.

The Sexually Abusive Family

The major difficulty in the assessment of the sexually abusive family is that the practitioner is asked to move from clinical to forensic assessment. There are key features common to both assessments such as isolation, abandonment, family discord, and victimization, but the clinical assessment is used to establish empathy and move toward a therapeutic relationship. The practitioner conducting a forensic assessment, even if trained as a clinician, is being asked to determine the truth within the parameters of the law. This assessment is legal fact finding. It collects and interprets evidence though placing it in some clinical perspective.

In that this assessment is forensic, most sexual abuse cases are more akin to investigations than clinical evaluations. Unfortunately, the weight of this investigation falls upon the child victim in most cases. There is often a secondary investigation in this process through repetitive examinations by frightening authority figures such as police or physicians in strange places such as emergency rooms and through the use of odd playthings such as anatomically correct dolls. The individual being assessed (the child) may also be a difficult study.

There has been a blanket belief in the sexual abuse area that children do not lie about this event. Very few children do lie about sexual contact in the home. It is also unlikely that many fantasize extra-familial contact. But, children, like everyone else, are sometimes not completely accurate. As Conte (1986) notes, it is not the absolute truth or falsehood of a child's statement that is critical: It is the reliability of the information that is most important. The practitioner must ask some reasonable questions of children's testimony.

Overall, it has been suggested that children are no better and no worse in eyewitness accuracy than adults. However, these studies are conducted in experimental settings that may not replicate the stress and crisis of the sexual abuse situation. In addition, measurement of retention of information about single events, as has been the typical design, differs from measurement of information about events which have occurred over time. Basically, the practitioner must ask themself whether there is any reason for the child to be less than accurate in their statement. Consideration must also be given to the age of the child, the description of the act, and the quality of the child's report (Rosenfeld, Nadelson, & Krieger, 1979; Summit, 1985). Undeutsch's (1982) "statement reality analysis," mentioned earlier, appears to be one assessment technique that cuts through some of the these questions about the child's report. If the child is living in a divorced family, facing pressures from both sides and possibly being coached, the difficulty in validating the report may be even greater.

Sexual abuse allegations in the postdissolution shared-custody situation are on the increase. In this situation there is a win/lose orientation between the parents that often requires near microscopic analysis of the relationship between parents and between both parents and the child. The child almost always loses in this situation. Given the intense anger that accompanies dissolution and child custody arrangements, skepticism must remain high. Coaching does take place in some cases. There are also situations in which the parent making the accusation has actually perpetrated the sexual abuse against the young and noncommunicative child in an effort to punish a former spouse. In these situations, particularly in light of the protracted and devastating litigation that follows, it may be best to protect the child from both parents. Keeping the child in parental custody may result in the entanglements of the process overwhelming the child completely (Kaplan & Kaplan, 1981). The greatest difficulty comes from the fact that many of these cases involve preschool children. Other than a questionable reliance upon the child's randomized responses to anatomically correct dolls, the evaluator is left with little choice than to make an educated guess about the accused parent's potential for sexual abuse.

Summit (1985) has noted that there is no objective way to recognize an individual who will sexually assault a child. Additionally, when the child first discloses, it will include only the most recent act and describe the least humiliating experience. The evaluator must remember that this disclosure may promise the victim that they are going to lose the only source of support they have ever known. This is not an allegation made lightly.

Both Summit (1985) and Sgroi (1982) indicate that the largest single barrier to adequate evaluation is a reluctance to accept the possibility of sexual abuse. The result is acceptance of a less uncomfortable alternative to explain the child's story. The evaluator must consider poor supervision, poor choice of surrogate caretakers, inappropriate role boundaries, blurred family roles, and confused expectations within the family before they dismiss the possibility of sexual abuse. If there is an antagonistic response from the family, the evaluator must dig even more deeply (Sgroi, 1982).

Assessment of the entire family, and their complete living situation, is wise even in the event in which the child was allegedly molested by a person outside the home (Brandt & Tisza, 1980, p. 53). These elements, when added to knowledge of the child's intellectual level, developmental progress, strengths, and vulnerabilities may help to achieve understanding of the lack of protectiveness that might have contributed to the problem (Kempe & Kempe, 1984, p. 192).

The evaluator must keep one thought in mind. *There is a reluctance to criminalize family events.* It is hoped that there are less impersonal means for mediating such problems (Finkelhor, 1984, p. 101). Yet sexual abuse is a criminal act committed by an individual often not suitable for diversion and one who requires a totally controlled environment to contain his or her near-obsessional drive toward children (James & Nasjleti, 1983, p. 14). Only about one in ten perpetrators is suitable for diversion. If there is the use of or threat of physical force during the act, bizarre or ritualistic actions, complementary antisocial activity in other areas, psychopathology, or denial of the inappropriate nature of the act, incarceration may be necessary (Groth et al., 1982, p. 142). A very high Pd or 4–9 profile in the MMPI may also suggest unsuitability for diversion programs (Anderson & Shafer, 1979, p. 40).

James and Nasjleti (1983, pp. 112–113) have encapsulated the evaluation of the sexually abusive family. At the socioecological level they suggest the need to understand support networks, family structure, and family interaction. Specific points of study include geographic isolation, household density, social supports, social participation, and decision making in the family. The family itself may be defined by confused role and task performance, tenuous mother-child bonds, and poor communication.

At the individual level, James and Nasjleti (1983) encourage examination of the quality of the marital and sexual relationships, personality variables, and sexual attitudes and knowledge. In all of this, impulse control, hostility, self-concept, and affection appear critical. Prior experiences of victimization, separation from parents, and generalized life stresses are additionally important considerations. All these elements play upon both in-home and out-of-home assault. In the out-of-home molestation it is critical that the adults understand how their reaction to the situation will predict the child's response (Flammang, 1980, pp. 180–183). As will be evident in the following, assessment is a functional element of working with the violent conjugal couple as well.

The Conjugally Violent Couple

The evaluation of the conjugal violence situation is more behavior and resource focused than in other areas of family violence. It is true that intrapsychic factors such as depression do inhibit or facilitate constructive solutions to the problem in some cases. However, environmental factors such as economic problems or educational differences merit equal footing with psychodynamic issues in the analysis of this home (Hilberman, 1980, p. 1344).

Recognizing that both victim and perpetrator will minimize the number and lethality of abusive events (Boyd & Klingbell, 1979; Roberts, 1984, p. 9), the evaluation must begin with an assessment of how far the abuse has gone. This is violence that will only increase in frequency and severity. If the events seem chronic, irrational, sudden, and of a serious nature, it is important to determine just how dangerous the perpetrator may be (for example, homicidal) to all concerned.

In order to assess perpetrator dangerousness, Walker (1979) suggests that evaluators turn their attention to whether the perpetrator has had experience with violence as a child, in the military, or through criminal activity. His degree of temper control, jealousy, and expectation of attention from the victim are critical points. Rigidity is important. The greater the rigidity, more in-grained the use of violence, greater the misperception of family roles, and more repetitive the violence, the less he is likely to change. If the victim is unable/unwilling to leave this situation, the evaluators should resign themselves to a very long, and probably unsuccessful, therapeutic course.

Mistreatment of the Elderly

There are specific assessment tools available for the elder mistreatment problem (Ferguson & Beck, 1983), but for the most part the evaluator's task rests with the determination of the problems encountered by a specific family in caring for a specific elderly individual.

The evaluator must conduct a mental status examination of the elderly victim. In this situation, the examination is a comprehensive effort which includes a consideration of general appearance and attitude, current and past behavior, short- and long-term memory, sensorium (the ability to draw information from sense organs), intellectual functioning, mood/affect, perceptual processes, thought content, and insight/judgment (Daiches, 1982; Maloney & Ward, 1976).

In the course of this examination the evaluator may use the Face-Hand test (Kaufman & Kaufman, 1977) to determine the older person's ability to sense their physical self by touching their face, a Bender Gestalt to measure mental state (Folstein, 1975), or specialized instruments that relate to the ability to function day to day (Lawton & Brody, 1969). These are often not precise measurements, but do give some perspective on persons otherwise difficult to reach.

It is too easy to view the older person as impaired if there is a lack of rapport, personality problem, or physical problem (such as deafness). Similarly, stereotyping of older persons as under-performing may convince the evaluator that any older person who can establish rapport with them is completely functional. If this person had been younger, the evaluator might have probed much more deeply to reach the conclusion that they were functional (Daiches, 1982).

One special role for the evaluator in elder mistreatment is the search for potential dementia due to aging or disease process such as Organic Brain Syndrome or Alzheimer's Disease. Some of these problems are acute and reversible and others are essentially permanent, signaling the beginning stages of a permanent decline (Luppens & Lau, 1983, p. 206).

In most cases involving physical problems, the persons around the older person will complain of the individual's memory loss, confusion, poor judgment, disorientation, and shallow affect. The clinician must rule out malnutrition, anemia, alcohol, and the overloading of prescription drugs before coming to the conclusion that a problem has developed in the brain (Butler, 1975).

If the evaluator finds an untreatable brain disorder, they should endeavor to provide all the information possible about the disorder to the family. Give the caretaker absolute permission to meet his or her own needs. Be available to respond to emergencies. Arrange alternative and respite care. Find local support groups for families. Finally, help the family to maximize the abilities the older person retains (Luppens & Lau, 1983, p. 207).

With the evaluation of the older person completed, the assessment of the social and interpersonal relationships held by family members can begin. Family resources, unresolved family conflict, a history of poor adjustment, and inadequate community support or resources all must be considered before the development of a treatment plan can begin (Langley, 1981, p. 17).

In speaking with the caretakers in the family, it is important to gain an understanding of their perceptions of the family stresses, the impact of role reversals that might be felt, their feelings about the support they receive from other family members, and any financial or marital stress that they believe has grown out of having the older person in the home (Chen et al., 1981, p. 15). This individual's memory of the parenthood practices of the older person may reveal an anger they were unaware of or had forgotten. Similarly, control issues and nonverbal communications may take place in their interaction with the older person which require some interpretation (Rathbone-McCune & Voyles, 1982, p. 192).

In sum, the elder mistreatment victim must be evaluated in light of their behavioral appropriateness, restlessness, aggression/passivity, responsiveness, orientation, isolation, grief, anxiety, depression, and paranoia (Falcioni, 1982, p. 211). The family environment must be assessed for physical and mental health problems, functional barriers, reliability of family and community support, and dangerous situations (Daiches, 1982). Most important, any intervention strategy that developed as a result of this assessment must consider the fact that this victim is an adult. They are not children and dependencies cannot be assumed. These are individuals who have a right to make choices. One of the worst offenders is the well-intentioned service provider who views this person as if they were childlike in every case (Douglas, 1983, p. 401).

The elder mistreatment victim is an older individual who has experienced loss, may have had many hopes disappointed, has a high degree of stress, and may be disabled physically. But these individuals are adults who have the right (if competent) to make decisions for themselves (Renvoize, 1978). Like the battered adult female who elects to stay in a violent situation, mistreated elderly persons have a right to stay where they are. This is only one of the special elements of working with the violent family. The following sections will reveal many others.

Part VI

Capturing the Family Violence
Practitioners' Environment (III):
Special Issues in Working with
the Violent Family—Attorney
and Clinician

16

Special Issues in Working with the Violent Family

Working with the Child

Relating to the child in the violent family demands unique skills and talents. Interviewing a child is far different than interviewing an adult, not only in level of response expected, but in the type of information sought and the techniques used for gathering that information. Seeking personal or intrapsychic data from a child, especially a very young child, is a fruitless undertaking. At best, the information will be sketchy and subject to misunderstanding. At worst, the information may be distorted and lead the evaluator to misinterpretation. As a result, it is likely that the parent will be a major source of information about the child. This can be problematic in the violent family.

Even in the functional family, when asked about the child(ren), adults tend to present what is important to them and be unaware of the child's interactions and behaviors in other settings such as school. Different persons will draw different conclusions regarding a child based on their various contacts and observations. Consequently, *it is imperative that the practitioner in the family violence case gather information about the child from the widest possible number of sources* (Costello, 1984, p. 16). Even having accomplished that, it is best to interpret the information with caution. The practitioner must recall that reported differences in the child are as much a part of the informant's perceptions as they are genuine features of the child's behavior. A thorough knowledge of the persons providing the data on the child may be helpful in putting that information in perspective. Additionally, confirmation of these perceptions may come from both structured and unstructured interviewing of the child him or herself.

Greenspan (1981, p. 1) describes the child practitioner's major talent as knowing when to get out of the child's way so he or she can introduce important features of his or her world. This refers to the major tool of the child-centered interview, observation. Recently clinicians have reported that direct interviewing of the child, when presented in a nonthreatening and understandable way, is productive (Costello, 1984, p. 16), but none has found the direct interview to be a replacement for observation.

Greenspan (1981, p. 2) describes the wealth of information to be found in the child's behavior. He suggests that every interview demands attention to style and depth of behavior toward the clinician, moods and emotions experienced and manifested, the style of movement, what is attended to and what is ignored, the themes of conversation, play and questioning, and general affect. In order to capture that information, Greenspan offers an observational checklist:

(1) *Physical and neurological development*: posture, gait, balance, motor coordination, speech, and general body size and use.
(2) *Mood*: emotional tone, facial expression, and subjectively reported feelings.
(3) *Human relationship capacity*: relating to the clinician, verbal and eye contact, spatial distances, and emotional reactions.
(4) *Affect*: emotions during the interview, depth of affect, and interview content at the time emotions rise.
(5) *Themes*: organization, depth, age-appropriateness, logical linkages or blockages.
(6) *Clinical reactions:* how the clinician feels about the subject and the feelings held by the clinician as the child left the office (e.g., worried, relieved, or angry).

Every child leaves an impression. It is important that the practitioner gather the data for that impression in an organized way. To do otherwise is to be left with a collection of unvalidated feelings. Several writers have offered suggestions in this regard.

Morgan and Burkholder (1982, p. 41) indicate that it is important to keep the purpose of the interview uppermost in mind when approaching a child. Most children are expert at quickly changing the topic. Age level differences can also be frustrating. Several different techniques help the practitioner to retain control.

A friendly informal tone is essential to the success of the child-centered interview. A discussion of activities that interest the child can help set the stage and provide an opportunity for practitioners to demonstrate their respect for the child. The child's faith that the practitioner respects his or her feelings and need for privacy must be in place before approaching critical issues.

The practitioner dealing with a child must be both a good listener and a careful informer (Morgan & Burkholder, 1982, p. 43). The child has virtually no experience with attorneys or clinicians other than media exposure. As a result, it is important for practitioners to explain their role clearly to the child. Some attorneys, for example, desensitize a child by having them visit the empty courtroom, practice in a mock trial setting, or actually observe a trial being held on a nontraumatic issue. These are not appropriate strategies for all children, but for some they may help reduce anxiety. At the conclusion of the explanation the child must understand that they are not powerless, have no reason to feel guilty, and that the practitioner is there to help them.

Open-ended rather than leading questions seem to be the most useful for children. Avoid abstraction and present every thought slowly and clearly. The use of paraphrases will assure the child that the practitioner wants to be clearly understood and to understand the child's thoughts on the matter before moving into a new issue. The initial interview is not necessarily a time to resolve issues. Dealing with information gathering and happenings of the moment rather than dwelling on the future will be helpful to the child (Morgan & Burkholder, 1982, p. 44).

If the child becomes tired or anxious, it is time for the interview to stop. If it is stopped, practitioners should tell children what will happen next and how they can get in contact if they have any questions. If they do call, answer the call or return the call immediately; they will be waiting anxiously for the call (Morgan & Burkholder, 1982, p. 45).

The Preschool Child

Preschoolers are among the most difficult children to deal with in the interview setting. Most feelings in this age group are acted out behaviorally or posturally rather than discussed (Morgan & Burkholder, 1982, p. 45). Play is the vehicle to experiment with feelings, to learn, and to express thoughts. Having some toys available to the child, especially toys that can be used to simulate events and people in their lives will be found to facilitate such play (Thompson, 1985, p. 25).

Several characteristics of children of preschool age will influence the interview. For example, time has little meaning to the preschooler. Things are only reliably remembered for a short time. Any memory of events extending beyond the previous year is of questionable validity. A child of three or older has a logical grasp of relationships, but feelings about people will override logic when traumatic events occur. It is wise to expect interviews with a child of this age to be slow, easily sidetracked, and full of physical movement.

A critical assessment point in the child of this age is the interaction with any parent or family member present in the interview setting. A secure child will demonstrate responsiveness, curiosity, exploration, and a warm and happy affect toward the individual (Thompson, 1985, p. 26). The adult's availability to the child, the frequency, quality, and type of play or physical contact between them are all important observational points to be recorded (Thompson, 1985, p. 26). Inappropriate contact between parent and child will frequently be sensed by the practitioner long before specific problems are identified.

The functional preschooler is helpful, predictable, and flexible. There is an appropriate level of self-esteem, and they report outside friendships (Thompson, 1985, pp. 28–29). On the other hand, if there are extremes in their environment, temperament, cognitions, or developmental progress, their behavior in the interview setting should provide immediate clues. Attention to issues such as temperament, attachment behaviors, adaptability, affect, attention span, and stimulus thresholds will be informative (Thompson, 1985, p. 26). This is information that only becomes available through systematic and intense observation.

The School-Age Child

The school-age child is a somewhat less difficult interview subject than the preschooler, but still a bit obtuse. If a problem does exist, it may manifest itself in school, family, or peer relations. The environment in which the problem occurs may not be the environment that is causing the behavior; it may simply be the only safe place to manifest feelings. Most problems in children of this age are due to a mismatch between expectations of persons in a given environment and the child's inability to meet those expectations (Brent, 1985, p. 30).

As was the case with the preschool child, multiple data sources are mandatory in determining with any accuracy what might be happening in the school-aged child's life. At a minimum, parents and teachers, as well as the child, need to be approached on the same issues. These adults may be accurate in their reports of the child's behavior, but are frequently in error when describing the thoughts and feelings of the child. This is particularly true if these adults have an inability to empathize with the child, as is characteristic of adults in violent families (Brent, 1985, p. 30).

Rapport is the key to the interview with the school-aged child. Play is not necessary unless the child has some language or communication impairment, as many maltreated children will. It is of utmost importance to gain the child's understanding of why he or she thinks the interview is being conducted, what he or she believes the problem is that brought him or her there, and his or her understanding of the practitioner's role. Misconceptions should, of course, be corrected. Confidentiality exists in this relationship, and any departure from that must be explained to the child or the trust level will quickly decay (Brent, 1985, p. 31).

School, friends, and activities are all good openers and there is no need to stress the child with confrontation of sensitive issues immediately. Discord in the family and the quality of the relationship between this child and each family member can be explored in a nonthreatening way. Discussion of disciplinary styles is almost always a necessary part of this conversation. Included in this discussion is the child's view of whether the parent's disciplinary style is appropriate. Many maltreated children will describe extremes in punishment and then make an effort to justify their parent's actions. Remember that not only conflict but affection between family members requires exploration (Brent, 1985, p. 31). It is best if the descriptions of family interaction can be confirmed or denied through an unobserved viewing of the child and parent in the waiting room, office, or school setting. Even though the school-aged child is capable of accurate description, there is no substitute for direct observation.

The Adolescent

The adolescent is among the most difficult and obstructionistic interview subjects. They are suspicious of the motives of the adult interviewer. The independence/dependence struggles normal to this age group make for an interview subject who is usually less than agreeable. It is the rare contact that will not bring a new concern, attitude, misunderstanding, or failed assignment from adolescents as they continually test the practitioner.

These interviews must, in many ways, be led by the adolescents. The affective tone and topic of the interview may be taken over by them. This is the result of the extra emotional space required by adolescents to enable them to play both child and adult roles. Flexibility in the interview is important in gaining adolescents' trust. Adolescents must be free to be many different persons during the course of a single interview.

The flat affect that only adolescents can demonstrate may be an additional feature of the interview. Boredom and sullenness seem to pervade. What is really occurring is fear and a hopefulness that the interviewer will leave them alone. The longer the child has lived in a maltreating environment, the more likely this response. This is often frustrating for the practitioner, but consideration must be given to the adolescent's lack of affective vocabulary and inexperience at discussing feelings honestly with an adult. Observation of these flat adolescents with a group of their peers would find them to be entirely different individuals.

The success of the interview process with adolescents rests with the practitioner's ability to convince the adolescent that this relationship is a safe place to be genuine. These adolescents have lived with distrust for some time and will require demonstration of the safe nature of this relationship. Simple availability will be a beginning. A consistently accepting and understanding attitude toward these adolescents, even in the face of their repeated rejections, should help. Avoidance of value-laden statements and judgmental attitudes is mandatory if the adolescent is to stay involved in the process (Bolton, 1980, pp. 190–192).

Stay out of adolescents' ways, answer their questions, talk to them in a respectful manner, and never indicate that you know what they are feeling. Transparency of thought is a fear of adolescents, and an adult who can read their minds is threatening. Adolescents may not be the most articulate of interview subjects, but the wise and patient investigator will find that they have a great deal to say (Morgan & Burkholder, 1982, p. 47).

The Sexually Abused Child: A Special Interview

Jones and McQuiston (1984, pp. 165–167, 1985) suggest that the sexually abused child presents a two-stage mandate for the practitioner: investigation and evaluation. Unfortunately, the helping professional is not as well prepared for the investigation phase as the evaluation phase. The normally uncritical and accepting interview of the helping professional is not the skeptical and cautious interview of the investigator. Given that recent information from Jones (1985) suggests that as many as 8 percent of the child sexual abuse cases seen today may involve fictitious reporting, the mandate to investigate and be skeptical is a strong one. At issue in these interviews is the child's recall ability, suggestibility, the training of the use of reconstruction devices, and the credibility of the child's statement. Fortunately, there are some general rules.

As with all child interview subjects, practitioners must explain who they are and why they are dealing with the child. Although sometimes uncomfortable, it is important to gather accurate and difficult information about the allegation at this early stage. The topics of the interview must include the painful details as well as a more general sense of the means used to elicit cooperation, any threats or use of violence, the victim's role in the event(s), and the perceived intentions and emotional condition of the alleged perpetrator. The child's response to free recall are the most valuable, although some structured questioning may be necessary. In some cases, reconstructive props such as dolls and dollhouses are useful.

In this interview, as in any child-centered interview, some information is gained from direct conversation and some from the interviewer's observation of play patterns, behavior changes, mood shifts, and topics or individuals repeatedly avoided. Any attempt made by the child to change the topic or distract the interviewer should be noted as well as any points that seem particularly agitating. Nonverbal communication and the use of first- or third-person pronouns can be telling (Jones & McQuiston, 1984, p. 174); drawing with the child or looking out the window together may take some of the sting out of having to relive the experience (Winnicott, 1971). It is important to gain a great deal of information in the first interview,

but 20 minutes is about the best that can be hoped for when dealing
with younger children. After a short rest the child can be approached
again.

Sexually abused children, like maltreated children generally, may
attempt to relieve the strain of the interview by saying virtually
anything. With the increased number of reports originating in
preschool children enmeshed in custody battles, there is an
uncomfortable sense that an increasing number of unfounded (i.e.,
coached) reports are occurring. This does not suggest that large
numbers of children lie in such situations. It is still accurate to
suggest that almost all children are telling the truth in these matters,
but children can and do lie on occasion. In fact, children are not only
better at lying, but they are more convincing when they do as they
are more easily able to tell themselves that they are telling the truth
than adults (Yuille, 1986). The current view is that children are more
credible as witnesses than previously believed, but they can be
coached, are subject to recall and memory errors, and may even be
less than truthful. It is the interviewer's role to pick from these
alternatives in helping to arrive at accurate testimony. The
fundamental reality is that the utility of the child's testimony is
dependent upon the appropriateness of the interview.

Overall, it is wise to remember that children feel themselves to be
incompetent and look to adults for cues and answers. They are not
usually misled about things about which they are very certain, but
they are suggestible in matters that are somewhat unclear to them
(Yuille & King, 1986). As has been noted previously, there is a
tendency in child sexual abuse matters for the child to retract prior
disclosures, leaving the interviewer at a loss. In reality, when a
contradictory statement or retraction does occur, the interviewer can
point out the discrepancy by noting the exact points of disagreement.
This should be only a light reminder and the child should not be led.
It is important to let the child know that the pressure they are feeling
is appreciated and that the pacing is up to the child. The approach
should be a quiet and level one that allows the child to be whomever
he or she needs to be at that time. Direct techniques will not prove
very productive until trust and safety are assured. That will be slow
in coming.

As Table 16.1 indicates, critical issues abound in viewing children
and the statements they provide. In almost every case the entire
interview should be recorded with audiotape and possibly videotape
as well. This does sometimes influence the interviewer's style, but

TABLE 16.1
Critical Issues in the Child Sexual Abuse Interview

I. General Issues Regarding the Child [Alleged Victim]

(1) Is the child developmentally competent to provide adequate recall?

(2) Does the child have the cognitive/intellectual capacity to provide adequate and accurate recall?

(3) Is/are there any feature(s) of the child's relationship with the alleged perpetrator that might motivate or encourage false accusations?

(4) Is/are there any feature(s) of the child's relationship with the reporting adult that might motivate or encourage false accusations?

(5) Is there anything in the personality of the child that might provide a motive for false accusations?

(6) Is there anything in the living situation of the child that might provide a motive for false accusations?

(7) Is there anything in the personality of the child that might preclude their ability to remember the event(s) clearly?

(8) Are there any coercive features of the relationship with the alleged perpetrator, or within the environment, that might prevent the child from maintaining the accusation?

(9) Does the child have the capacity to understand the event he or she is describing?

(10) Does the child have the language capacity to associate accurate verbal descriptions with the alleged events/behaviors?

(11) Does the child have the language capacity to understand the meaning of the events/behaviors he or she is describing?

(12) How might the child's statement be influenced by previous interviews?

(13) Does the child's level of social and cognitive competence allow for the assimilation of events/behaviors being described?

(14) Has the child show susceptibility to suggestion?

(15) Does the child display inappropriate affect? Is there an absence of the type of affect that would be expected?

II. General Issues Surrounding the Child's Statement

(1) Are there major elements of the story that are simply not possible? For example, contradictory to the laws of nature?

(2) Are there major elements of the story that are contradictory?

(3) Are there major elements of the story that are contradicted by physical evidence?

(4) Does the statement include language or concepts that are thought to be beyond the normal capacity of a child of that age or experience?

(5) Was there significant suggestion, coercion, or leading questioning offered by previous interviewers?

(continued)

TABLE 16.1 *(continued)*

(6) Is there any pattern in the child's statement that might suggest coaching or suggestibility?

(7) Have there been any leading questions or suggestions in previous interviews?

(8) Has the child's information, at any point or in any interview, been altered through the use of props and cues (for example, anatomically correct dolls of other reconstruction devices such as dollhouses)?

(9) Do the child's responses to free-report opportunities differ markedly from those prompted by the interviewer (from specific questions or reconstruction devices)?

III. Specific Issues Surrounding the Event(s)/Behavior(s)

(1) What was the exact type of sexual abuse alleged?

(2) What was the range of sexual activities alleged (for example, voyeurism, frottage, masturbation, fellatio, intercourse)?

(3) What was the duration and frequency of the alleged activity?

(4) What was the alleged perpetrator's alleged means of coercion?

(5) If incestuous activity is alleged, what was the method of concealment used by the family? That is, how incestuogenic is the family? Is there cooperation between the adults? Secretiveness? Seductiveness?

(6) What are the physical indicators of the event(s)/behavior(s) (expected in only 15 percent of the cases).

(7) What are the behavioral indicators and responses in the child?

(8) Can a pattern of precipitating events be identified?

(9) What was the timing and place of the event(s)?

(10) Were other children involved?

(11) Have there been any disclosures to other persons?

(12) What is the history of sexual development in all family members?

(13) Is there anything unusual or telling in the family's response to the problem? to the allegation?

(14) Is there anything unusual, unexpected, or telling in the child's response to the problem, to the allegation?

(15) What is the prognosis for normal functioning?

IV. Specific Issues with the Child's Statement

(1) Is the statement a coherent whole?

(2) Is the content logical?

(3) Do the differing segments of the statement fit together?

(4) Does the statement seem spontaneous?

(5) Is the action/content described without constraint or does it seem rehearsed?

(6) Are the details of good quality (i.e., specific) or are they general and noninformative?

TABLE 16.1 (*continued*)

(7) Are people and objects described in detail?

(8) Are the actions described sequential?

(9) Are there specific descriptions of time and place?

(10) Are the events and conversations associated with the event connected, overlapping, or related in some way?

(11) Is there evidence of unplanned interruption or unanticipated difficulties that would not likely to be a part of a contrived story?

(12) Are there details of objects or events that are unusual yet meaningful in this context?

(13) Does the child describe subjective states?

(14) Did the child consider escape or resistence?

(15) Is there spontaneous correction of details as the interview goes forward?

(16) Does the child describe wrong or inappropriate behavior on his or her part suggesting some self-deprecation?

(17) Does the child make excuses for the perpetrator?

(18) Does the child attribute unacceptable motives to the perpetrator?

(19) Are there sufficient details characteristic of the action that would only be known to someone involved?

References: Berliner and Barbieri (1984); Fote (1985); Loftus and Davies (1984); Goodman (1984a); Goodman (1984b); Johnson & Foley (1984); Stellar (1986); Stellar & Raskin (1986); Yuille & King (1986).

frequently serves as an educational device for the interviewer as well as a solid mechanism for maintaining accurate historical data on cases. In the final analysis, it seems that the interviewer's primary skills in this area are taking the time to review case records and preparing a list of questions beforehand, a true effort not to lead the child, and patience and caring during the actual interview process. This is the same patience and caring that must be exercised in working with the lower SES families which predominate the officially reported population of violent families. As will be evident from the following section, these families are no better prepared for the practitioner's intervention than the children just described.

Working with the Low-Income and Minority Family

The prevalence of low-income and minority families, at least within officially reported populations, is a factor in the practitioner's approach to violent families. This prevalence may represent a bias in reporting, but it results in a number of these families being referred to both clinical and legal practitioners. For the practitioner, this may be an unfamiliar population both personally and professionally.

Acosta, Yamamoto, and Evans (1982) have conducted an extensive review of the problems of service delivery to low-income and minority populations. Their work deals primarily with clinical settings, but their concepts may be applied across both clinical and legal practice with the violent family. Whether attorney or clinician, effective family violence practitioners must assess the influence of each family's sociocultural and ethnic background on the process and outcomes of each case. They must also recognize the implications of that background in their own relationship with a given family. Even practitioners who work hard to recognize and respond to their own prejudices sometimes underestimate how important a particular social or ethnic identification may be in their assessment of, or performance in, a given case (Acosta et al., 1982; Lorion, 1974; Sue, 1977). This personal issue is exacerbated by the fact that neither the traditional legal nor clinical orientation/training is especially well suited for dealing with these families.

With the possible exception of some social work training, most practitioner orientations are constructed to be most effective when the individuals involved are not only intelligent but sensitive and verbal. The classic reference to this appropriate individual is found in the acronym YAVIS (Schofield, 1964), young, attractive, verbal, intelligent, and sensitive (or successful). This is an individual who seeks out the practitioner, becomes an active participant, is insightful, and understands not only the stress of personal change, but the time commitment implied (Goldstein, 1973, pp. 5–6). *It is a virtual certainty that the members of a violent family will not fit this stereotype.* Even should the intelligence, verbal ability, and sensitivity be present, this family is probably not with the practitioner voluntarily. In fact, they may hope to be out of the practitioner's influence as quickly as possible. This opens the door to resistance and manipulation as will be discussed in the following section. When this resistance is added to the existing characteristics of the family, the practitioner is likely to be presented with what Goldstein (1973, p. 6) calls "Mr. NonYAVIS."

Mr. NonYAVIS is described as physically unexceptional; verbally reticent; intellectually unremarkable, dull, or frankly delayed; and vocationally marginal or unsuccessful. The problem that led him or her to the practitioner is seen as concrete and related to the social environment as opposed to his or her own thinking or behavior. The expectation held is that the practitioner will provide immediate help or guidance. Mr. NonYAVIS' role is passive, and a solution to the problem will be furnished almost immediately. The practitioner in the family violence case will meet virtually none of these expectations.

The predominant professional model in this individual's experience has been the physician. This physician, and the family violence practitioner by association was a smart/rich person to whom Mr. NonYAVIS had previously presented with a problem. Mr. NonYAVIS was passive while examined, and in minutes a concise problem statement and solution was forthcoming (i.e., "You have the flu. Take these pills for ten days"). The low-income and/or minority family holds the same expectation for the family violence practitioner which also means that they feel they do not have to worry about helping themselves. This is not a productive set of expectations within the family violence situation. Added to this problem is the fact that practitioners' expectations of the family may also not match.

Most practitioners have adopted the goal of at least adequate functioning. Goldstein (1973, p. 4) describes the practitioner's belief in adequate functioning as a search for vertical mobility, competition, ambition, self-discipline, prudence, rationality, and foresight. In short, practitioners have, in their own lives, learned to attack their environment in an effort to gain mastery over it. If practitioners are seeking this in the poor and/or minority family, they will be disappointed.

The poor and/or minority individual has often experienced a great deal more adversity than the YAVIS individual. They are also likely to have been previously disappointed by professional practitioners. There has been greater anxiety in their lives, more rejection, an increased likelihood of academic or social inadequacy, and a consistently higher level of stress. They are not only tired of dealing with stress, they never really learned how to deal with it very well (Goldstein, 1973, p. 66). The result is an attitude of trying to live in the present, make do with what they have, and an absence of concern about future planning (Schneiderman, 1965). This is a set of attitudes difficult for many practitioners to understand or accept. On the other hand, many of these families will be much more serious about certain family issues than their middle-class counterparts.

Poor and working-class parents show some tendency to value obedience more than middle-class parents. There are externally imposed rules for their children, and any transgression may result in physical punishment (Belskey, 1984). While the middle-class family may be oriented toward self-control through understanding, the lower-income family may measure the rightness of behavior through overt behavior as it fits the rules (Goldstein, 1973, p. 33). There are rules for all family members; rules that are violated result in punishment, frequently physical punishment.

As a result of basic differences in thinking and values, the practitioner and the family may not be speaking the same language both literally and figuratively (Goldstein, 1973, p. 51). This mismatch may be why some practitioners feel that working with lower income families is a waste of time. It is most certainly one of the major reasons why many minority and lower income families drop out of treatment almost immediately (Baekeland & Lundwall, 1975).

The fact that lower income individuals are unpopular with professional practitioners is not a new insight. In their now-classic research on mental illness and poverty, Redlich, Hollingshead, and Bellie (1955) noted that therapists disliked the lack of responsibility that seemed to be present in the low-income individual. The apparent lack of self-discipline, extreme dependency, and inability to deal with emotional problems were also areas that reportedly created frustration and disappointment in professionals working with these persons. When the need to bring concrete solutions into the therapy setting became apparent, for example, finding a place to live, the classically and psychodynamically trained therapists tended to move on to other issues. No practitioner with that narrow orientation will survive working within family violence.

McMahon and Shore (1968) found the issues of deprivation, squalor, dirt, and disease to arouse negative emotions in many professionals. Perhaps that is why diagnosticians have been described by Kadushin (1969) as more likely to ascribe extreme diagnoses to their lower class patients than their middle-class patients. This is a class-linked bias well known to those working in family violence. It is little wonder that professional services offered to lower income and minority families are often described by negative outcomes, differential treatment, underutilization, and noncompliance (Acosta et al., 1982, p. vii).

The practitioner in the family violence area must orient to the family's way of thinking. They are not going to come around to the practitioner's way of thinking. These families are accustomed to crisis and stress. They will not be as upset about their inability to deal with problems as the practitioner is likely to be. This family's assumption is that the practitioner will take care of the problem, and the solution will soon be forthcoming. This is a solution, by the way, that does not come from talking but from action (Acosta et al., 1982, p. 5).

Any practitioner unwilling to involve multiple community agencies, concentrate on the solving of environmental rather than psycho-dynamic or knotty legal problems, and be available around the clock should not become involved with violent families. If family violence practitioners must be anything, they must be flexible in operating style. Each meeting with the violent family may well be the last (Acosta et al., 1982, p. 48). If something useful is not presented at each meeting, the practitioner will not see this family again, at least voluntarily.

Acosta and colleagues (1982, p. 6) suggest that there will always be "psychosocial therapy" when working with low-income and minority families, no matter what else is occurring. Psychosocial therapy implies having a grasp of social realities and taking an active stance for the family in overcoming them. This is a family that may feel a great distance between themselves and the practitioner. They may be reluctant to express or disclose feelings, attitudes, or problems (Acosta et al., 1982, p. 15). They will not be afraid to ask for help with concrete problems because the practitioner is seen as an individual who can get them corrected. If the practitioner does fix these problems, the family will become attached. If the practitioner is unwilling, or unable, to fix these psychosocial difficulties, the family will terminate.

The key, then, is to allow the family to define the problems, as they see them, in concrete terms. The practitioner's response must be equally concrete. Being successful in this role not only places the family in a better position to deal with the nonconcrete family issues that led to the violence (in that environmental stress will be reduced), it allows practitioners to prove their abilities and gain the family's trust. If this, or any other family, is sent to practitioners against their will and contains an individual with the abrasive or resistant personality described in the next section, a set of additional problems are introduced to the clinical setting. These will be described following a summary view.

Low-Income Families: A Summary View

Many of the problems found in working with the low-income or minority family rest squarely on the shoulders of the practitioner. Practitioners, as individuals, are quite different in many cases than the persons they hope to serve. There is a gap in life experience, values, and expectations between them, and there are both stylistic and personal belief differences that require reflection.

It is hoped that practitioners in the family violence area hold an extra measure of interpersonal sensitivity, perceptiveness, depth of understanding and patience. While these are virtues, their presence also creates a preference for working with persons who have qualities that allow the exercise of these skills. That demands an affective orientation not usually available in the low-income and/or minority population of violent families (Goldstein, 1973, p. 16). That may be why Brody (1968) found practitioners to be pessimistic, annoyed, remote, and anxious around low-income clients/patients. In the family violence area especially, practitioners cannot afford to be bored or distant as that will give license to the family to move forward with their desire to terminate contact.

Many low-income individuals are not familiar with professional practitioners. They are frightened of the authority held by these individuals. It is questionable that they understand what is expected of them in the court or clinic, and no one has taken the time to explain it to them. They have, in many cases, been too intimidated to ask. The authority of the clinician may be more difficult to deal with than the more direct and understandable authority of the officer of the court. A little forethought will enable the practitioner to avoid some practical mistakes in dealing with this population.

First, do not use buzz words. "Touchy-feely" approaches will fall flat or be manipulated. If the individual is slow to respond to a question, wait. There is an annoying tendency among middle-class (i.e., hurried) practitioners to jump in and explain the individual's thoughts to them. Aggressiveness and impatience of this type will erode any hope of progress and eliminate the already-slim chance of disclosure and discussion, especially with minority individuals. Such lecturing has been learned by this individual as something to be tolerated and discarded. Finally, do not pretend to understand. If words or concepts are used which do not make sense, ask about them. It might be that this individual is testing, waiting to see the pretense if it is there.

On the other hand, it is equally unwise to modify familiar therapeutic techniques too greatly. There is obvious negative bias in such efforts that is sometimes so transparent that it becomes offensive. Being poor does not indicate a lack of intelligence, but many practitioners who do shift seem to move their expectations significantly downward for this group. If alterations in style are to be made, trust those that have been tested, such as those described by Goldstein.

Goldstein (1973, p. 17) has found that greater authority and direction, activity rather than introspection, concrete structure and organization rather than symbolism, and objectively demonstrable explanations will be better received than some of the more obscure approaches sometimes taken in the professional setting. A combination of modeling, role playing, social reinforcement, and homework assignments seems to show positive results (1973, p. 20). This does not represent the destruction of traditional practice. Rather, it is the directing of known techniques to specific families in a way that is consistent with their strengths and abilities. An awareness of environmental constraints, sociocultural factors, needs, and perspectives of a given family can create the most positive of therapeutic atmospheres (Acosta et al., 1982, p. 43). It is when adjustment is made across the board, as though the professional were dealing with a different species of person, that problems arise.

Low-income persons appear in professional settings with different needs and expectations than those more fortunate. There is a need for both concrete and therapeutic intervention. The therapeutic content is time-limited, supportive, and direct. The concrete services are wide ranging and defined by the survival needs of the family. According to Acosta and colleagues (1981, p. 6), these persons are seeking specific answers to specific problems, including:

(1) help in dealing with other agencies,
(2) specific guidance in personal and nonpersonal matters,
(3) help in putting thoughts into some perspective,
(4) referral to other services,
(5) help in gaining control over a life that is out of control,
(6) help in setting limits that are consistent,
(7) help in understanding why they think a certain way,
(8) help in putting childhood experiences into perspective,
(9) making certain that they are not "crazy," and
(10) an opportunity to ventilate and use the practitioner for nurturance [Acosta et al., 1982, pp. 13–14].

Since these families are likely to visit only briefly, unless court-ordered treatment is involved, the best strategy seems to be to educate them thoroughly about services and follow through with short-term goals directly targeting symptom relief and problem solving (Acosta et al., 1982, pp. 43, 147). Assertiveness training and behavioral techniques have been shown to be especially effective. *Approach each visit with this family as if they will never be seen again.* Be brief and be active. The critical features of performance are the taking of whatever actions are necessary to solve problems, being careful to respond to all questions, clarifying all viewpoints, and reaching beyond insight therapies. Do not attempt to speak this family's language in some gratuitous way. Instead speak your own in a way they can understand and act through goals that can be met. In this way success will not be assured, but it will at least be possible.

Hostility and Resistance

Violent families hold a unique ability to test the practitioner's personal and professional limits. This is both the most challenging and most frustrating element of working with such families. The violent family's daring the practitioner to help them is always there.

Although the hostility toward authority present in the violent family is most frequently demonstrated in passive-aggressiveness, it is sometimes overt. In either case, there are likely to be a series of ambivalent and oppositional interactions with the family. Stern (1984, p. 12) describes this "push-pull" form of relating as the ability to "hold on to others while rubbing them raw with behavior." For the perpetrator of family violence, this is a simple matter of carrying over into the professional setting a behavioral style that has been used in the family for some time.

There is an ambivalence in the perpetrator of family violence, a simultaneous desire for and fear of contact as well as a need for nurturance and a reluctance to be open to it. He or she wants human contact but knows neither how to reach for it nor how to sustain it. These persons have little sensitivity to others' cues, are selfish and intrusive, and *attention* not *communication* is the goal of interaction (Stern, 1984, p. 13). Consequently, this individual is isolated, frustrated, and angry even in their own family. The only continuous feature of the person's life is his or her ability to generate anger and misery in the people closest to them. These are not easy individuals to deal with in any professional situation, but even more difficult if their presence is involuntary (e.g., court-ordered).

Resistance in the family violence case is difficult to predict. In some court-ordered visits, compliance and acceptance is improved. In others there is a "stone-wall" quality; still others may present an artificial compliance for a period of time, followed by a decline into obstructionism. This resistance has many points of origin.

In the violent family resistance may be a symptom of a generalized inability to deal with problems. This is often compounded by a reluctance to admit to a problem, and in some cases, especially those in which legal decisions hinge upon admission of guilt, such as sexual abuse, resistance may be purposeful and strategic.

The family's feelings about change are always a consideration in resistance. There is great pessimism in the violent family about the possibility of positive change. In fact, change is sometimes frankly fear producing. In other cases, the root cause is fatigue, a fatigue that has convinced this family that the distance between them and being normal is so great that there is no reason to even begin the seemingly endless therapeutic journey (Goldfried, 1982, pp. 103–105).

All people find issues in their life that seem so impossible that they must be denied or avoided. The violent family is masterful at this defense. When the clinician asks these individuals to admit to and confront these problems directly, there is a perception of threat (Wachtel, 1982, p. xix). When this natural reluctance is superimposed upon a group (violent families) who are uniquely underprepared for the clinical experience, the oppositional inclinations are magnified.

A summary view of the etiology of resistance in the family violence case would find its origins in characteristics of the individuals such as defensiveness; characteristics of their interpersonal style such as abrasiveness; characteristics of the environment, (e.g., stressful), and/or characteristics of the clinical environment, for example, clinician personality or technique (Lazarus & Fay, 1982, p. 124).

All persons, violent families included, wish to be shown the path to balance in their world without having to make too many basic changes. In many areas of their lives they are simply not that uncomfortable. No matter how bizarre the family may appear, its members may not feel that there is anything wrong. Since psychic pain is the prime motivator for clinical cooperation, and there is none in some of these families, arriving at a motivational structure is difficult. This may be particularly true if the treatment was court-ordered.

The behavior that brings the violent family to the attention of authorities is usually the result of the perpetrator's protecting him or herself from a self-perceived danger. In asking them to strip away that protection, the clinician is really asking that they leave themselves exposed and vulnerable (Basch, 1982, pp. 2–3). This is a very difficult request for the insecure and controlling perpetrator. It may occur over a period of time, but not without a great deal of struggle. This struggle on the part of the perpetrator, is often involuntary.

Warner (1982) has reviewed what he terms the "defeating patient." This is an individual described as being intent on "squeezing you (the practitioner) out" and waiting until "you have exhausted yourself." Some family violence perpetrators hope that the practitioner will eventually give up on them. Others seek to prove they are as unworthy as they feel. Still others are persons who use people in any setting (e.g., abrasive personalities).

In a curious way, the defeatist will destroy the relationship with the practitioner and, having been rejected, will receive self-confirmation. The *abrasive* individual will, on the other hand, seek to destroy the relationship, and, if blessed with an understanding practitioner, will not be rejected, allowing them to feel safe (Barlevav, 1984, p. 85). This safety is short-lived and the limits will be tested again and again. After a period of dealing with such an individual, many practitioners will begin to question their own stability.

In the violent family member, resistance and abrasiveness are not always psychodynamic in origin. Many cases are nothing more than behavioral inadequacy. These individuals may deny the existence of a problem and resist treatment throughout, but it is more likely that they will show the resistance through missed appointments, being late, rationalizing negative behaviors, blowing practitioner comments out of proportion, or verbally battering the practitioner (Lathrop, 1984, pp. 63–64; Lazarus & Fay, 1982, pp. 115–117). This does, irrespective of origin, wear down the practitioner. The only defense is to remember its origins.

The therapeutic process and the violent family member are not a good match. The practitioner and this individual may not be able to establish rapport, and in family violence cases, it is rare that resources provide the availability of referral to someone else. There is no reason to believe that this individual will use social networks appropriately. They are not likely to select the most advantageous behavior when dealing with anyone. There is often a psychological and intellectual (fund of knowledge) deficit that makes it hard to advise these persons. These are not individuals who are highly invested in acting the way the practitioner wishes they would act toward others, and there is no reason to expect that these persons will be any more successful in their interactions with the practitioner than they have been with anyone else in their life. In the final accounting, *the weight of tolerance is on the practitioner* (Lazarus & Fay, 1982, p. 120).

If the individual in the violent family has (1) a long history of problems with little evidence of change, (2) a history of unsuccessful encounters with other practitioners, (3) never experienced competent family functioning, (4) been overly critical and impatient with the clinical/legal process, (5) been uncommitted and apathetic about the process, (6) been socially anxious or withdrawn, (7) been minimally communicative, or (8) procrastinated, the battle will be a long and probably ill-fated one. On a positive note, a few strategies do offer hope.

Behind the abrasive and self-defeating behaviors of the violent family member is a pathological fear. These are also individuals with a deep-seated need for closeness with a person who can be trusted and who will protect them. This may sound overly kind toward persons who have been violent toward an essentially defenseless family member, but in many cases they are afraid of the world. They seek to establish some sense of control, but in doing so select a hugely inappropriate behavior. This does not overlook the fact that, in some small number of cases, perpetrators behave aggressively toward others simply because they enjoy it, and professional time with those who enjoy inflicting pain is wasted.

For the individual who is responding out of fear, Meichenbaum and Gilmore (1982, p. 40) suggest that they are not the aggressive and defeating individual they seem to present. Rather these are persons who consider themselves so incompetent that they are destined to continuing fear and loneliness. The practitioner must help these individuals understand that change in a positive direction is possible (Goldfried, 1982, p. 97). This will require the establishment of a positive atmosphere by tailoring the therapeutic and daily living tasks to the individual's competencies. Any intervention must be structured for feasibility and the maximization of probable success. There will be inevitable setbacks, and the tendency for this individual to defeat their own purposes must be monitored (Meichenbaum &

Gilmore, 1982, pp. 42–46). The interventions must be understood, accepted, and goals jointly developed before moving forward. Importantly, this individual must be absolutely clear in the knowledge that even the most diligent efforts toward positive change occasionally result in uneven progress (Goldfried, 1982, p. 103).

The practitioner's caring and trustworthiness are the two fundamental tools for success (Goldfried, 1982, p. 99), but nurturance must be developed slowly for any hurried response to this individual's needs may be anxiety producing (Wepman & Donovan, 1984, p. 18). Although not appearing fragile, these individuals are in fear of the authority of the practitioner. This is a fragility and powerlessness that is exacerbated by the genuine power held by the practitioner in the family violence case (i.e., deciding when, or if, to return the child).

Gedo and Goldberg (1973) have suggested a specific therapeutic hierarchy for getting some sense of control back into the lives of these persons; this will be the type of power that allows them to deal constructively with problems rather than abrasively or in other self-defeating ways. First, the practitioner must protect the individuals from overstimulation. This is a crisis-intervention procedure in which continuous availability and direct advice keep the entire family stable after an explosive incident. Second, the practitioner must help the individuals achieve a sense of order and find those areas of their lives in which they do have control, an increased sense of self-respect being the hoped-for result. Third, once some order and sense of self is restored, the individuals must be exposed to parts of their personality or actions that have been denied. Fourth, the individuals must be given an explanation as to why their aberrant patterns developed and what they will mean in the future if continued. Obviously, this type of confrontation demands the presence of a strong relationship and should not be undertaken prematurely (Basch, 1982, p. 17).

If, in addition to the foregoing, there are opportunities to practice new behaviors that fit some aspects of the individual's regular routine (Goldfried, 1982, p. 103), and they are reinforced strongly, progress should be made. This combination of crisis intervention, cognitive restructuring, behavior modification, and reality therapy seems, as has been noted in other sections, the best combination of therapies to get the violent family moving in more positive directions. This is assuming, of course, that no other conditions impinge upon the therapeutic process. For, if economic conditions, psychopathology, or incipient dangerousness are additional features in the abrasive and self-defeating individual, additional considerations must apply. Some of these considerations will be noted in the sections to follow.

Treating the Personality and Affective Disorder

Personality Disorders

Historically, personality disorders were thought to have an unremitting and untreatable course (Reid, 1981, p. 155). Since recent work suggests that these disorders are treatable, the problem seems to have been one of misdiagnosis (Craft, 1965, p. 98). Correction of this misdiagnosis problem is not a simple process of establishing uniform testing or evaluation procedure (Estroff et al., 1984; Gabinet, 1983, p. 399; Schwemer & Bendel, 1976). Each of the personality disorders has a slightly different etiology and treatment. Consequently, each must be established and dealt with on a case-by-case basis.

Violent families that contain personality disordered individuals exist at two extremes. One extreme is described by inertia, futility, low self-esteem, and a lack of control over life events. At the opposite extreme is the family that is involved in constant antisocial activity. These families range from a depressed affect on one end to a chaotic lack of impulse control at the other (Wells, 1981, p. 115). Critical to the family violence practitioner are those families who exhibit dyscontrol internally.

A *dyscontrol* act is precipitous and of short duration. There is a complex interaction of affects, memories, predictions, and perceptions that cause the individual to generalize inappropriately and act without forethought. In some cases a secondary dyscontrol occurs in which time passes between the stimulus for the violent act and the act itself. Unable to decide how to respond, the perpetrator vacillates between acting upon and restraining his or her violent impulse. As these indecisive ruminations accumulate the amount of rage, fear, and depression in this individual increases. Given sufficient time, or the introduction of inhibition reducers such as alcohol, an explosion can occur (Monroe, 1982, pp. 373–377).

In treating the dyscontrol patient, it is important to determine any neurological precursors to the loss of control and treat these medically if possible. Following that, an identification of the specific drives or urges behind the act must be made. The appropriateness of the motivations for or goals of the act must become a topic of discussion. The clinician must assume the potential for future dyscontrol and provide a plan for handling these eventualities. The goal is to intercept the act and bring internal or external control to bear on the situation before it exceeds the individual's ability to control the response.

In the periods between dyscontrol acts, confrontation of the prior act is required. This confrontation includes an examination of disguised motivation, fears, and rebellious drives, not just the precipitating environmental events that will describe the patient's view of what went on (Monroe, 1982, p. 377). This is an individual who requires constant monitoring.

The opposite of the overtly explosive individual is the *passive-aggressive* individual who sends conflicting and incompatible messages to others. There is typically a facade of mutuality that only superficially hides the resentments and antagonisms that fester under the surface. This leaves other persons never quite certain of their position and unclear about the choice of actions or reactions that might please this individual. Communications cannot be understood and interpretations are dangerous (Million, 1981, p. 267). This is crazy-making behavior for members of this person's family.

The dynamics that generate passive-aggressive behavior include guilt, fear, and a perceived need for retaliation against dependency. It is a mixture of needing the persons in the environment and having that need create anger toward those necessary persons. This anger creates aggressiveness toward others in the environment, but never enough to cause them to leave.

Passive-aggressive persons require a firm hand to guide them toward facing their fear and ambivalence. These are very difficult patients. Fortunately, some behavior modification and cognitive restructuring strategies are showing promise. In these techniques, the goal is nothing more than a more consistent and predictable approach to important individuals. Even in the clinical setting, the patient will demonstrate submission in one session and resentment in the next (Million, 1981, p. 267). The clinician must do some interpretation for the passive-aggressive individual. The goal is to differentiate hostile from assertive behavior and to encourage the acceptance of some dependency. Typically, managing dependency in the family is learned through working through dependency upon the clinician. Fears of dependency and aggression must be dealt with and appropriate skill training introduced (Malinow, 1981, p. 126). These patients must, above all things, come to understand their own contribution to the frustrations, inadequacies, and behaviors that trouble them.

Working with the *antisocial personality* is a difficult task. Both authority and warmth must be balanced in a way that indicates to these individuals that the clinician is in control; at the same time, they must be able to trust the clinician. These individuals will view this clinical quandary as a challenge. The response to the clinical setting from the antisocial personality is likely to be one of testing clinical skills, confronting inconsistencies across sessions, and taking every possible opportunity to humiliate the clinician. The only way to contain the anger brought about by this antisocial style is to remind oneself that it was these individuals' harsh up-bringing that led them to this behavior.

The therapeutic goals in working with the antisocial personality can be found in increased use of appropriate reason, fairness, and rational expectations. This is a long-term clinical effort that must remain calm and nonconfrontational. It is also one of endless trial-and-error learning about the patient and his or her problem. Change can occur, but only after a protracted clinical experience.

The remaining personality disorders typically found in the violent family *(borderline, avoidant, dependent, and narcissistic person-alities)* present with some common therapeutic needs. These needs include repetitive crisis intervention, reality-based interactions, confrontation of destructive behaviors, and the development of a more rewarding environment (Gallahorn, 1981, p. 83; Million, 1981, p. 119).

Supportive treatment may be helpful in dealing with realistic self-worth. Psychopharmacological treatment may help control anxieties or depressions. Behavior modification serves to teach new responses to previously fear-producing situations, and cognitive restructuring may serve to combat erroneous self-attitudes and distorted social expectations (Kernberg, 1975; Kohut, 1975; Million, 1981, p. 119). Overall, it does not appear that traditional individually oriented insight therapies are particularly successful here; group or family therapy may be a better choice (Prodgers, 1984, p. 42). There must be an emphasis upon stating problems in behavioral terms; directives work better than interpretations or catharsis, and a strong symptom-focused approach must be adopted until there has been time given for insightful self-change and a reduction in self-destructive behavior (Harbin, 1982). Once symptoms have become controllable, it is possible to move toward confrontation, interpretation, and a more cognitive/affective focus, but a pattern of repetitive and consistent confrontation of behavior will mark most of the clinical time spent with the personality disordered individual (Harbin, 1982, p. 482).

Affective Disorders

Affective disorders, predominantly depression, pervade the lives of violent family members, parents and children alike. It may be found in the neglecting mother, the battered or sexually abused child, the battered conjugal partner, the mistreated elder, and in many perpetrators of these acts. In addition, depression itself occurs most frequently in the lower SES groups, which predominate in officially reported groups of violent families (Val et al., 1982, p. 103).

There are many treatments for depression. In the violent family, the initial work is in separating out the symptoms (i.e., sadness and immobility) from the consequences (family dysfunction) and the development of a treatment plan that deals with both. Often, the administration of antidepressant medication may aid in symptom reduction. This allows other therapies to influence the social disabilities (Lehmann, 1983, p. 4; Val et al., 1982, p. 103). Success is more likely in reactive (exogenous) depressions, which are in response to events than in autonomous (endogenous) depressions, which follow an unrelenting course irrespective of favorable environmental events (Paykel, 1982, p. 36; Wetzel, 1984, p. 5).

The clinician must be alert to the likelihood that both depression and anxiety are operating in the violent family member (Paykel, 1982). Such anxiety may be dealt with through pharmacotherapy, behavior therapy, cognitive reconceptualization, or reassurance, depending upon severity (Lehmann, 1983, p. 4). The cornerstone of treating the depression itself is an accurate identification of its origin.

The early theories on etiology of depression pointed toward anger that was misdirected at the self, anger *which should have been* directed at an object or individual. In some cases, the appropriate object (for the anger) is perceived as having been lost. In others, low self-esteem prevents the safe outward expression of the anger (Greenberg & Silverstein, 1983, p. 189). In either case, the violent family presents frequent opportunity for these dynamics to develop.

Sussman and colleagues (1985, p. 247) term the environment of the violent family "depressogenic" in that the highly stressful, sometimes dangerous, and often overwhelming (i.e., out of control) environment may overpower parent and child. This hostile, disruptive, and negative environment provides fertile ground for the development of depression (Orvaschel, Weissman, & Kidd, 1980; Winokur & Morrison, 1973). If nothing else, the repression of women in these families and the fear and anxiety that pervades should be sufficient to create a reactive depression in some (Deschner, 1984, p. 202; Gordon & Ledray, 1985, p. 30; Reavely & Gilbert, 1979).

Deschner (1984, p. 203) points toward the adult in the violent family feeling helpless and unable to cope with feared situations. This is followed by self-condemnation. In some cases defensive rage and counterattack focused on a child or spouse may be the result, More often, however, the result is self-condemning ruminations about others in the family that build until an explosion occurs. This is an individual who is out of control, and control is what must be introduced into his or her life.

In addition to the control introduced by chemical therapies of depression, some cases respond well to a combination of behavioral and cognitive approaches. Behavioral work applies to mood or social competence, cognitive therapies to more appropriate interpretation of events (Gordon & Ledray, 1985, p. 30). Also useful, in the clinical setting, is Lewison's (1974) suggestion that depression is related to the absence of reinforcing events in the environment. The depressed individual lives within an environment that is limited in the amount of reinforcements available. Additionally, this individual lacks the personal and intellectual skills necessary to draw out those reinforcements that are available. Focusing the individual's attention on the pleasant events that are available is one therapeutic approach. This is not easy in the barren environment of the violent family, but if applied as one of multiple therapies, this may show some success (Greenberg & Silverstein, 1983).

The cognitive therapies also seem to hold promise in the specialized treatment of the depressed member of a violent family. Depressed persons selectively recall events, all of which are recalled in a negative light. In giving meaning to situations, there is the anticipation of a negative outcome. Added to this burden is the disqualification of any prior success or previously positive events. This individual overgeneralizes from previous negative situations to all situations, loses the ability to discriminate between positive and negative events, and draws negative conclusions about events in the absence of negative evidence. This is an individual who needs to be taught a new way of thinking.

Cognition, according to Beck (Kovacs & Beck, 1978) includes the ways in which facts are perceived and processed, mechanisms for and content of memory recall, and problem-solving attitudes and strategies. There is a general schemata which is that set of previous life experiences (negative) that become the frame through which all life is perceived by the depressed person. This is especially true of the depressed individual in the violent family where there are negative expectations of self, of environment, and of the future (Val et al., 1982, p. 207). There is a misinterpretation and exaggeration of negative meanings/possibilities in life that must be changed. Gaining control over these thoughts and replacing them with more functional ones is one part of the solution to depression.

Ultimately, what were seen in the past as intractable clinical problems have fallen to the increasing strength of psychotrophic medications and cognitive/behavioral therapies. This does not suggest an easy course of treatment nor success. What it does guarantee is the demand for the family violence practitioner to draw upon the knowledge of all other clinicians in approaching the problems presented by their patients. *Whether the problem is environmental, emotional, physical, or legal, it will find a home in the violent family.* The practitioner is the only thing standing between this incompetent family and its own ability to incorporate problems. Unfortunately, as the next section will illustrate, the practitioner's ability to predict the outcome of work with these families is not as well defined as might be hoped.

Perpetrator Psychopathology and the Prediction of Violence/Dangerousness

Increased awareness of personality/situational variables in the violent family (e.g., psychopathology, personality disorders, and dyscontrol syndromes) brings a new area of responsibility to the family violence practitioner: prediction of violence/dangerousness. The child maltreatment practitioner in a dependency or severance hearing is being asked, "What is the potential for future violence in this parent?" The clinician in co-habitor violence may be asked not only about current violence, but about past violence as well. In spousal murders, for example, the issue may be whether the alleged murderer's fear of the spouse was justified; was he truly as dangerous as she felt he was? Most problematic among questions asked regarding violence is the question of when treatment is complete. At what point, for example, will sexual abuse not recur and the family be reunited? These are not questions either easily or reliably answered by today's techniques.

Monahan (1981) has described the clinical prediction of violent behavior as being "under sustained attack" (p. 27). It has been attacked on the grounds that it (1) is empirically impossible, (2) violates civil liberties, and (3) is a form of social control that is inconsistent with the clinician's "helping" orientation. Criticisms originate, then, in moral realms that view the prediction of dangerousness as an extension of discrimination against the poor, powerless, and minority elements of society, and in scientific realms through the knowledge that prediction of any "rare" (low base rate) event is questionable (Monahan, 1981, p. 11). These are not new criticisms.

More than ten years ago (1974) an American Psychiatric Association task force dealing with clinical aspects of the violent individual concluded that "the state of the art regarding predictions of violence is very unsatisfactory" (American Psychiatric Association, 1974; Monahan, 1981). Four years later the American Psychological Association (1978; Monahan, 1981) described the psychological prediction of violent behavior as "extremely poor." Although the American Psychological Association's report referred specifically to sentencing and release, the implication for other assessments of violence was clear: Most were inadequate. The problem for the family violence practitioner is that predictions of future violence *must* be made. Some of the problems in that prediction will be discussed here.

Monahan (1981, pp. 58–59) suggests that clinicians seeking to predict violence fail in several areas. First, they are dealing with a low base rate situation (something that does not happen very often) despite the requirement of a high base rate (at least 50 percent across the population) necessary for accurate prediction. Second, definitions of violence and dangerousness are unclear in most situations. Third, most clinicians fail to incorporate situational or environmental information into their predictions. Some of these issues, although still problematic, are better handled within the family violence situation.

Family violence has an incredible incidence. The numbers of cases are staggering, but compared to the total population, it is a relatively low base rate phenomenon. However, most family violence practitioners will only be asked to predict future violence in a perpetrator *who has already been violent.* The question here, "what is the likelihood of violence in this perpetrator as compared to other perpetrators?" is somewhat more easily answered. Second, the definition of the act (physical abuse, sexual abuse, or co-habitor battering) may be more clear than global criminal constructs. A notable exception to this is emotion/psychological violence in the family, a situation which has defied definition to this point. Third, the inclusion of situational and environmental elements is an automatic element of the family violence assessment. Finally, there is a guiding principle in work with violent families that aids in the decision: *Err in the direction of the victim* (especially if its a child). Although still a very difficult task, it seems that the family violence practitioner has a somewhat more manageable set of variables to work with than the general criminal violence practitioner. At least the options are more easily captured.

Violent and dangerous behavior is a relatively context-bound circumstance that includes individual predispositional and situational factors (Mulvey & Lidz, 1984, p. 380); it is the product of the interaction of forces within these two areas, both of which are multifaceted. Assessment demands a view of personality and situational factors as well as their intersection (Mischel, 1973; Monahan, 1981, p. 50). While it seems clear that mental illness is not a significant predisposing factor in violent behavior (Monahan & Steadman, 1983; Rabkin, 1979), other unique features of the individual may be predictive.

The most commonly noted predictor of violence in the individual has been the individual's past history of violence (Gutheil & Appelbaum, 1982). Some of this can be seen in the individual's childhood (Mulvey & Lidz, 1984, p. 393). The intergenerational transmission of violence within the family has already been discussed in this work as it pertains to later violence in the family. Outside the family violence literature, early experience with violence is frequently described as a contributor to later violent behavior of all descriptions (Goldstein, 1974; Justice et al., 1974). In fact, across the span of all historical features considered in assessing the violent individual, the family circumstances, both past and present, remain predictive of the possibility of violence.

The experience of growing up in a family that used violence to solve both internal and external problems is seen by clinicians as influential in understanding both the initiation and maintenance of later violent acts (Mulvey & Lidz, 1984, p. 396). The study of the family of origin can provide clues as to how reliant the individual is upon violence as a mechanism to solve problems, achieve goals, and cope with stress. In addition, inconsistent, harsh, and punishing parent-child relationships have been correlated with later juvenile and adult criminal violence (Farrington, 1978; McCord, 1979). The combination of learning to apply violence as a problem-solving tool, and being a perpetrator/recipient of violence from childhood forward, seems to be a partnership that is influential in electing to use violence as an adult.

In addition to the presence of violence in the childhood of the individual under study, other historical features merit consideration. The history of past dangerous acts, intentions, and thoughts remains important. The dangerous acts are obvious predictors through their presence (Pfohl, 1977). But aggressive fantasies (Monahan, 1981, pp. 55–56) and delusions (American Psychiatric Association, 1974; Dix, 1976) must also be given consideration. Membership in violence-prone groups might also be critical. This is of greater concern if membership involves the ownership, use, or training in the use of weapons against other persons. Previous criminal acts, especially if involving weapons, may be predictive of a violent mental set difficult to alter.

Williams and Miller (1977, p. 248) describe "mental status and perceived guilt or remorse" as telling. Both the ability to resolve stress-producing situations in a constructive manner and the recognition of the seriousness of consequences of acts are seen as cognitive skills that are necessary before risk can be considered to have been reduced in any way (Dix, 1976). The tendency to externalize problems and act precipitously and aggressively in solving problems may also suggest an inability to prevent future violence (Gutheil & Appelbaum, 1982). Within this, the motivation of the individuals as well as their internal inhibitions against a violent act must be studied. *Habitual use of violence becomes intractable* (Margargee, 1976).

Obviously, when inhibitions exceed motivations, violence will not occur. Yet, even in such an individual, when situational variables, habit, or substance misuse reduce inhibitional control, violence may be the result (Monahan, 1981, p. 50). Finkelhor (1984), for example, has noted the absence of internal inhibitions as a key feature of the sexually abusive act. It is wise to note, however, that individuals who succumb to violent behavior are not simply thrown into it. They may well have placed themselves in a likely position for the occurrence of such violence. This is frequently done with the full knowledge that the possibility of violence existed. In fact, it may have been hoped that the situation would serve to explain the occurrence of the violence (Toch, 1969).

Mulvey and Lidz (1984) have summarized the 1974 American Psychiatric Association task force report through the reminder that not all violence is related to mental disorder; other personal and situational variables must be considered. The American Psychiatric Association's report delineated the components of a "violence-potential" evaluation as:

(1) the dynamics of and techniques for anger resolution selected by the individual,
(2) the possibility of organic disorder,
(3) the past history of violence,
(4) the present use of drugs,
(5) the relationship to the potential victim (family membership increases the risk),
(6) the availability of weapons,
(7) medical conditions, and
(8) the social environment.

Goldstein (1974) suggests that maternal deprivation, poor paternal identification, and parental brutalization should be added to the list of critical variables.

In the past, with the possible exception of prior dangerous acts, most variables (i.e., age, sex, race, and psychiatric/criminal history) used to predict violence have been demographic/dispositional (Monahan, 1981, p. 64). Today it appears that evaluating individuals through personality, environment, or coping styles may be more productive (Mulvey & Lidz, 1984, p. 396). Also to be considered is the use of biological factors to explain violent behaviors, although the search for the biological origins of violent behavior is somewhat inconclusive at this point (Mulvey & Lidz, 1984, pp. 382–383).

Mulvey and Lidz (1984, pp. 383–385) have reviewed the literature on personality characteristics in violent individuals and offer several possible marker variables for consideration. Early in this literature, DeLeon (1961) described a "preassaultive state" that included:

(1) difficulty in using leisure time pleasurably and constructively,
(2) excessive alcohol use during leisure time,
(3) repetitive disputes with significant others,

(4) evidence of violent encounters with strangers,
(5) a penchant for weapons, and
(6) youthfulness.

Menninger and Modlin (1971) later found the personality characteristics of violent offenders to include:

(1) a low tolerance for anxiety,
(2) immediate action rather than thinking or discussion,
(3) shallow and ambivalent relations with others,
(4) egocentricity, and
(5) a tendency to make suspicious assumptions about the hostile nature of other's motives or intents.

The most critical feature of the Menninger and Modlin perspective suggests that this individual has a unique way of looking at the world; *it is a threatening place that must be guarded against.*

Mulvey and Lidz (1984, p. 384) see violent individuals as responding to events with a consistent cognitive and affective style. Since they view their environment as a stressful and threatening place, it only makes sense to these individuals to respond to perceived threats with violence. This becomes repetitive. Toch (1969) found two major themes in the violent perpetrator's psychological set. First, he found this individual to view violence as a self-preserving strategy used to enhance or bolster the ego in the eyes of self and others. This is characteristic of the battering husband. Second, this violent individual views his or her needs as the only important element of a given situation; this is familiar in the parent whose needs are met at the expense of a child. Megargee (1982) describes the individuals who succumb to violence as being either under- or overcontrolled. Again, concepts that hold application in the family violence world. In these concepts are found the co-habitor who cannot enter any conflictual situation without losing control to the escalating spiral of violence and the overcontrolled and "perfect" parents who are eventually overwhelmed by the responsibility they force upon themselves. Other perpetrator and situational descriptions fit well within both of these psychological "sets" in the potentially violent individual.

Evaluating Violence: A Summary View

The technology of the clinician, as it pertains to predicting violence, is currently suspect. Psychometric instrumentation alone will not accomplish the task. Traditional clinical approaches to psychodynamic issues do not reveal sufficient information. The family violence practitioner, with an orientation to both diathesis (dynamics) and stress (environment and demographics) seems to have an edge on the criminal practitioner. Additionally, the more confined questions asked of the family violence practitioner seem to promise a better predictive possibility. Overall, the prediction of violence within a family that has previously experienced violence is a greater possibility than prediction of violence in the world at large. The variables in victims, perpetrators, and family process that have been described in this work provide the necessary raw materials. What remains is the partnership of clinician and attorney in the courtroom setting to apply the evaluation to a productive end.

The Role of the Expert Witness

The glamour and excitement of the fictional courtroom are conspicuously absent from family violence work. In their place is hard work, obsessive attention to detail, and being asked to answer almost unanswerable questions. For most clinicians the courtroom side of family violence is uncomfortable. The adversarial atmosphere in which attorneys thrive is antithetical to the mediator in the clinician. In fact, many clinicians are not only frightened but offended. Discomfort notwithstanding, the clinician who does not wish to become involved in court proceedings should not become involved in family violence cases. Working within family violence will eventually demand that the clinician take the stand as an expert witness. Blau (1984) has offered some good advice for those who will be playing this unfamiliar role.

The clinician is selected as an expert witness because, due to professional knowledge and expertise, he or she holds the ability to draw inferences from facts that a jury would not be competent to draw. These are facts that will aid the trier of fact in the search for truth (Blau, 1984, p. 4). As such, it is wise to keep the clearest possible factual record from the outset in any work with a violent family.

Blau suggests that the clinician "err in the direction of excessive detail" (1984, p. 36) in recording every element of every interaction with this family. The record should be in chronological order, every contact noted (including phone calls), all conferences and contact with collateral professionals, all examination materials and results, all letters, time expended, and notes should be catalogued (p. 37). This is wise, for the title of "expert" does not imply immediate acceptance of what the clinician has to say.

The clinician should expect opposing attorneys to attempt to discredit his or her credentials and manipulate all elements of testimony in an effort to negate the expert opinion (Shapiro, 1984, p. 74). This will feel like a personal attack. To the attorney, it is not personal at all. The only way to avoid some sense of violation, devastation, and hostility is careful preparation by and for the attorney on the expert's side.

One major attack is likely to be for a lack of objectivity: "More art than science" is a favorite phrase (Haralambie, 1982, p. 291). The counter to this argument is empirical data drawn from standard texts, research, and test results. In some cases the strength of the expert's credentials will give immediate credence to the testimony. In this situation many attorneys will "stipulate" to the witness, which may mean that the attorney does not want the full extent of the expert's qualifications known. The strength of those credentials may be greater than that of their expert or simply lend too much weight to the testimony. If the clinician's credentials are strong, the expert's attorney may not agree to stipulation so that the qualifications may be heard (Shapiro, 1984, p. 84). Some of the expert's strategies change, however, depending upon whether he or she is testifying voluntarily or has been ordered to testify.

Blau (1984, pp. 298–299) suggests four steps to be taken after receipt of a subpoena. First, call the patient and advise him or her to notify his or her attorney. This is the point at which compulsive attention to detail should begin, if it has not already. Get permission or denials for everything in writing from this point forward. Second, ask the patient if you may contact his or her attorney and do so. Third, review all that has gone on to that point in your work with this patient. Point out any potentially damaging material you may have and discuss it with both patient and attorney. Finally, review all current statutes regarding practice in this area and contact your own attorney with any questions. This initiates the frustrating interaction between clinician, clinical records, and the court process, the seeming contradiction between therapist and reporting source.

In child maltreatment in every state and elder mistreatment in many, reporting is not a choice but an obligation. Once reported, records or notes associated with the case may become subject to review of the court. Every state has specific guidelines in the use of clinical records and confidentiality, and it is wise to learn and follow them after a report is made.

Some of the rules of confidentiality change in the family violence case. In child maltreatment, for example, confidentiality is usually only upheld in the attorney-client relationship. In individual cases (see *In re Lifschuta* 2 Cal. 3d 415, 467 P.2d 557, 85 Cal.Rptr. 829, 1970) it has been held that "limited intrusion into the psychotherapist/patient privilege when it is properly justified" is permissible (Shapiro, 1984, pp. 133–134). This permission is most often applied where there is an identifiable threat to harm or injure a third party (i.e., family violence). In some unique situations, the record may be sealed, a protective order entered, or a motion to certify questions might be honored (Blau, 1984, p. 299), but these are atypical in family violence cases.

Important in cases where there is identifiable intent to harm someone is the situation in which the patient reported such intent to the clinician. The clinician must err on the side of the potential victim. Knowledge of impending harm indicates a clear responsibility to warn the individual even though this may seem a breech of ethics and a violation of privileged communication (Blau, 1984, p. 308; Shapiro, 1984, p. 149). This has been legally tested and the responsibility to warn upheld *(Tarasoff v. Regents of the University of California,* 13 Cal. 3rd 177, 529 P.2d 553. 118 Cal. Rptr. 129, 1974).

Returning to the role of expert, the clinicians must remember that they are not an advocate for any person. That is difficult in viewing the defenseless victims of family violence. The clinician's only role is the defense of their opinion. The best mechanism for defending that opinion is an objective assessment of the facts and competent preparation of the attorney who must direct those facts into testimony.

The Clinician's Role in Preparing the Attorney

After, and only after, the report has been submitted to both attorneys and the court, is it appropriate to ask for a pretrial meeting with the attorney. The reason for delaying the meeting is to avoid any allegation that the clinician was influenced by the attorney in arriving at a decision. That is another reason for keeping exact dates, topics, and conclusions drawn in any contacts made between the date of report submission and the trial. It is destructive to speak with anyone but the attorney (Blau, 1984, p. 33; Shapiro, 1984), but it is not inappropriate to begin preparation of the attorney by evaluating all information from the clinical point of view, helping with discovery issues, providing a strengths and weaknesses analysis, and providing a list of the critical points that must be made in testimony (Haralambie, 1982). Submit questions that elicit the expert opinion itself, practice them together, and seek out advantages and disadvantages in their use (Shapiro, 1984, p. 75). Anticipate attacks on the clinical direction of the arguments and develop defenses. Finally, let the attorney know of the weak points in the clinical argument and the probable direction that attack will take (Shapiro, 1984, pp. 75–76). Be as honest and self-critical as possible. It will be easier in this setting than later in court.

Any information that may help the attorney to work with the opposing side's argument should be given. The attorney will not know the scientific credibility of their position. Study this and advise. Study the opposing expert's credentials, experience, type of practice, and look for holes in his or her reports or testimony as indicated by deposition. The fewer surprises in court the better for both clinician and attorney (Haralambie, 1982, p. 292).

The review of the opposing expert's work should include consideration of the quality of evaluation data, methods, the volume of data used in drawing conclusions, and any important omissions or alternative explanations for the conclusions offered (Haralambie, 1982, p. 293). The clinician in the family violence case is also an investigator. Any omission in preparing for the case, such as ignoring police reports, social work histories, or school data should and will, receive appropriate criticism in the courtroom setting. There are strategies that the attorney will want to transmit to the expert before trial as well.

The Attorney's Role in Preparing the Clinician

Expert witnesses may provide a deceptively calm exterior. They may have full control of their topical knowledge and absolutely no knowledge of the expert's role. This professional witness requires the same "sandpapering" as does the lay witness before throwing them into the courtroom.

Haralambie (1982, 1983) and Shapiro (1984) have provided several areas that cannot be overlooked in preparing experts for the trial experience. First, although elementary, experts must understand their role as being limited to providing and interpreting information for the judge and jury if applicable. It is also wise to counsel that the failure of the judge to follow their recommendation does not indicate personal failure; only a combination of evidence that led to a different conclusion (Haralambie, 1982, p. 294).

Following that discussion, it is wise to educate clinicians as to differences between direct and cross-examination. One may describe direct examination as involving open questions and the cross as involving closed questions. Make certain that experts know that the opponent will attempt to "put words in their mouth" as well as "lull them into error" during cross-examinations (Haralambie, 1982, pp. 294-295). Regular reassurance is helpful.

Let the clinicians know that you will seek an opportunity for them to state the basis upon which their opinion was offered after every major point. They must be made to realize that their reasoning will be questioned. Consequently, they must be prepared to describe not only the information used in decision making, but the process used to reach the conclusion. It is important to caution them against the use of overly technical language. But, it is also wise to encourage them to use some clinical language to allow the listener (i.e., the judge) to understand that they are from a specific technical area and to establish an adequate and precise record should appeal occur (Haralambie, 1982, p. 30; Shapiro, 1984, p. 92).

Regarding the behavior of opposing counsel, clinicians must realize that they will tend to take single features of the victim or perpetrator and apply them disproportionately. The solution to an expert's reaction to this ploy rests with an adequate role play of probable approaches to be used, including (1) questions that will be asked by your side, (2) probable questions from the opponent, and (3) adequate responses to both sets of questions (Shapiro, 1982, pp. 92-95).

Finally, prepare experts for the following courtroom traps: (1) *The use of professional jargon*: Encourage clinicians to use clear and straightforward language (Shapiro, 1984, p. 86) and to avoid clinical words with popular meanings (e.g., paranoid). Also, any use of the word "normal" must be explained, or it could play against the expert at some point. (2) *Avoidance of speculative or hypothetical questions*: Alert experts to listen for phrases such as "isn't is possible that" or "suppose that." Teach experts not to respond to "what ifs?" (Haralambie, 1982; Shapiro, 1984, pp. 78, 90). Shapiro calls these "hostile questions" and warns against the expert's tendency to be flippant in response. He suggests that the witness answer with "If what you are saying is . . ." followed by a rephrasing of the questions (p. 87). He also suggests that, before answering, witnesses first indicate which features of the questions can be agreed upon, what they disagree with, and what needs to be changed before it can be answered (p. 87). Teach experts that speculation on the stand is deadly. (3) *The sudden introduction of information*: The opponent may say "Would it change your opinion if . . .?" Clinicians must be advised never to change their opinion on the stand in this event. Shapiro (1984, p. 77) suggests that the expert acknowledge the new information as worthy of consideration, if it is, but note that it would have to be studied to place it in perspective. (4) *Dependence on notes and tests*: Experts must understand that notes taken to the stand may be used against them (Shapiro, 1984, p. 89). They must also view tests as supplemental and not the answer. They must be clear on such test issues as validity, reliability, methods of administration, and adequacy of conclusions, but they must not develop either opinion or testimony solely on the test scores (Haralambie, 1982, pp. 310–311). (5) *The yes/no answer*: Reassure experts that a question limited to a yes/no answer can be dealt with. If they cannot answer, encourage them to say so. If an answer would distort their perspective of the problem, encourage them to tell the judge, who may allow elaboration. If not, let them know that the issues will be picked up in later, more friendly examination. (6) *Sparring with opposing counsel*: Let experts know that sparring with the opposing attorney is a zero-sum game (Haralambie, 1982, p. 295; Shapiro, 1984, p. 78). Warn them that the opposing counsel will attack opinions, credentials, and personal issues. Alert experts that moving up this ladder of assault is a good sign, for it means that the opposing counsel is probing for, and not finding, weaknesses (Haralambie, 1982, p. 296; Shapiro, 1984, p. 80).

As a final point in working with clinicians, remind them periodically that they really are the *experts*. In the face of a solidly prepared opponent with a withering examination style, this is something that is easy to forget. Few clinicians are prepared for what appears to be hostility from opposing counsel. Few are prepared to have their opinions questioned and discarded. And few are prepared for the fact that the victim of family violence might be secondarily wronged, not based on the facts of a case, but upon a rule of law or inappropriate judicial/jury decision. As a result, work with experts must continue after the hearing/trial, especially if court opinion has gone against their own. Even as clinicians see themselves as those who bring about understanding of persons, the attorney is the professional who brings understanding of the systems within which these persons must live. Those two roles, if nothing else, describe the partnership that must exist between attorney and clinician in the family violence situation.

The Final "Summary View"

This work began with a review of the unmet promises of nearly a quarter of a century of work and study with violent families. These promises remain unmet, but this review has not been a pessimistic one. Strides have been and will continue to be made with violent families. In a sense, it may be beneficial to have unmet promises placed before us to encourage our continued reaching for new answers. Consider what might be lost otherwise.

If the early treatment of the then-known violent family had been immediately successful, it is possible that we would still accept single-factor etiologies. Our current-day understanding of the violent family's complex ecology would be absent. Family violence treatment, too, might have remained in the clinic and the social pressures which face so many families may have gone unrecognized or, at least, under-appreciated.

If the narrow initial definitions of family violence had been solidified, the secrecy of the process may have led to numerous unknown victims. Consider, for example, if child maltreatment theorists had not pressed for recognition and inclusion of the sexual abuse of children in our definitions, how many children would have suffered in silence. Consider, too, if gerontologists had not looked beyond institutional inadequacy toward family dysfunction in the care of the elderly. How many victims would have gone undiscovered? True, family protection services might have amassed a better record of service with more circumscribed definitions, but if only major incidents are dealt with, would we have been able to honestly speak of prevention?

Finally, if we had adopted an ''exception'' view of families which became violent; a view which saw their stresses as wholly different from all other families, would our knowledge of all families have grown to its current level? How many families with lesser problems would have gone unaided?

We have made strides. And, it has been the intent of this work to present some of the thinking and work that has led to those forward steps in the past twenty-five years. It was our hope that, through this work, clinical and legal practitioners will better understand each other. It was our hope that practitioner and researcher would better understand the synergism which must be between them in order to progress. No practitioner of any description, working with the violent family, can afford to work in isolation. The clinician needs the attorney and the researcher needs the practitioner. It seems clear that, beyond the unmet promises of yesterday, there is the promise of tomorrow. That promise is that it is only through the combined efforts of all that a new and better understanding of these families will be available for the future.

A Reference Guide to the Tables:
Appendices A-H

Appendix A

References for Table 2.3:
Marker Variables Correlated with Intra-Familial
Violence

SOCIAL ENVIRONMENT

(1) Multiple Environmental Stressors

Physical Maltreatment

Gil, 1970, p. 135
Giovannoni & Billingsley, 1970
Giovannoni, 1971
Steele & Pollack, 1972, p. 8
Friedrich & Boriskin, 1976, p. 581
Garbarino, 1977, p. 572
Rosenfeld & Newberger, 1979, p. 83
Straus et al., 1980
Wolfe et al., 1981, p. 27
Steele, 1982, p. 486
Rosenberg & Reppucci, 1983
Belsky, 1984, p. 83
Garbarino, 1984
Herrenkohl et al., 1984, p. 647
Howze & Kotch, 1984, p. 401
Pagelow, 1984, p. 125

Sexual Abuse

Russell, 1984, p. 236

Conjugal Violence

Straus, 1977
Ganley & Harris, 1978

Walker, 1979
Straus et al., 1980
LaViolette, 1984, pp. 3, 14
Neidig et al., 1984, p. 8
Roberts, 1984, pp. 1–2, 66–67

Mistreatment of the Elderly

Renvoize, 1979
Chen et al., 1981, p. 10
Langley, 1981, pp. 7, 13–14, 16
Cazenave & Woodburn, 1982, p. 1
Falcioni, 1982, p. 209
Douglas, 1983, p. 147
Steinmetz, 1983, p. 138

(2) Social Isolation

Child Maltreatment

Holter & Friedman, 1968
Giovannoni & Billingsley, 1970
Kempe & Helfer, 1972, p. xiv
Parke & Collmer, 1975
Garbarino, 1977a, p. 569
Milner & Wimberly, 1979
Garbarino & Sherman, 1980
Wolfe et al., 1981, p. 16
Star, 1983, p. 37
Herrenkohl et al., 1984, p. 647
Martin, 1984, p. 389
Alexander, 1972, p. 23
Morris & Gould, 1974, p. 45
Garbarino, 1977, p. 45
Bourne, 1975, p. 10
Rosenfeld & Newberger, 1979, p. 83
Garbarino & Stocking, 1980
Gaudin & Pollane, 1983
Cicchetti & Rizley, 1984, p. 44
Howze & Kotch, 1984, p. 401

Sexual Abuse

Gebhard et al., 1965
Henderson, 1972
Finkelhor, 1979, p. 26
Finkelhor, 1981, p. 2
Bauman et al., 1983
Tierney & Corwin, 1983, pp. 109–110

Ferracuti, 1972
Herman & Hirschman, 1977
Justice & Justice, 1979
Groth et al., 1982, p. 130
Star, 1983, p. 37
Kempe & Kempe, 1984, pp. 51,53

Conjugal Violence

Dobash & Dobash, 1979
Parke & Lewis, 1981
Deschner, 1984, p. 30
Pagelow, 1984, pp. 76–80, 326
Gelles & Straus, 1979
Star, 1983, p. 37
Neidig et al., 1984, p. 4
Roberts, 1984, pp. 1–2

Mistreatment of the Elderly

Chen et al., 1981, p. 4
Falcioni, 1982, p. 209
Douglas, 1983, p. 146
Luppins & Lau, 1983, p. 204
Langley, 1981, pp. 13–14
Cazenave, 1983, pp. 194–196, 200
Kosberg, 1983, p. 264
Pagelow, 1984, pp. 76–80

(3) Inadequate Survival Skills

Child Maltreatment

Kaufman, 1962, p. 21
Helfer, 1973
Milner & Wimberly, 1983
Steele, 1982, p. 486
Herrenkohl et al., 1984, p. 647
Mulford & Cohen, 1967, p. 9
Morris & Gould, 1974, p. 39
Restak, 1979, p. 19
Garbarino, 1984
Howze & Kotch, 1984, p. 401

Sexual Abuse

Groth et al., 1982, pp. 137–138
James & Nasjleti, 1983, p. 17
Kempe & Kempe, 1984, p. 52
Bauman et al., 1983, p. 80

Finkelhor, 1984
Russell, 1984

Conjugal Violence

Elbow, 1977
Walker, 1979, pp. 37–40
Deschner, 1984, p. 21
LaViolette, 1984, p. 14
Roberts, 1984
Fleming, 1979, pp. 295,304,320
Shapiro, 1980, p. 52
Ferraro, 1984, p. 3
Pagelow, 1984, pp. 99,326

Mistreatment of the Elderly

Chen et al., 1981, p. 10
Solomon, 1983, p. 152
Falcioni, 1982, p. 209

(4) Financial Stress

Child Maltreatment

Mulford & Cohen, 1967, p. 9
Johnson & Morse, 1968
Giovannoni & Billingsley, 1979
Garbarino & Crouter, 1978, p. 613
Bourne, 1979, p. 7
Straus, 1979
Miller & Challas, 1981, p. 7
Gabinet, 1983, p. 399
Star, 1983, p. 37
Herrenkohl et al., 1984, p. 642
Brody, 1968
Gil, 1970
Giovannoni, 1971
Pelton, 1978
Giovannoni & Bercera, 1979
Garbarino & Gilliam, 1980
Burgess & Garbarino, 1983, p. 95
McCord, 1983, p. 270
Green, 1984, p. 676

Sexual Abuse

Brown, 1978
Star, 1983, p. 37
Finkelhor, 1984, pp. 29, 163

Brown & Holder, 1980
Conte, 1984, p. 259

Conjugal Violence

Straus et al., 1980
Deschner, 1984, p. 29
Star, 1983, p. 37
Roberts, 1984, pp. 1–2

Mistreatment of the Elderly

Steinmetz, 1978, 1983, p. 138
Chen, 1981, p. 4
Falcioni, 1982, p. 209
Douglas, 1983, p. 149
Cazenave & Straus, 1979
Langley, 1981, pp. 13–14
Cazenave, 1983, pp. 194–196
Giordano & Giordano, 1984, p. 4

(5) Employment/Occupational Difficulty

Child Maltreatment

Light, 1973
Bourne, 1979, p. 10
Straus, 1979
Steinberg et al., 1981
Gil, 1970, p. 34
Holmes, 1978
Rosenfeld & Newberger, 1979, p. 83
Feshback, 1980, p. 53
Bronfenbrenner & Crouter, 1982
Belsky, 1984, p. 84

Sexual Abuse

Kempe & Kempe, 1984, p. 52

Conjugal Violence

Hornung et al., 1980, p. 26
LaViolette, 1984, p. 14
Straus et al., 1980

Mistreatment of the Elderly

Block & Sinnott, 1979
O'Rourke, 1981
Anderson, 1981, p. 78
Giordano & Giordano, 1984

(6) Educational Barriers

Child Maltreatment

Mulford & Cohen, 1967, p. 10
Holmes, 1978
Terr, 1970
Caplan et al., 1984, p. 349

Sexual Abuse

Finkelhor, 1979
Kempe & Kempe, 1984, p. 52

Conjugal Violence

Hornung et al., 1980, p. 27

(7) Racial/Ethnic Over-Representation

Child Maltreatment

Newberger et al., 1977
Giovannoni & Bercerra, 1979
Daniel et al., 1983
Hampton & Newberger, 1983
Bourne, 1979, p. 3
Friedrich & Einbender, 1983, p. 246
Hampton, 1984, p. 1

Sexual Abuse

Pagelow, 1984, p. 404
Pierce & Pierce, 1984, p. 111

Mistreatment of the Elderly

Staples, 1976
Kosberg, 1983
Cazenave, 1983, pp. 188, 190, 193, 199
Galbraith & Zdorkowski, 1984, p. 22

(8) Overcrowded Living Environment

Child Maltreatment

Light, 1983

Sexual Abuse

Lukianowicz, 1972
Renshaw & Renshaw, 1977
Russell, 1984
Boothe, 1976
Finkelhor, 1984

Mistreatment of the Elderly

Douglas, 1983, p. 146

PSYCHOLOGICAL ENVIRONMENT

(1) Psychopathology

Elmer, 1967
Zalba, 1967
Johnson & Morse, 1968
Laury, 1970
Kempe & Helfer, 1972, p. xii
Helfer, 1973, 1975
Blumberg, 1974
Kempe & Kempe, 1978
Milner & Wimberly, 1979
Friedman et al., 1981
Belsky, 1984, p. 83
Green, 1984, p. 675
Mulford & Cohen, 1967, p. 13
Holter & Friedman, 1968
Gil, 1970, pp. 43, 135
Court & Kerr, 1971
Spinetta & Rigler, 1978
Wasserman, 1973
Garbarino, 1977, p. 725
Newberger & Newberger, 1978
Oates, 1979
Friedrich & Wheeler, 1982
Estroff et al., 1984
Sloan & Meier, 1982

Sexual Abuse

Groth et al., 1982
James & Nasjleti, 1983, pp. 17–18
Russell, 1984, p. 259
Bauman et al., 1983
Tierney & Corwin, 1983, p. 109

Conjugal Violence

Fleming, 1979, p. 309
Deschner, 1984
Johnston, 1984
Neidig et al., 1984
Walker, 1979, p. 40
Ferraro, 1984, p. 3

LaViolette, 1984
Pagelow, 1984

Mistreatment of the Elderly

Kay, 1977
Chen et al., 1981, p. 10
Falcioni, 1982, p. 208
Solomon, 1983, p. 150
Giordano & Giordano, 1984, p. 4
Ban, 1978
Langley, 1981, p. 13
Cazenave, 1983, p. 194
Steinmetz, 1983

(2) Dependency Problems

Child Maltreatment

Morse et al., 1970
Oates, 1979
Milner & Wimberly, 1979
Bavolek, 1981, p. 42
Steele, 1982, pp. 486, 489
Star, 1983, p. 37
Friedrich & Einbender, 1983, p. 248
Martin, 1984, p. 389

Sexual Abuse

Lewis-Herman, 1981, p. 87
Baumann et al., 1983, pp. 79–80
Star, 1983, p. 37
Kempe & Kempe, 1984, p. 53
Pretky, 1984
Summit, 1984, p. 2
Mitkus, 1982, p. 10
James & Nasjleti, 1983, p. 6
Browne & Finkelhor, 1984, p. 2
Pagelow, 1984, p. 404
Stone et al., 1984, p. 28

Conjugal Violence

Elbow, 1977
Falk, 1979
Walker, 1979, p. 21
Straus, 1980, p. 202
Deschner, 1984, pp. 8, 21, 32
Johnston, 1984, p. 8

Ganley, 1978
Fleming, 1979, pp. 10, 288
Hilberman, 1980, p. 1339
Star, 1983, p. 37
Ferraro, 1984, pp. 4–5
Pagelow, 1984, p. 307

Mistreatment of the Elderly

Steinmetz, 1978, 1983, p. 138
Douglas et al., 1980
Hickey & Douglas, 1981a, p. 503, 1981b, p. 174
O'Rourke, 1981
Douglas, 1983, p. 144
Block & Sinnott, 1979
Chen et al., 1981, p. 10
Langley, 1981, pp. 13–14
Falcioni, 1982, p. 209

(3) Low Self-Esteem & Poor Self-Image

Child Maltreatment

Steele & Pollack, 1972, p. 5
Holmes et al., 1975
Bourne, 1979, pp. 7N8, 10
Miller & Challas, 1981, p. 7
Egeland et al., 1983, p. 460
Howze & Kotch, 1984, p. 401
Oates & Forrest, 1985
Morris & Gould, 1974, p. 39
Rodriquez, 1977, p. 9
Restak, 1979, p. 19
Steele, 1982, p. 486
Snyder et al., 1983
Martin, 1984, p. 389

Sexual Abuse

Groth et al., 1982, p. 130
Star, 1983, p. 37
Alford et al., 1984, p. 40
James & Nasjleti, 1983, p. 16
Tierney & Corwin, 1983, p. 109

Conjugal Violence

Gayford, 1975
Boyd, 1978
Labell, 1979

Ferraro, 1984, pp. 2,5
LaViolette, 1984, p. 14
Pagelow, 1984, pp. 99, 326
Elbow, 1977
Fleming, 1979, pp. 304, 325
Star, 1983, p. 37
Johnston, 1984, p. 7
Neidig et al., 1984, p. 21

Mistreatment of the Elderly

Chen et al., 1981, p. 10
Steinmetz, 1983
Solomon, 1983a, p. 165

(4) Feelings of Helplessness

Child Maltreatment

Miller & Challas, 1981, p. 7
Star, 1983, p. 37
Steele, 1982, p. 489

Sexual Abuse

Groth et al., 1982, p. 136
Star, 1983, p. 37

Conjugal Violence

Fleming, 1979
Star, 1983, p. 37
Walker, 1979
Roberts, 1984, pp. 1–2

Mistreatment of the Elderly

Solomon & Zinke, 1981
Pagelow, 1984, p. 100
Solomon, 1983a, p. 160

(5) Immaturity

Child Maltreatment

Gil, 1970, p. 34
Rodriquez, 1977, p. 9
Milner & Wimberly, 1979
Steele, 1982, pp. 486, 489
Morse et al., 1970
Shorkey, 1978
Oates, 1979

Sexual Abuse

Summit & Kryso, 1978
Groth et al., 1982, pp. 130,133
Tierney & Corwin, 1983, p. 109
Russell, 1983, pp. 253–259
Swift, 1979
Snyder et al., 1983
Alford et al., 1984, p. 40

Conjugal Violence

Fleming, 1979
Deschner, 1984

Mistreatment of the Elderly

Chen et al., 1981, pp. 10–11
Falcioni, 1982, p. 205

(6) Depression

Child Maltreatment

Milner & Wimberly, 1979
Belsky, 1984, p. 85
Steele, 1982, p. 485
Martin, 1984, p. 389

Sexual Abuse

Browne & Finkelhor, 1984
Conte, 1984

Conjugal Violence

Roberts, 1984, p. 2

Mistreatment of the Elderly

Kosberg, 1983, p. 269
Solomon, 1983, p. 165
Luppins & Lau, 1983, p. 207
Chen et al., 1981, p. 10

(7) Failure to Control Aggression and Anger

Child Maltreatment

Wasserman, 1967
Laury, 1970
Milner & Wimberly, 1979
Martin, 1984, p. 389
Steele & Pollack, 1968

Spinetta & Rigler, 1972
Star, 1983, p. 37

Sexual Abuse

Baumann et al., 1983, p. 80
Kempe & Kempe, 1984, p. 52
Star, 1983, p. 37

Conjugal Violence

Star, 1983, p. 37
Pagelow, 1984, p. 326
LaViolette, 1984, p. 14
Roberts, 1984, pp. 1–2

Mistreatment of the Elderly

Solomon, 1983, p. 165

(8) Anhedonia

Child Maltreatment

Rodriquez, 1977, p. 9
Star, 1983, p. 37
Steele, 1982, p. 486

Sexual Abuse

Star, 1983, p. 37

Conjugal Violence

Star, 1983, p. 37

(9) Defensiveness

Child Maltreatment

Kaufman, 1962, p. 21
Hill, 1975, p. 20
Martin, 1984, p. 389
Morris & Gould, 1974, p. 39
Feshback, 1980, p. 53

Sexual Abuse

James & Nasjleti, 1983, pp. 17–18
Russell, 1984, p. 254

Conjugal Violence

Walker, 1979

(10 & 11) Low Physiological Stimulus Threshold and Hypersensitivity

Child Maltreatment

Steele & Pollack, 1972, pp. 7–8
Lamp & Frodi, 1980
Bauer & Twentyman, 1985
Knutson, 1978
Wolfe et al., 1983

Conjugal Violence

Deschner, 1984

FAMILY PROCESS

(1) Pervasive Family/Marital Stress and Dysfunction

Child Maltreatment

Mulford & Cohen, 1967, p. 11
Bennie & Sclar, 1969
Gayford, 1975
Smith & Hanson, 1975
Bourne, 1979, p. 10
Milner & Wimberly, 1979
Kimball et al., 1980
Stacey & Shupe, 1983
Deschner, 1984, p. 34
Johnson & Morse, 1968
Gil, 1970, p. 35
Helfer, 1975
Roy, 1977
Reavely & Gilbert, 1979
Rosenfeld & Newberger, 1979, p. 83
Burgess & Garbarino, 1983
Belsky, 1984, pp. 84–87
Martin, 1984, p. 389

Sexual Abuse

Molnar & Cameron, 1975, p. 373
Finkelhor, 1979, p. 28
Lewis-Herman, 1981, p. 43
Tierney & Corwin, 1983, p. 109
Pagelow, 1984, p. 404
Summit & Kryso, 1978
Justice & Justice, 1979
Baumann et al., 1983, p. 79
Kempe & Kempe, 1984, pp. 5–53

Conjugal Violence

Gayford, 1975
Allen & Straus, 1980
Walker, 1983, 1985
Giles-Sims, 1984
Neidig et al., 1984, p. 6
Boyd & Kingbell, 1979
Star, 1980
Deschner, 1984
LaViolette, 1984, p. 14
Pagelow, 1984

Mistreatment of the Elderly

Block & Sinnott, 1979
O'Rourke, 1981
Solomon, 1983
Lau & Kosberg, 1979
Douglas, 1983
Giordano & Giordano, 1984, p. 4

(2) Poor/Distorted Family Communication Patterns

Child Maltreatment

Mulford & Cohen, 1967, p. 10
Smith et al., 1973
Burgess & Conger, 1976, 1977
Garbarino, 1977
Burgess et al., 1981
Burgess & Garbarino, 1983
Star, 1983, p. 37
Johnson & Morse, 1968
Smith & Hanson, 1975
Justice & Justice, 1976
Gaensbauer & Sands, 1980
Lewis & Schaeffer, 1981
Wasserman et al., 1983

Sexual Abuse

Star, 1983, p. 37

Conjugal Violence

Star, 1983, p. 37

Mistreatment of the Elderly

Falcioni, 1982

(3) Distorted/Elevated Expectations of Victim

Child Maltreatment

Laury, 1970
Martin, 1976
Bourne, 1979, pp. 7–8
Straus, 1979, p. 5
Bavolek, 1981, pp. 4, 42
Twentyman & Plotkin, 1982
Trowell, 1983, p. 392
Kempe & Helfer, 1972, p. xiv
Garbarino, 1977, p. 725
Milner & Wimberly, 1979
Feshback, 1980, p. 53
Steele, 1982, pp. 486, 489
Star, 1983, p. 37
Pagelow, 1984, p. 24

Sexual Abuse

Groth et al., 1982, p. 137
Star, 1983, p. 37

Conjugal Violence

Fleming, 1979, pp. 288–289
Star, 1983, p. 37

Mistreatment of the Elderly

Anderson, 1981, p. 80
Steinmetz, 1983, p. 141
Chen, 1981, p. 10

(4) Deprivation and Hostility in Family of Origin

Child Maltreatment

Johnson & Morse, 1968
Oliver & Taylor, 1971
Spinetta & Rigler, 1972
Ebeling et al., 1975, p. 70
Helfer, 1975
Conger et al., 1979
Miller & Challas, 1981, p. 7
Steele, 1982, p. 487
Snyder et al., 1983
Garbarino, 1984
Steele & Pollack, 1968, 1973, p. 9
Kempe & Helfer, 1972, p. xiv

Frommer & O'Shea, 1973
Morris & Gould, 1974, p. 28
Parke & Collmer, 1975
Milner & Wimberly, 1979
Wolfe et al., 1981, p. 17
Bolton, 1983
Star, 1983, p. 37
Herrenkohl et al., 1984, p. 647

Sexual Abuse

Kaufman et al., 1954
Rossaman, 1976
Groth & Burgess, 1979
Seghorn & Boucher, 1980
Groth et al., 1982, pp. 130, 138
James & Nasjleti, 1983, pp. 16–17
Star, 1983, p. 37
Conte, 1984, p. 259
Russell, 1984, pp. 23, 239
Gebhard et al., 1965
Burgess & Holstrom, 1978
Swift, 1979
Pelto, 1981
Langevin, 1983
Alford et al., 1984, p. 40
Finkelhor, 1984, p. 40

Conjugal Violence

Walker, 1979, p. 38
Rosenbaum & O'Leary, 1981
Deschner, 1984, p. 8
Pagelow, 1984, pp. 253, 326
Hilberman, 1980, pp. 1338–1339
Star, 1983, p. 37
Johnston, 1984, p. 2
Roberts, 1984, pp. 1–2, 159

Mistreatment of the Elderly

Harden, 1980
Hickey & Douglas, 1981, p. 175
Steinmetz, 1983, p. 137
Anderson, 1981, p. 78
Falcioni, 1982, p. 209
Fulmer & Cahill, 1984, p. 18

(5) Power Imbalances

Child Maltreatment

Shorkey, 1978
Feshback, 1980, p. 53
Baumann et al., 1983, p. 80
Martin, 1984, p. 389
Milner & Wimberly, 1979
Bavolek, 1981, p. 42
Star, 1983, p. 37

Sexual Abuse

Lewis-Herman, 1981, p. 87
Star, 1983, p. 37
Kempe & Kempe, 1984, p. 53
Russell, 1984, p. 258
James & Nasjleti, 1983, p. 16
Finkelhor, 1984, p. 34
Pagelow, 1984, p. 404

Conjugal Violence

Whitehurst, 1974
Fleming, 1979, p. 309
Star, 1983, p. 37
Ferraro, 1984, p. 6
Pagelow, 1984, p. 326
Elbow, 1977
Kalmus & Straus, 1982
Falk, 1984
Neidig et al., 1984, p. 5

Mistreatment of the Elderly

Chen et al., 1981, pp. 10–11

(6) Role Confusion/Disturbance

Child Maltreatment

Morris & Gould, 1974, p. 44
Solnit & Provence, 1979
Steele, 1982, p. 488
Bourne, 1979, pp. 7–8
Bavolek, 1981, p. 43

Sexual Abuse

Lustig et al., 1966
Browning & Boatman, 1977

Molnar & Cameron, 1975
Summit & Kryso, 1978

Mistreatment of the Elderly
Steinmetz, 1983

(7) Competitiveness and Jealousy

Child Maltreatment
Mulford & Cohen, 1967
Bolton, 1983, 1984

Conjugal Violence
Allen & Straus, 1983
Pagelow, 1984, p. 326
LaViolette, 1984, p. 3

Mistreatment of the Elderly
Douglas, 1983, p. 146

(8) Difficulty in Trusting

Child Maltreatment
Kempe & Helfer, 1972, p. xiv
Steele, 1982, p. 486
Kinard, 1980, p. 453

Sexual Abuse
Lewis-Herman, 1981
Stone et al., 1984, p. 28
Brown & Finkelhor, 1984, p. 4
Summit, 1984, p. 2

Conjugal Violence
Walker, 1979
LaViolette, 1984, p. 3
Arndt, 1984

(9) Inadequate Caregiving Knowledge

Child Maltreatment
Johnson & Morse, 1968
Bourne, 1979, pp. 7–8
David & Appel, 1979
Garbarino, 1984
Spinetta & Rigler, 1972
Garbarino, 1977, p. 725

Burgess & Conger, 1978
Crittendon, 1981
Herrenkohl et al., 1984, p. 647

Mistreatment of the Elderly

Chen et al., 1981, p. 10
Kosberg, 1983, p. 267
Douglas, 1983, pp. 141, 146, 149
Pagelow, 1984, p. 100

(10) Religiousness

Child Maltreatment

Gelles, 1982

Sexual Abuse

Baumann et al., 1983, p. 79

Conjugal Violence

Pagelow, 1984, p. 326

(11) Nonbiological Parent

Child Maltreatment

Burgess & Garbarino, 1983
Bolton, 1983

Sexual Abuse

Pozanski, & Blos, 1975
Finkelhor, 1979
Finkelhor, 1984, pp. 7, 29
Finkelhor et al., 1976
Tierney & Corwin, 1983, p. 108
Giles-Sims, 1984

(12) Single Parenthood

Child Maltreatment

Friedrich & Einbender, 1983, p. 246
Caplan et al., 1984

Sexual Abuse

Finkelhor, 1984
Summit, 1985

(13) Over-Valuation of Physical Punishment

Child Maltreatment

Gil, 1970, p. 136
Friedrich & Boriskin, 1976, p. 581
Bavolek, 1981, p. 42
Herrenkohl et al., 1984, p. 647
Laury, 1970
Dubanoskir et al., 1978
Reid et al., 1981

(14) Victim Characteristics that Contribute to the Problem

Child Maltreatment

Millowe & Lourie, 1964
Gil, 1970, p. 135
Robson & Moss, 1970
Thompson et al., 1971
Helfer, 1973
Korner, 1974
Sameroff & Chandler, 1975
Buchanan & Oliver, 1977
Lynch, 1977
Bourne, 1979, pp. 9–10
Mulhern & Passman, 1979
Ainsworth, 1980, p. 43
Frodi, 1981
Kadushin & Martin, 1981
Burgess & Garbarino, 1983, p. 97
Lerner & Lerner, 1983
Trowell, 1983, p. 392
Belsky, 1984, p. 83
Green, 1984
Elmer & Gregg, 1967
Morse et al., 1970
Klein & Stern, 1971
Kempe & Helfer, 1972, p. xiv
Stern, 1973
Hill, 1975, p. 19
Friedrich & Boriskin, 1976, p. 581
Brown & Bakeman, 1977
Garbarino, 1977, p. 725
Hunter et al., 1978
George & Main, 1979
Straws, 1979, p. 5
Bavolek, 1981, p. 42

Greenvoeller et al., 1981
Lennington, 1981
Kotelchuck & Newberger, 1983
Snyder et al., 1983
Wolfe & Mosk, 1983
Bousha & Twentyman, 1984
Hoffman-Plotkin & Twentyman, 1984

Appendix B

References for Table 5.1: Commonalities in Victims of Family Violence

(1) Poor Self-Concept and Low Self-Esteem

Child Maltreatment

Martin & Beezley, 1977
Elmer, 1979, p. 69
Hjorth & Ostrow, 1982
Friedrich & Einbender, 1983, p. 248
Bourne, 1979, p. 9
Kinard, 1980, pp. 453, 458
Escland et al., 1983, p. 460

Child Sexual Abuse

Tsai & Wagner, 1979
Herman, 1981, p. 14
Janas, 1983
Finkelhor, 1984, p. 194
Stone et al., 1984, p. 2
Burgess et al., 1981
James & Nasjleti, 1983, p. 7
Lewis-Herman, 1981
Kilpatrick & Amick, 1984, p. 78
Summit, 1984

Conjugal Violence

Seligman & Rosellin, 1975
Hilberman, 1980, p. 1342
Pagelow, 1984, p. 309
Walker, 1979, p. 31
Deschner, 1984, p. 35

Rosewater, 1984, p. 4

Mistreatment of the Elderly

Anderson, 1981, p. 81
Kosberg, 1983, p. 286
Chen et al., 1981, p. 11
Luppens & Lau, 1983, p. 209

(2) Dependency

Child Maltreatment

Egeland et al., 1983
Galambos & Dixon, 1984, p. 286
Friedrich & Einbender, 1983, p. 248

Child Sexual Abuse

(Female Victim)
Mitkus, 1982, pp. 10, 13
Browne & Finkelhor, 1984, p. 2
Stone et al., 1984, p. 78
James & Nasjleti, 1983, p. 6
Pretky, 1984
Summit, 1984, p. 2
(Male Victim)
Sussman, 1980, p. 346

Conjugal Violence

Richardson, 1977
Walker, 1979, pp. 31, 34
Straus, 1980, p. 702
Ferraro, 1984, p. 4
Fleming, 1979, p. 10
Hilberman, 1980, p. 307
Deschner, 1984, p. 32
Pagelow, 1984, p. 1339

Mistreatment of the Elderly

Blenker, 1979
Anderson, 1981, p. 81
Hickey & Douglas, 1981, pp. 174, 122
Falcioni, 1982, p. 209
Steinmetz, 1983, p. 138
Block & Sinnott, 1979
Chen et al., 1981, p. 11
Langley, 1981, pp. 13–14
Luppens & Lau, 1983, p. 208

Giordano & Giordano, 1984

(3) Difficulty in Trusting

Child Maltreatment

Kinard, 1980, p. 453

Child Sexual Abuse

Lewis-Herman, 1981
Stone et al., 1984, p. 28
Browne & Finkelhor, 1984, p. 4
Summit, 1984, p. 2

Conjugal Violence

Walker, 1979
LaViolette, 1984, p. 3
Arndt, 1984

(4) Revictimization

Child Maltreatment

Friedrich & Boriskin, 1976, p. 581
Herrenkohl & Herrenkohl, 1979
Bourne, 1979, p. 9
Herrenkohl et al., 1979

Child Sexual Abuse

Lewis-Herman, 1981, p. 29
Finkelhor, 1984, p. 194
Alford et al., 1984, p. 41
Summit, 1984, p. 2

Conjugal Violence

Fleming, 1979, pp. 10, 19
Straus, 1980, p. 702
Pagelow, 1984, p. 307
Hilberman, 1980, p. 1336
Giles-Sims, 1983, p. 25

Mistreatment of the Elderly

Solomon, 1983, p. 161

(5) Denial-Defensiveness-Withdrawal-Isolation

Child Maltreatment

Martin & Beezley, 1977
Kinard, 1980, p. 459

Elmer, 1979, p. 69
Egeland et al., 1983, p. 460

Child Sexual Abuse

(Female Victim)
Finkelhor, 1979, p. 31
Burgess & Holstrom, 1980, p. 81
James & Nasjleti, 1983, p. 3
Tsai & Wagner, 1979
Lewis-Herman, 1981
Summit, 1985
(Male Victim)
Landis, 1956
Nasjleti, 1980, pp. 270, 272
James & Nasjleti, 1983, p. 8
Russell, 1984, p. 194
Finkelhor, 1980, 1979, p. 68
Swift, 1980, p. 23
Kempe & Kempe, 1984, p. 73

Conjugal Violence

Hilberman, 1980, p. 1345
Pagelow, 1984, p. 320

Mistreatment of the Elderly

Anderson, 1981, pp. 78, 81
Falcioni, 1982, p. 209
Steinmetz, 1983, p. 145
Chen et al., 1981, p. 11
Kosberg, 1983, p. 286
Galbraith & Zdorkowski, 1984, p. 23

(6) Emotional and Psychological Trauma

Child Maltreatment

Elmer, 1979, p. 69
Straker & Jacobson, 1981
Martinez-Ruiz et al., 1983, p. 261
Kinard, 1980, p. 459
Hjorth & Ostrow, 1982

Child Sexual Abuse

DeFrancis, 1969, p. 5
Blumberg, 1978
Courtois, 1979
Tsai & Wagner, 1979

Koch, 1980
Leaman, 1980
Glasner, 1981
Silbert & Pines, 1981
Byrne & Valdiserie, 1982
DeJong, 1983
Kempe & Kempe, 1984, p. 22
Lourie, 1984
Seider & Calhoun, 1984
Summit, 1985
Burgess & Holmstrom, 1974
Anderson & Shafer, 1979
Finkelhor, 1979
Brown, 1980
LaBarbera & Dozier, 1980
Anderson, 1981
Pomeroy & Behar, 1981
Adams & Tucker, 1982
Romanik & Goodwin, 1982
Browne & Finkelhor, 1984, pp. 1–2, 6–7, 17
Kilpatrick & Amick, 1984, p. 2
Pagelow, 1984, p. 400
Stone et al., 1984, p. 78
(Additional)
(Female Victim)
Tsai et al., 1979
Kahn & Sexton, 1983
Felman & Nikitas, 1983
Summit, 1984, p. 5
(Male Victim)
Wahl, 1960
Nasjleti, 1980, p. 271
Russell, 1984, p. 195
Guttmacher, 1962
James & Nasjleti, 1983
(No Major Effects)
Bender & Grugett, 1952
Landis, 1956
Peters, 1976
Glasner, 1981
Gagnon, 1956
Yorokoglu & Kemph, 1966
Koch, 1980
Bender & Blau, 1984

Conjugal Violence

Walker, 1979, pp. 31, 35
Arndt, 1984
Ferraro, 1984, p. 4
Rosewater, 1984, p. 5
Hilberman, 1980, pp. 1341–1342
Douglas, 1984, p. 3
Pagelow, 1984, p. 309

Mistreatment of the Elderly

Anderson, 1981, pp. 78, 81
Chen et al., 1981, p. 11
Luppens & Lau, 1983, p. 206
Cazenave, 1981
Falcioni, 1982, p. 211

(7) Subsequent Deviance

Child Maltreatment

Bolton, Reich & Gutierres, 1978
McCord, 1983, p. 270
Garbarino, 1983

Child Sexual Abuse

(Female Victim)
Benward & Densen-Gerber, 1975
Weber, 1977
Allen & Finkelhor, 1979
Koch, 1980
Brown, 1981
Lewis-Herman, 1981, p. 30
James & Nasjleti, 1983, p. 6
Finkelhor, 1984, pp. 15, 189
Pagelow, 1984, p. 386
Stone et al., 1984, p. 28
James & Meyerding, 1977
Blumberg, 1978
Reich & Gutierres, 1979
Rush, 1980
Goodwin, 1982
Browne & Finkelhor, 1984, p. 2
Harrison & Lumry, 1984, p. 1
Pretky, 1984, p. 1
Summit, 1984, p. 1
(Male Victim)
Bell & Weinberg, 1978, 1981

Nasjleti, 1980, p. 277
Groth et al., 1982
Swift, 1979
DeYoung, 1982
James & Nasjleti, 1983
Pretky, 1984

Conjugal Violence

Hilberman, 1980, p. 1342
Deschner, 1984, p. 32

Behavioral Problems

Child Maltreatment

Martin & Beezley, 1976
Martin & Beezley, 1977
Kinard, 1980, pp. 453, 359, 460
George & Main, 1977
Egeland et al., 1980, 460
Hjorth & Ostrow, 1982

Child Sexual Abuse

Brown, 1981
Browne & Finkelhor, 1984, p. 3
James & Nasjleti, 1983
Pagelow, 1984, p. 396

Child Maltreatment

Elmer & Gregg, 1969
Martin & Rodeheffer, 1976
Rosenfeld & Newberger, 1979, p. 83
Burgess & Garbarino, 1983
Friedreich & Einbender, 1982, p. 248
Martin et al., 1974
Lynch, 1978
Kinard, 1980, p. 459
Egeland et al., 1982, p. 248
Perry et al., 1983

Sexual Maladjustment

Child Sexual Abuse

(Female Victim)

Blumberg, 1978
Finkelhor, 1979, p. 26; 1984, p. 192
Brown, 1981

Lewis-Herman, 1981
Silbert & Pines, 1981
Browne & Finkelhor, 1984, p. 3
Kilpatrick & Amick, 1984, p. 2
Pretky, 1984, p. 1
Courtois, 1979
LaBarbera et al., 1980
Glasner, 1981
Pomeroy et al., 1981
Felman & Mitkus, 1983
Kempe & Kempe, 1984, p. 55
Pagelow, 1984, p. 386

(Male Victim)

Finkelhor, 1979
Pretky, 1984, p. 1
Herman, 1981

(8) Social and Interpersonal Problems

Child Maltreatment

Martin & Beezley, 1977
Elmer, 1979, p. 69
Straker & Jacobsen, 1981
Egeland et al., 1983
Blager, 1979
Kinard, 1980, p. 453
Hjorth & Ostrow, 1982
Burgess, 1985

Child Sexual Abuse

Janas, 1983
Lourie, 1984
Kempe & Kempe, 1984, p. 54

Appendix C

References for Table 6.1:
Commonalities Across Perpetrators of Family Violence

(1) Psychopathology

Child Maltreatment

Gil, 1970, p. 34
Steele, 1982, p. 489
Oates, 1979

Child Sexual Abuse

Groth et al., 1982, p. 133
Russell, 1984, p. 259
James & Nasjleti, 1983, pp. 17–18

Conjugal Violence

Fleming, 1979, p. 304
Ferraro, 1984, p. 3
Walker, 1979, p. 40

Mistreatment of the Elderly

Chen, 1981, p. 10
Steinmetz, 1983
Falcioni, 1982, p. 208

(2) Unresolved Interpersonal Conflict

Child Maltreatment

Kaufman, 1962, p. 10
Steele, 1972, p. 32; 1982, p. 488
Ebeling & Hill, 1975, p. 20
Cicchetti & Rizley, 1984
Gil, 1970, p. 30

Pollack & Steele, 1972, p. 4
Herzberger, 1983

Child Sexual Abuse

Gebhard & Gagnon, 1964
Groth, 1979, p. 146
Groth et al., 1982, p. 138
Finkelhor, 1981
James & Nasjleti, 1983, pp. 16–17
Finkelhor, 1984, p. 40
Rossaman, 1976
Swift, 1979
Pelto, 1981
Alford et al., 1984, p. 40
Russell, 1984, p. 239

Conjugal Violence

Carlson, 1977
Harper, 1979
Deschner et al., 1980
Pagelow, 1984, p. 324
Fleming, 1979, p. 288
Walker, 1979, p. 39
Stacey & Shupe, 1983

Mistreatment of the Elderly

Steinmetz, 1983, p. 137

(3) Inappropriate and Distorted Dependencies

Child Maltreatment

Steele, 1970, p. 32
Oates, 1979
Steele, 1982, pp. 486, 489
Milner & Wimberly, 1979
Bavolek, 1981, p. 42
Martin, 1984, p. 389

Child Sexual Abuse

Lewis-Herman, 1981, p. 87
James & Nasjleti, 1983, p. 16
Bauman et al., 1983, p. 80
Alford et al., 1984

Conjugal Violence

Falk, 1974

Fleming, 1979, p. 288
Hilberman, 1980, p. 1339
Ferraro, 1984, pp. 2, 5
Elbow, 1977
Walker, 1979, p. 38
Deschner, 1984, pp. 8, 21

Mistreatment of the Elderly

Kosberg, 1983

(4) Immaturity

Child Maltreatment

Gil, 1970, p. 34
Oates, 1979
Shorkey, 1978

Child Sexual Abuse

Summit & Kryso, 1978
Groth et al., 1982, p. 133
Russell, 1984, pp. 253, 259
Swift, 1979
Alford et al., 1984, p. 40

Conjugal Violence

Falk, 1979
Harper, 1979
Fleming, 1979, p. 295
Deschner, 1984, p. 21

Mistreatment of the Elderly

Chen et al., 1981, pp. 10–11
Falcioni, 1982, p. 205

(5) Low Self-Esteem

Child Maltreatment

Mulford & Cohen, 1967, p. 13
Steele & Pollack, 1972, p. 5
Restak, 1979, p. 19
Steele, 1970, p. 32
Morris & Gould, 1974, p. 39

Child Sexual Abuse

James & Nasjleti, 1983, p. 16
Alford et al., 1984, p. 40

Conjugal Violence

Elbow, 1977
Ferraro, 1984, pp. 2, 5
Fleming, 1979, pp. 304, 325
Pagelow, 1984, p. 99

Mistreatment of the Elderly

Chen et al., 1981, p. 10
Steinmetz, 1983

(6) Lack of Personal and Experiential Family Role Preparation

Child Maltreatment

Minuchin, 1968
Terr, 1970, p. 29
Oates, 1979
Steele, 1970, p. 32
Morris & Gould, 1974, p. 39
Restak, 1979, p. 19
Steele, 1982, p. 489
Herzberger, 1983

Child Sexual Abuse

Summit & Kryso, 1978
Groth et al., 1982, p. 138
Finkelhor, 1984, p. 13
Swift, 1979
James & Nasjleti, 1983, pp. 17–18
Russell, 1984, pp. 238, 258

Conjugal Violence

Elbow, 1977
Walker, 1979, p. 36
Fleming, 1979, pp. 287, 304
Ferraro, 1984, pp. 2–3

Mistreatment of the Elderly

Chen et al., 1981, pp. 10–11
Luppens & Lau, 1983, pp. 125, 215
Anderson, 1981, p. 80
Kosberg, 1983, p. 268
Steinmetz, 1983, pp. 136, 141

(7) Need for Dominance and Control

Child Maltreatment

Alexander, 1972, p. 28
Feshback, 1980, p. 53
Shorkey, 1978
Bavolek, 1981, p. 42

Child Sexual Abuse

Lewis-Herman, 1981, p. 87
Finkelhor, 1984, p. 34
James & Nasjleti, 1983, p. 16
Russell, 1984, p. 258

Conjugal Violence

Falk, 1974
Fleming, 1979, p. 304
Elbow, 1977
Ferraro, 1984, p. 6

Mistreatment of the Elderly

Chen et al., 1981, pp. 10–11

(8) Approval of the Use of Violence

Child Maltreatment

Steele & Pollack, 1972, p. 4
Feshback, 1980, p. 53
Restak, 1979, p. 19

Conjugal Violence

Fleming, 1979, pp. 83, 295–296, 304, 325
Harper, 1979
Walker, 1979, p. 36
Deschner, 1984, p. 2
Ferraro, 1984, p. 8

(9) Lack of Social and Interpersonal Skills

Child Maltreatment

Kaufman, 1962, p. 21
Minuchin, 1968
Restak, 1979, p. 19
Mulford & Cohen, 1967, p. 9
Morris & Gould, 1974, p. 39

Child Sexual Abuse

Groth et al., 1982, pp. 137–138
James & Nasjleti, 1983, p. 17
Bauman et al., 1983, p. 80

Conjugal Violence

Elbow, 1977
Walker, 1979, pp. 37, 40
Deschner, 1984, p. 21
LaViolette, 1984, p. 14
Fleming, 1979, pp. 295, 304, 320
Shapiro, 1980, p. 52
Ferraro, 1984, p. 3
Pagelow, 1984, p. 99

(10) Denial and Defensiveness

Child Maltreatment

Kaufman, 1962, p. 21
Hill, 1975, p. 20
Morris & Gould, 1974, p. 39
Feshback, 1980, p. 53

Child Sexual Abuse

James & Nasjleti, 1983, pp. 17–18
Russell, 1984, p. 254

Conjugal Violence

Walker, 1979, p. 36

(11) Distorted View of the Victim

Child Maltreatment

Mulford & Cohen, 1967, p. 13
Hill, 1975, p. 19
Ainsworth, 1980, p. 43
Bavolek, 1981, p. 42
Trowell, 1983, p. 392
Steele & Pollack, 1972, p. 4
Straus, 1979, p. 5
Feshback, 1980, p. 53
Steele, 1982, p. 489

Child Sexual Abuse

Groth et al., 1982, p. 137

Conjugal Violence

Fleming, 1979, pp. 288–289

Mistreatment of the Elderly

Anderson, 1981, p. 80
Steinmetz, 1983, p. 141
Chen et al., 1981, pp. 10–11

Appendix D

References for Table 7.1:
Shared Characteristics of Adolescent Parents,
Maltreating Parents, and Their Children

DEMOGRAPHIC CHARACTERISTICS

(1) Over-Representation of Lower Socioeconomic Status Groups

Gil, 1970
Reiss, 1976
Lincoln et al., 1976
Holmes, 1978

(2) High Unemployment and Low Occupational Level

Young, 1964
Holmes, 1978
Nye, 1976

(3) Lowered Educational Levels

Nye, 1976
Holmes, 1978

(4) Large Numbers of Children Born in Close Succession

Light, 1973
Anastasiow et al., 1978
Klerman, 1975
Trussell & Menken, 1978

(5) Over-Representation of Single Parent, Female Head-of-Household

Hertz, 1977
Caplan et al., 1984
Holmes, 1978

(6) Youthfulness at First Birth

Lincoln et al., 1976
Holmes, 1978

(7) High Rates of Relationship Disruption

Lorenzi, 1977
Card & Wise, 1978

DYNAMIC CHARACTERISTICS

(1) Unrealistic Expectations of the Child

Steele & Pollack, 1974
DeLissovoy, 1973

(2) Ignorance of Child-Care Techniques

Fontana, 1973
Furstenberg, 1976

(3) Unfulfilled Dependency Needs and Role Reversals

Steele, 1975
Osofsky & Osofsky, 1978

(4) An Environment in Which the Child is Unwanted

Martin, 1976
Card & Wise, 1978

(5) Lack of Knowledge of Child Development

Vincent, 1961
Helfer, 1979

(6) Deprivation, etc.

Kempe & Helfer, 1972
Cheetham, 1977

(7) Low Self-Esteem

Pannor et al., 1971
Helfer, 1975

(8) Fear of Rejection

Abernathy, 1974
Holmes, 1978

(9) Low Frustration Tolerance

Pannor et al., 1971

Holmes, 1978

(10) Isolation

Vincent, 1961
Giovannoni & Billingsley, 1970
Malmquist, 1966

CHILD CHARACTERISTICS

(1) Complications of Pregnancy

Robson & Moss, 1970
Ryan & Schneider, 1978

(2) Premature Birth

Friedrich & Boriskin, 1976
Hunter et al., 1978
Brown & Bakeman, 1977
Minde, 1980

(3) Poor Health and Nutrition

Wallace, 1970
Plionis, 1975

(4) School and Behavior Problems

Elmer & Gregg, 1967
Hardy et al., 1978
Martin, 1976

Appendix E

References for Table 7.2:
Psychological Resources in the Divorced Single Parent
and Parent at Risk for Child Maltreatment

(1) Immaturity

Hetherington et al., 1977

(2) Unrealistic Expectations

Conger et al., 1982
Weiss, 1979

(3) Low Self-Esteem

Helfer, 1976
Hetherington, 1979

(4) Fear of Continued Rejection

Helfer, 1976
Hetherington, 1979

(5) Unfulfilled Dependency Needs

Steele, 1975
Longfellow, 1979
Bolton, 1983
Hetherington, 1979
Belsky, 1980

(6) Feelings of Being Out of Control or Overwhelmed

Holmes, 1978
Francke, 1983

(7) Depression

Briscoe et al., 1973
Orraschel et al., 1980
Pearlin & Johnson, 1977
Colletta, 1984

(8) Reduced Responsiveness to Their Children

Hetherington, 1979

(9) Difficulty in Trusting

Pearlin & Johnson, 1977
Holmes, 1978

(10) Poor Impulse Control and Impulsiveness

Steele & Pollack, 1972
Bolton, 1978
Hetherington, 1979
Hetherington et al., 1977
Burgess & Garbarino, 1983

(11) Less Verbal Interaction with the Child(ren)

Weiss, 1979

(12) High Levels of Disapproval of Child(ren)'s Behavior

Carter & Glick, 1976
Weiss, 1979
Hetherington, 1979

(13) Previous Negative Family Experience

Parke & Collmer, 1975
Hetherington, 1979
Weiss, 1975

(14) Attachment Difficulty

Steele, 1975
Belsky, 1980
Longfellow, 1979
Bolton, 1983

(15) Role Reversals with Child

Wallerstein & Kelly, 1975
Holmes, 1978

Appendix F

References for Table 7.3:
The Recently Divorced Parent and the Parent at High
Risk for Child Maltreatment: Contextual Stress and
Support

(1) Absence of Intrafamilial and Extrafamilial Support Systems
Bloom et al., 1979
Straus, 1980

(2) Employment Difficulty or Dissatisfaction
Bane, 1979
Hetherington, 1979

(3) Pervasive Financial Stress
Helfer, 1975
Hodges et al., 1978

(4) The Responsibilities of Single Parenthood
Wallerstein & Kelly, 1975
Steinberg et al., 1981
Hetherington et al., 1977

(5) Disruptive Emotional Relationships
Helfer, 1975
Bloom et al., 1979

(6) Generalized Isolation
Light, 1973
Hodges et al., 1978
Helfer, 1975

Appendix G

References for Table 7.4:
The Recently Divorced Parent and the Parent at Risk
for Maltreatment: Stress-Producing Child Behaviors
and Characteristics

(1) Difficult Temperament

Martin, 1976
Learner & Learner, in press
Hetherington, 1979

(2) Being Perceived by Parent as Difficult

Bloom et al., 1979
Belsky, 1984

(3) Problems in School

Martin, 1976
Hetherington et al., 1977

(4) Behavior Problems

Martin, 1976
Hetherington, 1979
Hetherington et al., 1977

(5) Discipline Problems

Millions, 1978
Martin, 1979
Bates, 1979

(6) Seen as Competitor by Parent

Brandwein et al., 1974
Kinard, 1982

(7) Lack of "Fit" with Parental Expectations

Hetherington, 1972
Friedrich & Einbender, 1983
Friedrich & Boriskin, 1976

Appendix H

References for Table 8.1:
Commonalities in Family Operations Across Violent Families

(1) Confused and Distorted

Child Maltreatment

Morris & Gould, 1963
Steele & Pollack, 1972
Parke & Collmer, 1975
Justice & Justice, 1976
Lynch & Roberts, 1977
Egeland & Vaughn, 1979
Oatman, 1979
Emde, 1980
Egeland & Sroufe, 1981
Burgess & Garbarino, 1983
Spinetta & Rigler, 1972
Ounstead et al., 1974
Helfer & Kempe, 1976
Garbarino, 1977, p. 722
DeLozier, 1979
Newberger, 1979, p. 15
Ainsworth, 1980
Kinard, 1980
Bolton, 1983, 1985

Child Sexual Abuse

Finkelhor, 1979, pp. 26–27
Giaretto, 1980, p. 40
Stern & Meyer, 1980
Lewis-Herman, 1981
Rosenfeld, 1979

Herman & Hirschman, 1980
Summit & Kryso, 1980
Kempe & Kempe, 1984, pp. 49, 59

Conjugal Violence

Brandon, 1976
Pagelow, 1984

(2) Unequal Power and Status Distributions

Child Maltreatment

Garbarino, 1977, p. 724
Ainsworth, 1980, p. 42

Child Sexual Abuse

Cormier et al., 1963
Summit & Kryso, 1978
Herman, 1981
Groth et al., 1982, p. 137
Finkelhor, 1984, p. 39
Russell, 1984
Hunter et al., 1985, p. 24
Maisch, 1973
Burgess et al., 1981
Lewis-Herman, 1981, p. 3
Tierney & Corwin, 1983, p. 108
Kempe & Kempe, 1984, p. 60
Summit, 1984, p. 3

Conjugal Violence

O'Brien, 1971
Carlson, 1977
Allen & Straus, 1983
Walker, 1983, pp. 47, 83
LaViolette, 1984, p. 3
Tidmarsh, 1976
Steinmetz, 1977
Giles-Sims, 1983
Deschner, 1984, p. 29
Pagelow, 1984, pp. 75, 99

Mistreatment of the Elderly

Hickey & Douglas, 1981, p. 174
Kosberg, 1983, p. 268
Douglas, 1983, p. 143
Luppins & Lau, 1983, pp. 209–210, 212

O'Malley et al., 1984, pp. 362, 366, 368
Pagelow, 1984, p. 78

(3) Frustration

Child Maltreatment

Steele & Pollack, 1972
Feshback, 1980, pp. 50–51

Child Sexual Abuse

Giaretto, 1978, 1980

Conjugal Violence

Giles-Sims, 1983, p. 27
Deschner, 1984, p. 70

Mistreatment of the Elderly

Anderson, 1981, p. 79
Block, 1983, p. 221
Hickey & Douglas, 1981, p. 504
Pagelow, 1984, p. 369

(4) Distorted Cognitions and Attributions

Child Maltreatment

Johnson & Morse, 1968, p. 151
Schneider et al., 1976
Feshback, 1980, pp. 50–54
Steele & Pollack, 1972, p. 11
Ainsworth, 1980, pp. 42–43
Steele, 1982, p. 488

Child Sexual Abuse

Finkelhor, 1979, p. 28
Groth et al., 1982
Finkelhor, 1981
Russell, 1984, p. 242

Conjugal Violence

Haley, 1976
Giles-Sims, 1983, p. 26
Ferraro, 1984, pp. 2–3
Hilberman, 1980, p. 1339
Deschner, 1984, pp. 71–75

(5) Role Incompetence in the Face of Stress

Child Maltreatment

Johnson & Morse, 1968, p. 151
Galdston, 1970, p. 28
Patterson, 1976
Garbarino, 1977, pp. 723–724
Burgess et al., 1981
Herrenkohl et al., 1981
Parke & Collmer, 1975
Elder, 1977
George & Main, 1979
Cicchetti & Rizley, 1984, p. 44
Kadushin & Martin, 1984

Child Sexual Abuse

Samuels, 1977
Finkelhor, 1984, 1979, p. 26
Tierney & Corwin, 1983, pp. 106, 110
Russell, 1984, p. 252

Conjugal Violence

Pinta, 1978
Walker, 1979
Giles-Sims, 1983, p. 24
Fleming, 1979, p. 311
Hilberman, 1980, p. 1339
Deschner, 1984, pp. 13, 18, 77

Mistreatment of the Elderly

Anderson, 1981, p. 78
Hickey & Douglas, 1981, p. 504
Douglas & Hickey, 1983
Chen et al., 1981, p. 5
Cazenave & Woodburn, 1982
Steinmetz, 1983, p. 138
Giordano & Giordano, 1984, pp. 232–234

References

Abel, G., Becker, J., Murphy, W. D., & Flanagan, B. (1981). Identifying dangerous child molesters. In R. B. Stuart (Ed.), *Violent Behavior*, New York: Brunner/Mazel.

Able, G., Becker, J., Cunningham-Rathner, J., Rouleau, J., Kaplan, M., & Reich, J. (1984). *The Treatment of Child Molesters* New York: SBC-TM.

Abel, G. E. (1985). Chart from Tarrant County Child Abuse Council Presentation. Fort Worth, TX: May 1985. (K. Dolan, Texas College of Osteopathic Medicine).

Abernathy, V. (1974). Illegitimate conception among teenagers. *American Journal of Public Health, 64*, 662–665.

Acher, J. R., & Toch, H. (1985). Battered women, straw men, and expert testimony: A comment on *State v. Kelly. Criminal Law Bulletin, 21* (2), 125–155.

Acosta, F. X., Yamamoto, J., & Evans, L. A. (1982). *Effective Psychotherapy for Low Income and Minority Patients.* New York: Plenum.

Adams-Tucker, C. (1982). Proximate effects of sexual abuse in childhood: A report on 28 children. *American Journal of Psychiatry, 39*, 1252–1256.

Adams-Tucker, C. (1984). The unmet psychiatric needs of sexually abused youths: Referrals from a child protection agency and clinical evaluations. *Journal of the American Academy of Child Psychiatry, 23* (6), 659–667.

Ainsworth, M.D.S. (1980). Attachment and child abuse. In G. Gerbner, C. Ross, & E. Zigler (Eds.), *Child Abuse: An Agenda for Actions.* New York: Oxford University Press.

Albert, J. S. (1981). Sociocultural determinants of personality pathology. In J. R. Lion (Ed.), *Personality Disorders: Diagnosis and Management*, Baltimore: Williams & Wilkins.

Alexander, H. (1972). The social worker and the family. In C. H. Kempe & R. E. Helfer (Eds.), *Helping the Battered Child and His Family.* Philadelphia: Lippincott.

Alexander, H. (1980). Long term treatment. In C. H. Kempe & R. E. Helfer (Eds.), *The Battered Child.* Chicago: University of Chicago Press.

Alexander, R. D. (1975). The search for a general theory of behavior. *Behavioral Science, 20*, 77–100.

Alford, J. M., Bauman, R. C., & Kaspar, C. J. (1984). Diagnostic classification of sexual child offenders. *Journal of Correctional and Social Psychiatry, 2,* 40–45.

Allen, C. & Straus, M. A. (1980). Resources, power and husband-wife violence. In M. A. Straus & G. T. Hotaling (Eds.), *The Social Causes of Husband-Wife Violence.* Minneapolis: University of Minnesota Press.

American Bar Association. (1977). *Juvenile Justice Standards.* Washington DC: Ballinger.

American Humane Association. (1981). *National Study on Child Neglect and Abuse Reporting.* Denver: American Humane Association.

American Psychiatric Association. (1974). *Clinical Aspects of the Violent Individual: Task Force Report 8.* Washington, DC: American Psychiatric Association.

American Psychiatric Association. (1980). *Diagnostic and Statistical Manual of Mental Disorders,* (3rd ed.). Washington, DC: American Psychiatric Association.

American Psychological Association. (1978). Report of the task force on the role of psychology in the criminal justice system. *American Psychologist, 33,* 1099–1113.

Anastasiow, N. J., Everett, M., O'Shaughnessy, T. E., Eggleston, P. J., & Eklund, S. J. (1978). Improving teenage attitudes toward children, child handicaps, and hospital settings: A child development curriculum for potential parents. *American Journal of Orthopsychiatry, 48,* 663–671.

Anderson, C. L. (1981). Abuse and neglect among the elderly. *Journal of Gerontological Nursing, 7* (2), 283–294.

Anderson, L. M., & Shafer, G. (1979). That character-disordered family: A community treatment model for family sexual abuse. *American Journal of Orthopsychiatry, 49* (3), 453–458.

Anderson, L. S. (1981). Notes on the linkage between the sexually abused child and the suicidal adolescent. *Journal of Adolescence, 4* (2), 157–162.

Armstrong, L. (1983) *The Home Front.* New York: McGraw-Hill.

Arndt, N. Y. (1984, August). *Domestic violence: An investigation of the psychological aspects of the battered woman.* Paper presented at the second Family Violence Researchers Conference. Durham, NH.

Avery, N. C. (1975). Viewing child abuse and neglect as symptoms of family dysfunctioning. In N. B. Ebeling, & D. A. Hill (Eds.), *Child Abuse: Intervention and Treatment.* Acton, MA: Publishing Sciences Group.

Baekeland, F., & Lundwall, L. (1975). Dropping out of treatment: A critical review. *Psychological Bulletin, 82,* 738–783.

Biley, T. F., & Bailey, W. H. (1983). *Criminal or Social Intervention in Child Sexual Abuse: A Review and a Viewpoint.* Denver, CO: American Humane Association.

Baker, H. J., & Leland, B. (1967). *Examiner's Handbook: Detroit Tests of Learning Aptitude* (revised ed.). Indianapolis: Bobbs-Merrill.

Ball, P. G., & Wyman, E. (1978). Battered wives and powerlessness: What can counselors do? *Victimology, 2* (3/4), 545–552.

Bandura, A. (1973). *Aggression: A Social Learning Analysis.* Englewood Cliffs, NJ: Prentice-Hall.

Bane, M. (1979). Marital disruption and the lives of children. In G. Levinger & D. C. Moles (Eds.), *Divorce and Separation: Context, Causes, and Consequences.* New York: Basic Books.

Bar levav, R. (1984). A malicious sense of survival, In E. M. Stern (Ed.), *Psychotherapy and the Abrasive Patient.* New York: Haworth Press.

Barnard, C. P. (Ed.). (1983). Families, incest, and therapy (special issue). *International Journal of Family Therapy, 5* (2).

Basch, M. G. (1982). Dynamic psychotherapy and its frustrations. In P. Wachtel (Ed.), *Resistance: Psychodynamic and Behavioral Approaches.* New York: Plenum.

Bauer, W. T., & Twentyman, C. T. (1983). Abusing, neglectful, and comparison mothers' responses to child-related and non-child related stressors. *Journal of Consulting and Clinical Psychology,53* (3), 335–343.

Bauman, R. C., Kaspar, C. J., & Alford, J. M. (1983). The child sex abusers. *Journal of Social and Correctional Psychiatry,3*, 76–80.

Bavolek, S. J. (1981). Educational setting for the primary prevention of child abuse and neglect with school age children. *Monographs in Behavior Disorders* (Summer), 40–48.

Bayley, N. (1969). *Manual for the Bayley Scales of Infant Development.* New York: Psychological Corporation.

Beck, A. T. (1976). *Cognitive Therapy and the Emotional Disorders.* New York: International Universities Press.

Beck, A. T., Rush, A. J., & Shaw, G. F. (1979). *Cognitive Therapy of Depression.* New York: Guilford.

Bell, A., & Weinberg, M. (1978). *Homosexualities.* New York: Simon & Schuster.

Bell, A., & Weinberg, M. (1981). *Sexual Preference in Development Among Men and Women.* Bloomington: Indiana University Press.

Bellack, L., & Bellack, S. S. (1971). *Children's Apperception Test Manual* (5th Ed.). Larchmont, NY: CPS

Belsky, J. (1980). Child maltreatment: An ecological integration. *American Psychologist, 35*, 320–335.

Belsky, J. (1984). The determinants of parenting: A process model. *Child Development, 55*, 83–96.

Bemporad, J. R., & Lee, K. W. (1984). Developmental and psycho-dynamic aspects of childhood depression. *Child Psychiatry and Human Development, 14* (3), 1391–1396.

Bender, L. (1946). *Bender Motor Gestalt Test: Cards and Manual of Instruction.* New York: American Orthopsychiatric Association.

Bender, L., & Blau, A. (1937). The reaction of children to sexual relations with adults. *American Journal of Orthopsychiatry, 7* (XII), 500–518.

Bender, L., & Grugett, A. (1952). A follow-up report on children who had atypical sexual experiences. *American Journal of Orthopsychiatry, 22*, 825–837.

Bennie, E. H., & Sclare, A. B. (1969). The battered child syndrome. *American Journal of Psychiatry, 125*, (7), 975–979.

Berliner, L., & Barbieri, M. K. (1984). The testimony of the child victim of sexual assault. *Journal of Social Issues, 40*, 125–134.

Berliner, L., Blick, L. C., & Bulkley, J. (1984). Expert testimony on the dynamics of intra-family child sexual abuse and principles of child development. In J. Bulkley (Ed.), *Child Sexual Abuse and the Law* (5th Ed.), Washington DC: American Bar Association.

Berliner, L., & Roe, R. (1985). The child witness: The progress and emerging limitations. In *American Bar Association National Policy Conference on Legal Reforms in Child Sexual Abuse Cases*. Washington DC: American Bar Association.

Berliner, L., & Stevens, D. (1982). Clinical issues in child sexual abuse. In J. R. Conte & D. Shore (Eds.), *Social Work and Child Sexual Abuse*. New York: Haworth.

Besharov, D. J. (1985). Right versus rights: The dilemma of child protection. *Public Welfare,* (Spring), 19–27.

Billingsley, A. (1969). Family functioning in the low income Black community, *Casework, 50*, 563–572.

Black, L. (1979). Children of alcoholics. *Alcohol Health and Research World, 4* (1), 23–27.

Blager, F. B. (1979). The effect of intervention on the speech and language of abused children. *Child Abuse and Neglect 3*, (3/4), 991–996

Blau, T. H. (1984). *The Psychologist as Expert Witness*. New York: John Wiley.

Blenker, M. (1965). Social work and the family: Relationships in later life. In E. Shanus & G. Streib (Eds.), *Social Structure and the Family: Intergenerational Relationships*. Englewood Cliffs, NJ: Prentice-Hall.

Blenker, M. (1979). The normal dependence of aging. In R. Kalish (Ed.), *The Dependencies of Old People*. Occasional Papers in Gerontology, no. 6, Ann Arbor, MI: Institute on Gerontology.

Block, M. R. (1983). Special problems and vulnerability of elderly women. In J. I. Kosberg (Ed.), *Abuse and Mistreatment of the Elderly*. Boston, PSG.

Block, M. R., & Sinnott, J. (1979). *Battered Elder Syndrome: An Exploratory Study*. College Park: University of Maryland Center on Aging.

Bloom, B. L., White, S. W., & Asher, S. J. (1979). Marital disruption as a stressful life event. In G. Levinger & O. W. Moles (Eds.), *Divorce and Separation: Context, Causes, and Consequences*. New York: Basic Books.

Blumberg, M. L. (1974). Psychopathology of the abusing parent. *American Journal of Psychiatry, 28* (1), 21–29.

Blumberg, M. L. (1979). Character disorders in traumatized and handicapped children. *American Journal of Psychotherapy, 33* (2), 201–213.

Blythe, B. J. (1983). A critique of outcome evaluation in child abuse treatment. *Child Welfare, 62* (4).

Bochnak, E. (1981). *Women's Self-Defense Cases: Theory and Practice.* New York: Michie.

Bolton, F. G., Jr. (1978). Signals of family stress in high-risk families. In M. L. Lauderdale, R. N. Anderson, & S. E. Cramer (Eds.), *Child Abuse and Neglect: Issues on Innovation and Implementation.* Washington DC: DHEW Pub. NO (OHDS) 78–30148.

Bolton, F. G., Jr. (1980). *The Pregnant Adolescent: Problems of Premature Parenthood.* Beverly Hills, CA: Sage Publications.

Bolton, F. G., Jr. (1983). *When Bonding Fails: Clinical Assessment of the High-Risk Family.* Beverly Hills, CA: Sage Publications.

Bolton, F. G., Jr. (1984, August). *"Normal family violence": A diathesis-stress approach to assessment and treatment of child abuse.* Paper presented at the Second Family Violence Researchers Conference. Durham, NH.

Bolton, F. G., Jr. (1984). The recently divorced parent and child: Assessing risk to the relationship. In P. Bushard (Ed.), *Legal and Therapeutic Support of the Restructured Family.* Phoenix: International Association of Family and Conciliation Courts.

Bolton, F. G., Jr. (1985). The adolescent parent and child maltreatment: Bi-lateral victimization. *Child and Youth Service Review.* East Lansing, MI: American Humane Association.

Bolton, F. G., Jr., & Belsky, J. (1986). Adolescent fatherhood and child maltreatment. In A. Elster and M. Lamb (Eds.), *Adolescent Fatherhood.* Hillsdale, NJ: Erlbaum.

Bolton, F. G., Jr., Charlton, J. K., Gai, D. S., Laner, R. H., & Shumway, S. M. (1985). Preventive screening of adolescent mothers and infants: Critical variables in assessing risk for child maltreatment. *Journal of Primary Prevention, 5* (3), 17–25.

Bolton, F. G., Jr., Laner, R. H., & Kane, S. P. (1980) Child maltreatment risk among adolescent mothers: A study of reported cases. *American Journal of Orthopsychiatry, 50* (3), 489–504.

Bolton, F. G., Jr., & Laner, R. H. (1981). Maternal maturity and maltreatment: Expanding the definition of the abusive adolescent mother. *Journal of Family Issues, 2,* 485–508.

Bolton, F. G., Jr., & Laner, R. H. (in press). Children rearing children: A study of reportedly maltreating younger adolescents. *Journal of Family Violence.*

Bolton, F. G., Jr., Laner, R. H., Gai, D. S., & Kane, S. P. (1981). The study of child maltreatment: When is research—research? *Journal of Family Issues, 3* (4), 531–539.

Bolton, F. G., Jr., & MacEachron, A. (in press). Child maltreatment and the recently divorced parent: Issues in assessment. *Journal of Family Violence.*

Bolton, F. G., Jr., & Montagnini, M. W. (1975). Group diagnosis and treatment for parents in potentially abusive settings. *Proceedings of the Southwestern Psychological Association.* Phoenix: Southwestern Psychological Association.

Bolton, F. G., Jr., Reich, J., & Guiterres, S. (1978). Delinquency patterns in maltreated children and siblings. *Victimology, 2* (2), 349–357.

Booth, A. (1976). Crowding and family relations. *American Sociological Review, 41,* 308–321.

Bourne, R. (1979). Child abuse and neglect: An overview. In R. Bourne & E. H. Newberger (Eds.), *Critical Perspectives on Child Abuse,* Lexington, MA: Lexington Books.

Bourne, R., & Newberger, E. H. (Eds.). (1979a), *Critical Perspectives on Child Abuse.* Lexington, MA: D. C. Heath.

Bourne, R., & Newberger, E. H. (1979b). Family "autonomy" or "coercive intervention"? Ambiguity and conflict in the proposed standards for child abuse and neglect. In R. Bourne & E. H. Newberger (Eds.), *Critical Perspectives on Child Abuse.* Lexington, MA: Lexington Books.

Boyd, V. D. (1978). *Domestic violence: Treatment alternatives for the male batterers.* Paper presented at the American Psychological Association Meeting, Toronto, Canada.

Boyd, V. D., & Kingbell, K. S. (1979). *Behavioral Characteristics of Domestic Violence.* Unpublished Manuscript.

Bradley, S. J. (1979). The relationship of early maternal separation to borderline personality in children and adolescents: A pilot study. *American Journal of Psychiatry, 136* (4a), 424–426.

Brandt, R. T., & Tisza, V. (1977). The sexually misused child. *American Journal of Orthopsychiatry, 44,* 80–87.

Brandwein, R. A., Brown, C. A., & Fox, E. M. (1974). Women and children last: The social situation of divorced mothers and their families. *Journal of Marriage and the Family, 36,* 498–514.

Bratt, C. S. (1984). Incest statutes and the fundamental right of marriage: Is Oedipus free to marry? *Family Law Quarterly, 18* (3).

Brent, D. A. (1985). Psychiatric assessment of the school age child. *Psychiatric Annals, 15* (1), 30–35.

Briscoe, C. W., Smith, J. B., Robins, E., Marlens, S., & Gaskin, F. (1973). Divorce and psychiatric disease. *Archives of General Psychiatry, 29,* 119–125.

Brodsky, S. L. (1980). Understanding and treating sexual offenders. *Howard Journal of Penology and Crime Prevention, 19* (2), 102–115.

Brody, G. F. (1968). Socioeconomic differences in stated maternal child rearing practices and in observed maternal behavior. *Journal of Marriage and the Family, 30,* 656–660.

Bross, D. C. (Ed.).(1984). *Multidisciplinary Advocacy for Mistreated Children* Denver, CO: National Association of Counsel for Children.

Brown, F. E. (1980). Juvenile prostitution: A nursing perspective. *Journal of Psychiatric Nursing and Mental Health Services, 18* (12), 32–34.

Brown, J. V., & Bakeman, R. (1979, April). *Behavioral dialogues between mothers and infants: The effect of prematurity.* Paper presented at the American Pediatric Society and the Society for Pediatric Research, San Francisco. Reprinted by Center for Crime and Delinquency. NIMH, DHEW Pub No. (OHDS) 79–30225.

Brown, L. (1978, October). *Analysis of official reports of sexual abuse in 1976.* Paper presented to CAUSES Conference on Incest, Chicago.

Brown, L., & Holder, W. (1980). The nature and extent of sexual abuse in contemporary American society. In W. Holder (Ed.), *Sexual Abuse of Children.* Englewood, CO: American Humane Association.

Browne, A., & Finkelhor, D. (1984). *The Impact of Child Sexual Abuse: A Review of The Research.* Durham: University of New Hampshire Family Violence Research Program. (mimeo)

Browne, A., and Finkelhor, D. (1986). Initial and long term effects: A review of the literature. In D. Finkelhor (Ed). *A Sourcebook on Child Sexual Abuse..* Newbury Park, CA: Sage.

Browning, D., & Boatman, B. (1977). Incest: Children at risk. *American Journal of Psychology, 134,* 69–72.

Bruno v. Codd, 393 NE2d 976 (N.Y. 1979).

Buchanan, A., & Oliver, J. E. (1977). Abuse and neglect as a cause of mental retardation: A study of 140 children admitted to subnormality hospitals in Wiltshire. *British Journal of Psychiatry, 131,* 458–487.

Bulkley, J. (1984). *Child Sexual Abuse and the Law* (5th ed.). Washington, DC: American Bar Association.

Bulkley, J. A. (1985). Evidentiary and procedural trends in state legislation and other emerging legal issues in child sexual abuse cases. In *National Policy Conference on Legal Reforms in Child Sexual Abuse Cases.* Washington DC: American Bar Association (pre-publication edition) .

Bulkley, J. A., & Davidson, H. A. (1981). *Child Sexual Abuse: Legal Issues and Approaches.* Washington, DC: American Bar Association, Young Lawyers Division.

Burgess, A. W. (1984). *Child Pornography and Sex Rings.* New York: D. C. Heath.

Burgess, A. W., & Holmstrom, L. (1979). Sexual disruption and recovery. *American Journal of Orthopsychiatry,* 49, 648–657.

Burgess, A. W., Groth, A. N., & McCausland, M. (1981). Child sex initiation rings. *American Journal of Orthopsychiatry, 51,* 110–118.

Burgess, R. L. (1978). *Project Interact: A Study of Patterns of Interactions in Abusive, Neglectful, and Control Families.* Final Report to the National Center on Child Abuse and Neglect.

Burgess, R. L. (1985, January). Social incompetence and the victim of child maltreatment. Paper presented to the Arizona State Department of Economic Security Child Protective Services Training Academy, Tucson.

Burgess, R. L., Anderson, E. S., Schellenbach, C. J., & Conger, R. D. (1981). A social interactional approach to the study of abusive families. In J. P. Vincent (Ed.), *Advances in Family Intervention, Assessment, and Theory: An Annual Compilation of Research* (vol. 2). Greenwich, CT: JAI.

Burgess, R. L., & Conger, R. D. (1977). Family interaction patterns related to child abuse and neglect: Some preliminary findings. *Child Abuse and Neglect, 1,* 269–277.

Burgess, R. L., & Conger, R. D. (1978). Family interactions in abusive, neglectful, and normal families. *Child Development, 49,* 1163–1173.

Burgess, R. L., & Garbarino, J. (1983). Doing what comes naturally? An evolutionary perspective on child abuse. In D. Finkelhor et al. (Eds.), *The Dark Side of Families.* Beverly Hills, CA: Sage Publications.

Burgess, R. L., & Richardson, R. A. (1984). Child abuse during adolescence. In R. M. Lerner & N. L. Galambos (Eds.), *Experiencing Adolescence: A Sourcebook for Parents, Teachers, and Teens.* New York: Garland Publishing.

Burgess, R. L. & Youngblade, L. M. (1985). Social incompetence and the intergenerational transmission of abusive parental practices. Pennsylvania State University: Department of Individual and Family Studies (mimeo).

Burnside, I. M. (1973). Mental health in the aged: The nurse's perspective. In *Aging: Prospects and Issues* (revised). Los Angeles: Percey Andrus Gerontology Center, University of Southern California Press.

Buros, O. K. (Ed.). (1972). *The Seventh Mental Measurements Yearbook.* Highland Park, NJ: Gryphon.

Butcher, J. N. (1987). *Clinical Applications of the MMPI.* Minneapolis: University of Minnesota.

Butler, R. N. (1975). *Why Survive? Being Old in America.* New York: Harper & Row.

Byrne, J. P., & Valdiserri, E. V. (1982). Victims of childhood sexual abuse: A follow-up study of a noncompliant population. *Hospital and Community Psychiatry,* 938–940.

Caffey, J. (1972). On the theory and practice of shaking infants: Its potential residual effects of permanent brain damage and mental retardation. *American Journal of Diseases of Children, 24,* 161–169.

Calahan, D., & Room, R. (1974). *Problem Drinking Among American Men.* New Brunswick, NJ: Rutgers Center for Alcohol Studies.

Campbell, A. (1975). The American way of mating. *Psychology Today,* 37–43.

Caplan, D. J., Watters, J., White, G., Perry, R., & Bates, R. (1984). Toronto Multiagency Child Abuse Research Project: The abused and the abuser. *Child Abuse and Neglect, 8* (3), 343–351.

Card, J. J., & Wise, L. L. (1978). Teenage mothers and fathers: The impact of early childbearing on the parent's personal and professional lives. *Family Planning Perspectives, 10*, 199– 205.

Carlson, B. E. (1977). Battered women and their assailants. *Social Work, 22*, 455–460.

Carrillo, R., & Marrujo, B. (1984, August). *Acculturation and domestic violence in the Hispanic community.* Paper presented at the Second Family Violence Researchers Conference, Durham, NH.

Carter, H., & Slick, P. C. (1976). *Marriage and Divorce: A Social and Economic Study.* Cambridge, MA: Harvard University Press.

Cattell, R. B., Eber, H. W., & Tatsuoka, M. M. *Handbook for the Sixteen Personality Factor Questionnaire.* Champaign, IL: Institute for Personality and Ability Testing.

Caulfield, B. A. (1978). *Legal Aspects of Protective Services for Abused and Neglected Children.* Washington, DC: Government Printing Office.

Cazenave, N. A. (1983). Elder abuse and black Americans: Incidence, correlates, treatment and prevention. In J. I. Kosberg (Ed.), *Abuse and Maltreatment of the Elderly.* Boston: John Wright PSG.

Cazenave, N. A., & Woodburn, P. (1981, July). *Stress management and coping alternatives for families of the frail elderly.* Paper presented at the First Family Violence Researchers Conference, Durham, NH.

Chandler, S. M. (1982). Knowns and unknowns in sexual abuse of children. *Journal of Social Work and Human Sexuality, 1* (1–2), 51–68.

Chapman, S. B., & Terry, T. (1984). Treatment of sexually abused children from minority urban families: A socio-cultural perspective. *Clinical Proceedings, CHNMC, 40* (May–August), 244–259.

Cheetham, J. (1977). *Unwanted Pregnancy and Counseling.* London: Routedge & Kegan Paul.

Chen, P. N., Bell, S. L., Dolinsky, D. L., Doyle, J., & Dunn, M. (1981). Elderly abuse in domestic settings: A pilot study. *Social Work, 4* (1), 132–147.

Cicchetti, D., & Rizley, R. (1981). Developmental perspectives on the etiology, intergenerational transmission, and sequelae of child maltreatment. In C. Cicchetti & R. Rizley (Eds.), *New Directions for Child Development: Developmental Perspectives on Child Maltreatment.* San Francisco: Jossey-Bass.

Cicchetti, D., & Rizley, R. (1984). Developmental perspectives on the etiology, intergenerational transmission, and sequelae of child maltreatment. *New Directions for Child Development, 11*, 31–55.

Clawson, A. (1962). *The Bender Visual Motor Gestalt Test For Children.* Los Angeles: Western Psychological Services.

Clecky, H. (1964). *The Mask of Sanity.* St. Louis, MO: C. V. Mosby.

Cohen, M., Seghorn, T., & Calmus, W. (1969). Sociometric study of the sex offender. *Journal of Abnormal Psychology, 74*, 249–255

Cohn, A. H. (1979). Effective treatment of child abuse and neglect. *Social Work, 24* (6) 513–520.

Coleman, D. H., & Straus, M. A. (1979, August). *Alcohol abuse and family violence.* Paper presented at the American Sociological Association, Boston.

Colletta, N. D. (in press). At risk for depression: A study of young mothers. *Journal of Genetic Psychology.*

Conger, R. D., Burgess, R. L., & Barrett, C. (1979). Child abuse related to life change and perceptions of illness: Some preliminary findings. *Family Coordinator, 28,* 73–78.

Conte, J. (1982). Sexual abuse of children: Enduring issues for social work. In J. R. Conte & D. Shore (Eds.), *Social Work and Child Sexual Abuse.* New York: Haworth.

Conte, J. (1984a, November). *The effects of sexual abuse on children: A critique and suggestions for future research.* Paper presented to the Third International Institute of Victimology, Lisbon, Portugal.

Conte, J. R. (1984b). Progress in treating the sexual abuse of children. *Social Work, 29* (3), 258–263.

Conte, J. (1986, January). *Child sexual abuse: A historical overview.* Paper presented to the Child Protective Services Training Academy, Phoenix, AZ.

Conte, R., & Berliner, L. (1984). The impact of sexual abuse on children: Empirical findings. In L.E.A. Walker (Ed.), *Handbook on Sexual Abuse of Children.* New York: Springer.

Conte, J., Berliner, L., & Nolan, D. (1980). Police and social worker cooperation in child sexual assault cases. *F.B.I. Law Enforcement Bulletin, 49* (3), 7–10.

Coolsen, P., & Wechsler, J. (1984). Community involvement in the prevention of child abuse and neglect. In *Perspectives on Child Maltreatment in the Mid '80's.* Washington, DC: National Center on Child Abuse and Neglect.

Cormier, B., Kennedy, M., & Sangowicz, J. (1962). Psychodynamics of father-daughter incest. *Canadian Psychiatric Association Journal, 7,* 207–212.

Cornell, C. P., & Gelles, R. J. (1982). Adolescent to parent violence. *Urban Social Change Review, 15* (Winter), 8–14.

Costell, R. M. (1980). The nature and treatment of male sex offenders. In B. Jones (Ed.), *Sexual Abuse of Children: Selected Readings.* Washington, DC: National Center on Child Abuse and Neglect, (OHDS) 78–30161.

Costello, A. J. (1984). Assessment of children and adolescents: An overview. *Psychiatric Annals, 15* (11), 15–24.

Court, J., & Kerr, A. (1971). The battered child syndrome—2: A preventable disease? *Nursing Times, 67* (23), 695–697.

Courtois, C. (1979). The incest experience and its aftermath. *Victimology: An International Journal, 4,* 337–347.

Craft, M. (1965). *Ten Studies into Psychopathic Personality*. Bristol: John Wright and Sons.

Crites, J. D. (1964). Test review of C.P.I. and client personalities. *Journal of Counseling Psychology, 11*, 294–306.

Crittendon, O. M. (1981). Abusing, neglecting, problematic, and adequate dyads: Differentiating by patterns of interaction. *Merrill-Palmer Quarterly, 27*, 201–218.

D'Agnostino, P. (1975). Strains and stresses in protective services. In N. B. Ebeling & D. A. Hill (Eds.), *Child Abuse: Intervention and Treatment*. Acton, MA: Publishing Services Group.

Daiches, S. (1982, November). *Risk assessment: A guide for adult protective services workers*. Paper presented to Arizona State Department of Economic Security, Adult Protective Services Division, Phoenix, AZ. (mimeo)

Daly, M., & Wilson, M. I. (1980). Abuse and neglect of children in evolutionary perspective. In R. D. Alexander & D. W. Tinkle (Eds.), *Natural Selection and Social Behavior*. New York: Cheron.

Daniel, J. H., Hampton, R. L., & Newberger, E. H. (1983) Child abuse and accidents in Black families: A comparative study. *American Journal of Orthopsychiatry, 53* (4), 645–653.

Daniels, A. M. (1969). Reaching unwed mothers. *American Journal of Nursing, 69*, 332–335.

Davidson, H. A. (1980). *Representing Children and Parents in Abuse and Neglect Cases*. Washington, DC: American Bar Association/National Legal Resource Center for Child Advocacy and Protection.

Davidson, H. A. (1981). *The Guardian Ad Litem. An Important Approach to the Protection of Children and Legal Challenges in Child Protection-An Agenda for the 80's in Protecting Children Through the Legal System*. Washington, DC: American Bar Association/National Legal Resource Center for Child Advocacy and Protection.

DeFrancis, V. (1969). *Protecting the Child Victim of Sex Crimes Committed by Adults*. Denver, CO: American Humane Association.

DeJong, A. R. (1983, May). *Predictors of depression in sexually abused children*. Paper presented at Society for Developmental and Behavioral Pediatrics First Annual Meeting.

DeJong, A. R., Hervada, A. A., & Emmett, G. A. (1983). Epidemiologic variations in childhood sexual abuse. *Child Abuse and Neglect, 17* (2), 155–162.

DeLeon, C. A. (1961). Threatened homicide: A medical emergency. *Journal of the National Medical Association, 53*, 467–474.

deLissovoy, V. (1973). Child care by adolescent parents. *Children Today, 2*, 22–25.

Densen-Gerber, J. (1978, September). *Legislative response and treatment challenges*. Paper presented to Second International Congress of Child Abuse and Neglect, London.

Derdeyn, A. P. (1983). Depression in childhood. *Child Psychiatry and Human Development, 14* (1), 16–29.

Deschner, J. P. (1984). *The Hitting Habit: Anger Control for Battering Couples.* New York: Free Press.

Deschner, J. P., Geddes, C., Grimes, V., & Stancukas, E. (1980). *Battered women: Factors associated with abuse.* Arlington: University of Texas at Arlington/Graduate School of Social Work (duplicated).

DeYoung, M. (1982). *The Sexual Victimization of Children.* Jefferson, NC: McFarland.

Dibble, U. G., & Straus, M. A. (1980). Some social structure determinants of inconsistency between attitudes and behavior: The case of family violence. *Journal of Marriage and the Family, 42,* 71–80.

Dix, G. (1976). "Civil" commitment of the mentally ill and the need for data on the prediction of dangerousness. *American Behavioral Scientist, 19,* 318–334.

Dixen, J., & Jenkins, J. O. (1981). Incestuous child sexual abuse: A review of treatment strategies. *Clinical Psychology Review, 1* (2), 211–222.

Dobash, R. E., & Dobash, R. (1979). *Violence Against Wives.* New York: Free Press.

Dollard, J., Doob, L., Miller, N. E., Mower, O. H., & Sears, R. (1939). *Frustration and Aggression.* New Haven, CT: Yale University Press.

Douglas, R. L. (1983). Opportunities for prevention of domestic neglect and abuse of the elderly. *Prevention in Human Services, 3* (1).

Douglas, R. L. (1983). Domestic neglect and abuse of the elderly: Implications for research and services *Family Relations, 32,* 395–402.

Douglas, R. L., & Hickey, T. (1983). Domestic neglect and abuse of the elderly: Research findings and a systems perspective for service delivery planning. In J. I. Kosberg (Ed.), *Abuse and Maltreatment of the Elderly: Causes and Interventions.* Boston: John Wright PSG.

Drotar, D., Baskiewicz, A., Irvin, N., Kennell, J., & Klaus, M. (1974). The adaptation of parents to the birth of an infant with a congenital malformation: A hypothetical model. *Case Western Reserve Pediatrics, 56* (5), 710–717.

Dubanoski, R. A., Evans, I. M., & Higuchi, A. N. (1978). A behavioral approach to the analysis and treatment of child abuse. *Child Abuse and Neglect, 2* (1), 153–172.

Duberman, L. (1975). *The Reconstituted Family: A Study of Remarried Couples and Their Children.* Chicago: Nelson-Hall.

Dumas, J. E., & Wahler, R. G. (1983). Predictors of treatment outcome in parent training: Mother insularity and socioeconomic disadvantage. *Behavioral Assessment, 5,* 301–313.

Dunn, L. M. (1965). *Expanded Manual for the Peabody Picture Vocabulary Test.* Circle Pines, MN: American Guidance Service.

Duquette, D. N. (1981). The legal aspects of child abuse and neglect and legal roles. In K. C. Faller (Ed.), *Social Work with Abused and Neglected Children: A Manual of Interdisciplinary Practice*. New York: Free Press.

Dyas v. U.S., 376 A.2d 827 (D.C. 1977).

Ebeling, N. B., & Hill, D. A. (Eds.). (1975). *Child Abuse: Intervention and Treatment*. Acton, MA: Publishing Sciences Group.

Edleson, J. L. (1984). Working with men who batter. *Social Work, 29* (3), 237–242.

Egeland, B., Sroufe, L. A., & Erickson, M. (1983). The developmental consequence of different patterns of maltreatment. *Child Abuse and Neglect, 7* (4), 459–470.

Elbow, M. (1977). Theoretical considerations of violent marriages. *Social Casework, 58* (9), 515–526.

Ellis, A. (1970). *The Essence of Rational Psychotherapy: A Comprehensive Approach to Treatment*. New York: Institute for Rational Living.

Ellis, A. (1976). Techniques of handling anger in marriage. *Journal of Marriage and Family Counseling, 2*, 305–315.

Elmer, E. (1967). *Children in Jeopardy: A Study of Abused Minors and Their Families*. Pittsburgh: University of Pittsburgh.

Elmer, E. (1977). A follow-up study of traumatized children. *Pediatrics, 59* (2), 2730279.

Elmer, E., & Gregg, G. S. (1967). Developmental characteristics of abused children. *Pediatrics, 40*, 596–602.

Erickson, E. H. (1963). *Childhood and Society*. New York: Norton.

Estroff, T. W., Herrara, C., Gaines, R., Slaffer, D., Gould, M., & Green, A. (1984). Maternal psychopathology and perceptions of child behavior in psychiatrically referred and child maltreatment families. *Journal of the American Academy of Child Psychiatry, 23* (6), 649–652.

Fairborough, N., & Litman, R. E. (1975). Suicide prevention. In H.L.P. Resnick, H. L. Ruben, & D. D. Ruben (Eds.), *Emergency Psychiatric Care: The Management of Mental Health Crisis*. Bowie, MD: Charles Press.

Falcioni, D. (1982). Assessing the abused elderly. *Journal of Gerontological Nursing, 8* (4), 208–212.

Faller, K. C. (1981). *Social Work With Abused and Neglected Children: A Manual of Interdisciplinary Practice*. New York: Free Press.

Farrington, K. (1978). A general stress theory of intra-family violence. In M. A. Straus and G. Hotaling (Eds.), *The Social Causes of Husband-Wife Violence*. Minneapolis: University of Minnesota Press [reprinted, 1980].

Faulk, M. (1984). Men who assault their wives. *Medicine, Science, and the Law, 14*, 180–183.

Faulkner, L. R. (1982). Mandating the reporting of suspected cases of elder abuse: An inappropriate, ineffective, and ageist response to the abuse of older adults. *Family Law Quarterly, 16* (1), 69–91.

Felman, Y. M., & Nikitas, S. A. (1983). Sexually transmitted diseases and child sexual abuse. *New York State Journal of Medicine, 83* (5), 714–716.

Ferguson, D., & Beck, C. (1983). Half tool for assessment of elder abuse. *Geriatric Nurse,* (Sept.–Oct.), 301–304.

Ferracuti, F. (1972). Incest between father and daughter. In H.L.P. Reshick & M. E. Wolfgang (Eds.), *Sexual Behaviors.* Boston: Little-Brown.

Ferraro, K. J. (1983). Rationalizing violence: How battered women stay. *Victimology, 8* (3–4), 204–208.

Ferraro, K. J. (1984, August). *An existential approach to battering.* Paper presented to the Second Family Violence Researchers Conference. Durham: NH.

Feshback, S. (1980). Child abuse and the dynamics of human aggression and violence. In G. Gerbner, C. Ross, & E. Zigler (Eds.), *Child Abuse: An Agenda for Action.* New York: Oxford University Press.

Fields, M. (1978). Wife beating: Government intervention policies and practices. In U.S. Civil Rights Commission (Ed.), *Battered Women: Issues of Public Policy.* Washington, DC: Government Printing Office.

Finkelhor, D. (1979). *Sexually Victimized Children.* New York: Free Press.

Finkelhor, D. (1981). *Four pre-conditions of sexual abuse: A model.* Paper presented at first National Family Violence Researchers Conference, Durham, NJ.

Finkelhor, D. (1983). Common features of family abuse. In D. Finkelhor et al. (Eds.), *The Dark Side of Families: Current Family Violence Research.* Beverly Hills, CA: Sage Publications.

Finkelhor, D. (1984). *Child Sexual Abuse: New Theory and Research.* New York: Free Press.

Finkelhor, D. (1986). *A Sourcebook on Child Sexual Abuse.* Beverly Hills, CA: Sage Publications.

Finkelhor, D., Gelles, R. J., Hotaling, G. T., & Straus, M. A. (Eds.). (1984). *The Dark Side of Families: Current Family Violence Research.* Beverly Hills, CA: Sage Publications.

Flammang, C. J. (1980). Interviewing child victims of sex offenders. In L. G. Schultz (Ed.), *The Sexual Victimology of Youth.* Springfield, IL: Charles C Thomas.

Flannery, E. J. (1979). Synopsis: Standards relating to abuse and neglect. In R. Bourne & E. H. Newberger (Eds.), *Critical Perspectives on Child Abuse.* Lexington, MA: Lexington Books.

Fleming, J. B. (1979). *Stopping Wife Abuse.* Garden City, NY: Anchor Press/Doubleday.

Fletcher, G. J. O. (1984). Psychology and common sense. *American Psychologist, 39* (3), 203–213.

Folstein, M. G. (1975). Mini-mental state: A practical method for grading the cognitive state of patients for the clinician. *Journal of Psychiatric Research, 12,* 189–198.

Fontana, V. J. (1973). *Somewhere a Child is Crying: Maltreatment Causes and Prevention*, New York: Macmillan.

Fote, D. J. (1985). Child witness in sexual abuse criminal proceedings: Their capabilities, special problems, and proposals for reform. *Pepperdine Law Review, 13* (1), 157–184.

Francke, L. B. (1983). *Growing Up Divorced.* New York: Linden Press/Simon and Schuster.

Fraser, B. G. (1978). The Court's Role. In B. D. Schmitt (Ed.), *The Child Protection Team Handbook: A Multidisciplinary Approach to Managing Child Abuse and Neglect.* New York: Garland STPM Press.

Friedman, R. (1976). Child abuse: A review of the psychosocial research. In Hefner & Co. (Eds.), *Four Perspectives on the Status of Child Abuse and Neglect.* New York: Hefern.

Friedrich, W. N., & Borishin, J. A. (1976). The role of the child in abuse: A review of the literature. *American Journal of Orthopsychiatry, 46* (4), 580–590.

Friedrich, W. N., & Einbender, A. J. (1983). The abused child: A psychological review. *Journal of Clinical Child Psychology, 12* (3), 244–258.

Frodi, A. M. (1981). Contributions of infant characteristics to child abuse. *American Journal of Mental Deficiency, 85*, 341–349.

Frodi, A. M., & Lamb, M. B. (1980). Child abusers' responses to infant smiles and cries. *Child Development, 51*, 238–241.

Frommer, E., & O'Shea, G. (1973a). Antenatal identification of women liable to have problems in managing their infants. *British Journal of Psychiatry, 123*, 149–156.

Frommer, E., & O'Shea, G. (1973b). The importance of childhood experiences in relation to problems of marriage and family building. *British Journal of Psychology, 123, 157–160.*

Fulmer, T. T., & Cahill, V. M. (1984). Assessing elder abuse. *Journal of Gerontological Nursing, 10* (12), 16–20.

Funk, J. B. (1981). Consultation in the management of sexual molestation. *Journal of Clinical Child Psychology, 10* (2), 83–85.

Furniss, T. (1983). Mutual influence and interlocking professional-family process in the treatment of child sexual abuse and incest. *Child Abuse and Neglect, 7* (2), 207–224.

Furstenberg, F. F., Jr. (1976). *Unplanned Parenthood: The Social Consequences of Teenage Childbearing.* New York: Macmillan.

Furstenberg, F. F., Jr. (1981). Implicating the family: Teenage parenthood and kinship involvement. In T. Ooms (Ed.), *Teenage Pregnancy in a Family Context.* Philadelphia: Temple University Press.

Gabinet, L. (1979). MMPI profiles of high risk and outpatient mothers. *Child Abuse and Neglect, 3*, 373–379.

Gabinet, L. (1983). Child abuse treatment failures reveal need for redefinition of the problem. *Child Abuse and Neglect, 7* (4), 395–402.

Gaensbauer, T. J., & Sands, K. (1980). Distorted affective communications in abused/neglected infants and their potential impact on caretakers. *Journal of the American Academy of Child Psychiatry, 18*, 236–251.

Gagnon, J. (1965). Female child victims of sex offenses. *Social Problems, 13*, 176–192.

Galambos, N. L., & Dixon, R. A. (1984). Adolescent abuse and the development of a personal sense of control. *Child Abuse and Neglect, 8* (3), 285–293.

Galbraith, M. W., & Zdcrkowski, R. T. (1984). Teaching the investigation of elder abuse. *Journal of Gerontological Nursing, 10* (12), 21–25.

Galdston, R. (1975). Preventing the abuse of little children. *American Journal of Orthopsychiatry, 45*, 372–381.

Gallahorn, G. E. (1981). Borderline personality disorders. In J. R. Lion (Ed.), *Personality Disorders: Diagnosis and Management*. Baltimore: Williams & Wilkins.

Gambrill, E. (1981). The use of behavioral procedures in cases of child abuse and neglect. *International Journal of Behavioral Social Work and Abstracts, 1*, 3–26.

Ganley, A. L. (1981). Counseling programs for men who batter: Elements of effective programs. *Response, 4* (8), 3–4.

Ganley, A., & Harris, L. (1978, August). *Domestic violence: Issues in designing and implementing programs for male batterers*. Paper presented to American Psychological Association Annual Meeting, Toronto, Canada.

Garbarino, J. (1977a). The human ecology of child maltreatment. *Journal of Marriage and the Family, 39* (4), 721–735.

Garbarino, J. (1977b). The price of privacy in the social dynamics of child abuse. *Child Welfare, 56* (9), 567–575.

Garbarino, J. (1980). Meeting the needs of mistreated youths. *Social Work, 25* (2), 122–126.

Garbarino, J. (1984a). Adolescent maltreatment: A guide for practice and policy applications for adolescent mental health. *Adolescent Mental Health Abstracts, 2* (2), 1–110.

Garbarino, J. (1984b). What have we learned about child maltreatment? In *Perspectives on Child Maltreatment in the Mid '80's*. Washington, DC: National Center on Child Abuse and Neglect.

Garbarino, J., & Crouter, A. (1978). Defining the community context for parent-child relations: The correlates of child maltreatment. *Child Development, 49*, 604–616.

Garbarino, J., & Gilliam, G. (1980). *Understanding Abusive Families*. Lexington, MA: D. C. Heath.

Garbarino, J., & Sherman, D. (1980). High risk neighborhoods and high risk families: The human ecology of child maltreatment. *Child Development, 51*, 188–198.

Garbarino, J., & Stocking, S. H. (1980). *Protecting Children from Abuse and Neglect.* San Francisco, CA: Jossey-Bass.

Garmezy, N. (1974). The study of competence in children at risk for severe psychopathology. In E. J. Anthony & C. Koupernik (Eds.), *The Child in His Family: Children at Psychiatric Risk.* New York: John Wiley.

Gaudin, J. M., & Pollane, L. (1983). Social networks, stress, and child abuse. *Children and Youth Services Review, 5* (1), 91–102.

Gayford, J. J. (1975a) Wife battering: a preliminary survey of 100 cases. *British Medical Journal, 5951* (1), 194–197.

Gayford, J. J. (1975b). Battered wives. *Medicine, Science, and the Law, 15,* 237–243.

Gebhard, P. H., & Gagnon, J. H. (1964). Male sex offenders against very young children. *American Journal of Psychiatry, 121,* 576–579.

Gebhard, P. H., Gagnon, J. H., Pomeroy, W. B., & Christenson, C. V. (1965). *Sex offenders: An Analysis of Types.* New York: Harper & Row.

Gedo, J. E., & Goldberg, A. (1973). *Models of the Mind.* Chicago: University of Chicago Press.

Geller, J. A., & Walsh, J. C. (1977). A treatment model for the abused spouse. *Victimology, 2* (2), 627–632.

Gelles, R. J. (1973). Child abuse as psychopathology: A sociological critique and reformulation. *American Journal of Orthopsychiatry, 43* (4), 611–621.

Gelles, R. J. (1974). *The Violent Home.* Beverly Hills, CA: Sage Publications.

Gelles, R. J. (1976). Abused wives: Why do they stay? *Journal of Marriage and the Family, 38* (November), 659–668.

Gelles, R. J. (1978a). Violence toward children in the United States. *Journal of Orthopsychiatry, 48,* 580–592.

Gelles, R. J. (1978b). Violence in the American family. In J. P. Martin (Ed.), *Violence and the Family.* New York: John Wiley.

Gelles, R. J. (1979). *Family Violence.* Beverly Hills, CA: Sage Publications.

Gelles, R. J. (1980). Violence in the family: A review of research in the seventies. *Journal of Marriage and the Family,* (November), 873–885.

Gelles, R. J. (1982). Applying research on family violence to clinical practice. *Journal of Marriage and Family, 44* (1), 9–20.

Gelles, R. J., & Fedrick-Cornell, C. (1985). *Intimate Violence in Families.* Beverly Hills, CA: Sage Publications.

Gelles, R. J., & Straus, M. A. (1978). Determinants of violence in the family: Toward a theoretical integration. In W. Burr et al., (Eds.), *Contemporary Theories About the Family* (vol. I). New York: Free Press.

Gelles, R. J., & Straus, M. A. (1980). Physical violence in families. In E. Corfman (Ed.), *Families Today—A Research Sampler on Families.* Washington, DC: Government Printing Office.

George, C. E., & Main, M. (1979). Social interactions of young abused children: Approach, avoidance, & aggression. *Child Development, 50,* 306–318.

George, C., & Main, M. M. (1980). Abused children: Their rejection of peers and caregivers. In T. M. Field (Ed.), *High Risk Infants and Children: Adult and Peer Interactions.* New York: Academic Press.

Gerbner, G., Ross, C. J., & Zigler, E. (1980). *Child Abuse: An Agenda for Action.* New York: Oxford University Press.

Giaretto, H. (1976). Humanistic treatment of father-daughter incest. In R. Kempe & C. H. Kempe (Eds.), *Child Abuse and Neglect: The Family and Community.* Cambridge, MA: Ballinger.

Giaretto, H. A. (1982). *Integrated Treatment of Child Sexual Abuse.* Palo Alto, CA: Science and Behavior Books.

Gil, D. (1970). *Violence Against Children.* Cambridge, MA: Harvard University Press.

Giles-Sims, J. (1983). *Wife-Battering: A Systems Theory Approach.* New York: Guilford Press.

Giles-Sims, J., & Finkelhor, D. (1984). Child abuse in stepfamilies. *Family Relations, 33* (3), 407–413.

Giordano, N. H., & Giordano, J. A. (1984a). Elder abuse: A review of the literature. *Social Work, 29* (3), 232–237.

Giordano, N. H., & Giordano, J. A. (1984b, August). *Domestic violence: Profiles and predictors of five types of elder abuse.* Second Family Violence Researchers Conference, Durham, NH.

Giovannoni, J. M., & Bercerra, R. M. (1979). *Defining Child Abuse.* New York: Free Press.

Gionabboni, J., & Billingsley, A. (1970). Child neglect among the poor: A study of parental adequacy in families of three ethnic groups. *Child Welfare* 49 (4), 196–204.

Glasner, A. J. (1981). The incidence of adult sexual dysfunction in people who were sexually molested during childhood. *Dissertation Abstracts Int. 41* (8), 3159–8.

Glasser, W. (1965). *Reality Therapy: A New Approach to Psychiatry.* New York: Harper & Row.

Goldfried, M. R. (1982). Resistance and clinical behavior therapy. In P. L. Wachtel (Ed.), *Resistance: Psychodynamic and Behavioral Approaches.* New York: Plenum Press.

Goldstein, A. P. (1973). *Structured Learning Therapy: Toward a Psychotherapy for the Poor.* New York: Academic Press.

Goldstein, J., Freud, A., & Solnit, A. J. (1973). *Beyond the Best Interests of the Child.* New York: Free Press.

Goldstein, J., Freud, A., & Solnit, A. (1979). *Before the Best Interests of the Child.* New York: Free Press.

Goldstein, R. (1974). Brain research and violent behavior. *Archives of Neurology, 30,* 1–18.

Goode, W. J. (1971). Force and violence in the family. *Journal of Marriage and the Family, 33,* 624–636.

Goodman, G. S. (1984a). Children's testimony in historical perspective. *Journal of Social Issues, 40* (2), 9–32.

Goodman, G. S. (1984b). The child witness: Conclusions and future directions for research and legal practice. *Journal of Social Issues, 40* (2), 157–176.

Goodman, G. S. (1984c). The accuracies and inaccuracies of children's eyewitness reports. In *Multidisciplinary Advocacy for Mistreated Children.* Denver: National Association of Counsel for Children.

Goodman, G. S., & Helgeson, V. S. (1985). Child sexual assault: Children's memory and the law. In American Bar Association (Ed.), *National Policy Conference on Legal Reforms in Child Sexual Abuse Cases.* Washington, DC: National Legal Resource Center for Child Advocacy and Protection.

Goodwin, J., Cormier, L., & Owen, J. (1983). Grandfather-granddaughter incest: A trigenerational view. *Child Abuse & Neglect, 17* (2), 163–170.

Goodwin, J. (1982). *Sexual Abuse: Incest Victims and Their Families.* Boston: John Wright PSG.

Goodwin, J., & DiVasto, P. (1979). Mother-daughter incest. *Child Abuse and Neglect, 3* (3/4), 953–957.

Goodwin, J., McCarthy, T., & DiVasto, P. (1981). Prior incest in mothers of abused children. *Child Abuse and Neglect, 5*, 87–95.

Gordon, V. C., & Ledray, L. E. (1985). Depression in women: The challenge of treatment and prevention. *Journal of Psychosocial Nursing, 23* (1), 26–32.

Graham, M. H. (1985). Child sex abuse prosecutions: Hearsay and confrontation clause issues. In *American Bar Association National Policy Conference on Legal Reforms in Child Sexual Abuse Cases.* Washington, DC: National Legal Resource Center for Child Advocacy and Protection.

Green, A. (1983). Dimensions of psychological trauma in abused children. *Journal of the American Academy of Child Psychiatry, 22*, 231–237.

Green, A. H. (1984a). Child maltreatment: Recent studies and future directions. *Journal of the American Academy of Child Psychiatry*, 675–678.

Green, A. H. (1984b). Child abuse by siblings. *Child Abuse and Neglect, 8* (3), 311–317.

Green, A. H., Gaines, R. W., & Sandgrund, A. (1974). Child Abuse: Pathological syndrome of family interaction. *American Journal of Psychiatry, 131* (8), 882–886.

Green, A. H., Voeller, K., Gaines, R. W., & Kubie, J. (1981). Neurological impairment in maltreated children. *Child Abuse and Neglect, 3*, 129–134.

Greenberg, M. S., & Silverstein, M. C. (1983). Cognitive and behavioral treatments of depressive disorders: Interventions with adults. In H. C. Morrison (Ed.), *Children of Depressed Parents*, New York: Grune & Stratton.

Greenspan, S. I. (1981). *The Clinical Interview of the Child.* New York: McGraw-Hill.

Gregg, G. S., & Elmer, E. (1969). Infant injuries: Accident or abuse? *Pediatrics, 44*, 434–439.

Groth, A. N. (1978). Sexual trauma in the life histories of rapists and child molesters. *Victimology, 4* (1), 10–16.

Groth, A. N., Hobson, W., & Gary, T. (1982). The child molester: Clinical observations. In J. Conte & D. Shore (Eds.), *Social Work and Child Sexual Abuse*. New York: Haworth Press.

Gutheil, T. G., & Appelbaum, P. S. (1982). *Clinical Handbook of Psychiatry and the Law*. New York: McGraw-Hill.

Guerin, P. J., Jr. (Ed.), (1976). *Family Therapy: Theory and Practice*. New York: Gardner Press.

Guggenheim, M. (1984). The right to be represented but not heard: Reflections on legal representation for children. *New York University Law Review, 29*, April.

Guttmacher, M. (1960). *The Mind of the Murderer*. New York: Farrar, Straus, & Cudahy.

Guttmacher, M. S. (1961). *Sex Offenses: The Problem, Causes and Prevention.* New York: W. W. Norton.

Haley, J. (1976). *Problem-Solving Therapy*. New York: Harper & Row.

Hammer, E. F. (1960). *The Clinical Application of Projective Drawings*. Springfield, IL: Charles C Thomas.

Hampton, R. L. (1984, August). *Child maltreatment: A comparison of Black, White, and Hispanic cases.* Paper presented to the Second Family Violence Researchers Conference, Durham, NH.

Haralambie, A. M. (1982). Experts in custody cases. In National Association of Counsel for Children (Eds.), *Practical Child Advocacy*. Denver: National Association of Counsel for Children.

Haralambie, A. M. (1983). *Handling Child Custody Cases*. Colorado Springs: Shepard's/McGram-Hill Family Law Series.

Harbin, H. T. (1981). Family therapy with personality disorders. In J. R. Lion (Ed.), *Personality Disorders: Diagnosis and management (Revised for DSM-III*. Baltimore: Williams & Wilkins.

Harbin, H., & Madden, D. (1979). Battered parents: A new syndrome. *American Journal of Psychiatry, 136* (October), 1288–1291.

Hardy, J. B., Welcher, D. W., Stanley, J., & Dallas, J. R. (1978). Long range outcomes of adolescent pregnancy. *Clinical Obstetrics and Gynecology, 21*, 1215–1232.

Harper, S. (1979, May). *Violent men and fathers.* Paper presented to the Conference on Battered Women: Learning How to Help, University of Texas at Arlington.

Harrer, M. N. (1981). *Father-Daughter Incest: A Study of the Mother*. Ann Arbor, MI: Dissertation Abstracts International, 41 (12): 4665–B.

Harrison, P. A., & Lumry, A. E. (1984, August). *Female sexual abuse victims' perspectives on family dysfunction, substance use, and psychiatric disorders*. Paper presented to the Second Family Violence Researchers Conference, Durham, NH.

Heim, N. (1981). Sexual behavior of castrated sex offenders *Archives of Sexual Behavior, 10* (1), 11–19.

Helfer, R. E. (1975). *The Diagnostic Process and Treatment Programs*. Washington, DC: Government Printing Office.

Helfer, R. E. (1979). *Childhood Comes First: A Crash Course in Childhood for Parents*. East Lansing, MI: Author.

Henderson, J. (1972). Incest: A synthesis of data. *Canadian Psychiatric Association Journal, 17*, 299–313.

Herman, J. (1983). Recognition and treatment of incestuous families. *International Journal of Family Therapy, 5* (2), 81–91.

Herman, J., & Hirschman, L. (1977). Father-daughter incest. *Signs, 2*, 1–22.

Herrenkohl, E. C., & Herrenkohl, R. C. (1979). A comparison of abused children and their nonabused siblings. *Journal of the American Academy of Child Psychiatry, 18*, 260–269.

Herrenkohl, R. C., Herrenkohl, E. C., & Egolf, B. P. (1983). Circumstances surrounding the occurrence of child maltreatment. *Journal of Consulting and Clinical Psychology, 51* (3), 424–431.

Herrenkohl, R. C., Herrenkohl, E. C., Egolf, B. P., & Secch, M. (1979). The repetition of child abuse: How frequently does it occur? *Child Abuse and Neglect, 3*, 67–72.

Herrenkohl, E. C., Herrenkohl, R. C., Toedter, L., & Yanushefski, A. M. (1984). Parent-child interaction in abusive and non-abusive families. *Journal of the American Academy of Child Psychiatry, 23* (6), 641–648.

Hertz, D. G. (1977). Psychological implication of adolescent pregnancy: Patterns of family interaction in adolescent mothers-to-be. *Psychodynamics, 18*, 13–20.

Herzberger, S. D. (1983). Social cognition and the transmission of abuse. In D. Finkelhor et al. (Eds.), *The Dark Side of Families*. Beverly Hills, CA: Sage Publications.

Hetherington, E. M. (1979). Divorce: A child's perspective. *American Psychologist, 34* (10), 851–858.

Hetherington, E. M., Cox, M., & Cox, R. (1977). The aftermath of divorce. In J. H. Stevens & M. Matthews (Eds.), *Mother-Child-Father-Child Relations*. Washington, DC: National Association for the Education of Young Children.

Hickey, T., & Douglas, R. L. (1981a). Mistreatment of the elderly in the domestic setting: An exploratory study. *American Journal of Public Health, 71* (5), 500–507.

Hickey, T., & Douglas, R. L. (1981b). Neglect and abuse of older family members: Professional's perspectives and case experiences. *Gerontologist, 21* (2), 174–178.

Hilberman, E. (1980). Overview: The "wife beater's wife" reconsidered. *American Journal of Psychiatry, 137* (11), 1336–1345.

Hill, D. A. (1975). Child abuse: Early case finding in a hospital setting. In N. B. Ebeling & D. A. Hill (Eds.), *Child Abuse: Intervention and Treatment.* Acton, MA: Publishing Sciences Group.

Hindman, M. H. (1977). Child abuse and neglect: The alcohol connection. *Alcohol Health and Research World, 1* (3), 2–7.

Hindman, M. H. (1979). Family violence. *Alcohol Health and Research World, 4* (1), 2–10.

Hjorth, C. W., & Ostrow, E. (1982). The self-image of physically abused adolescents. *Journal of Youth and Adolescence, 11* (2), 71–76

Hoekstra, K.O.C. (1984). Ecologically defining the mistreatment of adolescents. *Children and Youth Services Review, 6* 285–298.

Hodges, F. C., Weschler, R. C., & Ballantine, C. (1978, August). *Divorce and the preschool child: Cumulative stress.* American Psychological Association Meeting, Toronto, Canada.

Hoffman-Plotkin, D., & Twentyman, C. F. (1984). A multimodal assessment of behavioral and cognitive deficits in abused and neglected preschoolers. *Child Development, 55,* 794–800.

Holmes, M. B. (1978). *Child Abuse and Neglect Programs: Practice and Theory.* Washington, DC: National Institute of Mental Health.

Holmes, T. H., & Rahe, R. H. (1967). The social readjustment rating scale. *Journal of Psychosomatic Research, 11* (2), 213–218.

Holter, J. C., & Friedman, S. B. (1968). Principles of management in child abuse cases. *American Journal of Orthopsychiatry, 38,* 127–136.

Hooyman, N. R. (1983). Abuse and neglect: Community interventions. In J. I. Kosberg (Ed.), *Abuse and Maltreatment of the Elderly.* Boston: John Wright PSG.

Hornung, C., McCullough, B., & Sugimoto, T. (1981). Status Relationships in marriage: Risk factors in spouse abuse. *Journal of Marriage and the Family, 43* (August), 679–692.

Horowitz, M. J. (1983). Post-traumatic stress disorders. *Behavioral Sciences and the Law, 1* (3), 9–24.

Horstman, P. M. (1975). Protective services for the elderly: The limits of parens patriae. In J. A. Weiss (Ed.), *Law of the Elderly.* New York: Practicing Law Institute.

Howells, K. (1981). Adult sexual interest in children: Considerations relevant to theories of etiology. In M. Cook & K. Howells (Eds.), *Adult Sexual Interest in Children.* New York: Academic Press.

Howze, D. C., & Kotch, J. B. (1984). Disentangling life events, stress, and social support: Implications for the primary prevention of child abuse and neglect. *Child Abuse and Neglect, 8* (4), 401–410.

Hunter, R. S., Kilstrom, N., Kraybill, E. N., & Loda, F. (1978). Antecedents of child abuse and neglect in premature infants: A prospective study in a newborn intensive care unit. *Pediatrics, 61* (4) 629–635.

Ibn-Tamas v. U.S., 407 A.2d 626 (D.C. 1979).

James, B., & Nasjleti, M. (1983) *Treating Sexually Abused Children and Their Families*. Palo Alto, CA: Consulting Psychologists Press.

James, J., & Meyerding, J. (1977). Early sexual experiences and prostitution. *American Journal of Psychiatry, 134*, 1381–1385.

Janas, C. (1983). Family violence and child sexual abuse. *Medical Hypnoanalysis, 4* (2), 68–76.

Jason, J. (1984). Centers for disease control and epidemiology of violence. *Child Abuse and Neglect, 8* (3), 279–283.

Jayaratne, S. (1977). Child abusers as parents and children: A review. *Social Work, 22* (1), 5–9.

Johnson, B., & Morse, H. A. (1968). Injured children and their parents. *Children, 15*, 147–152

Johnson, J. (1981). Program enterprise and official cooptation in the battered women's shelter movement. *American Behavioral Scientist, 24* (6), 827–842.

Johnson, J. M., & Ferraro, K. J. (1984). The victimized self: The case of battered women. In J. A. Kotarba & A. Fontana (Eds.), *The Existential Self in Society*. Chicago: University of Chicago Press.

Johnson, M. K., & Foley, M. A. (1984). Differentiating fact from fantasy: The reliability of children's memory. *Journal of Social Issues, 40* (2), 33–50.

Johnston, M. E. (1984, August). *Correlates of early violence experience among men who are abusive toward female mates*. Second Family Violence Researchers Conference, Durham: NH.

Jones, D.P.H., & McQuiston, M. (1984). Interviewing the sexually abused child: Principles and practice. In D. Bross (Ed.), *Multidisciplinary Advocacy for Mistreated Children*. Denver, CO: National Association of Counsel for Children.

Jones, D.P.H., & McQuiston, M. (1985). *Interviewing the Sexually Abused Child* (vol. 6). Denver: C. Henry Kempe National Center for the Prevention and Treatment of Child Abuse and Neglect.

Josiassen, R. C., Fantuzzo, J., & Rosen, A. C. (1980). Treatment of pedophilia using multistage aversion therapy and social skills training. *Journal of Behavior Therapy and Experimental Psychiatry, 11* (1), 55–61

Justice, B., & Duncan, D. F. (1976). Life crisis as a precursor to child abuse. *Public Health Reports, 91* (2), 110–115.

Justice, B., & Justice, R. (1976). *The Abusing Family*. New York: Human Sciences Press.

Justice, B., & Justice, R. (1979). *The Broken Taboo: Sex in the Family*. New York: Human Sciences Press.

Justice, B., & Justice, R. (1982). Clinical approaches to family violence. *Family Therapy Collections, 3*, 1–20.

Justice, B., Justice, R. & Kraft, J. (1974). Early warning signs of violence: Is a triad enough? *American Journal of Psychiatry, 131*, 457–459.

Kadushin, A., & Martin, J. A. (1981). *Child Abuse: An Interactional Event.* New York: Columbia University Press.

Kadushin, C. (1969). *Why People Go to Psychiatrists.* New York: Atherton.

Kahn, A. J., & Kammerman, S. B. (1980). Child abuse: A comparative perspective. In G. Gerbner et al. (Eds.), *Child Abuse and Agenda for Action.* New York: Oxford University Press.

Kalmuss, D. S., & Straus, M. A. (1983). Feminist, political, and economic determinants of wife abuse services. In D. Finkelhor et al. (Eds.), *The Dark Side of Families.* Beverly Hills, CA: Sage Publications.

Kaplan, S. L., & Kaplan, S. J. (1981). The child's accusation of sexual abuse during a divorce and custody struggle. *Hillside Journal of Clinical Psychiatry, 3* (1), 81–95.

Katz, K. D. (1980). Elder Abuse. *Journal of Family Law, 18* (4), 695–722.

Kaufman, A. S., & Kaufman, N. L. (1977). *Clinical Evaluation of Young Children with the McCarthy Scales.* New York: Grune & Stratton.

Kaufman, I. (1962). Psychiatric implications of physical abuse of children. In V. DeFrancis (Ed.), *Protecting the Battered Child.* Denver, CO: American Humane Association.

Kaufman, I., Peck, A. L., & Tagiuri, C. K. (1954). The family constellation and overt incestuous relations between father and daughter. *American Journal of Orthopsychiatry, 24,* 266–279.

Kelley, R. J. (1982). Behavioral re-orientation of pedophiliacs: Can it be done? *Clinical Psychology Review, 2,* 387–408.

Kempe, C. H., & Helfer, R. E. (1968). *The Battered Child* (3rd ed). Chicago: University of Chicago Press.

Kempe, C. H., & Helfer, R. E. (Eds.). (1972). *Helping the Battered Child and His Family.* Philadelphia: J.B. Lippincott.

Kempe, R. S., & Kempe, C. H. (1978). *Child Abuse.* Cambridge, MA: Harvard University Press.

Kempe, R. S., & Kempe, C. H. (1984). *The Common Secret: Sexual Abuse of Children and Adolescents.* New York: W. H. Freeman.

Kempe, C. H., Silverman, F. N., Steele, B. F., Droegemueller, W., & Silver, H. K. (1962). The battered child syndrome. *Journal of the American Medical Association, 181,* 17–24.

Kernberg, O. (1975). *Borderline Conditions and Pathological Narcissism.* New York: Jason Aronson.

Kilpatrick, D. G., & Amick, A. E. (1984, August). *Intrafamilial and extrafamilial sexual assault: Results of a random community survey.* Second Family Violence Researchers Conference, Durham, NH.

Kimball, W. H., Stewart, R. B., Conger, R. D., & Burgess, R. L. (1980). A comparison of family interaction in single-versus two-parent abusive, neglectful, and control families. In T. M. Field (Ed.), *High Risk Infants and Children: Adult and Peer Interactions.* New York: Academic.

Kinard, E. M. (1978). *Emotional Development in Physically Abused Children: A Study of Self-Concept and Aggression.* Palo Alto, CA: R & E Research Associates.

Kinard, E. M. (1980a). Emotional development in physically abused children. *American Journal of Orthopsychiatry, 50,* 686–696.

Kinard, E. M. (1980b). Mental health needs of abused children. *Child Welfare, 69* (8), 451–462.

Kinard, E. M. (1982). Experiencing child abuse: Effects on emotional adjustment. *American Journal of Orthopsychiatry, 52,* 82–91.

Kinard, E. M., & Klerman, L. V. (1980). Teenage parenting and child abuse: Are they related? *American Journal of Orthopsychiatry, 50,* 481–488.

Kirk, S. A., McCarthy, J. J., & Kirtz, W. D. (1968). *Examiner's Manual: Illinois Test of Psycholinguistic Abilities* (Rev. ed.). Urbana: University of Illinois Press.

Klein, M., & Stern, L. (1971). Low birthweight and the battered child syndrome. *American Journal of Diseases of Children, 122* (1), 15–18.

Klerman, G. L. (1975). Depression and adaptation. In R. J. Friedman & R. Katz (Eds.), *The Psychology of Depression: Contemporary Theory and Research.* Washington, DC: Government Printing Office.

Knutson, J. F. (1978). Child abuse research as an area of aggression. *Pediatric Psychology, 3* (1), 20–27.

Kocen, L., & Bulkley, J. (1984). Analysis of criminal child sex offense statutes. In J. Bulkley (Ed.), *Child Sexual Abuse and the Law* (5th Ed.). Washington, DC: American Bar Association.

Koch, M. (1980). Sexual abuse in children. *Adolescence, 15* (59), 643–648.

Kohut, H. (1975). *The Restoration of the Self.* New York: International Universities Press.

Koppotz, E. M. (1963). *The Bender-Gestalt Test for Young Children.* New York: Grune & Stratton.

Kosberg, J. I. (Ed.). (1983a). *Abuse and Maltreatment of the Elderly: Causes and Interventions.* Boston, MA: John Wright PSG.

Kosberg, J. I. (1983b). The special vulnerability of elderly parents. In J. I. Kosberg (Ed.), *Abuse and Maltreatment of the Elderly.* Boston, MA: John Wright PSG.

Kotelchuck, M., & Newberger, E. H. (1983). Failure to thrive: A controlled study of familial characteristics. *Journal of the American Academy of Child Psychiatry, 2,* 322–328.

Kovacs, M., & Beck, A. T. (1978). Maladaptive cognitive structures in depression. *American Journal of Psychiatry, 135,* 525–535.

Krauskopf, J. M. (1983). *Advocacy for the Aging.* St. Paul, MN: West Publishing.

Kroth, J. A. (1976). Family therapy impact on intrafamilial child sexual abuse. *Child Abuse and Neglect, 3* (1), 297–302.

LaBarbera, J. D., & Dozier, J. E. (1980). Hysterical seizures: The role of sexual exploitation. *Psychosomatics, 21* (11), 897–903.

LaBarbera, J. D., Martin, J. E., & Dozier, J. E. (1980). Child psychiatrists, view of father-daughter incest. *Child Abuse and Neglect, 4* (3), 147–151.

Labell, L. S. (1979). Wife abuse: A sociological study of battered women and their mates. *Victimology, 4* 258–267.

Lamb, M. E., Teti, D. M., Lewkowicz, K. S., & Malkin, C. M. (1985, June). *Intrafamilial child maltreatment and the child welfare system.* Paper presented for a Study Group, "Rethinking Child Welfare: International Perspectives," University of Minnesota, Minneapolis.

Landis, J. T. (1956). Experience of 500 children with adult's sexual relations. *Psychiatric Quarterly, 30*, 91–109.

Langevin, R. (1983). *Sexual Strands: Understanding and Treating Sexual Anomalies in Men.* Hillsdale, NJ: Lawrence Erlbaum Associates.

Langley, A. (1981). *Abuse of the Elderly.* Human Services Monograph Series, No. 27. Washington, DC: Project Share.

Langley, R., & Levy, C. R. (1977). *Wife-Beating: The Silent Crisis.* New York: Dutton.

Lanyon, R. F. (1985). Theory and treatment in child molestation. *Journal of Consulting and Clinical Psychology, 54* (2), 176–182.

Laszlo, A. T., & McKean, T. (1978). Court diversion: An alternative for spouse abuse cases. In *Battered Women: Issues of Public Policy.* Washington, DC: Commission on Civil Rights.

Lathrop, D. D. (1984). The care and feeding abrasiveness. In E. M. Stern (Ed.), *Psychotherapy and the Abrasive Patient.* New York: Haworth Press.

Latimer, P. R., & Sweet, A. A. (1984). Cognitive versus behavioral procedures in cognitive-behavior therapy: A critical review of the evidence. *Journal of Behavior Therapy and Experimental Psychiatry, 15*, (1), 9–22.

Lau, E. E., & Kosberg, J. I. (1979). Abuse of the elderly by informal care providers. *Aging, 299* (Summer), 10–15.

Laury, G. (1970). The battered child syndrome: Parental motivation, clinical aspects. *Bulletin of the New York Academy of Medicine, 46* (9), 676–685.

LaViolette, A. D., Barnett, O. W., & Miller, C. L. (1984, August). A classification of wife abusers on the *BEM* sex role inventory. Second Family Violence Researchers Conference, Durham, NH.

Lawton, M. P., & Brody, E. M. (1969). Assessment of older people: Self-maintaining and instrumental activities of daily living. *Gerontologist, 9*, 179–186.

Lazarus, A. A. (1981). *The Practice of Multi-Modal Therapy.* New York: McGraw-Hill.

Lazarus, A. A., & Fay, A. (1982). Resistance or rationalization? A cognitive-behavioral perspective. In P. L. Wachtel (Ed.), *Resistance: Psychodynamic and Behavioral Approaches.* New York: Plenum.

Leaff, L. A. (1981). Psychodynamic aspects of personality disorders. In J. R. Lion (Ed.), *Personality Disorders: Diagnosis and Management.* Baltimore: Williams & Wilkins.

Leaman, K. M. (1980). Sexual abuse: The reactions of child and family. In B. Jores (Ed.), *Sexual Abuse of Children: Selected Readings*. Washington, DC: National Center on Child Abuse and Neglect.

Lehmann, H. E. (1983). The clinician's view of anxiety and depression. *Journal of Clinical Psychiatry, 44* (8), 3–7.

Lennington, S. (1981). Child abuse: The limits of sociobiology. *Ethology and Sociobiology, 2*, 17–29.

Lerman, L. G. (1983). Legal help for battered women. In J. J. Costa (Ed.), *Abuse of Women: Legislation, Reporting, and Prevention*. Lexington, MA: Lexington Books.

Lerman, L. G. (1984). Mediation of wife abuse cases: The adverse impact of informal dispute resolution on women. *Harvard Women's Law Journal, 7*, 57–113.

Lerman, L. G., Landis, L., & Goldzweig, S. (1983). State legislation on domestic violence. In J. J. Costa (Ed.), *Abuse of Women: Legislation, Reporting, and Prevention*. Lexington, MA: Lexington Books.

Lerner, R., & Lerner, J. (1983). Temperament-intelligence reciprocities in early childhood: A contextual model. In M. Lewis (Ed.), *Origins of Intelligence* (2nd ed). New York: Plenum.

Levinger, G., & Moles, O. W. (Eds.). (1979). *Divorce and Separation: Context, Causes and Consequences*. New York: Basic Books.

Lewis-Herman, J. (1981). *Father-Daughter Incest*. Cambridge, MA: Harvard University Press.

Lewis, M., & Schaffer, S. (1981). Peer behavior and mother-infant interaction in maltreated children. In M. Lewis & L. A. Rosenblum (Eds.), *The Uncommon Child*. New York: Plenum.

Lewishon, P. M. (1974). A behavioral approach to depression. In R. Friedman & M. M. Katz (Eds.), *The Psychology of Depression: Contemporary Theory and Research*. Washington, DC: V. H. Winston.

Libai, D. (1980). The protection of the child victim of a sexual offense. In L. G. Schultz (Ed.), *The Sexual Victimology of Youth*. Springfield, IL: Charles C Thomas.

Light, R. (1974). Abused and neglected children in America: A study of alternative policies. *Harvard Educational Review, 43* (November), 556–598.

Liles, R., & Bulkley, J. (1984). Prior sexual acts of the defendant as evidence in prosecutions for child sexual abuse. In J. Bulkley (Ed.), *Child Sexual Abuse and the Law* (5th ed.). Washington, DC: American Bar Association.

Lincoln, R., Jaffe, F. S., & Ambrose, A. (1976). *Eleven Million Teenagers*. New York: Guttmacher Institute.

Lindberg, F. H., & Distad, L. J. (1985). Survival responses to incest: Adolescents in crisis. *Child Abuse and Neglect: The International Journal, 9*, 521–526.

Linnell, T., Zieman, G. L., & Romano, P. A. (1984). Treating abusive families in heterogeneous parent groups. *Family Therapy, 11* (1), 79–84.

Lion, J. R. (Ed.). (1981). *Personality Disorders: Diagnosis and Management (revised for DSM-III)* (2nd ed.). Baltimore: Williams & Wilkins.

Lloyd, D. W. (1984). The corroboration of sexual victimization of children. In J. Bulkley (Ed.), *Child Sexual Abuse and the Law* (5th ed.). Washington, DC: American Bar Association.

Lloyd, D. W. (1985). Practical issues in avoiding confrontation of a child witness and the defendant in a criminal trial. In American Bar Association (Ed.), *National Policy Conference on Legal Reforms in Child Sexual Abuse Cases.* Washington, DC: National Legal Resource Center for Child Advocacy and Protection.

Lofthus, E. F., & Davies, G. M. (1984). Distortions in the memory of children. *Journal of Social Issues, 40* (2), 51–68.

Long, L. L. (1982). When the client is a child: Dilemmas in the lawyer's role. *Journal of Family Law, 21*, 4.

Longfellow, C. (1979). Divorce in context: Its impact on children. In G. Levinger & O. W. Moles (Eds.), *Divorce & Separation: Context, Causes, and Consequences.* New York: Basic Books.

Lorenzi, M. (1977). Marital outcomes of adolescent pregnancy. *Adolescence, 12*, 13–22.

Lorion, R. F. (1974). Patient and therapist variables in the treatment of low-income patients. *Psychological Bulletin, 81*, 344–354.

Lourie, I. S. (1979). Family dynamics and the abuse of adolescents: A case for a developmental phase-specific model. *Child Abuse and Neglect, 3*, 967–974.

Lourie, I. S. (1984). The locus of emotional harm in incest: The study of "non-victims" of incestuous families. *Clinical Proceedings Children's Hospital National Medical Center Conference*, (January–April), 46–54.

Lukianowicz, N. (1983). Incest. *British Journal of Psychiatry, 120*, 301–313.

Luppens, J., & Lau, E. E. (1983). The mentally and physically impaired elderly relative: Consequences for family care. In J. I. Kosberg (Ed.), *Abuse and Maltreatment of the Elderly.* Boston: John Wright PSG.

Lynch, M. A. (1978). The critical path. In C. M. Lee (Ed.), *Child Abuse: A Reader and Sourcebook.* London: Open University Press.

Lystad, M. (1975). Violence at home: A review of the literature. *American Journal of Orthopsychiatry, 45* (3), 328–345.

MacAndrew, C., & Edgerton, R. B. (1969). *Drunken Comportment: A Social Explanation.* Chicago: Aldine.

MacFarlane, K. (1985). Diagnostic evaluations: Interview techniques and the uses of videotape. In American Bar Association (Ed.), *National Policy Conference on Legal Reforms in Child Sexual Abuse Cases.* Washington, DC: National Legal Resource Center for Child Advocacy and Protection.

MacFarlane, K., & Bulkley, J. (1982). Treating child sexual abuse: An overview of current program models. In J. Conte & D. Shore (Eds.), *Social Work and Child Sexual Abuse.* New York: Haworth.

MacFarlane, K., & Korbin, J. E. (1983). Confronting the incest secret long after the fact: A family study of multiple victimization with strategies for intervention. *Child Abuse and Neglect, 17* (2), 225–238.

Maisch, H. (1972). *Incest.* New York: Stein & Day.

Malin, N. R. (1981). Pathways to placement of adolescent children. *Social Work, 26,* 482–487.

Malinow, K. L. (1981a). Dependent personality. In J. R. Lion (Ed.), *Personality Disorders: Diagnosis & Management.* Baltimore: Williams & Wilkins.

Malinow, K. L. (1981b). Passive aggressive personality. In J. R. Lion (Ed.), *Personality Disorders: Diagnosis & Management.* Baltimore: Williams & Wilkins.

Malmquist, C. (1966). Personality characteristics of women with repeated illegitimacies—Descriptive aspects. *American Journal of Orthopsychiatry, 36,* 476–484.

Martin, D. (1976). *Battered Wives.* San Francisco: Glide Publications.

Martin, H. P. (1976). *The Abused Child: A Multidisciplinary Approach to Developmental Issues and Treatment.* Cambridge, MA: Ballinger.

Martin, H. P., & Beezley, P. (1977). Behavioral observations of abused children. *Developmental Medicine and Child Neurology, 19,* 373–387.

Martin, H. P., Beezley, P., Conway, E. F., & Kempe, C. H. (1974). The development of abused children. *Advances in Pediatrics, 21,* 25–73.

Martin, H. P., & Rodeheffer, M. (1976). Learning and intelligence. In H. P. Martin (Ed.), *The Abused Child.* Cambridge, MA: Ballinger.

Martin, J. (1983). Maternal and paternal abuse of children: Theoretical and research perspectives. In D. Finkelhor et al. (Eds.), *The Dark Side of Families.* Beverly Hills, CA: Sage Publications.

Martin, J. A. (1984). Neglected fathers: Limitations in diagnostic and treatment resources for violent men. *Child Abuse and Neglect, 8* (4), 387–392.

Martinez-Roiz, A., Domingo-Salvany, F., Liorvas-Terol, J., & Ibanez-Cacho, J. M. (1983). Psychologic implications of the maltreated child syndrome. *Child Abuse and Neglect, 7* (3), 261–263.

Masterson, J. F. (1976). *Psychotherapy and the Borderline Adult: A Developmental Approach.* New York: Brunner/Mazel.

Matlins, S. (1981). Services for children of alcoholics. Washington, DC: Government Printing Office.

Mattingly, R. (1975). Children at risk. *Health and Social Service Journal, 85* (4437), 1008–1015.

Mayer, J., & Black, R. (1977). Child abuse and neglect in families with an alcohol or opiate addicted parent. *Child Abuse and Neglect, 1,* 85–98.

McCord, J. (1979). Some childrearing antecedants to criminal behavior in adult men. *Journal of Personality and Social Psychology, 37*, 1477–1486.

McCord, J. (1983). A forty year perspective on the effects of child abuse and neglect. *Child Abuse and Neglect, 7* (3), 265–270.

McCord, W., & McCord, J. (1956). *The Psychopath: An Essay on the Criminal Mind.* Princeton, NJ: Van Nostrand.

McDermott, P., & McDermott, J. (1976). The treatment of child abuse: Play therapy with a 4 year old child. *Journal of the American Academy of Child Psychiatry, 15*, 430–440.

McGaghy, C. H. (1968). Drinking and deviance disavowal: The case of child molesters. *Social Problems, 16*, 43–49.

McGaghy, C. H. (1971). Child molesting. *Sexual Behavior, 1*, 16–24.

McMahon, A. W., & Shore, M. F. (1968). Some psychological reactions to working with the poor. *Archives of General Psychiatry, 18*, 562–568.

Medden, B. J. (1985). The assessment of risk in child abuse and neglect case investigations. *Child Abuse and Neglect, 9*, 57–62.

Megargee, E. I. (1976). The prediction of dangerous behavior. *Criminal Justice and Behavior, 3*, 3–21.

Megargee, E. I. (1982). Psychological determinants and correlates of criminal violence. In M. E. Wolfgang & N. A. Weiner (Eds.), *Criminal Violence.* Beverly Hills, CA: Sage Publications.

Mehrabian, A., & Weinstein, L. (1985). Temperament characteristics of suicide attempters. *Journal of Consulting and Clinical Psychology, 53* (4), 544–546.

Meichenbaum, D. (1977). *Cognitive-Behavior Modification: An Integrative Approach.* New York: Plenum.

Meichenbaum, D., & Gilmore, B. (1982). Resistance from a cognitive-behavioral perspective. In P. L. Wachtel (Ed.), *Resistance: Psychodynamic and Behavioral Approaches.* New York: Plenum.

Melton, G. B. (1984). Procedural reforms to protect child victim/witnesses in sex offense proceedings. In J. Bulkley (Ed.), *Child Sexual Abuse and the Law* (5th ed.). Washington, DC: American Bar Association.

Menninger, R. W., & Modlin, H. C. (1971). Individual violence: Prevention in the violence threatening patient. In J. Fawcett (Ed.), *Dynamics of Violence.* Chicago: American Medical Association.

Miller, S. H. (1983). *The Influence of Adolescent Childbearing on the Incidence, Type, and Severity of Child Maltreatment.* New York: Child Welfare League of America.

Miller, D., & Chalias, G. (1981, July). Abused children as adult parents: A 25 year longitudinal study. First Family Violence Researchers Conference, Durham, NH.

Million, T. (1981a). *Disorders of Personality: DSM-III: Axis-II.* New York: John Wiley.

Million, T. (1981b). The avoidant personality. In J. R. Lion (Ed.), *Personality Disorders: Diagnosis and Management*. Baltimore: Williams & Wilkins.

Milliones, D. (1978). Relationship between perceived child temperament and maternal behavior. *Child Development, 49*, 1255–1257.

Milner, J. S. (1980). *The Child Abuse Potential Inventory: Manual*. Webster, NC: Psytec.

Milner, J. S. (1981). *The child abuse potential inventory: Current status and uses*. First Family Violence Researchers Conference, Durham, NH.

Milner, J. S., & Wimberly, R. C. (1979). An inventory for the identification of child abusers. *Journal of Clinical Psychology, 35*, 95–100.

Milner, J. S., & Wimberly, R. C. (1980). Prediction and Explanation of Child Abuse. *Journal of Clinical Psychology, 36*, 875–884.

Milowe, I., & Lourie, R. (1964). The child's role in the battered child syndrome. *Society for Pediatric Research, 65*, 1079–1081.

Minde, K. L. (1980). Bonding of parents to premature infants: Theory and practice. In P. M. Taylor (Ed.), *Parent-Infant Relationships*. New York: Grune & Stratton.

Minuchin, S. (1968). *Families of the Slums: An Exploration of Their Structure and Treatment*. New York: Basic Books.

Mischel, W. (1973). Toward a cognitive social learning reconceptualization of personality. *Psychological Review, 80*, 252–283.

Mitchell, W. G., Gorlee, R. W., & Greenberg, R. A. (1980). Failure to thrive: A study in a primary care setting, epidemiology and follow-up. *Pediatrics, 65* (5), 971–977.

Mitkus, C. M. (1982, May) *Shadow figures in incest families: The reactions of siblings*. Second Annual Conference on Sexual Victimization of Children, Washington, DC.

Mlyniec, W. J. (1985). Presence, compulsory process, and pro se representation: Constitutional ramifications upon evidentiary innovation in sex abuse cases. In American Bar Association (Ed.), *National Policy Conference on Legal Reforms in Child Sexual Abuse Cases*. Washington, DC: National Legal Resource Center for Child Advocacy and Protection.

Mnookin, R. H. (1974). Foster care—in whose best interest? *Harvard Educational Review, 43* (4), 158–197.

Mohr, J. W. (1962). The pedophilias: Their clinical social and legal implications. *Canadian Psychiatric Association Journal, 7*, 255–260.

Mohr, J. W., & McKnight, C. K. (1971). Violence as a function of age and relationship with special reference to matricide. *Canadian Psychiatric Association Journal, 16* (1), 29–53.

Molnar, G., & Cameron, P. (1975). Incest syndromes: observations in a general hospital psychiatric unit. *Canadian Psychiatric Association Journal, 20*, 373–377.

Monahan, J. (1981). *Predicting Violent Behavior: An Assessment of Clinical Techniques*. Beverly Hills, CA: Sage Publications.

Monahan, J., & Steadman, J. J. (1983). Crime and mental disorder: An epidemiological approach. In N. Morris & M. H. Tonry (Eds.), *Crime and Justice: An Annual Review of Research*. Chicago: University of Chicago Press.

Monroe, R. R. (1982). The problem of impulsivity in personality disturbances. In J. R. Lion (Ed.), *Personality Disorders: Diagnosis and Management*. Baltimore: Williams & Wilkins.

Morgan, J. M., & Burkholder, R. B. (1982). Interviewing children and adolescents. In A. Haralambie (Ed.), *Practical Child Advocacy*. Denver: National Association of Counsel for Children.

Morris, M. G., & Gould, R. W. (1974). Role reversal: A necessary concept in dealing with the "battered child syndrome." *American Journal of Orthopsychiatry, 33* (2), 298–299.

Morrison, H. L. (Ed.). (1983). *Children of Depressed Parents: Risk, Identification, and Intervention*. New York: Grune & Stratton.

Morse, C. W., Sahler, O. J., & Friedman, S. B. (1970). A three year follow-up of abused and neglected children. *American Journal of Diseases of Children, 120*, 439–446.

Mouzakitus, C. M. (1984). Characteristics of abused adolescents and guidelines for intervention. *Child Welfare, 63* (2), 149–157.

Mrazek, P. B. (1980). Annotation: Sexual abuse of children. *Journal of Child Psychology and Psychiatry, 21* (1), 91–94.

Mulford, J., and Cohen, R. (1967). *Neglecting Parents: A Study of Psychosocial Characteristics*. Denver: American Humane Association, Children's Division.

Mulhern, R. K., & Passman, R. H. (1977). Maternal punitiveness affected by situational stress: An experimental analogue of child abuse. *Journal of Abnormal Psychology, 86*, 565–569.

Mulvey, E. P., & Lidz, C. W. (1984). Clinical considerations in the prediction of dangerousness in mental patients. *Clinical Psychology Review, 4*, 379–401.

Murphy, J. K., Jenkins, J., Newcombe, R. G., & Silbert, J. R. (1981). Objective birth data and the prediction of child abuse. *Archives of Disease in Childhood, 56*, 295–297.

Mussen, P. H., Conger, J. J., & Kagan, J. (1963). *Child Development and Personality*. New York: Harper.

Nasjleti, M. (1980). Suffering in silence: The male incest victim. *Child Welfare, 59*, 269–275.

National Center for Child Abuse and Neglect. (1981). *Study Findings: National Study of Incidence and Severity of Child Abuse and Neglect*. Washington, DC: Department of Health, Education and Welfare.

Neidig, P., Friedman, D. H., & Collins, B. (1984, August). *Attitudinal characteristics of males who have engaged in spouse abuse*. Paper presented at the Second National Conference for Family Violence Researchers, University of New Hampshire. Durham, NH.

Newberger, E. H. (1979). The myth of the battered child syndrome. In R. Bourne & E. H. Newberger (Eds.), *Critical Perspectives on Child Abuse.* Lexington, MA: Lexington Books.

Newberger, E. (1985a). *Child Abuse in 1985: A Medical Perspective.* Boston: Children's Hospital.

Newberger, E. (1985b). Courts, at times, add to damage: Prosecutorial approach often punishes children. *Boston Globe* (December 1).

Newberger, E. H., & Bourne, R. (Eds.). (1979a). *Critical Perspectives on Child Abuse and Neglect.* Lexington, MA: Lexington Books.

Newberger, E. H., & Bourne, R. (1979b). The medicalization and legalization of child abuse. In R. Bourne & E. H. Newberger (Eds.), *Critical Perspectives on Child Abuse.* Lexington, MA: Lexington Books.

Newberger, E. H., & Daniel, J. H. (1979). Knowledge and epidemiology of child abuse: A critical review of concepts. In R. Bourne & E. H. Newberger (Eds.), *Critical Perspectives on Child Abuse.* Lexington, MA: Lexington Books.

Newberger, E. H., & Hyde, J. N. (1979). Child abuse: Principles and implications of current pediatric practice. In R. Bourne & E. H. Newberger (Eds.), *Critical Perspectives on Child Abuse.* Lexington, MA: Lexington Books.

Newberger, C. M., & Newberger, E. H. (1978, November). *The search for a theory on child abuse.* Paper presented at the Conference on Child Abuse: Cultural Roots and Policy Options, Annenberg School of Communications, Philadelphia: University of Pennsylvania.

Newberger, E. H., Newberger, C. M., & Hampton, R. L. (1983). Child abuse: The current theory base and future research needs. *Journal of the American Academy of Child Psychiatry, 22* (3), 262–268.

Newberger, E. H., Reed, R. B., Daniel, J. H., Hyde, J. N., & Kotelchuck, M. (1980). Pediatric social illness: Toward an etiologic classification. *Pediatrics, 60,* (1), 178–185.

Norton, A. J., & Glick, P. C. (1979) Marital instability in America: Past, present, and future. In G. Levinger & O. W. Moles (Eds.), *Divorce and Separation: Context, Causes, and Consequences.* New York: Basic Books.

Novaco, R. W. (1975). *Anger Control: The Development and Evaluation of an Experimental Treatment.* Lexington, MA: Lexington Books.

Novaco, R. W. (1979). The cognitive regulation of anger and stress. In P. C. Kendall & S. D. Hollan (Eds.), *Cognitive-Behavioral Interventions: Theory, Research and Procedures.* New York: Academic Press.

Nye, I. F. (1976). School age parenthood. *Extension Bulletin 667.* Pullman, WA: Cooperative Extension Service, Washington State University.

Oates, M. R. (1979). A classification of child abuse and its relation to treatment and prognosis. *Child Abuse and Neglect, 3,* 907–915.

O'Brien, J. E. (1971). Violence in divorce prone families. *Journal of Marriage and the Family, 33* (November), 692–698.

Oliver, J. E., & Taylor, A. (1971). Five generations of ill-treated children in the family pedigree. *British Journal of Psychiatry, 119*, 473–480.

Olivira, O. H. (1981). Psychological abuse of the elderly. In D. Holden & F. Carey (Eds.), *Abuse of Older Persons.* Knoxville, TN: University of Tennessee Press.

O'Malley, T. A., O'Malley, H. C., Everitt, D. E., & Sarson, D. (1984). Categories of family-mediated abuse and neglect of elderly persons. *Journal of American Geriatrics Society, 32* (5), 362–369.

Orvaschel, H., Weissman, M. M., & Kidd, K. K. (1980). Children and depression: The children of depressed parents, the childhood of depressed patients, depression in children. *Journal of Affective Disorders, 2* (1), 1–16.

Osofsky, J. D., & Osofsky, H. J. (1978). Teenage pregnancy: Psychosocial considerations. *Clinical Obstetrics and Gynecology, 21*, 1161–1172.

Ounstead, C., Oppenheimer, R., & Lindsey, J. (1974). Aspects of bonding failure: The psychopathology and psychotherapeutic treatment of families of battered children. *Developmental Medical and Child Neurology, 16*, 447–456.

Pagelow, M. D. (1981). *Woman Battering: Victims and Their Experiences.* Beverly Hills, CA: Sage Publications.

Pagelow, M. D. (1982). *Mothers, maltreatment of children, and social policy.* Tenth World Congress of Sociology, Mexico City.

Pagelow, M. D. (1984). *Family Violence.* New York: Praeger Scientific.

Pannor, R., Massarik, F., & Evans, B. *The Unwed Father: New Approaches for Helping Unmarried Young Parents.* New York: Springer.

Parke, R. D., & Collmer, C. W. (1975). *Child Abuse: An Interdisciplinary Analysis.* Chicago: University of Chicago Press.

Parke, R. D., & Lewis, N. G. (1981). The family in context: A multilevel interactional analysis of child abuse. In R. W. Henderson (Ed.), *Parent-Child Interaction: Theory, Research, and Prospects.* New York: Academic Press.

Patterson, G. R., & Hops, H. (1972). Coercion, a game for two: Intervention techniques for marital conflict. In R. E. Ulrich & P. T. Mountjoy (Eds.), *The Experimental Analysis of Social Behavior.* New York: Appleton-Century-Crofts.

Patterson, G. R., Reid, J. B., Jones, R. R., & Conger, R. E. (1975). *Families with Aggressive Children.* Eugene, OR: Castalia Publishing.

Paulker, S. (1969). Girls pregnant out of wedlock. In M. LaBarre & W. LaBarre (Eds.), *Double Jeopardy, The Triple Crisis— Illegitimacy Today.* New York: National Council on Illegitimacy.

Paulson, M. J., Schwemer, G. T., & Bendel, R. B. (1976). Clinical applications of the Pd, Ma, and (Oh) Experimental MMPI Scales to further understanding of abusive parents. *Journal of Clinical Psychology, 32*, 558–564.

Paykel, E. S. (Ed.). (1982a). *Handbook of Affective Disorders*. New York: Guilford Press.

Paykel, E. S. (1982b). Life events and early environment. In E. S. Paykel (Ed.), *Handbook of Affective Disorders*. New York: Guilford Press.

Pearlin, L. I., & Johnson, J. S. (1977). Marital status, life strains, and depression. *American Sociological Review, 42*, 704–715.

Pedrick-Cornell, C., & Gelles, R. J. (1982). Elder abuse: The status of current knowledge. *Family Relations, 31* (May), 457–465.

Pelto, V. L. (1981). Male incest offenders and non-offenders: A comparison of early sexual history. *Dissertation Abstracts International, 42*(3), 1154–B Ann Arbor, MI.

Pelton, L. H. (1978). Child abuse and neglect: The myth of classlessness. *American Journal of Orthopsychiatry, 48* (4), 608–617.

Penna, M. W. (1981). Classification of personality disorders. In J. R. Lion (Ed.), *Personality Disorders: Diagnosis and Management*. Baltimore: Williams & Wilkins.

Perry, M. A., Doran, L. D., & Wells, E. A. (1983). Developmental and behavioral characteristics of the physically abused child. *Journal of Clinical Child Psychology, 12*, 320–324.

Peters, J. J. (1976). Children who are victims of sexual assault and the psychology of offenders. *American Journal of Psychotherapy, 30*, 398–421.

Peters, S. D. (1984). *The relationship between childhood sexual victimization and adult depression among Afro-American and White Women.* Unpublished Doctoral Dissertation, University of California, Los Angeles.

Pfeiffer, E., & Busse, E. W. (1973). Mental disorders in later life-affective disorders, paranoid, neurotic, and situational reactions. In E. W. Busse & E. Pfeiffer (Eds), *Mental Illness in Later Life*. Washington, DC: American Psychiatric Association.

Pfohl, S. J. (1977). The "discovery" of child abuse. *Social Problems, 24* (3), 310–323.

Phillips, J. A. (1981). Narcissistic personality. In J. Lion (Ed.), *Personality Disorders: Diagnosis and Management*. Baltimore: Williams & Wilkins.

Pierce, L. H., & Pierce, R. L. (1984, August). *Race as a factor in childhood sexual abuse.* Second Family Violence Researchers Conference, Durham, NH.

Pinderhughes, C. A. (1972). Managing paranoia in violent relationships. In G. Usdin (Ed.), *Perspectives in Violence*. New York: Brunner/Mazel.

Pinta, E. R. (1978). Pathological tolerance. *American Journal of Psychiatry, 135*, 698–701.

Pizzey, E. (1974). *Scream Quietly or the Neighbors Will Hear*. Harmondsworth, UK: Penguin.

Plummer, C. (1984). *Preventing sexual abuse: What in-school programs teach children*. Second Family Violence Researchers Conference, Durham, NH.

Plummer, K. (1981). Pedophilia: Constructing a sociological baseline. In M. Cook & K. Howells (Eds.), *Adult Sexual Interest in Children*. London: Academic Press.

Polansky, N., Borgman, D., & DeSaix, C. (1972). *Roots of Futility*. San Francisco: Jossey-Bass.

Polansky, N., DeSaix, C., & Sharlin, S. A. (1972). *Child Neglect*. New York: Child Welfare League of America.

Polansky, N. A., Hally, C., & Polansky, N. (1974). *States' knowledge of child neglect*. Athens: University of Georgia Regional Institute of Social Welfare Research.

Pollack, C., & Steele, B. (1972). A therapeutic approach to the parents. In C. H. Kempe & R. E. Helfer (Eds.), *Helping the Battered Child and His Family*. Philadelphia: J.B. Lippincott.

Pomeroy, J. C., Behar, D., & Steward, M. A. (1981). Abnormal sexual behavior in pre-pubescent children. *British Journal of Psychiatry, 138* (February), 119–125.

Poznanski, E. (1982). Depression in children and adolescents. In E. R. Val et al. (Eds.), *Affective Disorders: Psychopathology and Treatment*. Chicago: Year Book Medical Publishers.

Poznanski, E., & Blos, P. (1975). Incest. *Medical Aspects of Human Sexuality, 9*, 46–76.

Prescott, S., & Locko, C. (1977). Battered women: A social psychological perspective. In M. Roy (Ed.), *Battered Women a Psychosociological Study of Domestic Violence*. New York: Van Nostrand Reinhold.

Prentky, P. (1984, August). *Childhood physical and sexual abuse in the lives of sexually aggressive offenders*. Second Family Violence Researchers Conference, Durham, NH.

Prodgers, A. (1984). Psychopathology of the physically abusing parent: A comparison with the borderline syndrome. *Child Abuse and Neglect, 8* (4), 411–424.

Radbill, S. X. (1974). A history of child abuse and infanticide. In R. E. Helfer & C. H. Kempe (Eds.), *The Battered Child*. Chicago: University of Chicago Press.

Rabkin, J. (1979). Criminal behavior of discharged mental patients: A critical appraisal of the research. *Psychological Bulletin, 86*, 1–27.

Ramsey, S. H. (1983). Representation of the child in protection proceedings: The determination of decision-making capacity. *Family Law Quarterly, 17* (3), 287–326.

Rapaport, D., Gill, M. M., & Shafer, R. (1975). *Diagnostic Psychological Testing* (7th rev.). New York: International Universities Press.

Rathbone-McCuan, E. (1980). Elderly victims of family violence and neglect. *Social Casework, 61* (May), 296–304.

Rathbone-McCuan, E., & Hashimi, J. (1982). *Isolated Elders: Health and Social Intervention*. Rockville, MD: Aspen Systems.

Rathbone-McCuan, E., Travis, A., & Voyles, B. (1983). Family intervention: The task-centered approach. In J. I. Kosberg (Ed.), *Abuse and Maltreatment of the Elderly*. Boston: John Wright PSG.

Rathbone-McCuan, E., & Voyles, B. (1982). Case Detection of Abused Elderly Parents. *American Journal of Psychiatry, 139*, 2, 189–192.

Reavely, W., & Gilbert, M. T. (1978). The behavioral treatment approach to potential child abuse. In C. M. Lee (Ed.), *Child Abuse: A Reader and Sourcebook*. London: Open University Press.

Redlich, F. C., Hollingshead, A. B., & Bellis, E. (1955). Social class differences in attitudes toward psychiatry. *American Journal of Orthopsychiatry, 25*, 60–70.

Regan, J. J. (1981). Protecting the elderly: The new paternalism. *Hastings Law Journal, 32* (May), 1111–1132.

Regan, J. J. (1983). Protective services for the elderly: Benefit or threat? In J. I. Kosberg (Ed.), *Abuse and Maltreatment of the Elderly: Causes and Interventions*. Boston: John Wright PSG.

Reich, J. W., & Guiterres, S. E. (1979). Escape/aggression incidence in sexually abused juvenile delinquents. *Criminal Justice and Behavior, 6*, 239–243.

Reid, W. H. (1978). Diagnosis of antisocial syndromes. In W. H. Reid (Ed.), *The Psychopath: A Comprehensive Study of Antisocial Disorders and Behaviors*. New York: Brunner/Mazel.

Reid, W. H. (1981). The antisocial personality and related syndromes. In J. R. Lion (Ed.), *Personality Disorders: Diagnosis and Management*. Baltimore: Williams & Wilkins.

Reid, W. H., & Morrison, H. L. (1983). Risk factors in children of depressed parents. In H. L. Morrison (Ed.), *Children of Depressed Parents: Risk, Identification, and Intervention*. New York: Grune & Stratton.

Reiss, I. L. (1976). *Family Systems in America*. Hinsdale, IL: Dryden Press.

Renvoize, J. (1978). *Web of Violence*. London: Routledge & Kegan Paul.

Resnick, G. (1985). Enhancing parental competencies for high risk mothers: An evaluation of prevention effects. *Child Abuse and Neglect: The International Journal, 9*, 479–489.

Resnick, P. J. (1969). Child murder by parents: A psychiatric review of filicide. *American Journal of Psychiatry, 126*, 325–334.

Restak, R. M. (1979). *The Brain: The Last Frontier*. New York: Warner Books.

Richardson, L. A. (1977). *Women and altruistic madness: A study of sex-based vulnerability*. American Sociological Association Annual Meeting, Chicago.

Ripley, C. R. (1984). Clinical treatment of the non-disclosing Black client: A therapeutic paradox. *American Psychologist, 39* (11), 1234–1244.

Rivara, F. P. (1985). Physical abuse in children under two: A study of therapeutic outcomes. *Child Abuse and Neglect, 9* (1), 85–88.

Roberts, A. R. (Ed.). (1984). *Battered Women and Their Families: Intervention Strategies and Treatment Programs.* New York: Springer Publishing.

Robson, K. S., & Moss, H. A. (1970). Patterns and determinants of maternal attachment. *Journal of Pediatrics, 77* (6), 976– 985.

Rodenberg, M. (1971). Child murder by a depressed mother: A case report. *Canadian Psychiatric Association Journal, 16,* 821– 826.

Rodriquez, A. (1977). *Handbook of Child Abuse and Neglect.* Flushing, NY: Medical Examination Publishing.

Roe, R. J. (1985). Expert testimony in child sexual abuse cases. In American Bar Association (Eds.), *National Policy Conference on Legal Reforms in Child Sexual Abuse.* Washington, DC: National Legal Resource Center for Child Advocacy and Protection.

Rogers, Carl M. (1982). Child sexual abuse and the courts: preliminary findings. *Journal of Social Work and Human Sexuality, Fall-Winter,* 145-153.

Romanik, R. L., & Goodwin, J. (1982). Adaptation to pregnancy due to childhood sexual abuse. *Birth Psychology Bulletin, 3* (2), 2–9.

Rosenbaum, A., & O'Leary, K. D. (1981a). Marital violence: Characteristics of abusive couples. *Journal of Consulting and Clinical Psychology, 49* (1), 63–71.

Rosenbaum, A., & O'Leary, K. D. (1981b). Children, the unintended victims. of marital violence. *American Journal of Orthopsychiatry, 51* (4), 692–699.

Rosenberg, M. S., & Reppucci, N. D. (1983). Abusive mothers: Perceptions of their own and their children's behavior. *Journal of Consulting and Clinical Psychology, 51* (5), 671– 673.

Rosenberg, M. S., & Reppucci, N. D. (1985). Primary prevention of child abuse. *Journal of Consulting and Clinical Psychology, 53* (5), 576–585.

Rosenfeld, A. A. (1976). The clinical management of incest and sexual abuse of children. *Journal of the American Medical Association, 242* (16), 1761–1764.

Rosenfeld, A. A., Nadelson, C. C., & Krieger, M. (1979). Fantasy and reality in patients' reports of incest. *Journal of Clinical Psychiatry, 40* (4), 159–164.

Rosenfeld, A. A., & Newberger, E. H. (1977). Compassion vs. control: Conceptual and practical pitfalls in the broadened definition of child abuse. *Journal of the American Medical Association, 237* (19), 2086–2088.

Rosenfeld, A. A., & Newberger, E. H. (1979). Compassion vs. control: Conceptual and practical pitfalls in the broadened definition of child abuse. In Bourne and Newberger (Eds.), *Critical Perspectives on Child Abuse.* Lexington, MA: D.C. Heath.

Rosewater, L. B. (1984, August). *The MMPI and battered women.* Second Family Violence Researchers Conference, Durham, NH.

Rossman, P. (1980). The pederasts. In L. G. Schultz (Ed.), *The Sexual Victimology of Youth.* Springfield, IL: Charles C Thomas.

Roy, M. (Ed.). (1977). *Battered Women: A Psychosocial Study of Domestic Violence.* New York: Van Nostrand Reinhold.

Rush, F. (1980). *The Best Kept Secret: Sexual Abuse of Children.* Englewood Cliffs, NJ: Prentice-Hall.

Russell, D. (1984). *Sexual Exploitation: Rape, Child Sexual Abuse, and Sexual Harassment.* Beverly Hills, CA: Sage Publications.

Ryan, G. M., & Schneider, J. M. Teenage obstetric complications. *Obstetrics and Gynecology, 21,* 1191–1197.

Sameroff, A. J., & Chandler, M. J. (1975). Reproductive risk and the continuum of caretaking casualty. In F. D. Horowitz (Ed.), *Review of Child Development Research* (vol. 4). Chicago: University of Chicago Press.

Sampson, J. J. (1981). Statutory regulation of emergency taking of possession of a child by a state governmental entity. In American Bar Association (Ed.), *Protecting Children Through the Legal System.* Washington, DC: National Legal Resource Center for Child Advocacy and Protection.

Sandgrund, A., Gaines, R. W., & Green, A. H. (1975). Child abuse and mental retardation: A problem of cause and effect. *Journal of Mental Deficiency, 19* (3), 327–330.

Schmidt, W. C., Miller, K. G., Bell, W. G., & Elaine, B. (1981). *Public Guardianship and the Elderly.* Cambridge, MA: Ballinger.

Schmitt, B. D. (Ed.). (1978). *The Child Protection Team: A Multidisciplinary Approach to Managing Child Abuse and Neglect.* New York: Garland.

Schneiderman, L. (1965). Social class, diagnosis, and treatment. *American Journal of Orthopsychiatry, 35,* 95–105.

Schneider, C., Pollack, C., & Helfer, R. E. (1972). Interviewing the parents. In C. H. Kempe & R. E. Helfer (Eds.), *Helping the Battered Child and His Family.* Philadelphia: J. B. Lippincott.

Schofield, W. (1964). *Psychotherapy: The Purchase of Friendship.* Englewood Cliffs, NJ: Prentice-Hall.

Schudson, C. (1978). Court diversion: An alternative to spousal abuse cases. In U. S. Commission on Civil Rights, *Battered Women: Issues of Public Policy.* Washington, DC: U.S. Commission on Civil Rights.

Schultz, L. G. (1980a). *The Sexual Victimology of Youth.* Springfield, IL: Charles C Thomas.

Schultz, L. G. (1980b). The victim and the justice system—An introduction. In L. G. Schultz (Ed.), *The Sexual Victimology of Youth.* Springfield, IL: Charles C Thomas.

Schumm, W. R., Martin, M. S., Bollman, S. R., & Jurich, A. P. (1982). Classifying family violence: Whither the woozle? *Journal of Family Issues, 3* (3), 319–340.

Schwemer, F. T., & Bendel, R. B. (1976). Clinical application of the Pd. Ma, and (OH) Experimental MMPI Scales for further understanding of abusive parents. *Journal of Clinical Psychology, 32*, 558–564.

Seghorn, T. K. (1981). *The decision tree: Factors in the clinical subtyping of sexually dangerous persons.* American Psychological Association Annual Meeting, Los Angeles.

Seghorn, T. K., & Boucher, R. J. (1981) Sexual abuse in childhood as a factor in adult sexually dangerous criminal offenses. In J. M. Samson (Ed.), *Childhood and Sexuality: Proceedings of the International Symposium.* Montreal Editions Etudes Vivantes.

Seider, A. L., & Calhoun, K. S. (1984, August). Childhood sexual abuse: Factors related to differential adult adjustment. Second Family Violence Researchers Conference, Durham, NH.

Seligman, M. P. (1975). *Helplessness: On Depression, Development, and Death.* San Francisco: W. H. Freeman.

Sgrdi, S. (1982). *Handbook of Clinical Intervention in Child Sexual Abuse.* Lexington, MA: Lexington Books.

Shapiro, D. L. (1984). *Psychological Evaluation and Expert Testimony: A Practical Guide to Forensic Work.* New York: Van Nostrand Reinhold.

Sherman, L. W., & Berk, R. A. (1984). The Minneapolis domestic violence experiment. *Police Foundation Report, 1* (April), 1–8.

Shorkey, C. T. (1978). Psychological characteristics of child abusers: Speculation and the need for research. *Child Abuse and Neglect, 2*, 69–76.

Silbert, M., & Pines, A. (1981). Sexual child abuse as an antecedent to prostitution. *Child Abuse and Neglect, 5*, 407–411.

Silverstone, B., Hyman, H. K., & Kirschner, K. (1979). *You and Your Aging Parent.* New York: Pantheon.

Sloan, I. J. (1983a). *Governing Law and Legislation.* Dobbs Ferry, NY: Oceana Publications.

Sloan, I. J. (1983b). *The Law and Legislation of Elderly Abuse.* Dobbs Ferry, NY: Oceana Publications.

Sloan, M. P., & Meier, J. H. (1983). Typology for parents of abused children. *Child Abuse and Neglect, 7* (4), 443–450.

Smith, S. M., & Hanson, R. (1974). 134 battered children: A medical and psychological study. *British Medical Journal, 3* (5932), 666–670.

Smith, S. M., Hanson, R., & Noble, S. (1973). Parents of battered babies: a controlled study. *British Medical Journal, 4* (889), 388–391.

Snyder, J. C., Hampton, R., & Newberger, E. H. (1983). Family dysfunction, violence, neglect, and sexual misuse. In J. Levine et al. (Eds.), *Developmental Behavioral Pediatrics.* Philadelphia: Saunders.

Solnit, A. J. (1980). Too much reporting, too little service: Roots and prevention of child abuse. In G. Gerbner et al. (Eds.), *Child Abuse and Agenda for Action.* New York: Oxford University Press.

Solnit, A. J., & Provence, S. (1979). Vulnerability and risk in early childhood. In J. D. Osofsky (Ed.), *Handbook of Infant Development.* New York: John Wiley.

Solomon, K. (1983a). Victimization by health professionals and the psychologic response of the elderly. In J. I. Kosberg (Ed.), *Abuse and Maltreatment of the Elderly.* Boston: John Wright PSG.

Solomon, K. (1983b). Intervention for the victimized elderly and sensitization of health professional: Therapeutic and educational efforts. In J. I. Kosberg (Ed.), *Abuse and Maltreatment of the Elderly.* Boston: John Wright PSG.

Spence, J. T., & Helmreich, R. L. (1978). *Masculinity and Femininity: Their Psychological Dimensions Correlates and Antecedents* University of Texas Press: Austin.

Spinetta, J. J. (1978). Parental personality factors in child abuse. *Journal of Consulting and Clinical Psychology, 46,* 1409–1414.

Spinetta, J. J., & Rigler, D. (1972). The child-abusing parent: A psychological review. *Psychological Bulletin, 77* (4), 2986–3004.

Stacey, W., & Shupe, A. (1983). *The Family Secret: Domestic Violence in America.* Boston: Beacon.

Staples, R. (1978). Masculinity and race: The dual dilemma of Black men. *Journal of Social Issues, 34,* 1169–1228.

Star, B. (1983). *Helping the Abuser: Intervening Effectively in Family Violence.* New York: Family Service Association of America.

State v. Kelly, 478 A 2d 364 (NJ, 1984).

State v. Wanrow, 559 P2d 548 (Wash, 1977).

Steele, B. F. (1970). Violence in our society. *The Pharos of Alpha Omega Alpha, 33,* 42–48.

Steele, B. F. (1975). *Working with Abusive Parents from a Psychiatric Point of View.* Washington, DC: Government Printing Office.

Steele, B. F. (1982). Abusive fathers. In S. H. Cath et al. (Eds.), *Father and Child: Developmental and Clinical Perspectives.* Boston: Little-Brown.

Steele, B. V, & Pollack, C. B. (1968). A psychiatric study of parents who abuse infants and small children. In R. E. Helfer & C. H. Kempe (Eds.), *The Battered Child.* Chicago: University of Chicago Press.

Steele, B., & Pollack, C. (1972). A therapeutic approach to the parents. In C. H. Kempe & R. E. Helfer (Eds.), *Helping the Battered Child and His Family.* Philadelphia: J. B. Lippincott.

Steinberg, L. D., Catalano, R., & Dooley, D. (1981). Economic antecedents of child abuse and neglect. *Child Development, 52,* 975–985.

Steinmetz, S. K. (1977). The use of force for resolving family conflict: The training ground for abuse. *Family Coordinator, 26* (1), 19–26.

Steinmetz, S. K. (1978). The battered husband syndrome. *Victimology, 2* (3/4), 499–509.

Steinmetz, S. K. (1983). Dependency, stress, and violence between middle-aged caregivers and their elderly parents. In J. I. Kosberg (Ed.), *Abuse and Maltreatment of the Elderly.* Boston: John Wright PSG.

Steller, M., & Raskin, D. C. (1986, February). *Credibility assessment procedure.* Paper presented to the Assessing the Credibility of the Child Witness in the Sexual Abuse Case Seminar, St. Luke's Hospital Center for Behavioral Health and the Law, Scottsdale, AZ.

Steller, M. (1986, February). *Statement reality analysis.* Paper presented to the Assessing the Credibility of the Child Witness in the Sexual Abuse Case Seminar, St. Luke's Hospital Center for Behavioral Health and the Law, Scottsdale, AZ.

Stern, E. M. (Ed). (1984). *Psychotherapy and the Abrasive Patient.* New York: Haworth Press.

Stern, L. (1973). Prematurity as a factor in child abuse. *Hospital Practice, 8* (5), 117–123.

Stern, M. J., & Meyer, L. C. (1980). Family and couple interactional patterns in cases of father-daughter incest. In K. MacFarlane et al. (Eds.), *Sexual Abuse of Children: Selected Readings.* Washington, DC: Government Printing Office.

Sternberg, S. (1981). Admissibility of expert testimony on battering. In F. Bochnak (Ed.), *Women's Self Defense Cases, Theory and Practice.* Charlottesville, VA: Michie Co.

Stevens, D., & Berliner, L. (1980). Special techniques for child witnesses. In L. G. Schultz (Ed.), *The Sexual Victimology of Youth.* Springfield, IL: Charles C Thomas.

Stone, L. E., Tyler, R. P., & Mead, J. J. (1984). Law enforcement officers as investigators and therapists in child sexual abuse: Training model. *Child Abuse and Neglect, 8* (1), 75–82.

Straker, G., & Jacobson, R. S. (1981). Aggression, emotional maladjustment, and empathy in the abused child. *Developmental Psychology, 17* (6), 762–765.

Straus, M. A. (1973). A general systems theory approach to a theory of violence between family members. *Social Science Information, 12* (3), 105–125.

Straus, M. A. (1974). Leveling, civility, and violence in the family. *Journal of Marriage and the Family, 36* (February), 13–29.

Straus, M. A. (1976). Sexual inequality, cultural norms, and wife-beating. In E. C. Viano (Ed.), *Victims and Society.* Washington, DC: Visage.

Straus, M. A. (1978). Wife Beating: How common and why? *Victimology, 2* (3–4), 443–458.

Straus, M. A. (1979). Family patterns and child abuse. *Child Abuse and Neglect, 3,* 213–225.

Straus, M. A. (1980a). Stress and physical child abuse. *Child Abuse and Neglect, 4,* 75–88.

Straus, M. A. (1980b). Victims and aggressors in marital violence. *American Behavioral Scientist, 23*, 5, (May/June), 681–704.

Straus, M. A., Gelles, R. J., & Steinmetz, S. K. (1980). *Behind Closed Doors: Violence in the American Family.* Garden City, NY: Anchor Press.

Stuart, R. B. (1974). Behavioral remedies for marital ills: A guide to the use of operant-interpersonal techniques. In A. S. Gurman & D. G. Rice (Eds.), *Couples in Conflict: New Directions in Marital Therapy,* New York: Aronson.

Stubblefield, R. L. (1975). Antisocial personality in children and adolescents. In A. M. Friedman, H. I. Kaplan, & B. J. Sadock (Eds.), *Comprehensive Textbook of Psychiatry.* Baltimore: Williams and Wilkins.

Sue, S. (1977). Community mental health services to minority groups: Some optimism, some pessimism. *American Psychologist, 32*, 616–624.

Summit, R. C. (1983). The child sexual abuse accommodation syndrome. *Child Abuse and Neglect, 7* (2), 177–194.

Summit, R. C. (1984). The impact of child abuse: Psycho-social and educational implications. In S. Leuing (Ed.), *Mental health and the School.* Vancouver, BC: University of British Columbia.

Summit, R. C. (1985, April). *Child sexual abuse: New knowledge and treatment strategies.* Presented to the Arizona Child Protective Services Training Academy, Tucson, AZ.

Summit, R. C., & Kryso, J. (1978). Sexual abuse of children: A clinical spectrum. *American Journal of Orthopsychiatry, 48* (2), 237–251.

Sussman, A., & Cohen, S. J. (1975). *Reporting Child Abuse and Neglect: Guidelines for Legislation.* Cambridge, MA: Ballinger.

Sussman, E. J., Trickett, P. K., Iannotti, R. J., Hollenbeck, B. E., & Zahn-Waxler, C. (1985). Child rearing patterns in depressed, abusive and normal mothers. *American Journal of Orthopsychiatry, 55* (2) April.

Swanson, D. W. (1971). Who violates children sexually? *Medical Aspects of Human Sexuality, 5*, 184–197.

Swift, C. (1979). Prevention of sexual child abuse: Focus on the perpetrator. *Journal of Clinical Child Psychology, 8*, (2), 133–136.

Swift, C. (1980). Sexual victimization of children: An urban mental health center survey. In L. G. Schultz (Ed.), *The Sexual Victimology of Youth.* Springfield, IL: Charles C Thomas.

Taitz, L. S. (1980). Effects on growth and development of social, psychological, and environmental factors. *Child Abuse and Neglect, 4*, 55–65.

Tartar, R. E., Hegedus, A. M., Winsten, N. E., & Alterman, A. I. (1984). Neuropsychological, personality, and familial characteristics of physically abused delinquents. *Journal of American Academy of Child Psychiatry, 23* (6), 668–674c.

Taylor, J. W. (1984). Structured conjoint therapy for spouse abuse cases. *Social Casework, 65* (1), 11–18.

Terman, L. M., & Merrill, M. A. (1973). *Stanford-Binet Intelligence Scale: Manual for the 3rd Revision, Form L-M*. Boston: Houghton-Mifflin.

Terr, L. C. (1970). A family study of child abuse. *American Journal of Psychiatry, 127* (5), 665–671.

Thar, A. E. (1982). The admissibility of expert testimony of battered wife syndrome: An evidentiary analysis. *Northwestern University Law Review, 77* (3), 348–373.

Thompson, M.G.G. (1985). The developmental assessment of the preschool child. *Psychiatric Annals, 15* (11), 25–29.

Tierney, K., & Corwin, D. (1983). Exploring intra-familial child sexual abuse: A systems approach. In D. Finkelhor et al. (Eds.), *The Dark Side of Families*. Beverly Hills, CA: Sage Publications.

Toch, H. (1969). *Violent Men*. Chicago: Aldine.

Trowell, J. A. (1983). Emergency caesarian section: A research study of the mother-child relationship in a group of women admitted expecting a normal vaginal delivery. *Child Abuse and Neglect, 7* (4), 387–394.

Trussell, J., & Menken, J. (1981). Early childbearing and subsequent fertility. In F. Furstenberg, Jr. et al. (Eds.), *Teenage Sexuality, Pregnancy, and Childbearing*. Philadelphia: University of Pennsylvania Press.

Tsai, M., & Wagner, N. W. (1979). Therapy groups for women sexually molested as children. *Archives of Sexual Behavior, 7*, 417–427.

Tsai, M., Feldman-Summers, S., & Edgar, M. (1979). Childhood molestation: Variables related to differential impacts on psychosexual functioning in adult women. *Journal of Abnormal Psychology, 88*, 407–417.

Twentyman, C. T., & Plotkin, R. C. (1982). Unrealistic expectations of parents who mistreat their children: An educational deficit pertaining to child development. *Journal of Clinical Psychology, 38*, 497–503.

Tyler, A. H., & Brassard, M. R. (1984). Abuse in the investigation and treatment of intrafamilial child sexual abuse. *Child Abuse and Neglect, 8* (1), 47–53.

Ulbrich, P., & Huber, J. (1981). Observing parental violence: Distribution and effects. *Journal of Marriage and the Family, 43* (3).

Undeutsch, U. (1982). Statement reality analysis. In A. Trankell (Ed.), *Reconstructing the Past*. Deventer, The Netherlands: Kluver, Law & Takation.

U.S. Attorney General. (1984). *Family Violence in America: The Final Report of the Attorney General's Task Force on Family Violence*. Washington, DC: Attorney General's Office.

U.S. Commission on Civil Rights. (1978). *Battered Women: Issues of Public Policy: A Consultation Sponsored by the U.S. Commission on Civil Rights*. Washington, DC: Commission on Civil Rights.

U.S. Commission on Civil Rights. (1982). *The Federal Response to Domestic Violence: A Report of the U.S. Commission on Civil Rights*, Washington, DC: Commission on Civil Rights.

Uviller, R. K. (1980). Save them from their saviors: The constitutional rights of the family. In G. Gerbner et al. (Eds.), *Child Abuse: An Agenda for Action.* New York: Oxford University Press.

Val, E. R., Gaviria, F. M., & Flaherty, J. H. (1982). *Affective Disorders: Psychopathology and Treatment.* Chicago: Year Book Medical Publishers.

Van den Berghe, P. H. (1983). Human inbreeding avoidance: Culture in nature. *Behavioral and Brain Sciences, 6,* 91–123.

Vincent, C. (1961). *Unmarried Mothers.* New York: Macmillan.

Virkunnen, M. (1974). Incest offenses and alcoholism. *Medicine, Science, and the Law, 14,* 124–128.

Wachtel, P. L. (ed.). (1982). *Resistance: Psychodynamic and Behavioral Approaches.* New York: Plenum Press.

Wahl, C. W. (1960). The psychodynamics of consummated maternal incest. *Archives of General Psychiatry, 3* (188), 153–155.

Wald, M. S. (1976). State intervention on behalf of "neglected" children: Standards for removal of children from their homes, monitoring the status of children in foster care, and termination of parental rights. *Stanford Law Review, 28* (4) 623–.

Wald, M. S. (1980). Thinking about public policy toward abuse and neglect of children: Review of *Before the Best Interest of the Child. Michigan Law Review, 76* (March), 645–693.

Wald, M. S. (1982). State intervention on behalf of endangered children: A proposed legal response. *Child Abuse and Neglect, 6,* 3–45.

Wald, M. S. (1985, May) *Child abuse legislation: Current Status and recommendations for change.* Paper presented to the Arizona Child Protective Services Training Academy, Tucson, AZ.

Wald, M. S., Carlsmith, J. M., Leiderman, P., French, H., & Smith, C. (1985). *Protecting Abused/Neglected Children: A Comparison of Home and Foster Placement.* Palo Alto, CA: Stanford University Press.

Walker, L. E. (1978). Battered women and learned helplessness. *Victimology, 2,* 525–534.

Walker, L. E. (1979). *The Battered Woman.* New York: Harper Colophon.

Walker, L. E. (1984). Battered women, psychology, and public policy. *American Psychologist, 39* (10), 1178–1182.

Walker, L. E., Thyfault, R. K., & Browne, A. (1982). Beyond the juror's ken: Battered women. *Vermont Law Review, 7* (1), 1–14.

Wallace, H. (1979). Factors associated with perinatal mortality and morbidity. *Clinical Obstetrics and Gynecology, 13,* 13–43.

Wallerstein, J. S. (1984). Children of divorce: Preliminary report of a ten year follow-up of young children. *American Journal of Orthopsychiatry, 54* (3), 444–458.

Wallerstein, J. S., & Kelly, J. B. (1975). The effects of parental divorce: Experiences of the preschool child. *Journal of the American Academy of Child Psychiatry, 14,* 600–616.

Warner, S. J. (1984). The defeating patient and reciprocal abrasion. In E. M. Stern (Ed.), *Psychotherapy and the Abrasive Patient*. New York: Haworth Press.

Wasserman, S. (1967). The abused parent of the abused child. *Children, 14* (September–October), 175–179.

Weber, E. (1977). Sexual abuse begins at home. *Ms.* (April), 64–67.

Wechsler, D. (1967). *Manual for the Wechsler Preschool and Primary Scale of Intelligence*. New York: Psychological Corporation.

Wechsler, D. (1974). *Manual for the Wechsler Intelligence Scale for Children-Revised.* New York: Psychological Corporation.

Weinberg, S. (1955). *Incest Behavior*. New York: Citadel Press.

Weinerman, G. T. (1981). Improving practice to avoid unnecessary placement. In American Bar Association (Eds.), *Protecting Children Through the Legal System*. Washington, DC: National Resource Center for Child Advocacy and Protection.

Weissman, M. M., & Klerman, G. L. (1977). Sex differences in the epidemiology of depression. *Archives of General Psychiatry, 34*, 98–111

Wells, S. J. (1981). A model of therapy with abusive and neglectful families. *Social Work, 26* (2), 113–116.

Wepman, B. J., & Donovan, M. W. (1984). Abrasiveness: Descriptive and dynamic issues. In E. M. Stern (Ed.), *Psychotherapy and the Abrasive Patient*. New York: Haworth Press.

Wetzel, J. W. (1984). *Clinical Handbook of Depression*. New York: Gardner.

Whitcomb, D. (1985). Assisting child victims in the courts: The practical side of legislative reform. In American Bar Association (Ed.), *National Policy Conference on Legal Reforms in Child Sexual Abuse Cases*. Washington, DC: National Legal Resource Center for Child Advocacy and Protection.

Whitehurst, R. N. (1974). Alternative family structures and violence-reduction. In S. K. Steinmetz & M. A. Straus (Eds.), *Violence in the Family*. New York: Dodd and Mead.

Williams, W., & Miller, K. (1977). The role of personal characteristics in perceptions of dangerousness. *Criminal Justice and Behavior, 4*, 421.

Wilson, G. (1978). *The Secrets of Sexual Fantasy.* London: J. M. Dent & Sons.

Winnocott, D. W. (1971). *Therapeutic Consultations in Child Psychiatry*. London: Hogarth.

Winokur, G. (1979). Unipolar depression: Is it divisible into autonomous subtypes? *Archives of General Psychiatry, 36*, 47–52.

Winokur, G., & Morrison, J. (1973). The Iowa 500: Follow-up of 225 depressives. *British Journal of Psychiatry, 123*, 543–548.

Winokur, G., Morrison, J., Clancy, J., & Crowe, R. (1973). The Iowa 500: Familial and clinical findings favor two kinds of depressive illness. *Comprehensive Psychiatry, 14*, 99–106.

Wolfe, D. A. (1984). Child-abusive parents: An empirical review and analysis. *Psychological Bulletin, 97* (3), 462–482.

Wolfe, D. A., Fairbank, J. A., Kelly, J. A., & Bradlyn, D. (1981, July). *Child abuser's response to stressful and non-stressful parent-child interactions.* Paper presented at the First Family Violence Researchers Conference, Durham, NH.

Wolfe, D. A., Jaffe, P., Wilson, S. K., & Zak, L. (1985). Children of battered women: The relation of child behavior to family violence and maternal stress. *Journal of Consulting and Clinical Psychology, 53* (5), 657–665.

Wolfe, D. A., Kaufman, K., Aragona, J., & Sandler, J. (1981). *The Child Management Program for Abusive Parents: Procedures for Developing a Child Abuse Intervention Program.* Winter Park, FL: Anna.

Wolff, R. (1983). Child abuse and neglect dynamics and underlying patterns. *Victimology, 8,* (1–2), 105–112.

Wolff, S. (1984). The concept of personality disorder in childhood. *Journal of Child Psychology and Psychiatry, 25* (1), 5–13.

Wulkan, D., & Bulkley, J. (1984). Analysis of incest statutes. In J. Bulkley (Ed.), *Child Sexual Abuse and the Law.* Washington, DC: American Bar Association, National Legal Resource Center for Child Advocacy and Protection.

Wyatt, G. E. (1985). The sexual abuse of Afro-American and White American women in childhood. *Child Abuse and Neglect: The International Journal, 9* (4), 507–520.

Yates, A., Beutler, L. E., & Crago, M. (1985). Drawings by child victims of incest. *Child Abuse and Neglect, 9* (2), 183–190.

Yllo, K., & Straus, M. A. (1981). Interpersonal violence among married and cohabitating couples. *Family Relations, 30* (3), 339–347.

Yorokoglu, A., & Kempe, J. P. (1966). Children not severely damaged by incest with a parent. *Journal of American Academy of Child Psychiatry, 5,* 111–124.

Young, L. (1964). *Wednesday's Children: A Study of Child Neglect and Abuse.* New York: McGraw-Hill.

Yuille, J. C., & King, M. A. (1986). *Children as Witnesses.* Vancouver: University of British Columbia Eyewitness Research Project. (mimeo).

Zalba, S. R. (1966). Treatment of child abuse. *Social Work, 11* (4), 8–16.

Zalba, S. R. (1967). The abused child: II, A typology for classification and treatment. *Social Work, 12,* 70–79.

Zalba, S. R. (1971). Battered children. *Transactions, 8* (July–August), 58–61.

Zeifert, M. (1981). Abuse and neglect: The adolescent as hidden victim. In K. C. Faller (ed.), *Social Work with Abused and Neglected Children.* New York: Free Press.

About the Authors

Frank G. Bolton, Jr., is currently the Coordinator of Psychological Services for the Arizona Department of Economic Security. He is the author of more than forty articles and five books. His other Sage books in family violence and related areas are *The Pregnant Adolescent: Problems of Premature Parenthood* and *When Bonding Fails: Clinical Assessment of the High Risk Family.*

Susan R. Bolton is an attorney in private practice and a shareholder in the Phoenix, Arizona law firm, Shimmel, Hill, Bishop & Gruender, P.C.. She is a founding member and Past President of the Arizona Women Lawyers Association. Although her practice is predominantly in the area of commercial litigation, she has been active in both the Juvenile and Domestic Relations Courts through court appointment and pro bono representation.

NOTES

NOTES

NOTES